# HISTORIC PHOTOS OF
# FORT WORTH

TEXT AND CAPTIONS BY
QUENTIN McGOWN

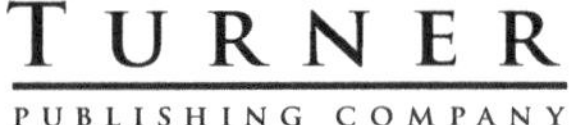

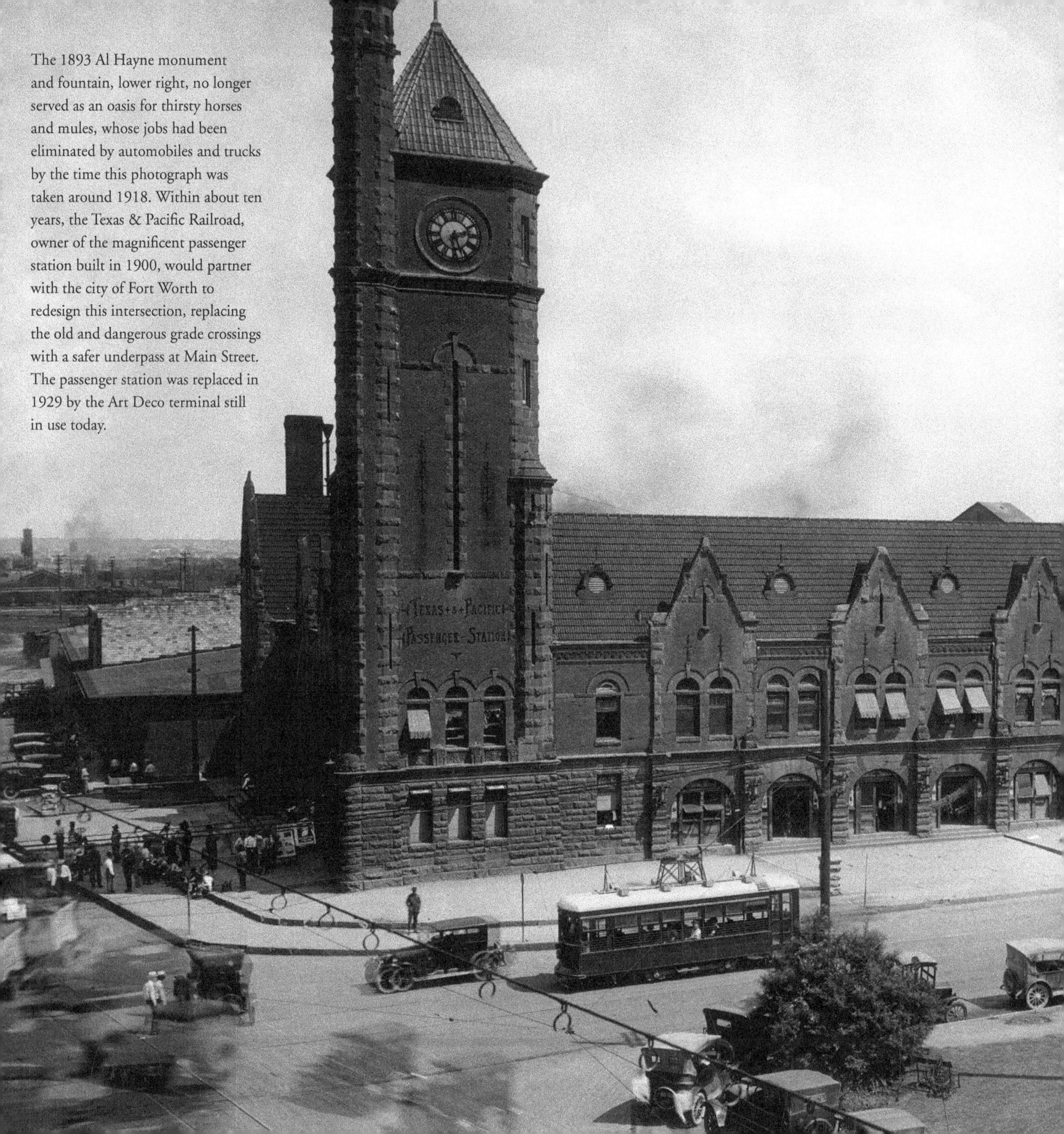


The 1893 Al Hayne monument and fountain, lower right, no longer served as an oasis for thirsty horses and mules, whose jobs had been eliminated by automobiles and trucks by the time this photograph was taken around 1918. Within about ten years, the Texas & Pacific Railroad, owner of the magnificent passenger station built in 1900, would partner with the city of Fort Worth to redesign this intersection, replacing the old and dangerous grade crossings with a safer underpass at Main Street. The passenger station was replaced in 1929 by the Art Deco terminal still in use today.

# HISTORIC PHOTOS OF
# FORT WORTH

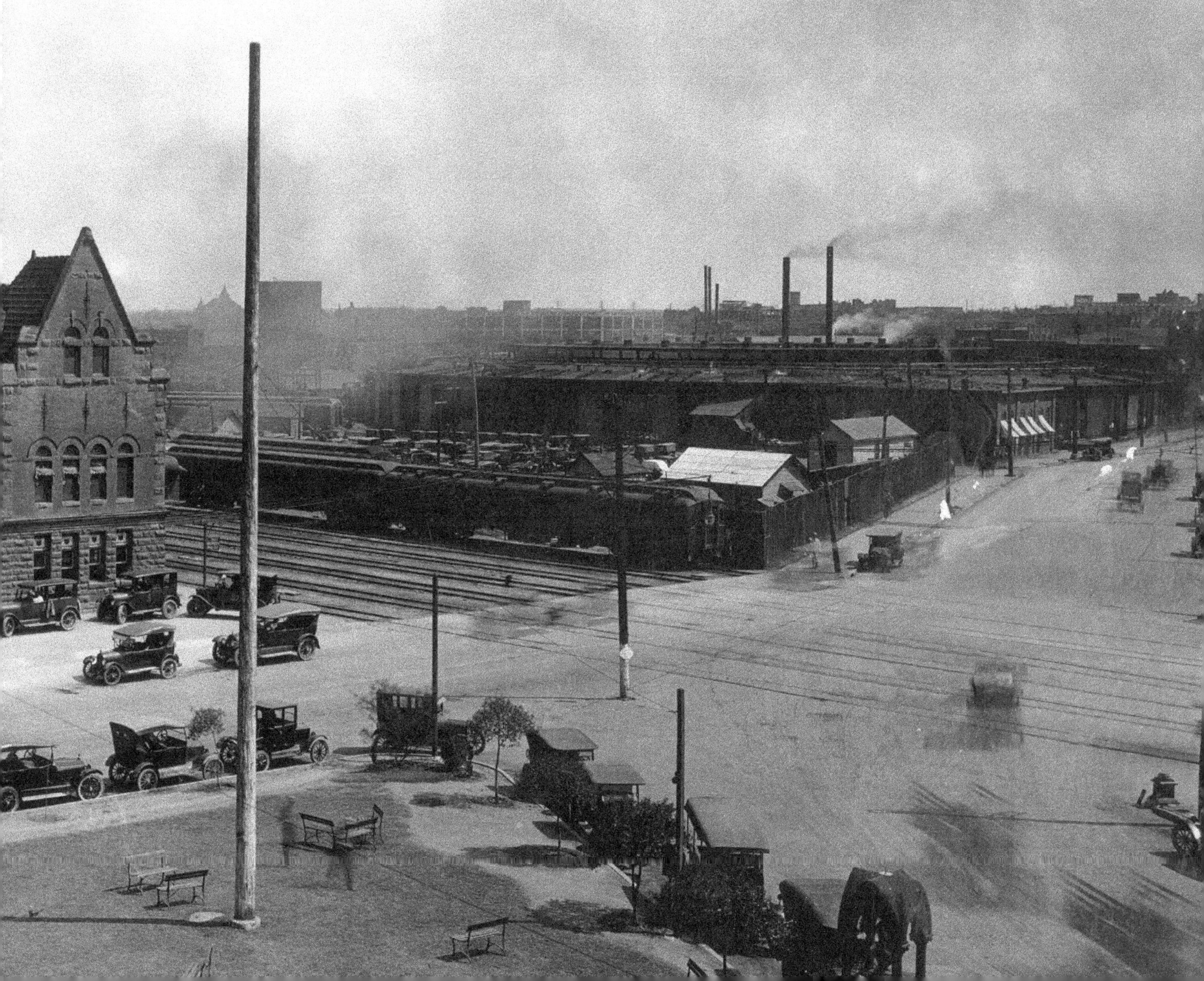

Turner Publishing Company
www.turnerpublishing.com

*Historic Photos of Fort Worth*



Library of Congress Control Number: 2006937031

ISBN: 978-1-59652-317-3

Printed in the United States of America

ISBN 978-1-68336-932-5 (hc)

# Contents

The life-size statue of humorist Will Rogers on his horse, Soapsuds, continues to preside over an ever-expanding Cultural District. Commissioned by Rogers's friend and Fort Worth titan Amon Carter, the bronze was completed by Electra Waggoner Biggs in 1939, but waited until 1947 to be unveiled by a dignitary Carter deemed important enough for the job—in this case, General Dwight D. Eisenhower.

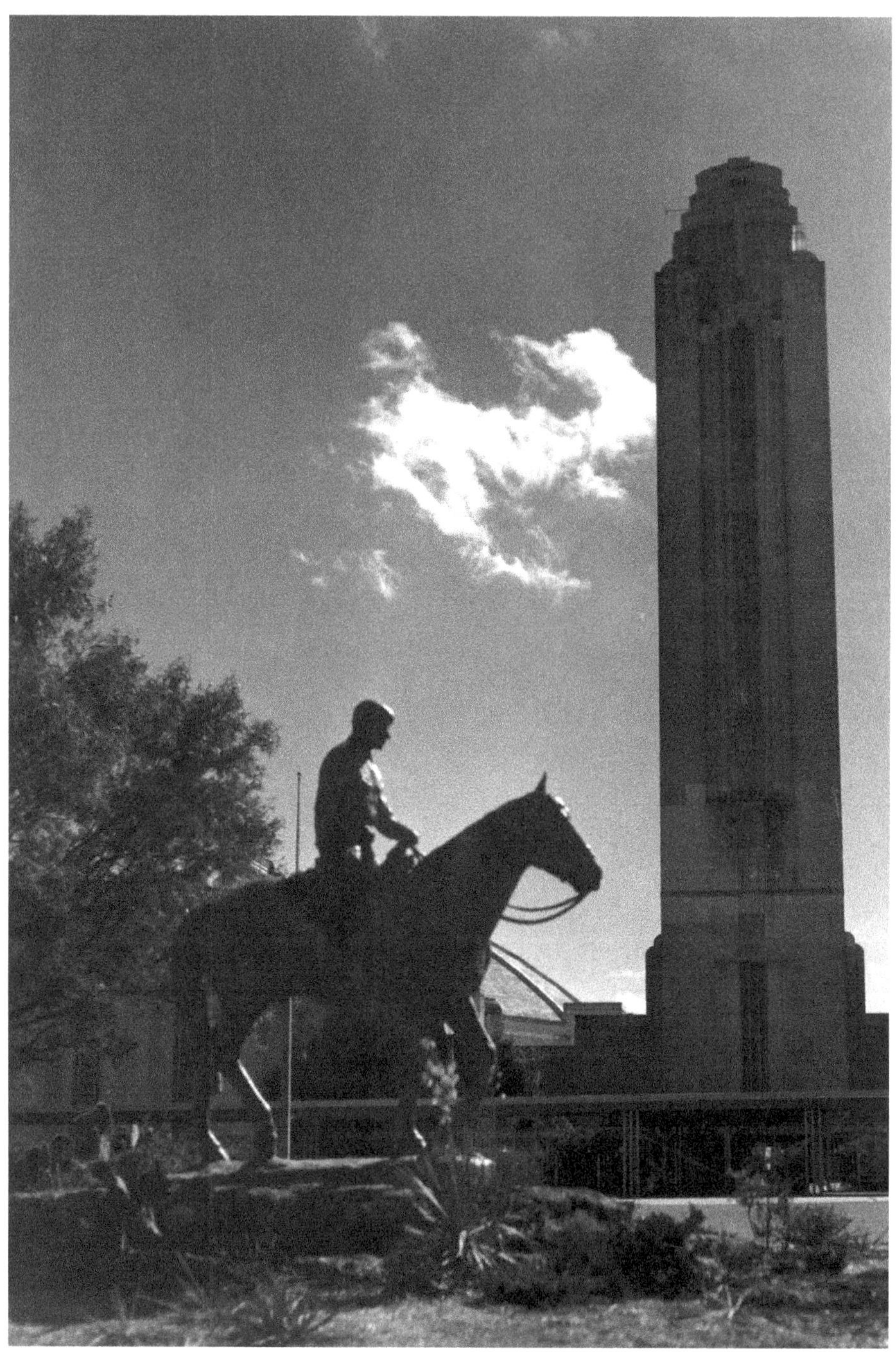

# Acknowledgments

This volume, *Historic Photos of Fort Worth,* is the result of the cooperation and efforts of a number of individuals.

Tom Wiederhold, Fort Worth Police Historical Association
Jim Noah
Jack White
Susan Pritchett, Tarrant County Archives
Donna Kruse, Tom Kellam, Jabari Jones and the staff of the
Fort Worth Public Library Genealogy and Local History Department
Louis Sherwood, Texas Wesleyan University Special Collections
Gilbert Anguiano
Pete Charlton, lectricbooks.com
Sarah Biles, North Fort Worth Historical Society
Beverly Washington
Sarah Walker
Brenda McClurkin, Ruth Callahan, and the staff of the University of Texas at Arlington Library, Special Collections
The staff at Turner Publishing
And, especially, my wife, Laurie, with deepest thanks.

—*Quentin McGown*

# Preface

Fort Worth has thousands of historic photographs that reside in archives, both locally and nationally. This book began with the observation that, while those photographs are of great interest to many, they are not easily accessible. During a time when Fort Worth is looking ahead and evaluating its future course, many people are asking, How do we treat the past? These decisions affect every aspect of the city—architecture, public spaces, commerce, infrastructure—and these, in turn, affect the way that people live their lives. This book seeks to provide easy access to a valuable, objective look into the history of Fort Worth.

The power of photographs is that they are less subjective than words in their treatment of history. Although the photographer can make decisions regarding subject matter and how to capture and present it, photographs do not provide the breadth of interpretation that text does. For this reason, they offer an original, untainted perspective that allows the viewer to interpret and observe.

This project represents countless hours of review and research. The researchers and writer have reviewed thousands of photographs in numerous archives. We greatly appreciate the generous assistance of those listed in the acknowledgments of this work, without whom this project could not have been completed.

The goal in publishing this work is to provide broader access to this set of extraordinary photographs which seek to inspire, provide perspective, and evoke insight that might assist people who are responsible for determining Fort Worth's future. In addition, the book seeks to preserve the past with adequate respect and reverence.

With the exception of touching up imperfections caused by the damage of time and cropping where necessary, no other changes have been made. The focus and clarity of many images is limited to the technology and the ability of the photographer at the time they were taken.

The work is divided into eras. Beginning with some of the earliest known photographs of Fort Worth, the first section records photographs from 1877 through the late nineteenth century. The second section spans the first decade of the twentieth century. Section Three carries the story forward to 1940. The last section covers the World War II era up to recent times.

In each of these sections we have made an effort to capture various aspects of life through our selection of photographs. People, commerce, transportation, infrastructure, religious institutions, and educational institutions have been included to provide a broad perspective.

We encourage readers to reflect as they go walking in Fort Worth, strolling through the city, its parks, and its neighborhoods. It is the publisher's hope that in utilizing this work, longtime residents will learn something new and that new residents will gain a perspective on where Fort Worth has been, so that each can contribute to its future.

*—Todd Bottorff, Publisher*

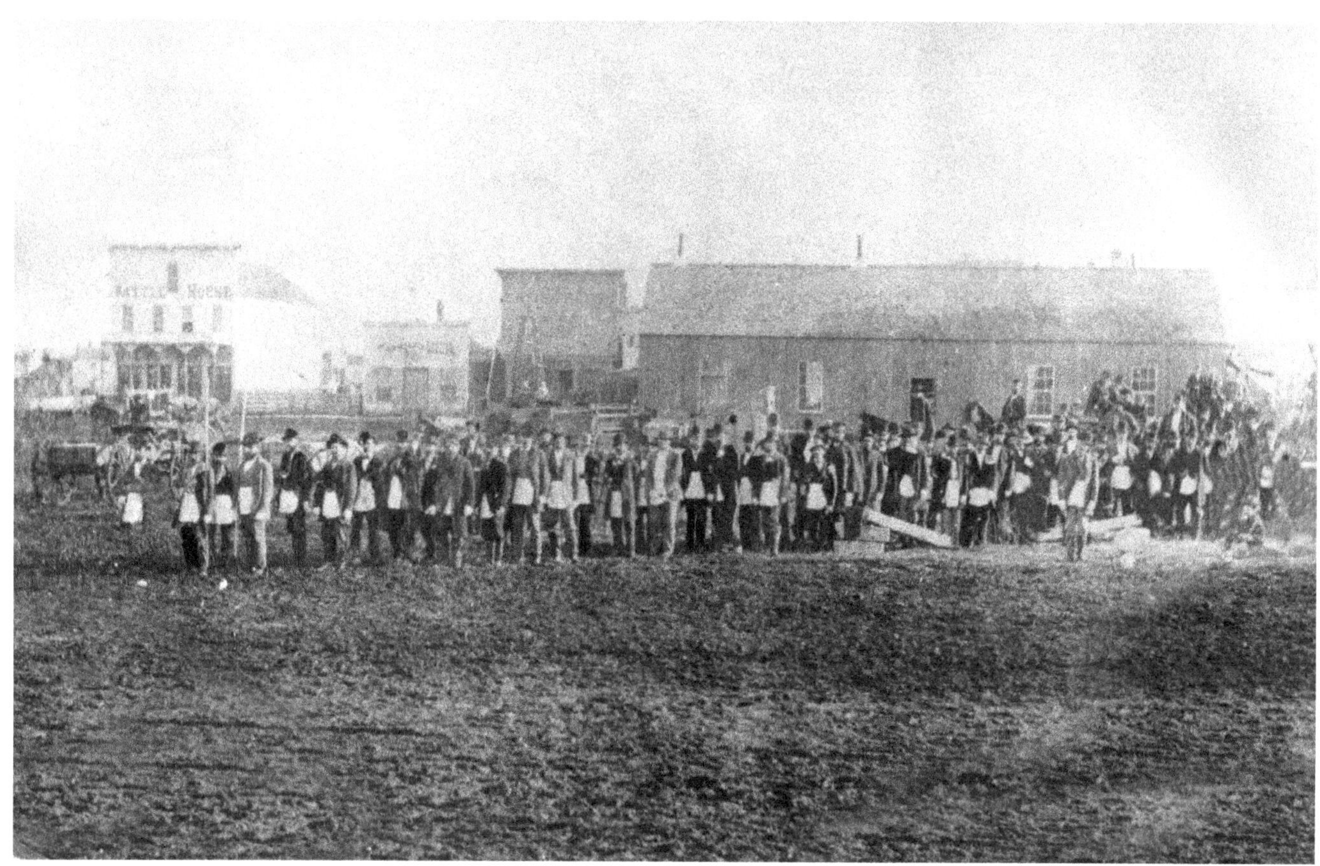

Following the March 29, 1876 fire that destroyed the first permanent Tarrant County courthouse and most of the records in it, commissioners hired architects and builders, Thomas and Werner, to oversee construction of a replacement. In November 1877, members of the Fort Worth Masonic Lodge, Number 148, gathered for the cornerstone laying ceremony. Between 1876 and the completion of the new courthouse in 1878, the county and courts operated out of a temporary 25 by 60 foot building seen here on the south side of the public square and behind the assembled masons. The Battle House at left stood on the present corner of Weatherford and Commerce Streets.

# Army Outpost to Railroad Town

## 1849–1899

On June 6, 1849, a detachment of United States Dragoons formally established a small fort on the northwest Texas frontier. The soldiers were sent to protect the first waves of determined settlers from the Comanche and Kiowa who claimed the land as theirs and who were equally determined to keep it. The unstoppable push westward of Anglo migration led to the abandonment of the outpost in 1853 after a relatively uneventful career. Civilians moving into the ramshackle buildings left behind then began the task of building a town, laying the foundations for the modern City of Fort Worth.

Fort Worth struggled through its early years, even after plucking the county seat designation from neighboring Birdville in 1856. The Civil War diverted attention and resources from frontier protection, and the town once again found itself uncomfortably close to the bloody clashes between settlers and native tribes. It was after the war's end that Fort Worth found its first real opportunity for success, one that would permanently shape its identity. Beginning in 1866, cowboys driving millions of Texas cattle up the trails to the Kansas railheads or to pastures farther north helped turn the town into a supply and entertainment center. A drover could find everything from boots to saddles to shirts, along with saloons and professional women more than ready to take that new shirt off his back.

Not content with just watching cattle pass through town on the way to someone else's railhead, Fort Worthians struggled to bring the railroad to town. When a national depression in 1873 halted rail construction, so many people left town that it was said a panther could sleep unmolested on Main Street, giving rise to the city's nickname "Panther City." The town patiently worked through the lean years, and the Texas & Pacific finally arrived in July 1876. Over the next year, the city's population swelled to almost ten thousand.

As the city grew, it tried hard to shake off the dust of its frontier days, but never strayed too far from its livestock roots and the willingness to provide whatever service, in whatever form, it could. Fort Worth established colleges, an opera house, hospitals and the magnificent and tragic Texas Spring Palace, all the while consolidating alternate entertainments in an infamous Hell's Half Acre at the south end of downtown.

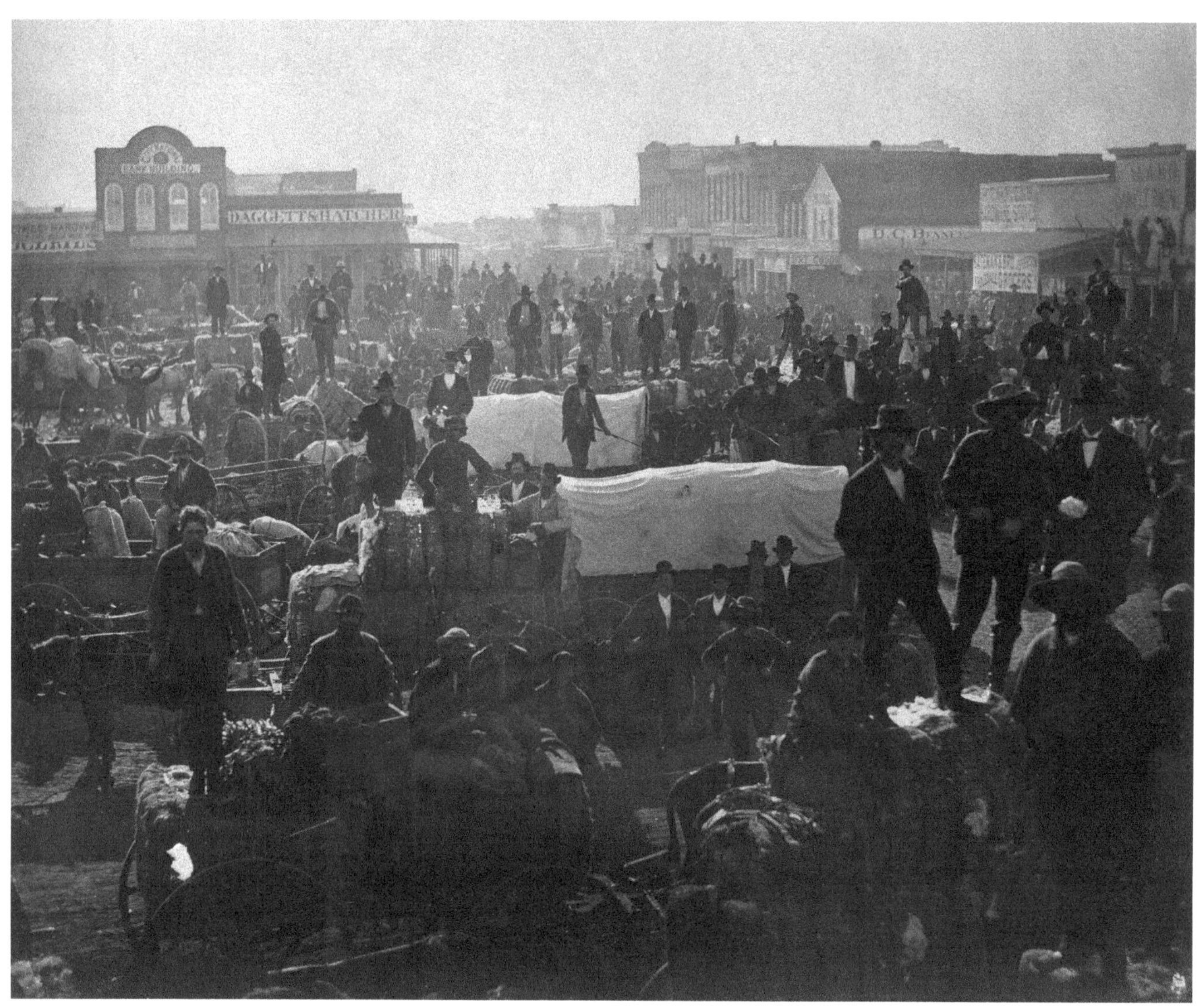


The Daggett and Hatcher store, at the corner of Houston and Weatherford streets, overlooks a bustling market scene about 1878. As cotton, produce, livestock and other goods arrived in town to coincide with the sessions of the district court, proud Tarrant Countians posed for an unknown photographer set up next to the courthouse.

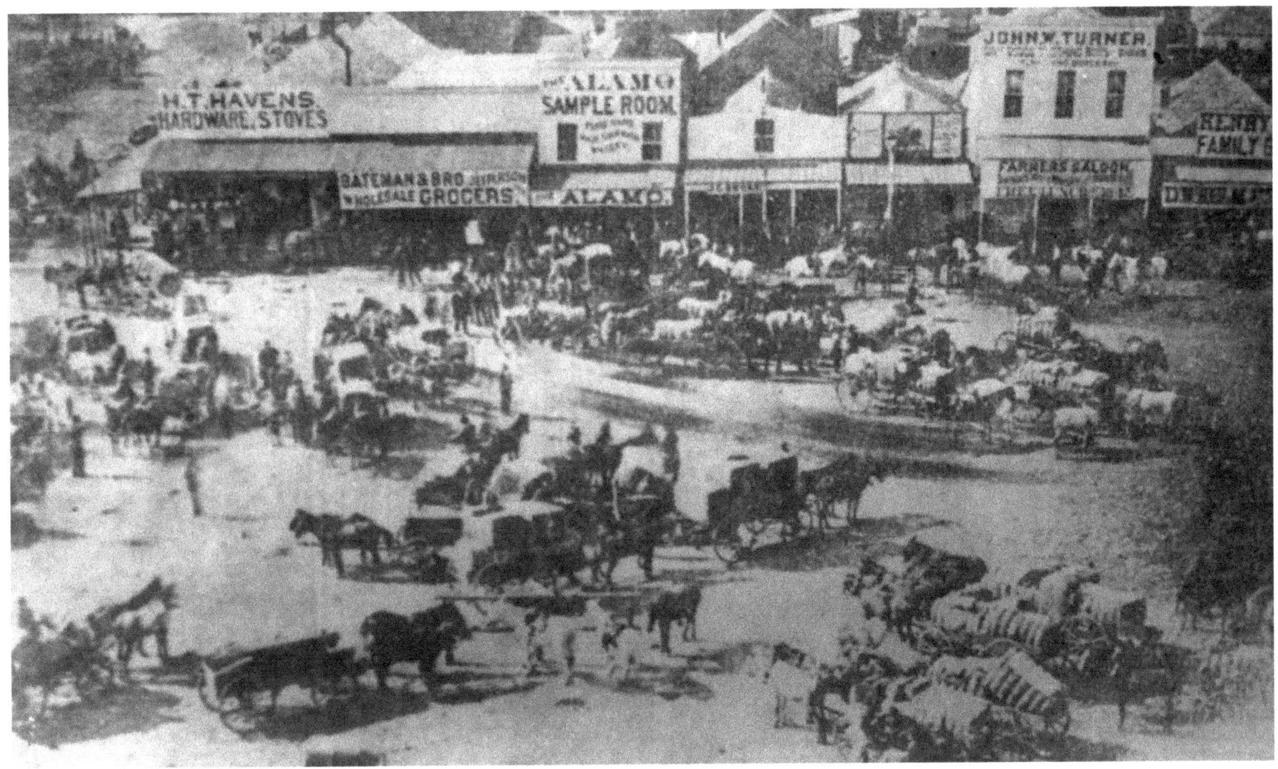


The west side of the public square surrounding the courthouse, now the 100 block of North Houston Street, offered everything from dry goods and groceries to guns and saddlery. Judging by the crowded storefronts, the Farmers Saloon with its free lunch and the Alamo Sample Room, with its "Pure Hand Made Sourmash Whisky," were the most popular places to do business on this market day about 1878.

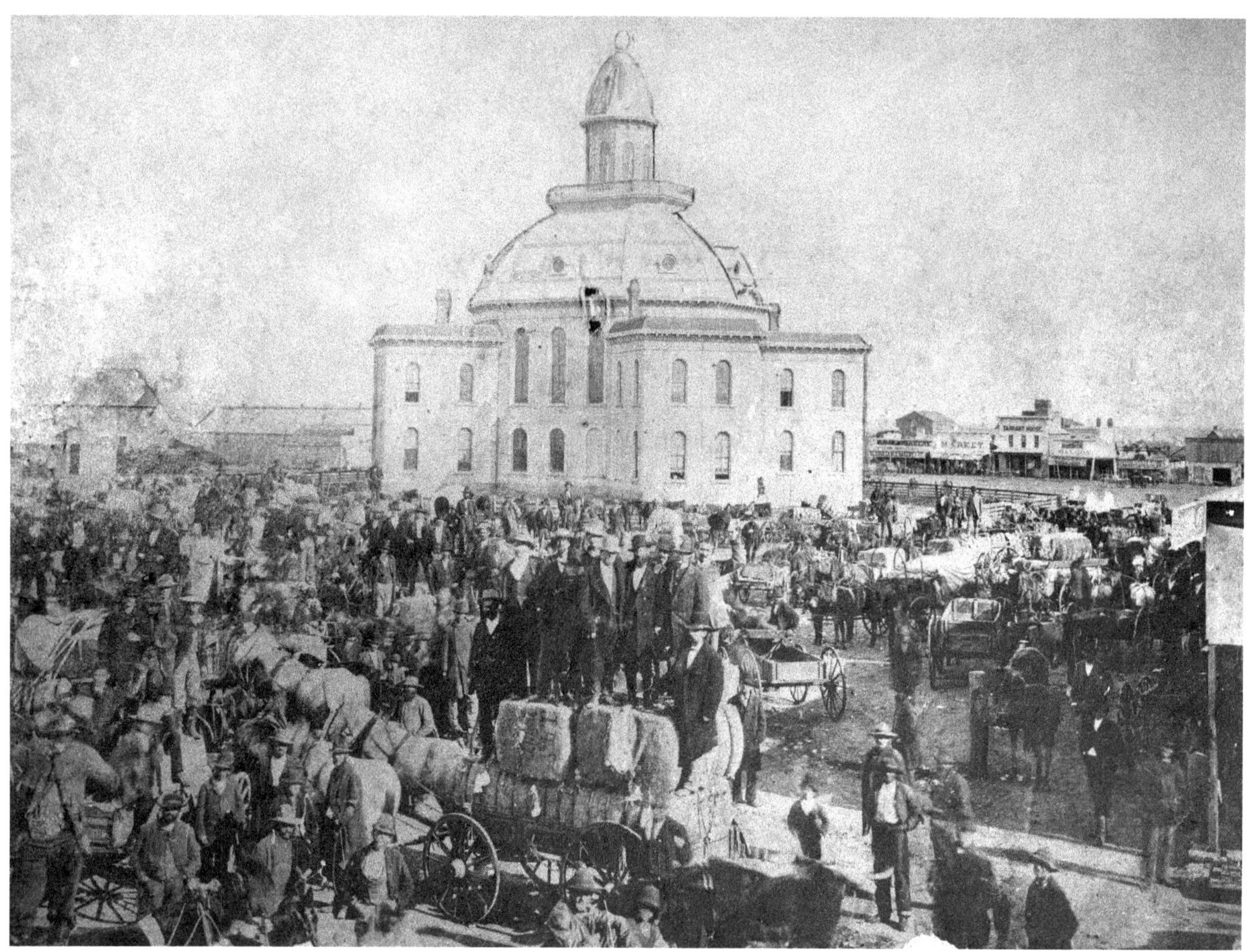

Looking east across the expansive public square from the intersection of Houston and Weatherford, this view shows the 1878 courthouse surrounded by a fence to keep stray animals out. The two-story building visible just to the right of the courthouse is the old Masonic Lodge, built in 1857, and used until 1878 for numerous community activities, including school and church sessions.

When Fort Worth incorporated in 1873, it moved municipal operations from temporary quarters on the public square to a new city hall and fire station at Rusk Street and 2nd. The old city hall shown here would be replaced by a new fire station in 1907, Rusk would be renamed Commerce, and in time the fire station would become a historic element nestled under the City Center Tower One. A streetlight hangs at upper right.

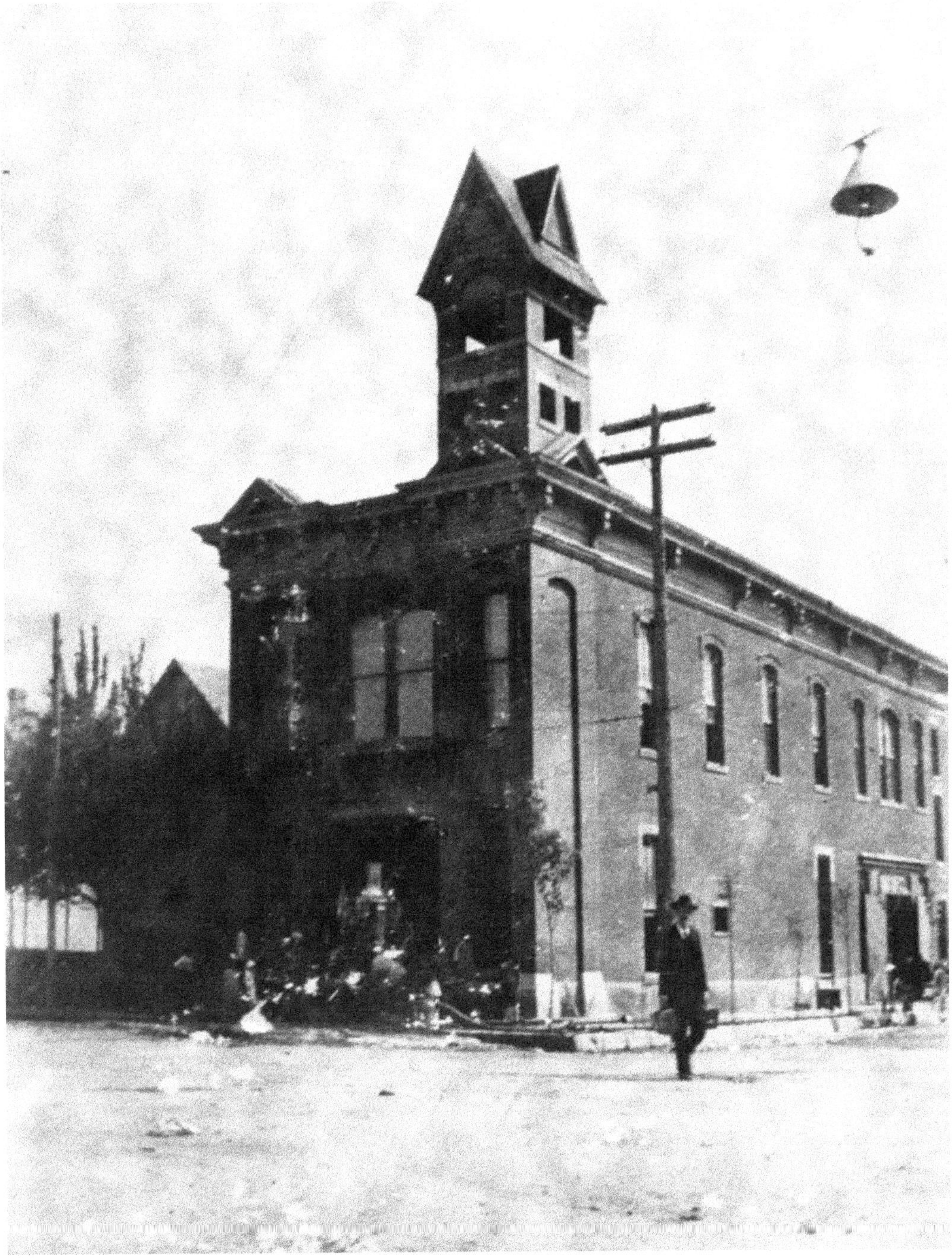

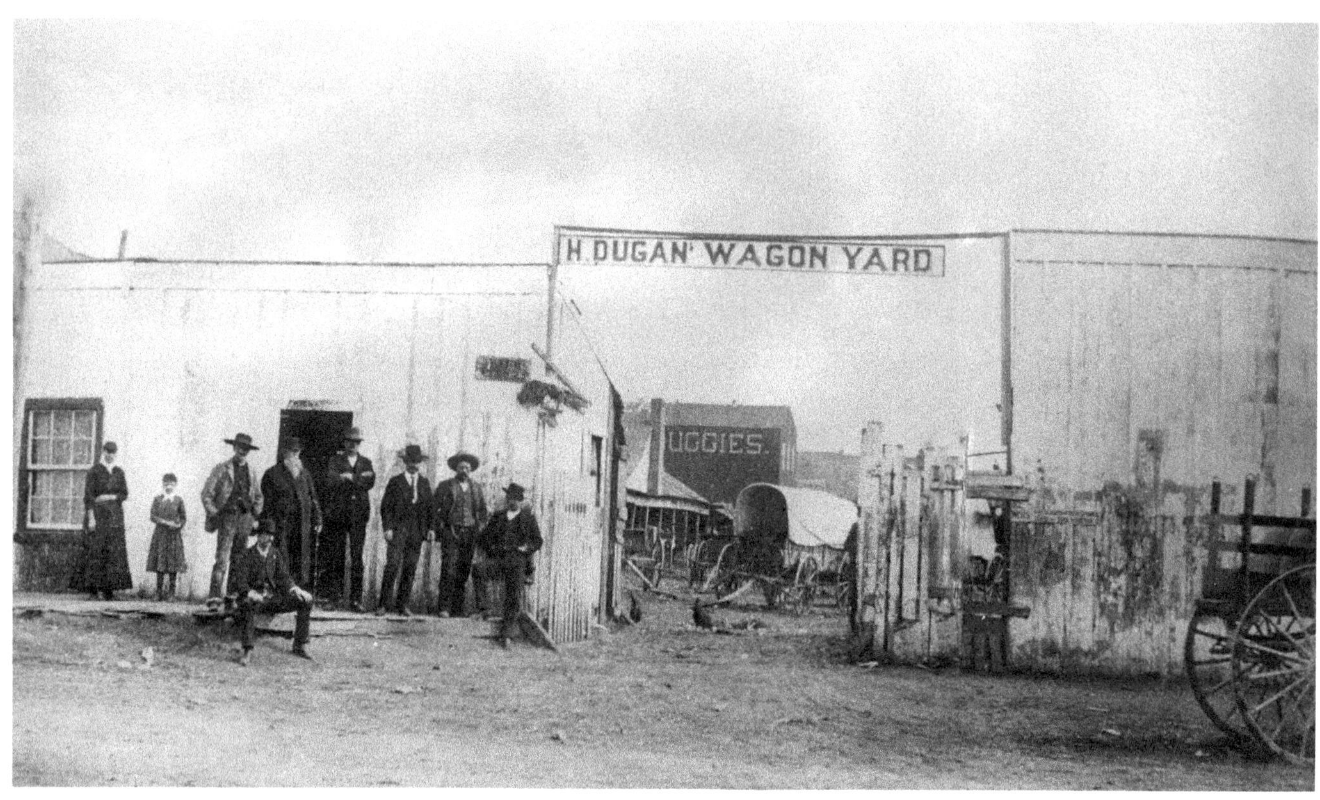


Hugh Dugan joined the flood of new residents in Fort Worth during the boom that followed the arrival of the Texas & Pacific railroad in 1876. He started a laundry business about 1878 and expanded his property on Weatherford Street at Taylor to accommodate the transportation needs of the rapidly growing town.

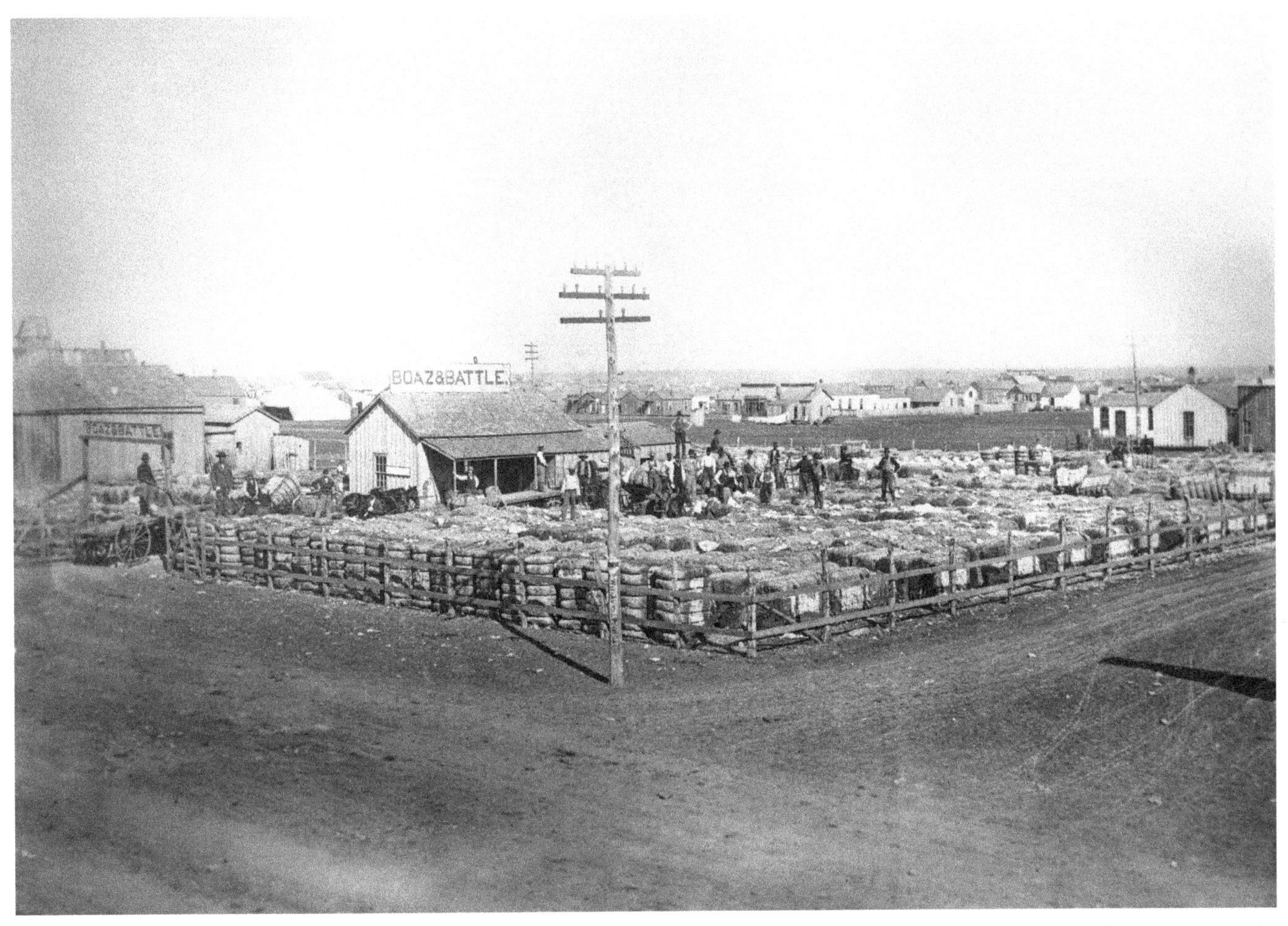


David Boaz settled in Tarrant County with his family in 1859. He returned after his service in the Confederate Army and built a cotton brokerage business. He later partnered with George Battle to expand the business in the early 1880s to include buffalo hides and wool and to build a yard between Main and Houston from 13th to 14th streets, across from the railroad depot. A vertical sign on the utility pole appears to be an advertisement for Wizard Oil, a popular patent medicine.

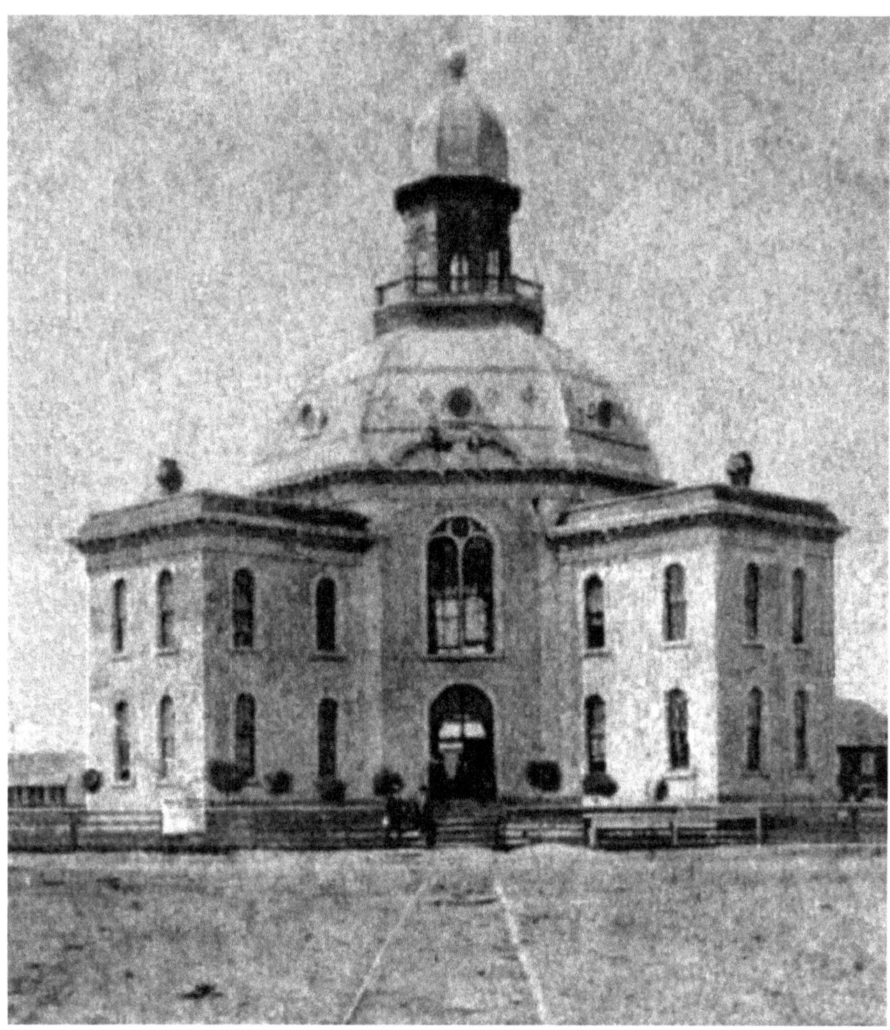

Following the devastating 1876 fire that destroyed Tarrant County's first permanent courthouse, county leaders immediately built a new, larger structure to accommodate the growing community. Visitors atop the dome had a panoramic view.

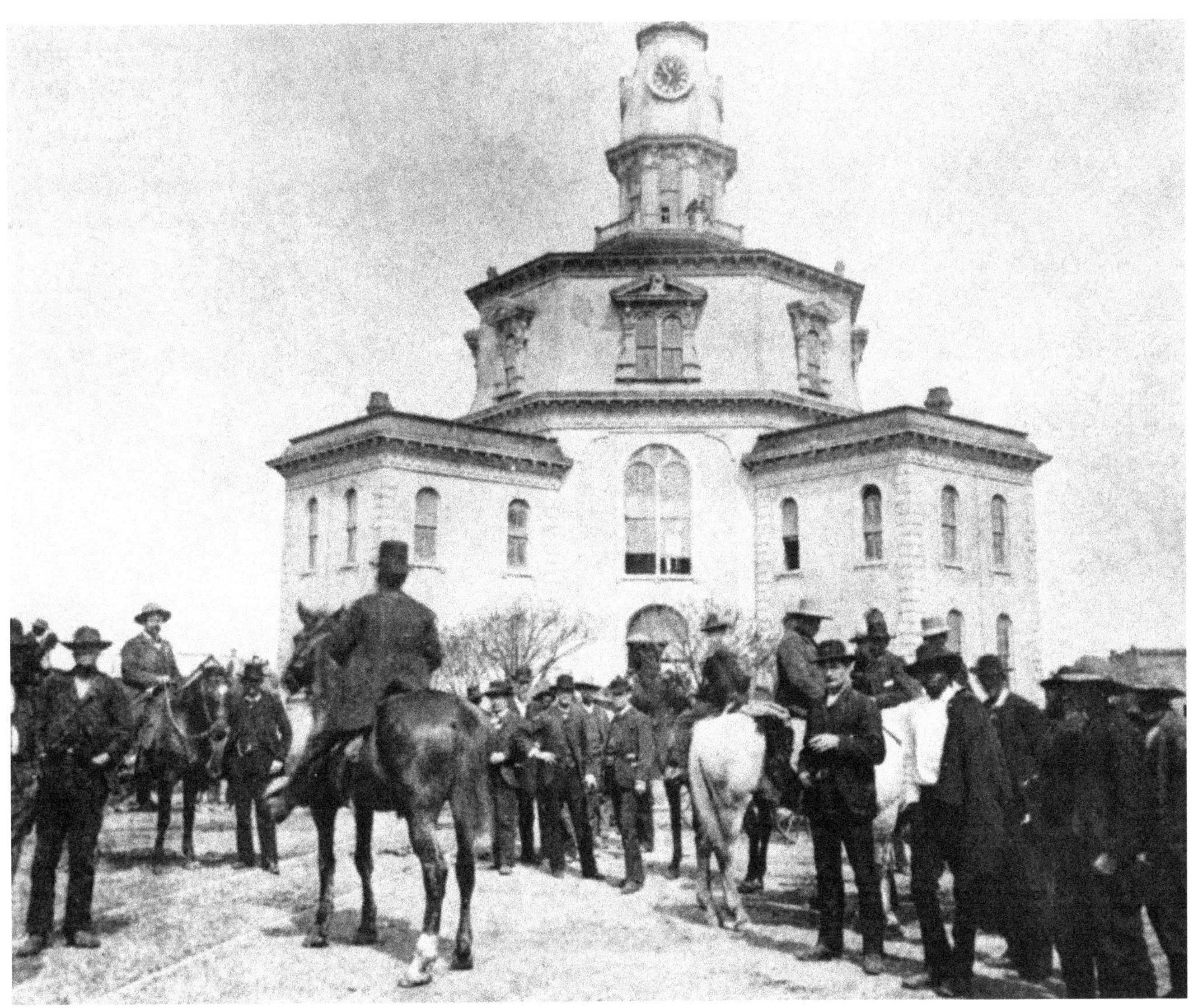

It wasn't long before the 1878 Courthouse ran out of space for the growing county business, prompting an 1882 remodeling that replaced the old dome with a new third floor and a clock tower. Local architect J. J. Kane designed the new additions. Even expanded, the courthouse had a tough time meeting the needs of a growing community and would be replaced a decade later.

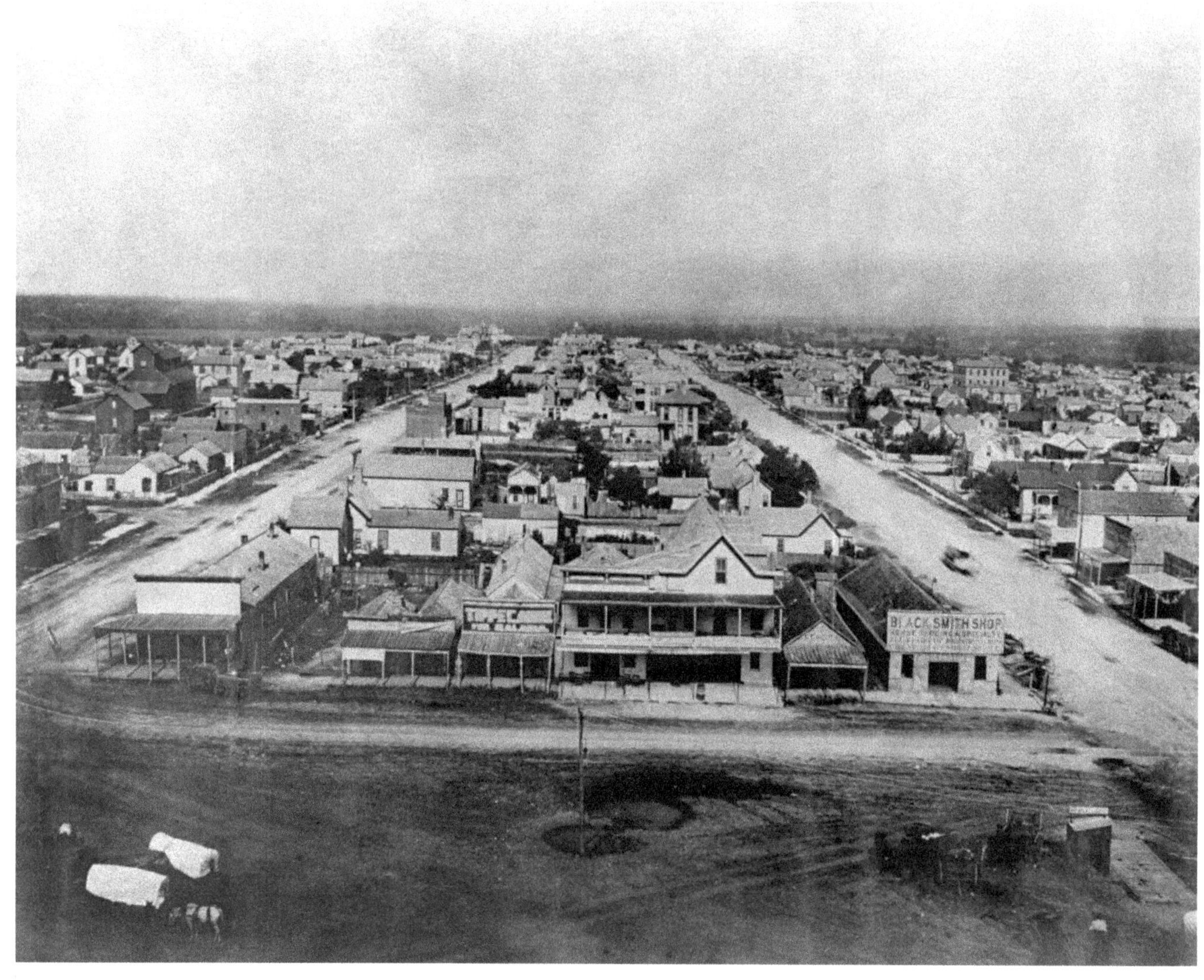


Not long after the 1882 expansion of the courthouse, a photographer captured this view of the east side of the square and the growing city beyond. A new advertisement for Tippecanoe Bitters, a malaria "cure" patented in 1883, adorns a frame storefront typical of Fort Worth's early architecture. Next door stood the two-story Illinois Boarding House, successor to the Tarrant House. The blacksmith on the corner of what is now Commerce and Weatherford streets touted his services as "cheap and on short notice."

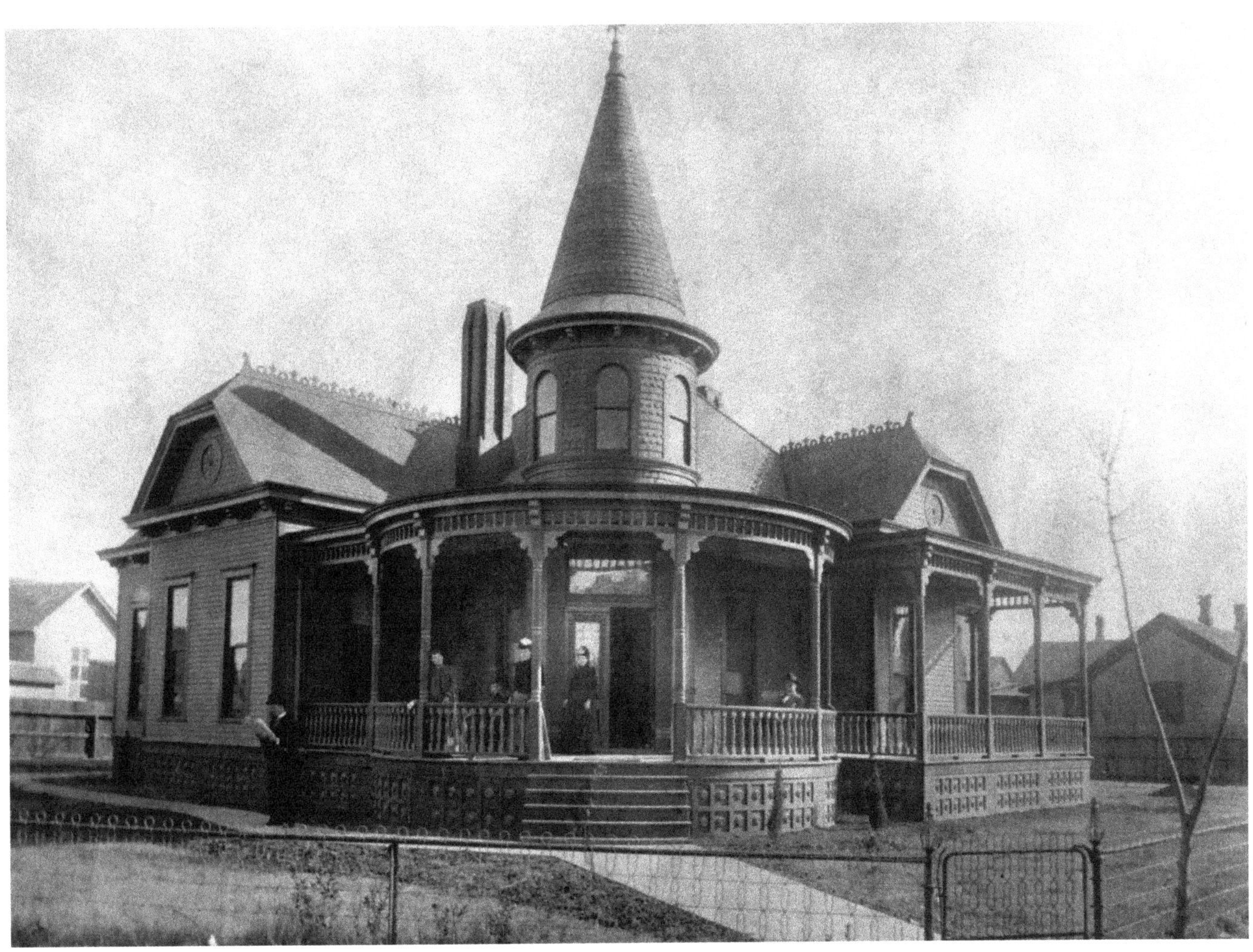

In 1893, German-born Sam Levy purchased this house on the southeast corner of Lamar and 7th streets from the heirs of John S. Hirshfield, whose 1874 addition to the city, with its grid aligned to true north, created the odd street angles in that section of downtown. Levy later served as president of the Casey-Swasey Cigar Company, one of the largest wholesale liquor and tobacco firms in the region. In 1903, he was a founder and the first president of Temple Beth-El, Fort Worth's first Reform Judaism congregation. He sold his home in 1919 to Bernie Anderson and Morris Berney, who erected the Neil P. Anderson building on the site.

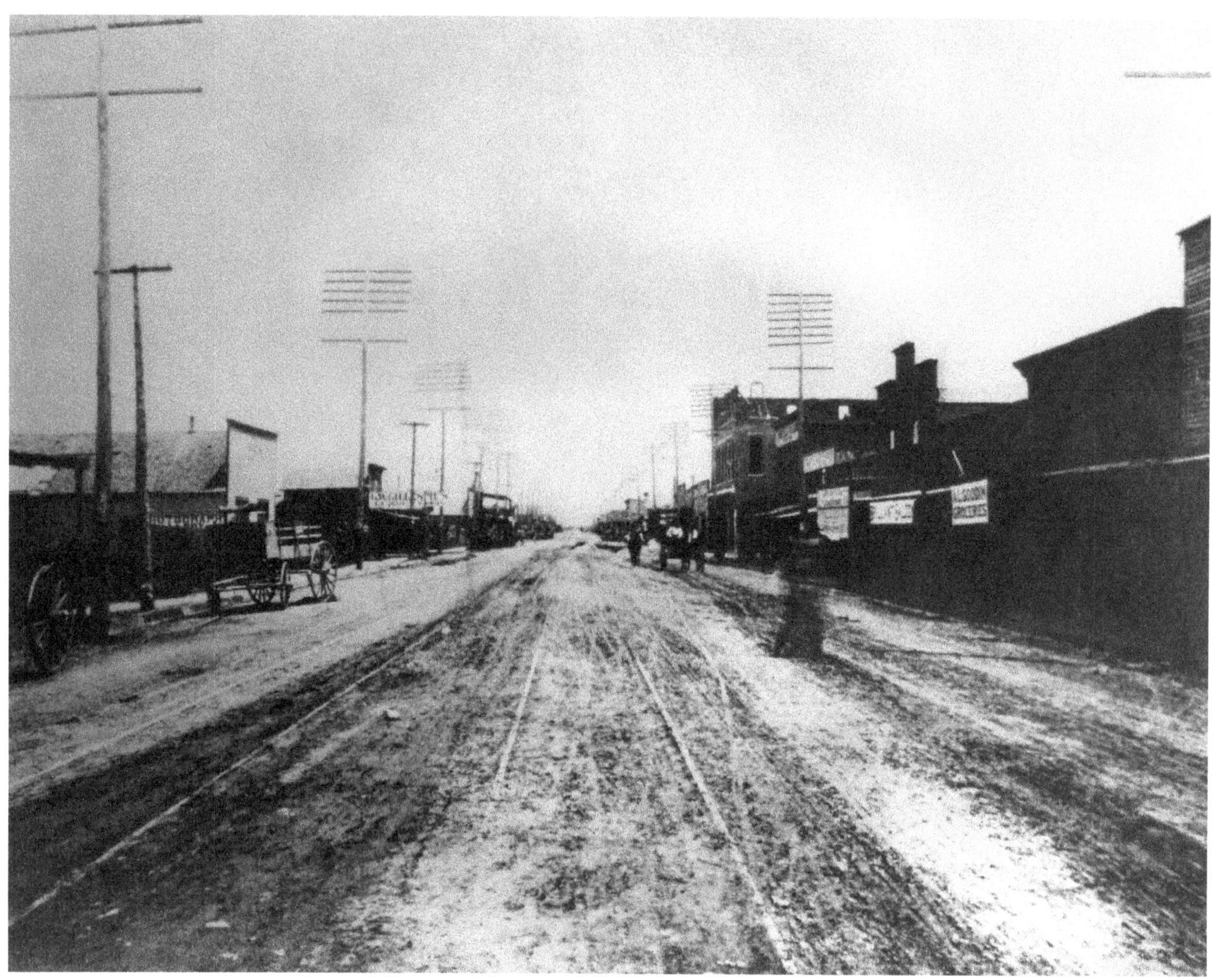

The view down Houston Street, looking south from 6th in early 1889, shows a street on the verge of major change as the brick-and-sandstone Board of Trade Building at 7th Street, under construction at right center, replaces the old wood-frame structures from the city's pioneer days. Gillespie's Lumber Yard and Hardware business occupies most of the east side of the street, surrounding the small studio of photographer J. H. Mignon.

In 1881, the Knights of Pythias, a charitable and fraternal organization chartered in Washington D.C. in 1864 and established in Texas in 1872, built its first permanent lodge in Fort Worth at the corner of 3rd and Main. Damaged by fire in 1901, the building was rebuilt in Flemish style, complete with knight, and still presides over Main Street as the signature building in Sundance Square.

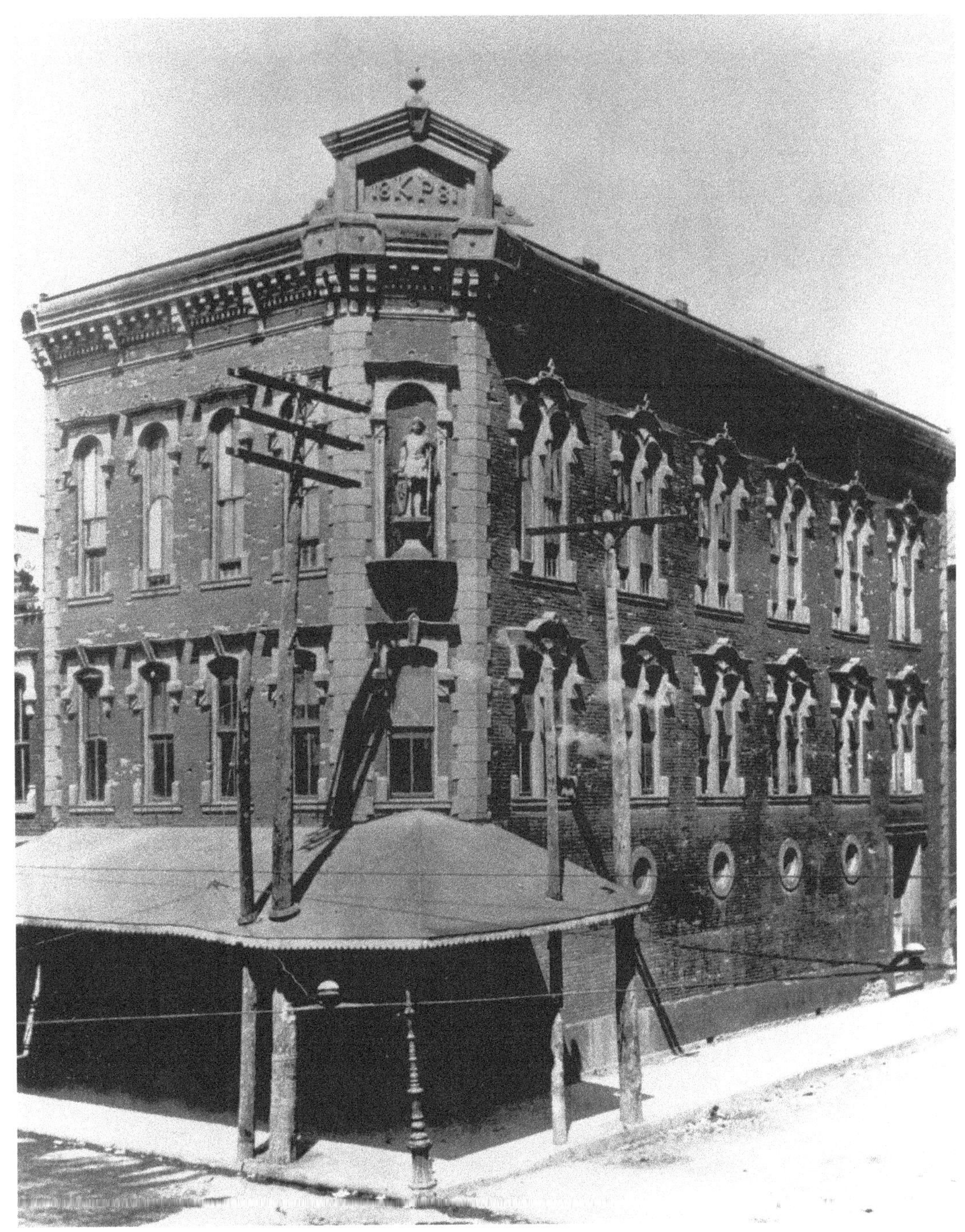

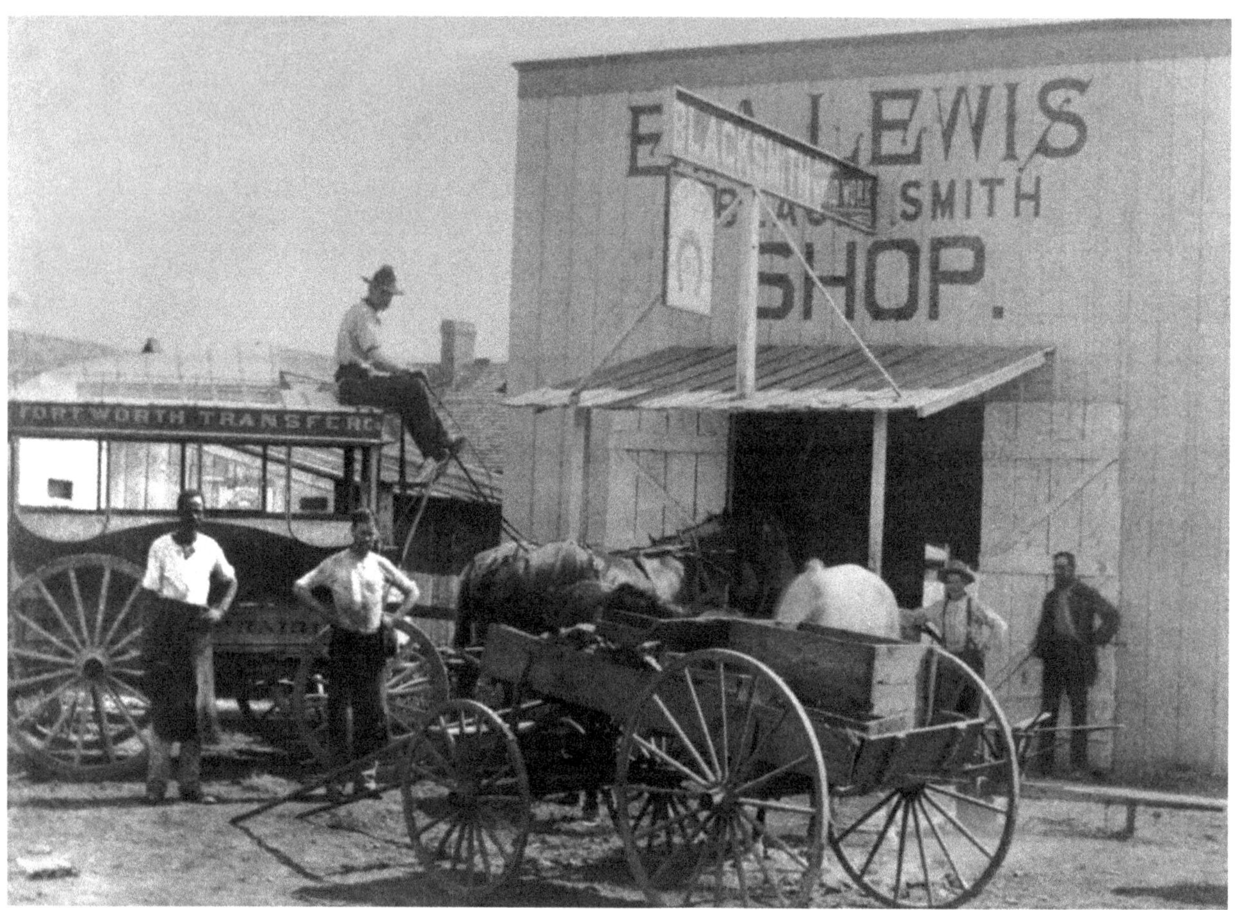


From its headquarters on lower Jones Street near the train depots, the Fort Worth Transfer Company delivered goods all over the growing town. E. A. Lewis, and other blacksmiths, kept the vehicles in good working order and occasionally worked on the draft animals as well.

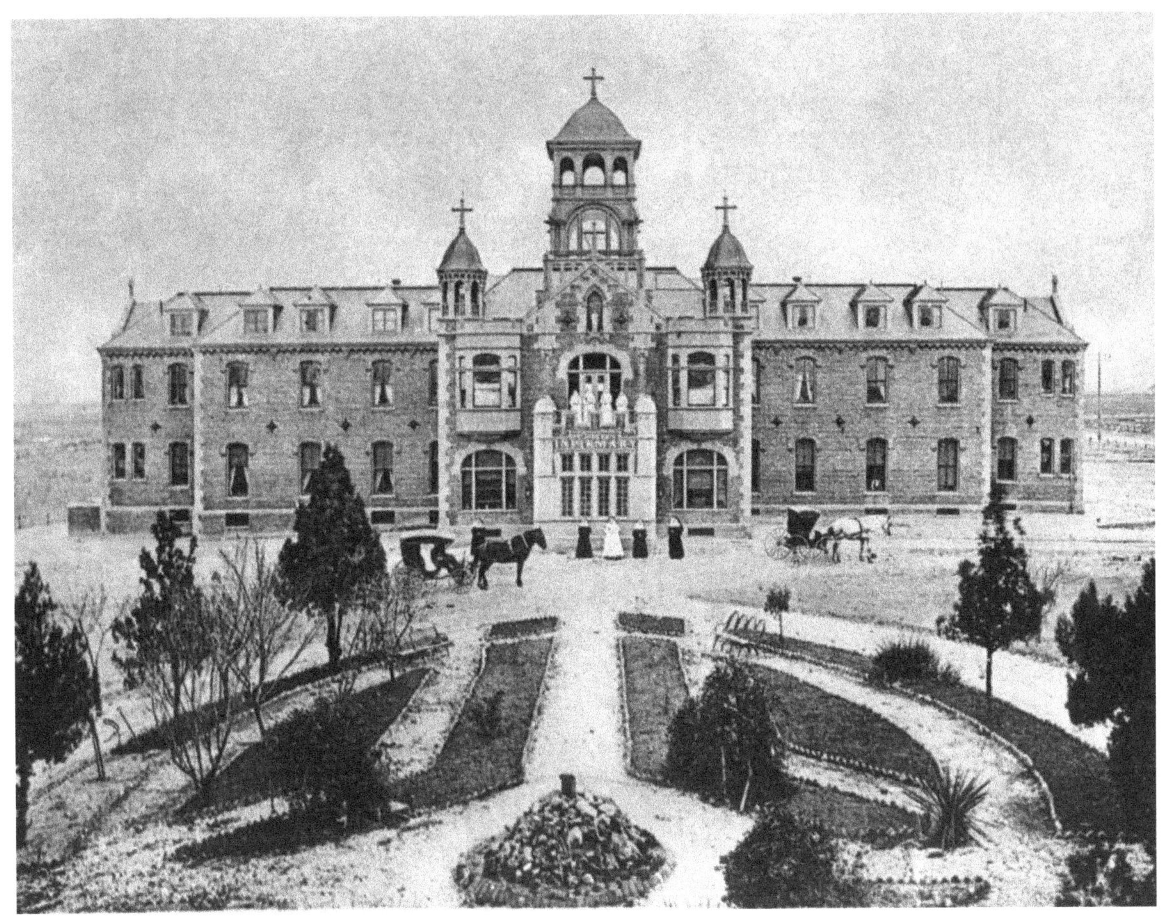

Tracing its roots to a private hospital built in 1883 on the far southern outskirts of town to serve the employees of the Missouri Pacific Railroad, St. Joseph's Infirmary (later St. Joseph's Hospital), was under the direction of the Sisters of Charity of the Incarnate Word. Here, the sisters pose proudly in front of their new building, dedicated in 1898. They provided care to all who sought it regardless of ability to pay and, remarkable for the time, regardless of race.

As Fort Worth continued to grow with the expansion of livestock activities and an ever-increasing number of railroads linking the city with the rest of the country, the single streetcar track down Main Street accommodated a mule-drawn car that made the seventeen-block trip eighty times a day—unless the mule bolted or the car got stuck in the mud.

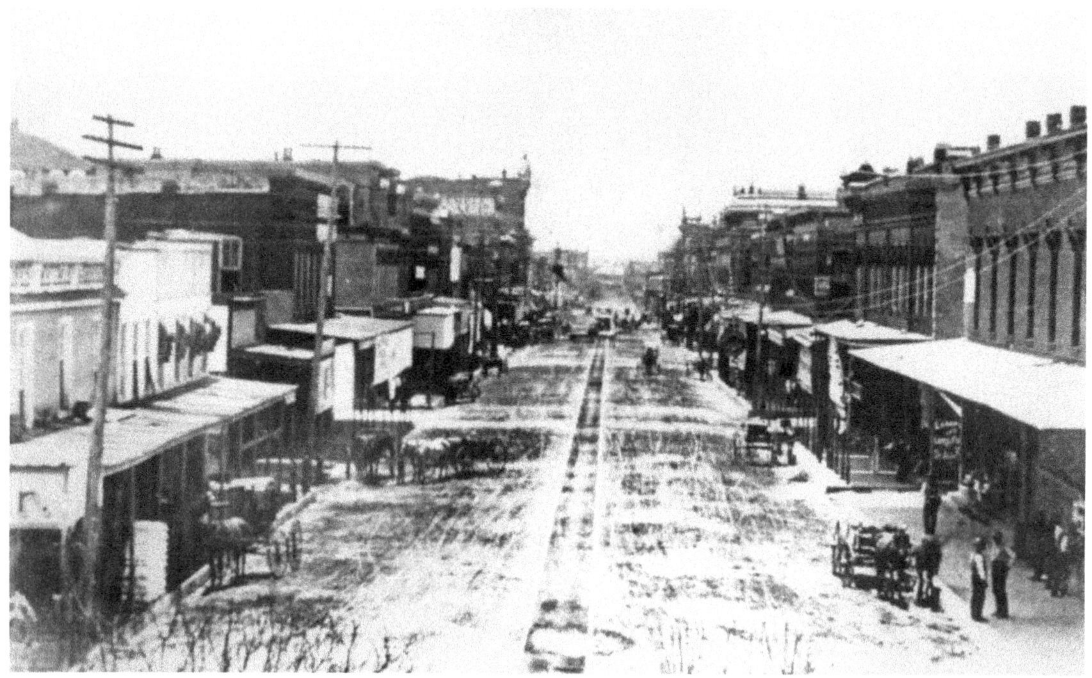

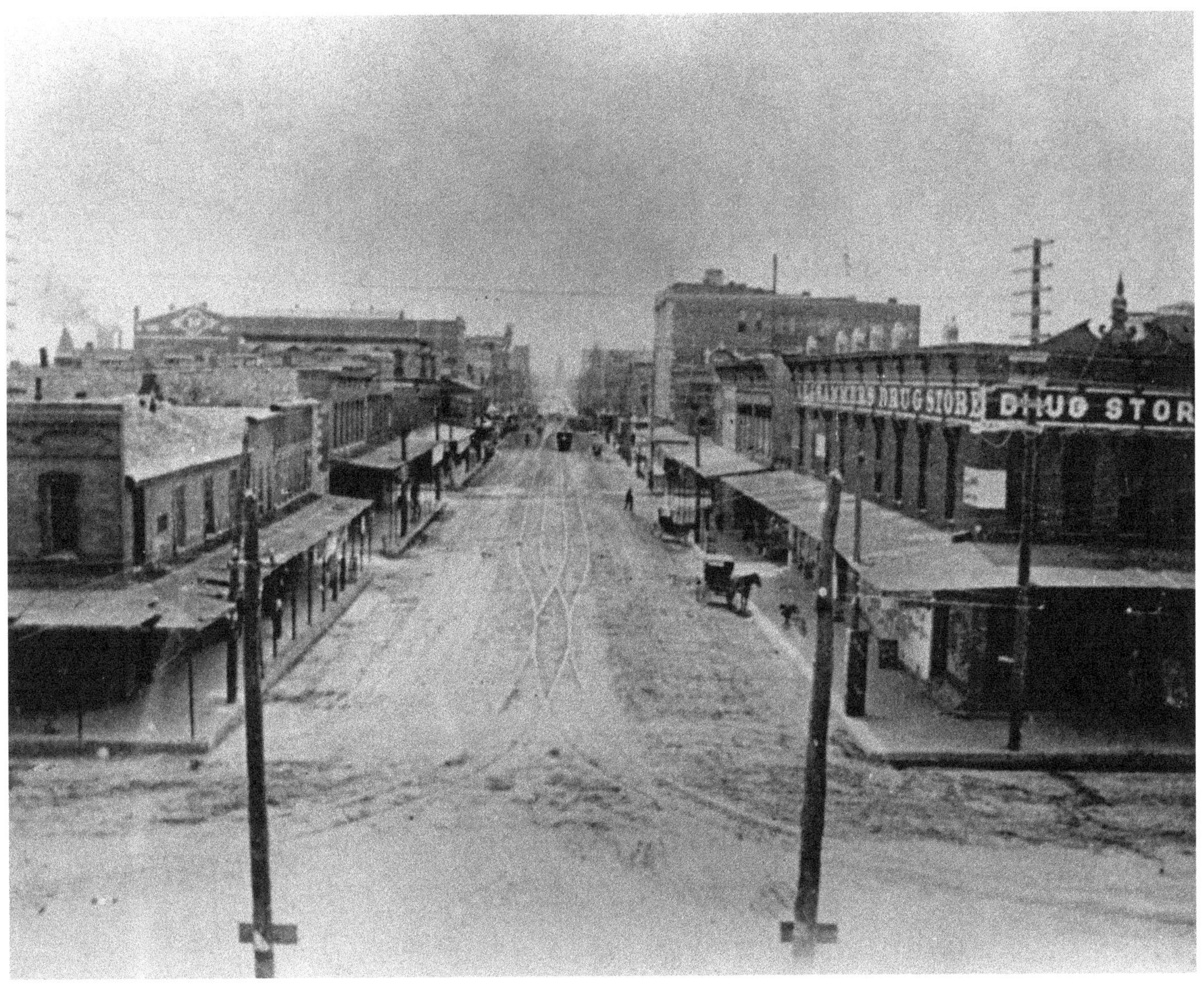


In 1889, Fort Worth became the first Southwestern city to power its street railway with electricity. This 1900 view from the courthouse shows the expansion of the streetcar tracks from one to two lines. Prominent at the far end of Main Street is the newly constructed Texas & Pacific Union Passenger Station, a fitting architectural bookend to the 1895 courthouse.

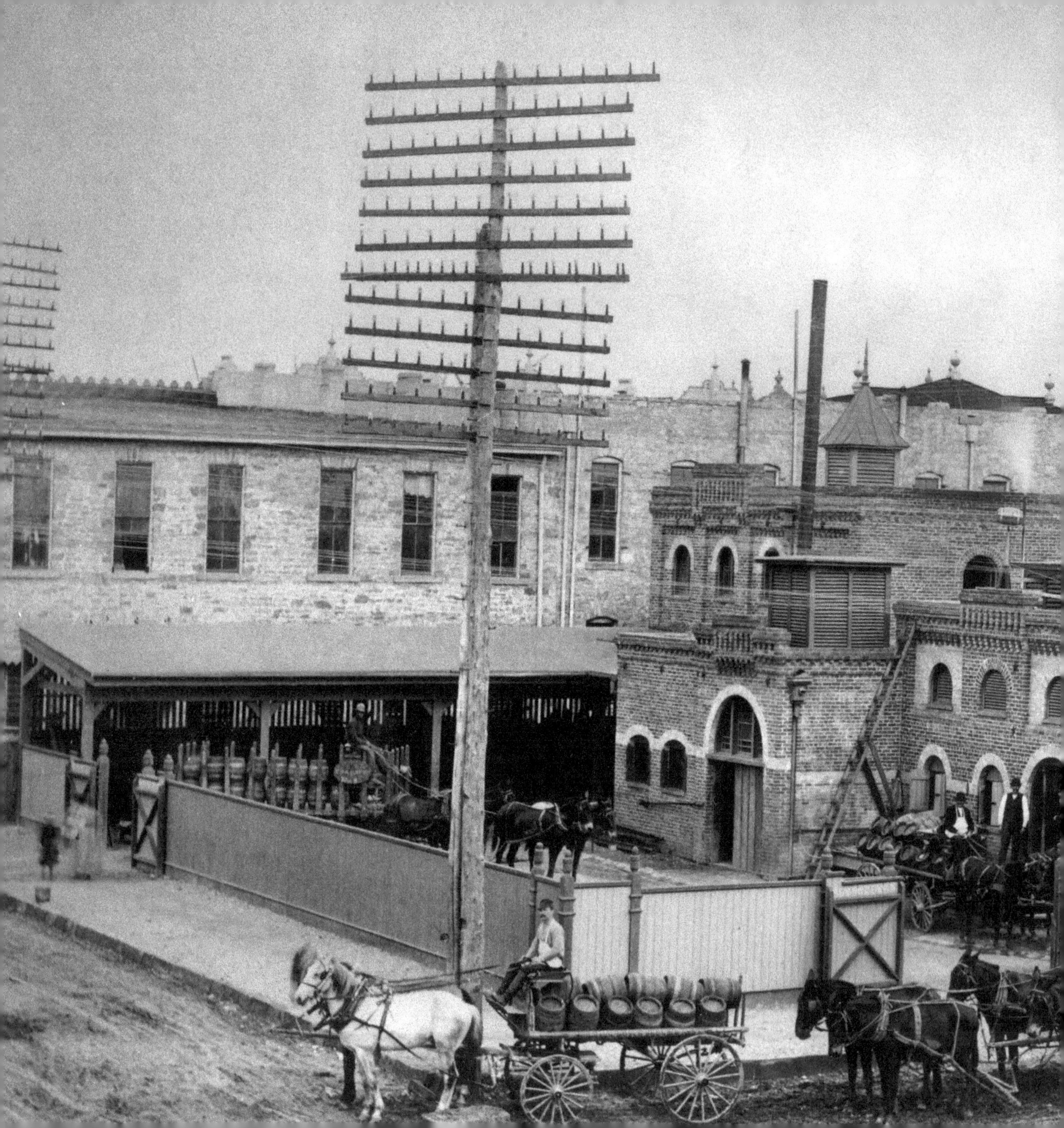

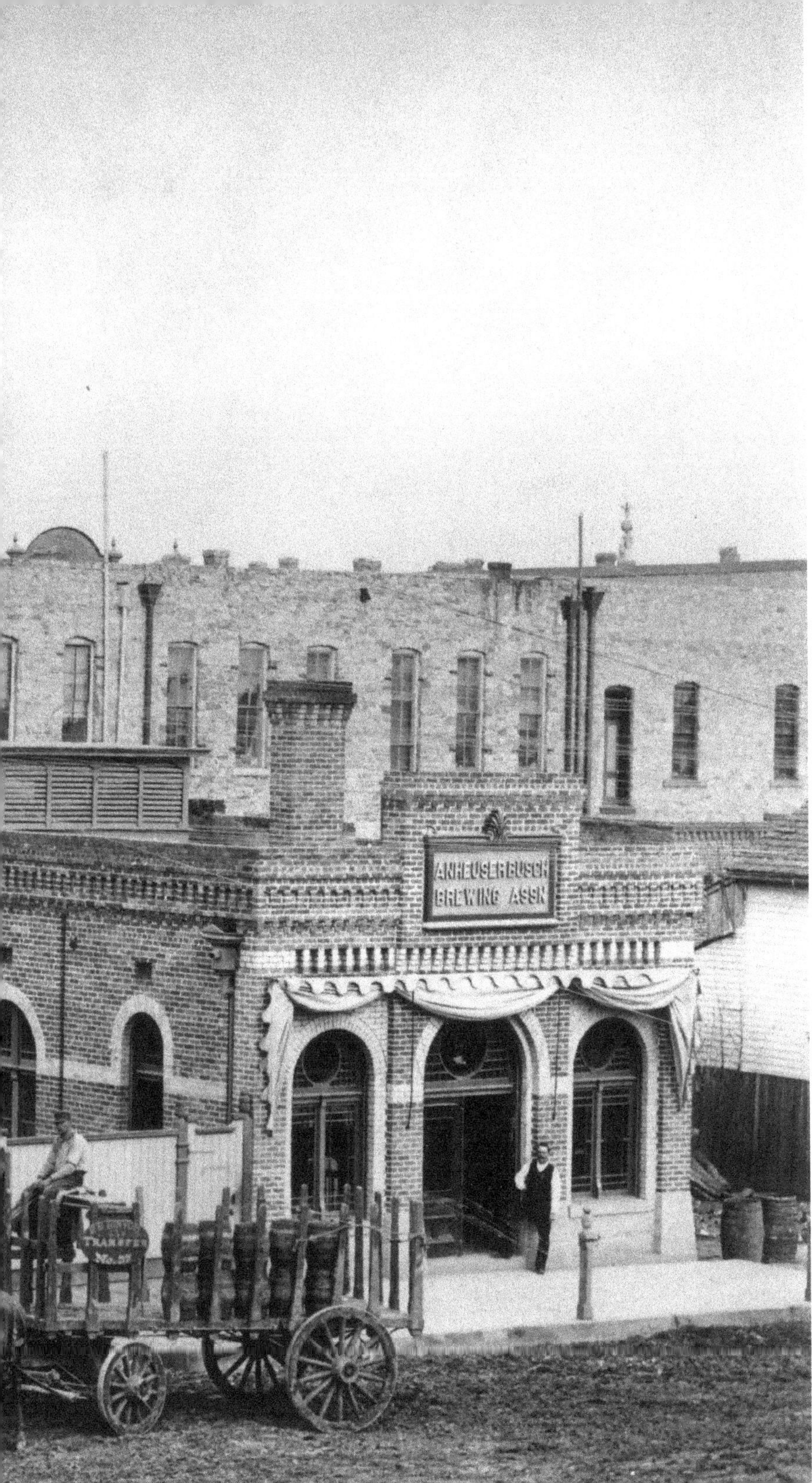


The Eberhard Anheuser Company Brewing Association opened its first office in Fort Worth about 1878, a year before the firm changed its name to include Anheuser's son-in-law and partner, Adolphus Busch. The popular business quickly outgrew its small office and depot on Main Street and by 1885 expanded to the location shown here on the southeast corner of 3rd and Throckmorton streets. Delivery wagons kept local saloons and hotels supplied with the company's signature Budweiser beer. The company remained at this location until about 1892, when it left its German Gothic "castle" for larger facilities at Taylor and Front, now Lancaster Avenue.

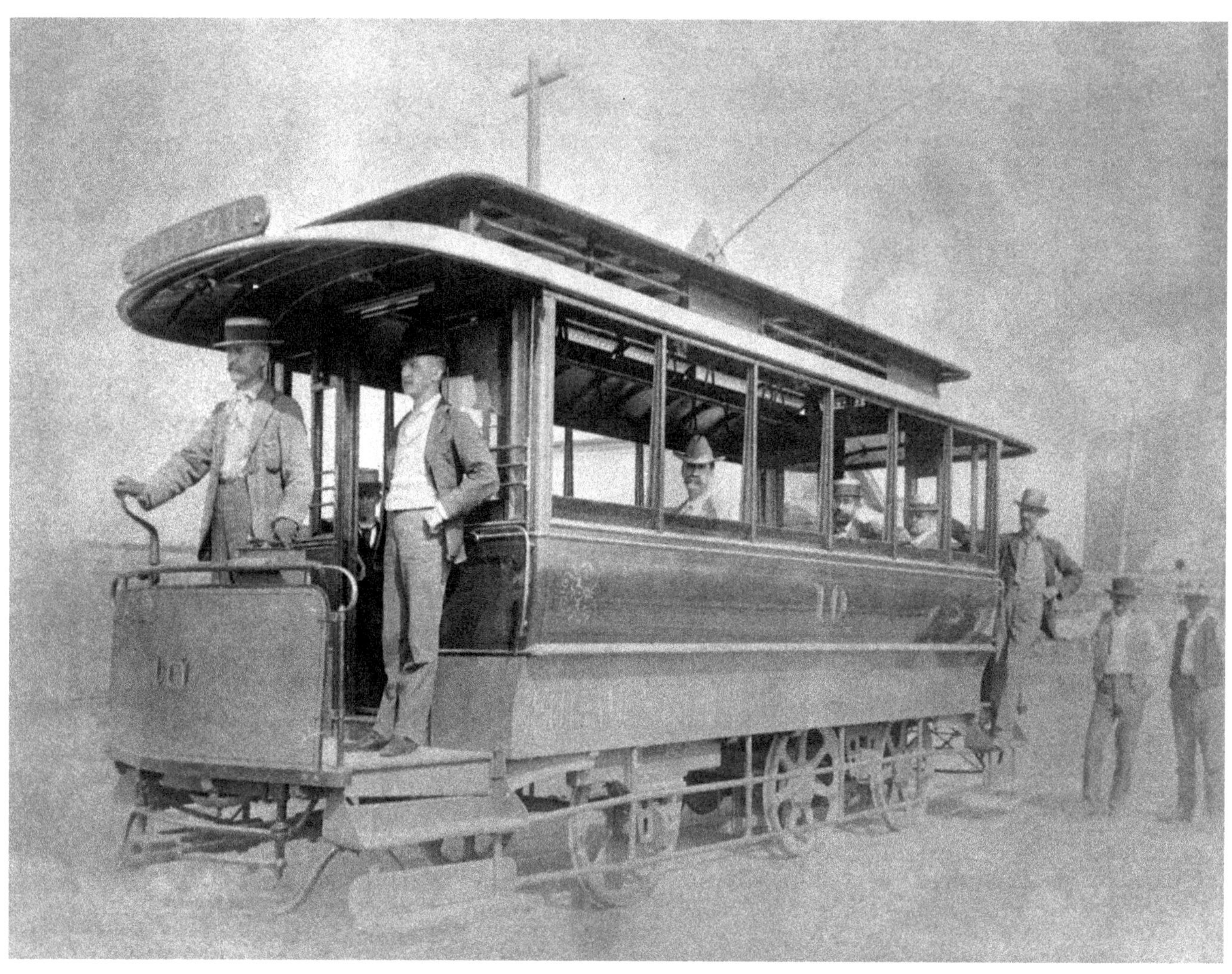

The operator switched from reins and temperamental animals to a handle controlling the electric current on his new streetcar. While not dramatically different in appearance from the old mule-drawn cars, the powered one was the pride of the city. Electric streetcar companies sprang up to provide connections to the growing city. The last trolley in Fort Worth would make its final run in the late 1930s.

When a site selection committee of the Methodist Episcopal Church, South, explored potential locations for its new Polytechnic College, it settled on a parcel of donated land four miles east of Fort Worth. Chartered in 1890 and opening for classes in this building the following year, the college sparked residential and commercial development in the surrounding area that led to the incorporation of the City of Polytechnic. Fort Worth eventually annexed the small city and the college evolved into today's Texas Wesleyan University.

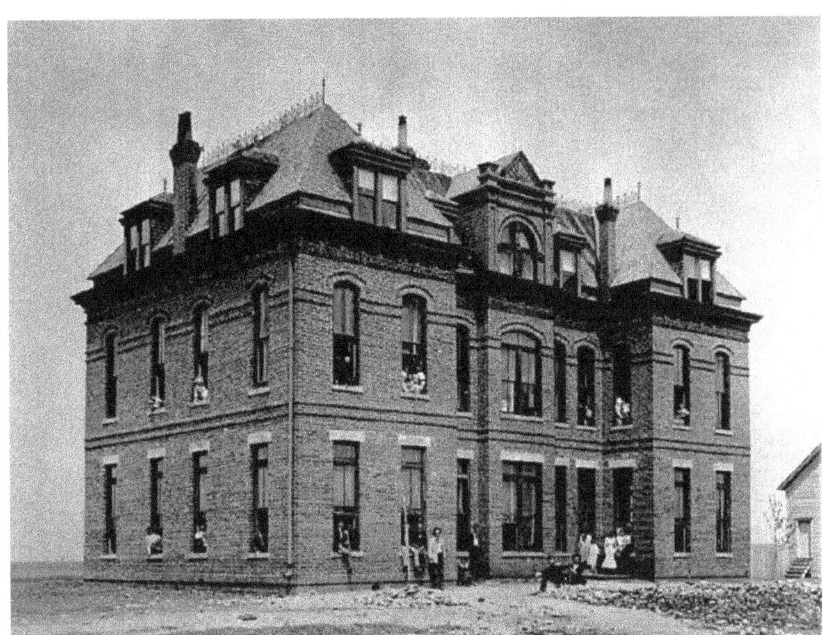

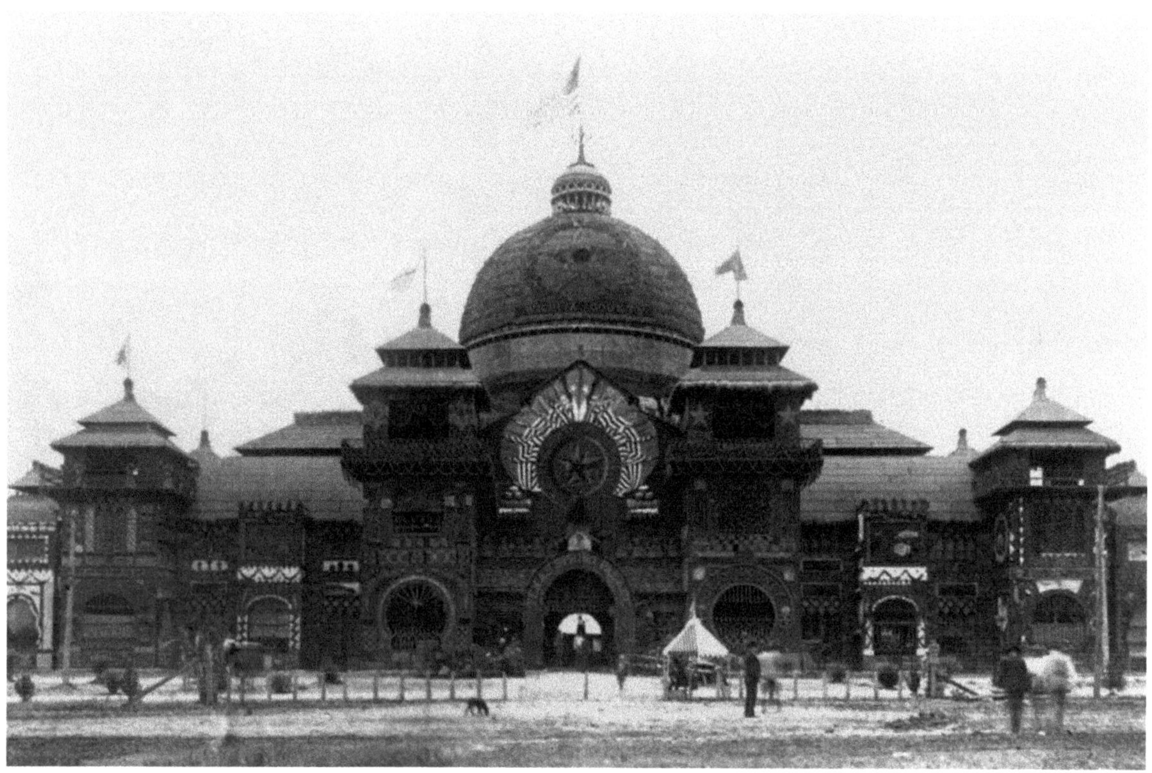

The Texas Spring Palace opened to great fanfare during the Spring of 1889 near the present intersection of West Vickery and Galveston, south of the railroad tracks downtown. Designed to showcase the seemingly limitless natural resources of Texas, the massive building of more than 100,000 square feet housed exhibits from counties across the state. The inaugural season proved so popular that the Spring Palace was expanded by another hundred feet on each end and reopened for the 1890 season.

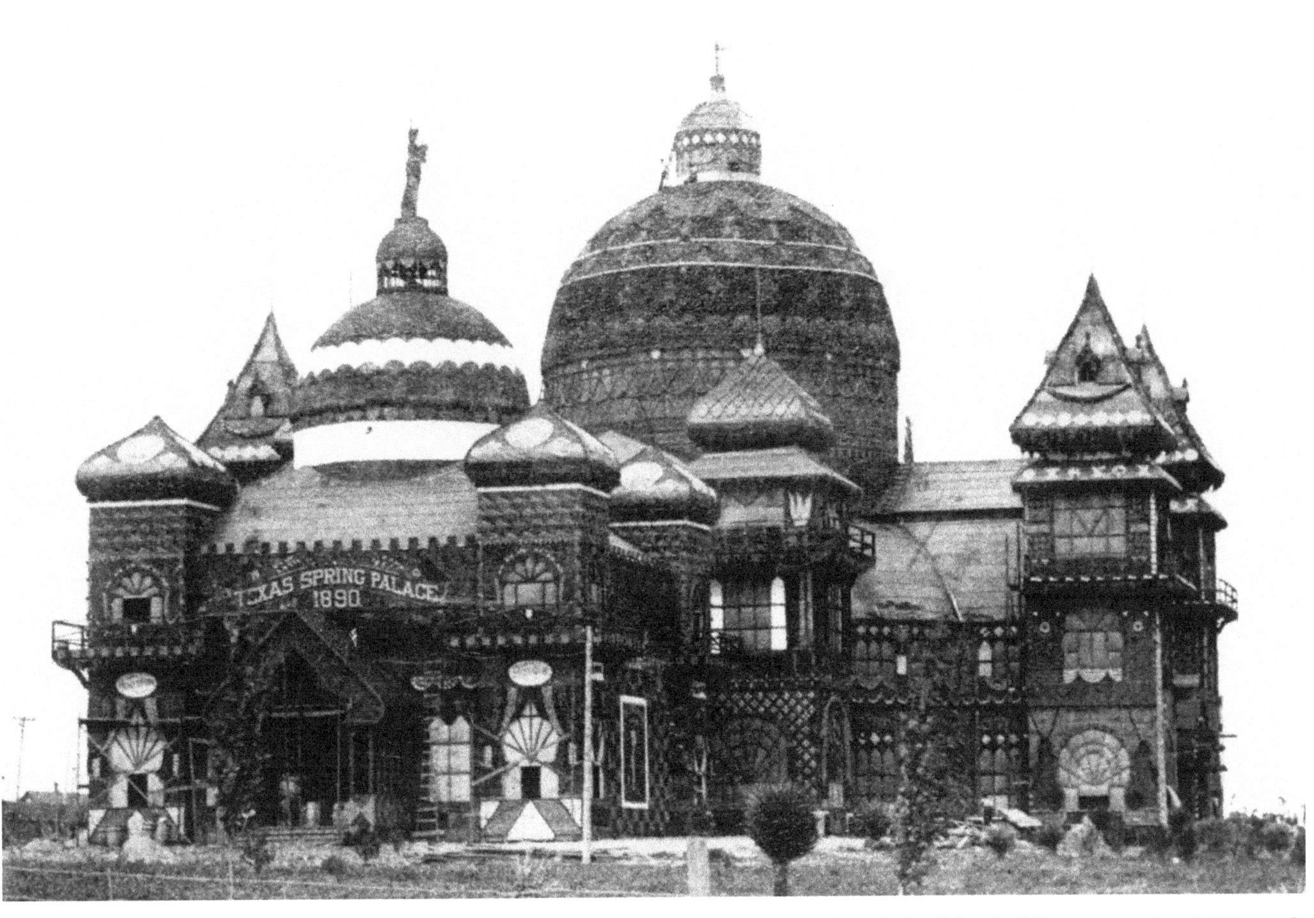


On the night of May 30, 1890, fire broke out in the Texas Spring Palace building as more than 7,000 people enjoyed the fancy dress ball on the 16,000-square-foot dance floor. Miraculously, all but one escaped as the building was completely engulfed by flames in less than fifteen minutes. Al Hayne stayed behind to direct people out of the burning building and was fatally injured when he finally was forced to jump from a second-story window.

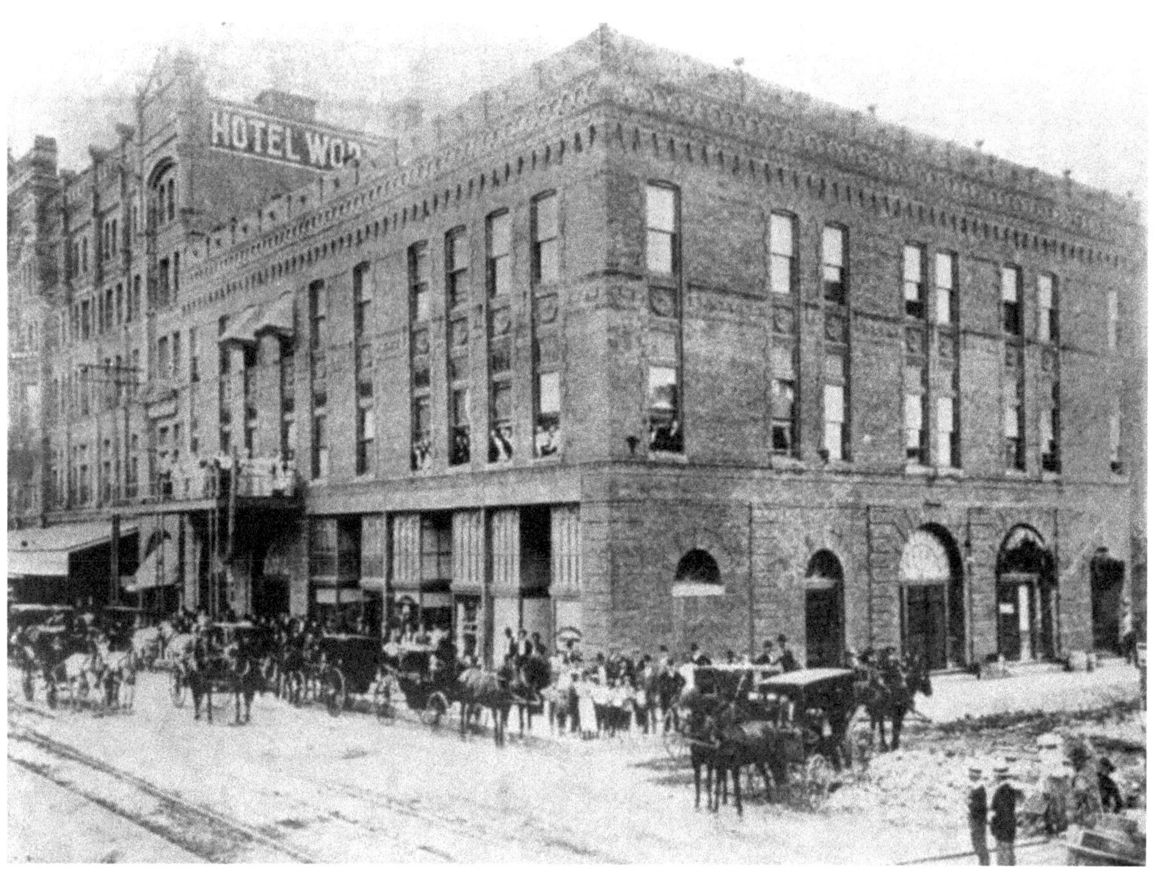


Texas cattleman John Scharbauer opened his Worth Hotel in 1894 with a three-story addition to the adjacent five-story Hendricks office building at 7th and Main. The new hotel quickly became the city's finest, but was replaced in 1927 by a newer Worth Hotel at 7th and Taylor. The old Hendricks Building found new life as the Worth Building until it was destroyed by fire in 1945. Today, the Hilton Hotel, formerly the 1921 Texas Hotel, stands on the site of the three-story Worth at 8th and Main.

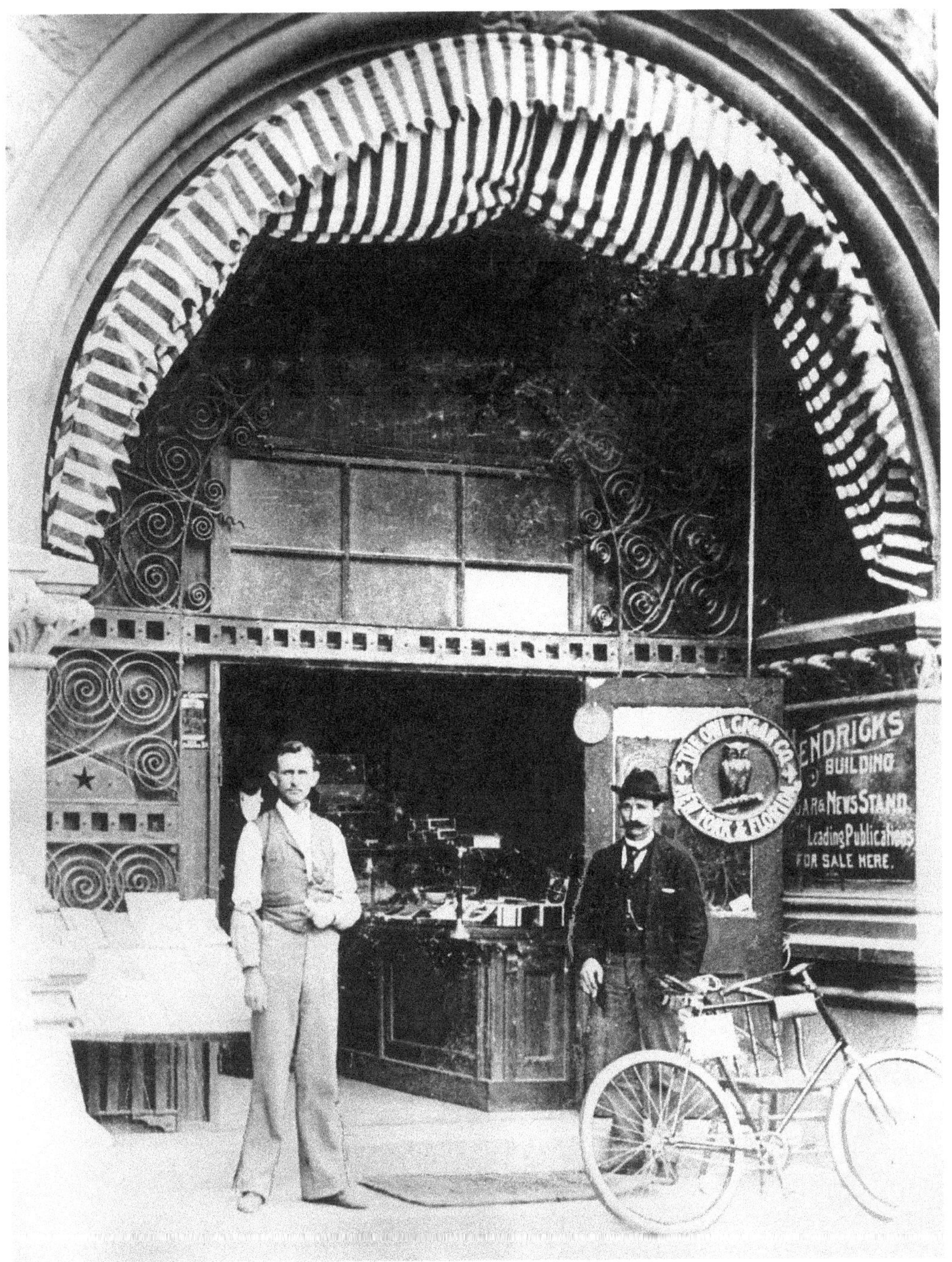


Before its expansion and conversion into the Worth Hotel, the Hendricks Building was among the early "skyscrapers" in Fort Worth. Its five floors provided offices for some of the leading businesses in town. Soon after the building opened in the early 1890s, Pryor McDaniel greeted customers at his cigar store and newsstand at 807 Main. The lowered awning of the shop can be seen at far left in the preceding image.

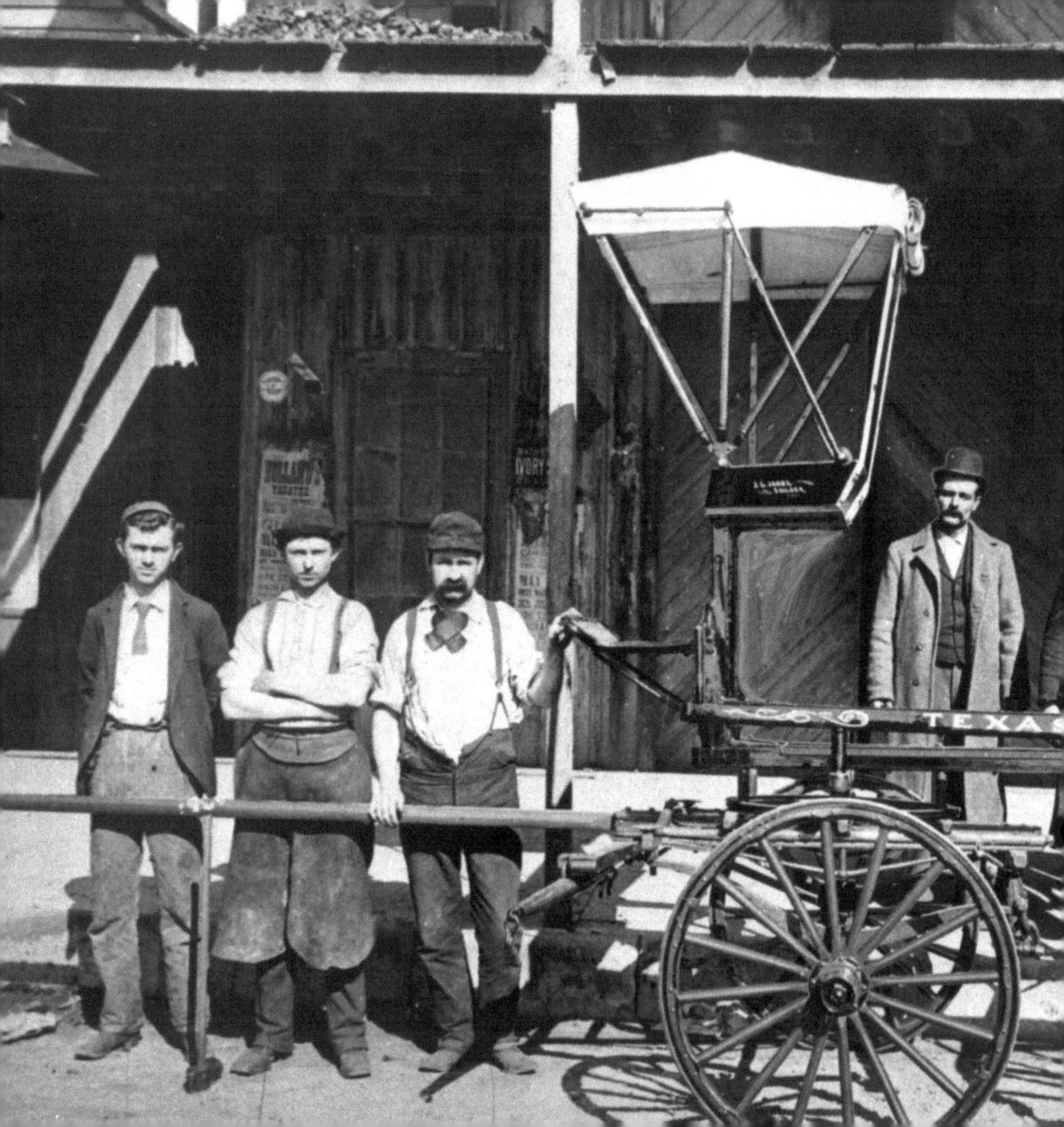
IVORY
TEXAS

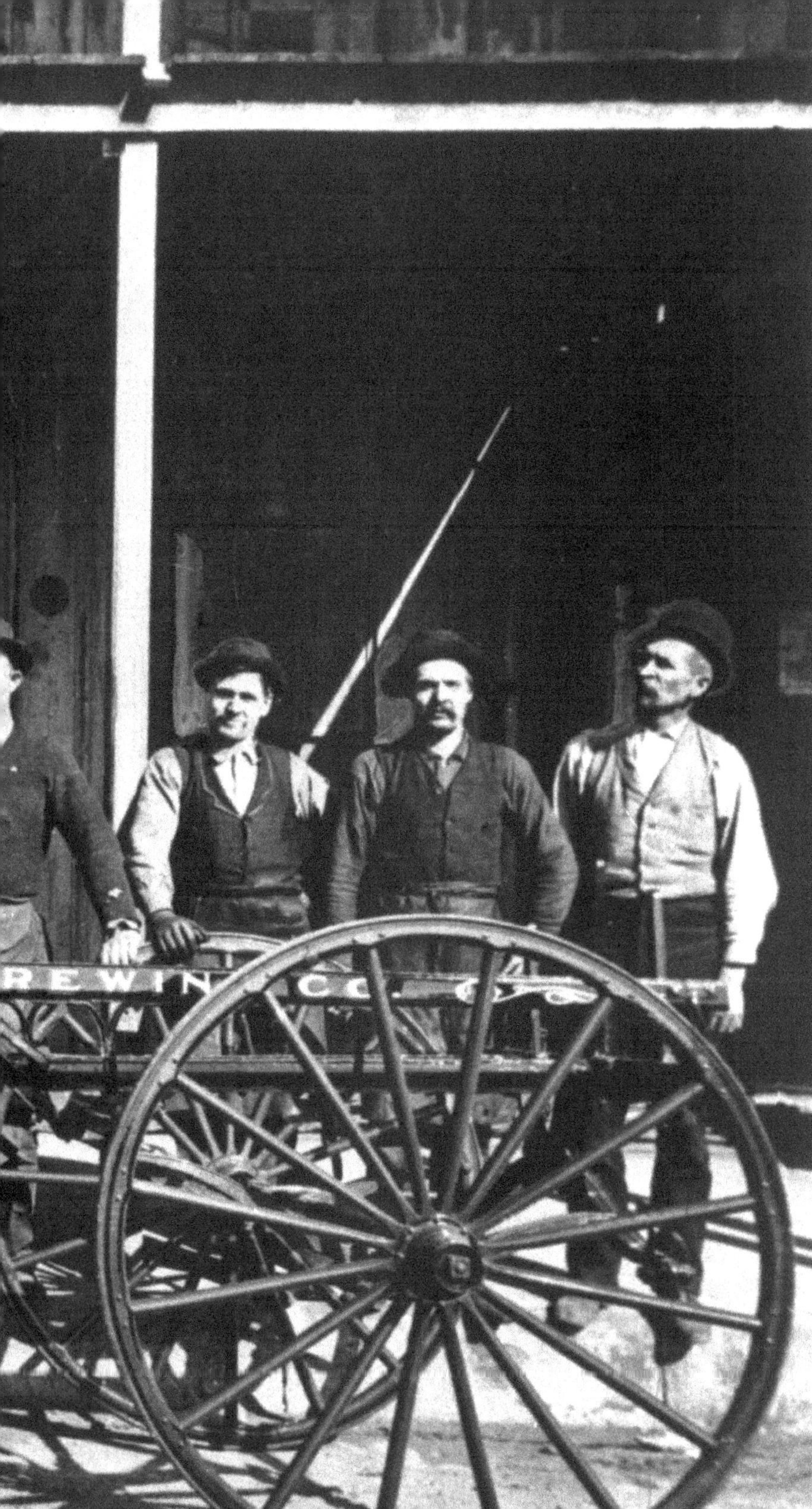


The Texas Brewing Company's enormous plant on Jones Street (site of today's Intermodal Transportation Center) sent delivery wagons out across the city and kept businesses liberally supplied in Hell's Half Acre, near the present site of the Fort Worth Convention Center. The sprawling vice district covered much of the south end of downtown and was the chief source of problems for the city's lawmen.

In 1893, Tarrant County voters approved a $500,000 bond package to build a new courthouse to replace the outdated and outgrown 1878 courthouse. Designed along the lines of the 1888 State Capitol, and constructed of Texas pink granite, the building remains one of the most important structures in Fort Worth and is considered one of the finest of Texas' historic courthouses.

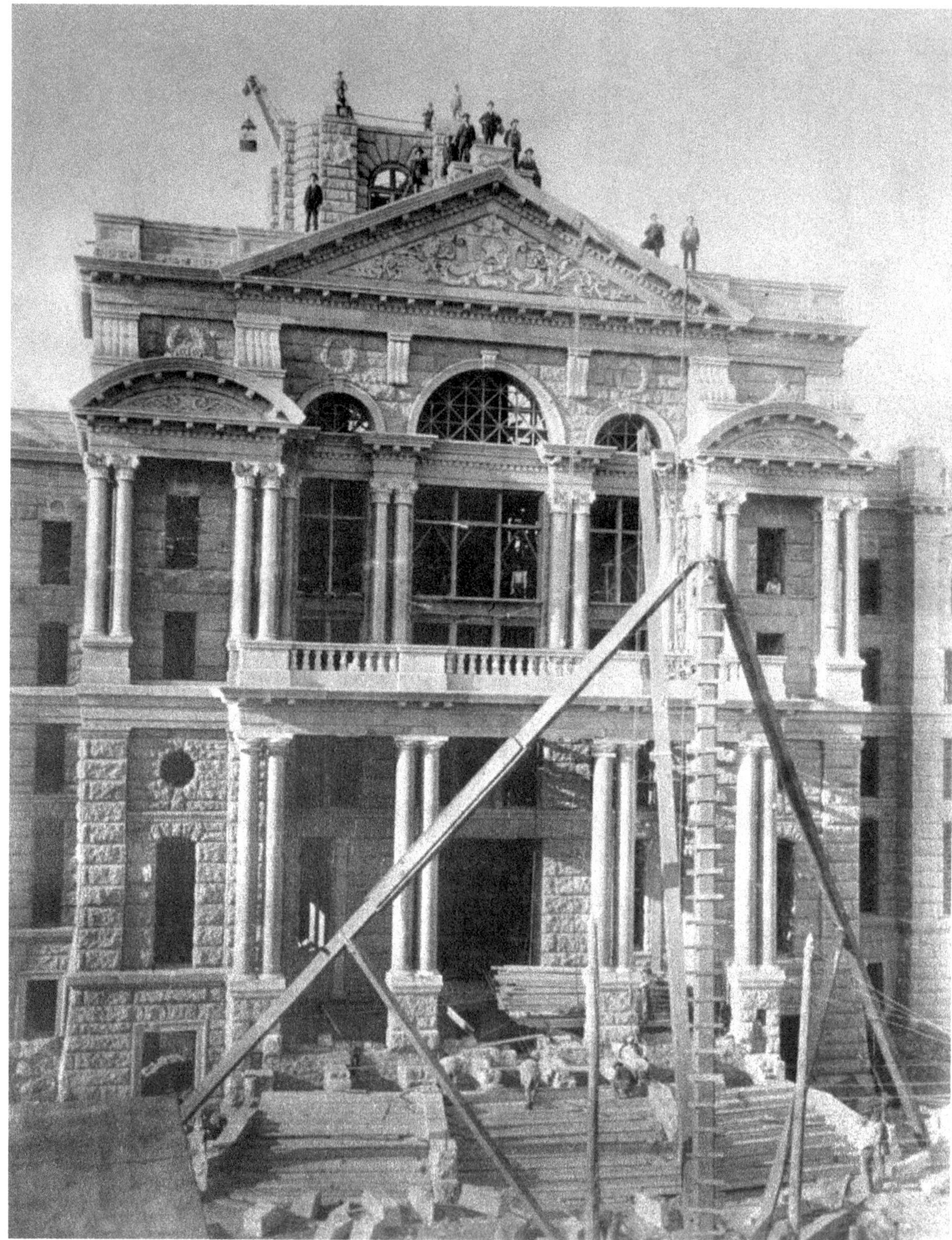

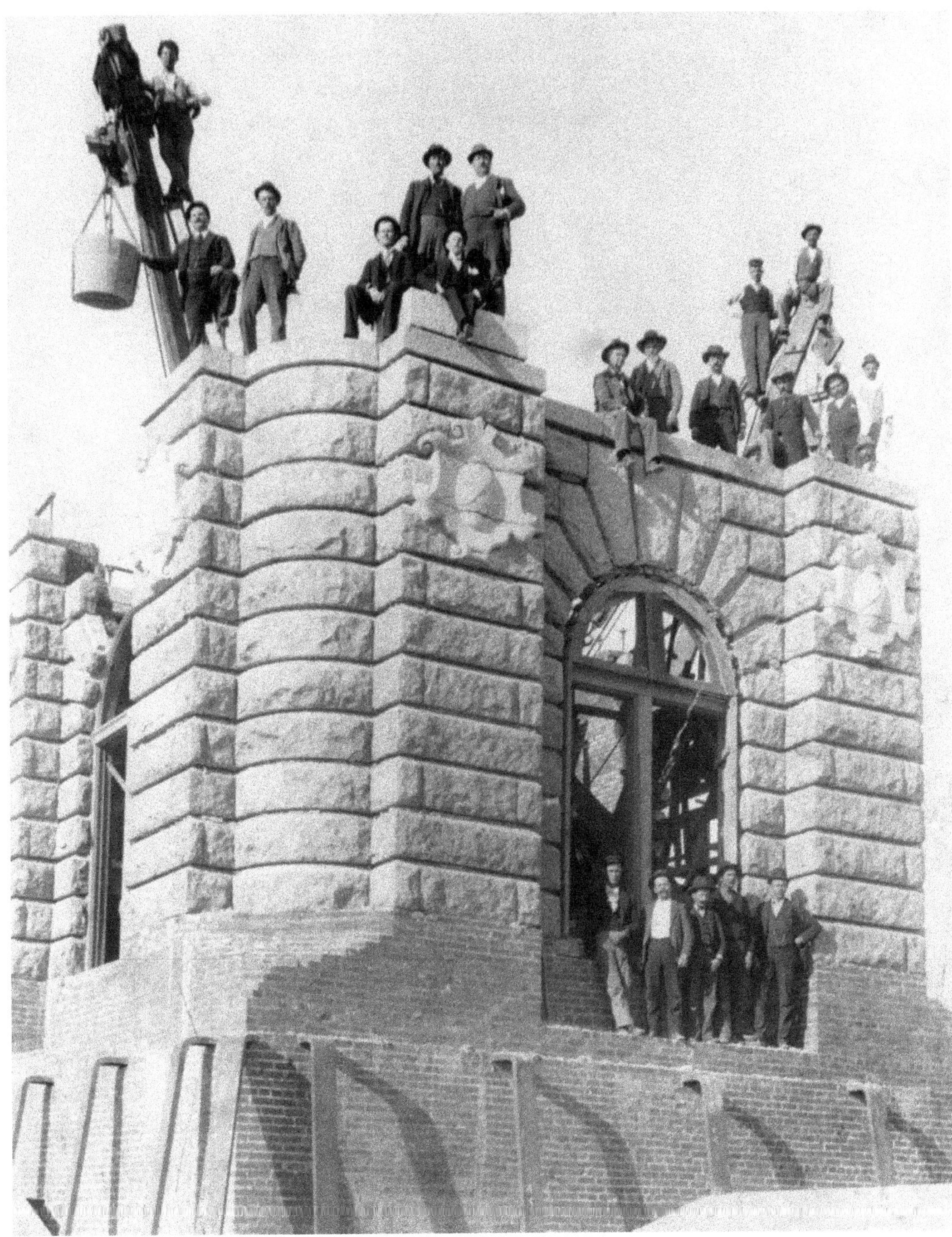

Construction foremen and proud county leaders braved the climb to the top of the courthouse during construction. At top, and standing third from left, is L. D. Nichols, granite foreman. Joining him are members of the commissioners court. Local lore says citizens outraged at the size and expense of the building voted all of them out of office the following year, even though it came in under budget. County Judge Robert G. Johnson sits on the ledge over the window right of center.

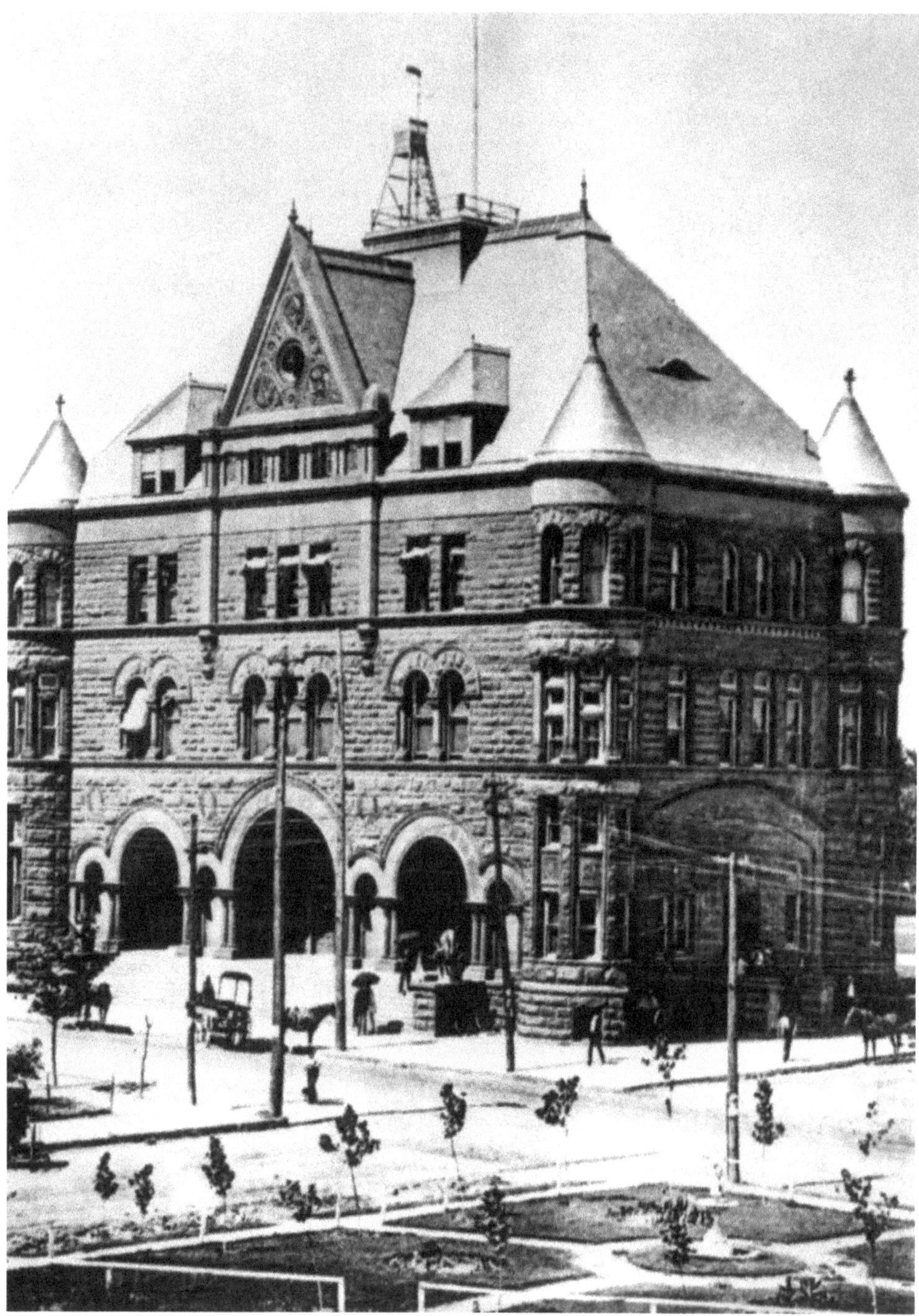

In 1896, a year after completion of the Tarrant County Courthouse, the Federal Government opened a new Post Office and Court building at Jennings and 11th to house the United States District Court of the just-created Fort Worth Division of the Northern District of Texas. Postal operations headquartered in the building oversaw mail service throughout Texas, Arkansas, Oklahoma and Louisiana. In 1898, the U.S. Weather Bureau set its collecting instruments on the roof.

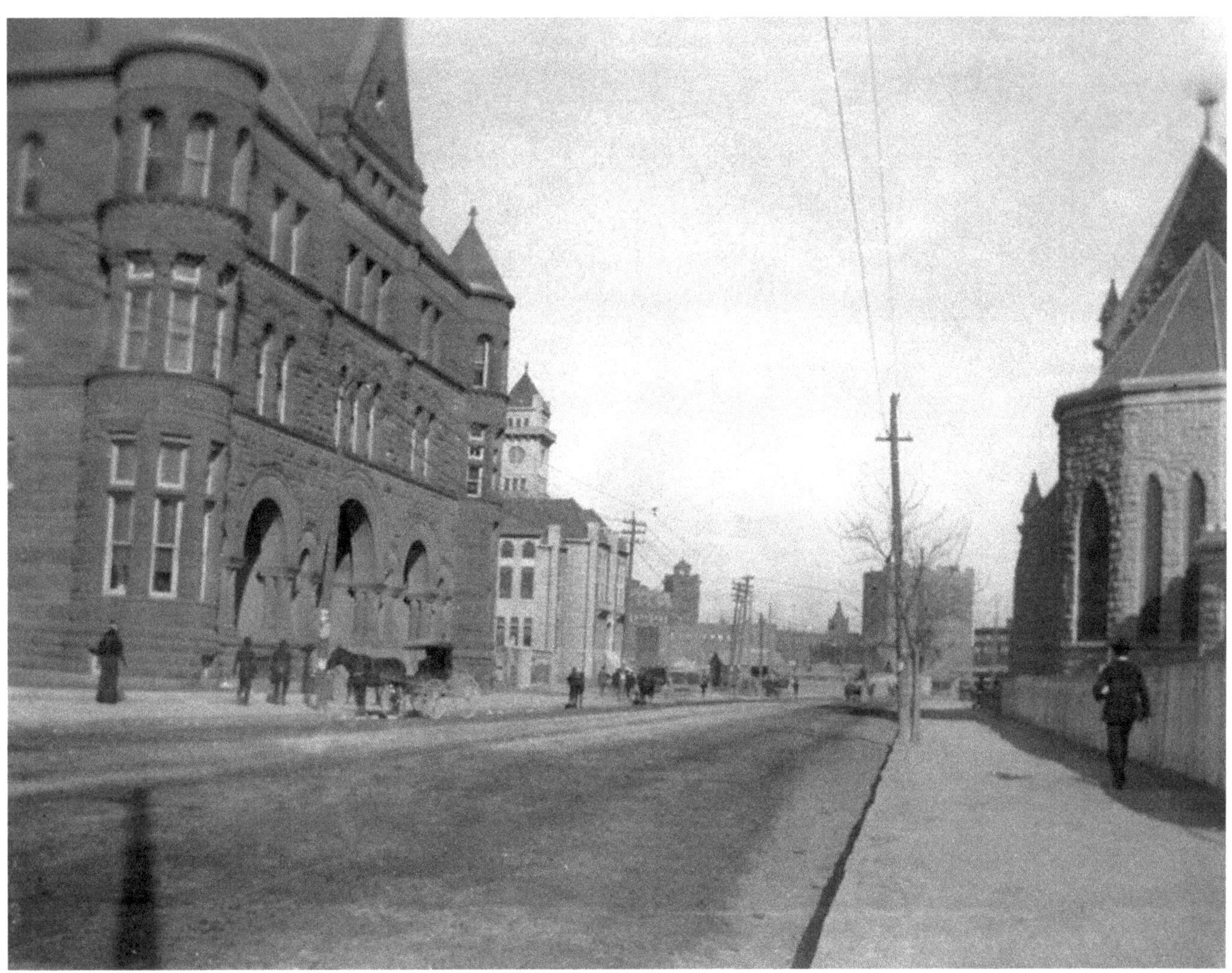

This image, taken in December 1896, looks north on Jennings, past the just-opened red sandstone Federal Building and the 1893 Fort Worth City Hall beyond. Of all the buildings shown here, only the 1888 St. Patrick Cathedral, at right, remains today.

In order to stock his store at 7th and Burnett, Louis Bicocchi would ride out early to meet farmers as they came into town to sell at the market. Selecting the best produce to complement his wide selection of imported goods, he became one of the city's leading early grocers, catering to the wealthy families building their homes along Lamar and Burnett streets during the 1880s. Bicocchi later partnered with J. B. Laneri to found Fort Worth Macaroni Company in 1899. His store, shown here in 1894, was the first in town with electric lights and a cash register.

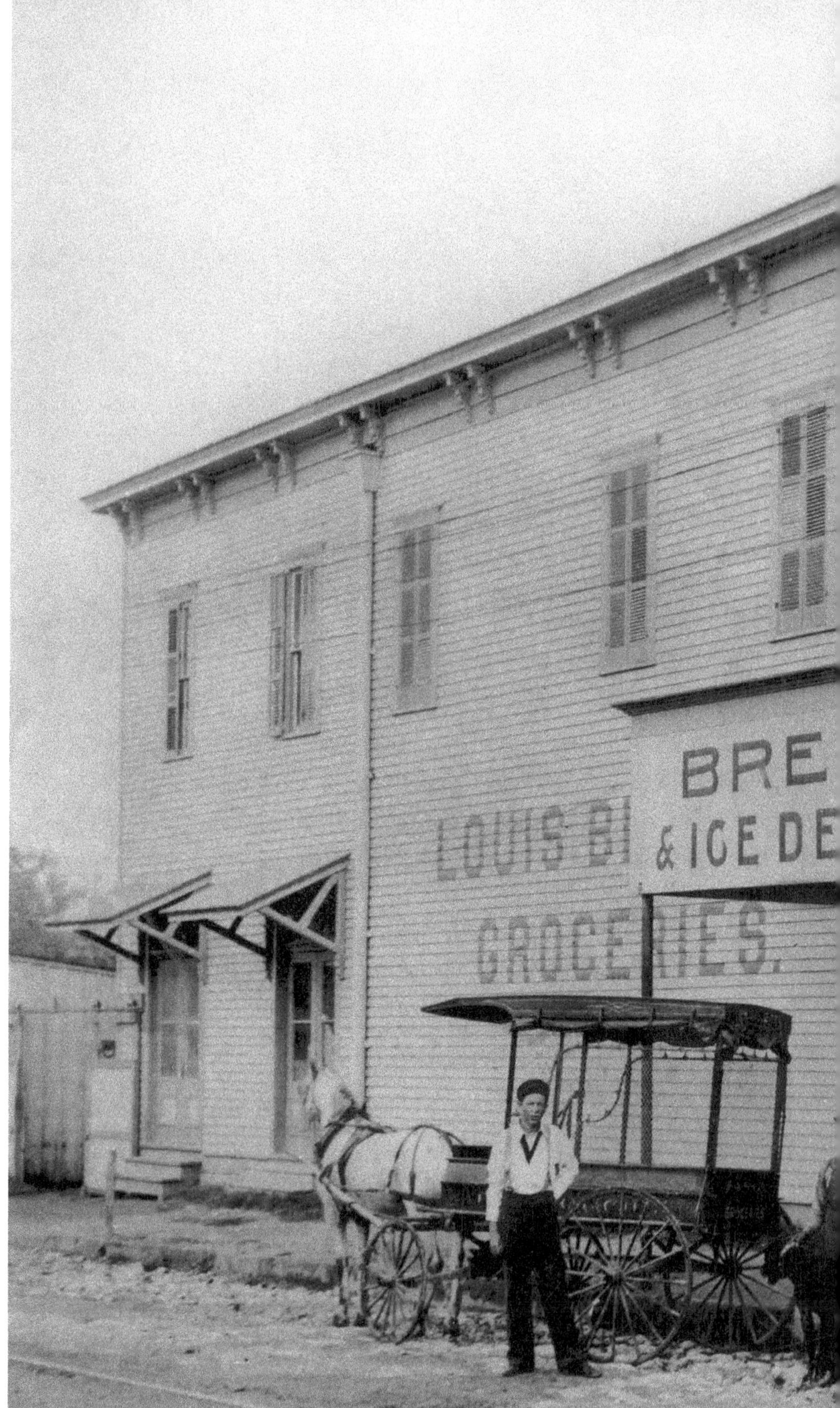

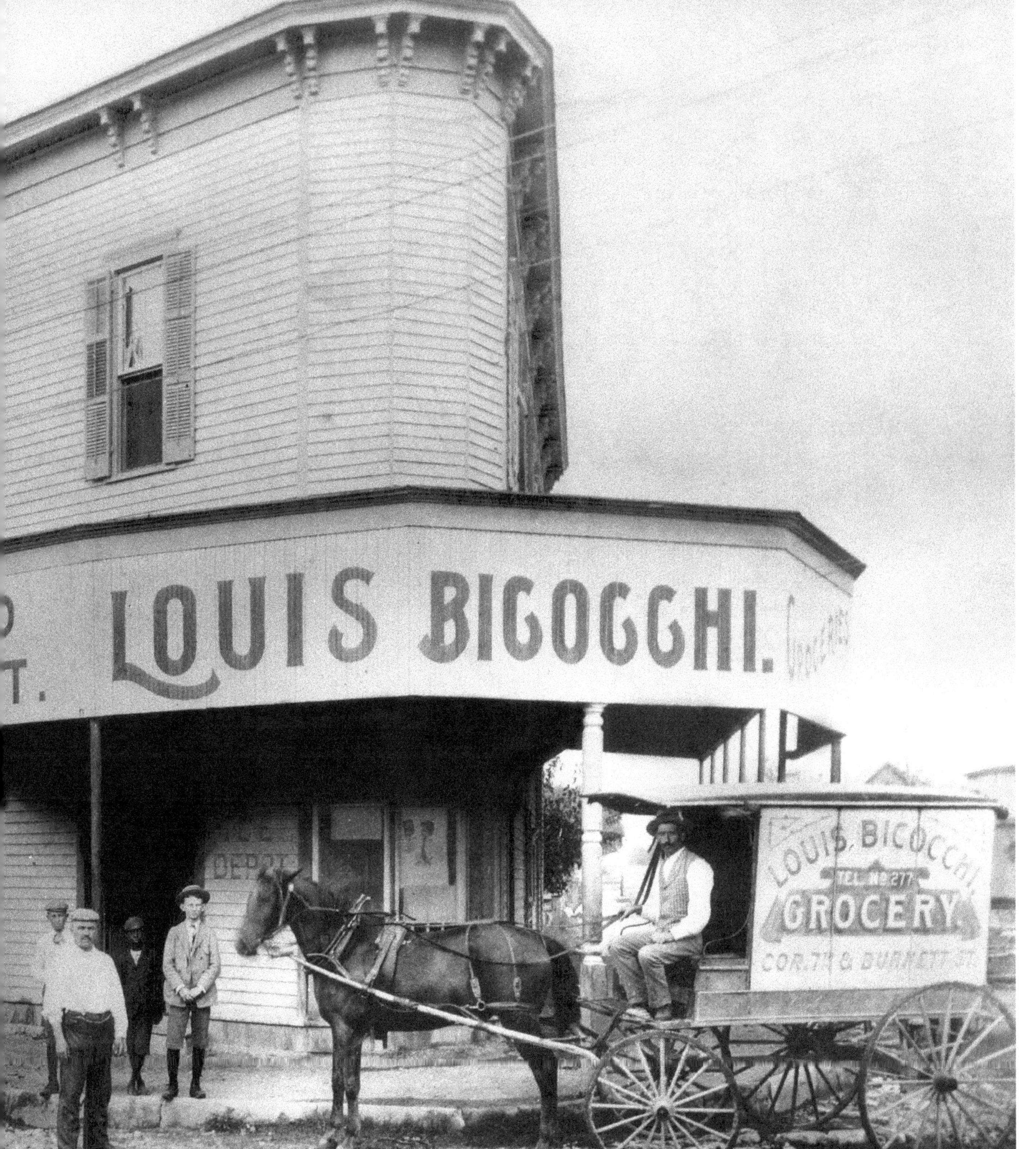
LOUIS, BICOCCHI
GROCERY

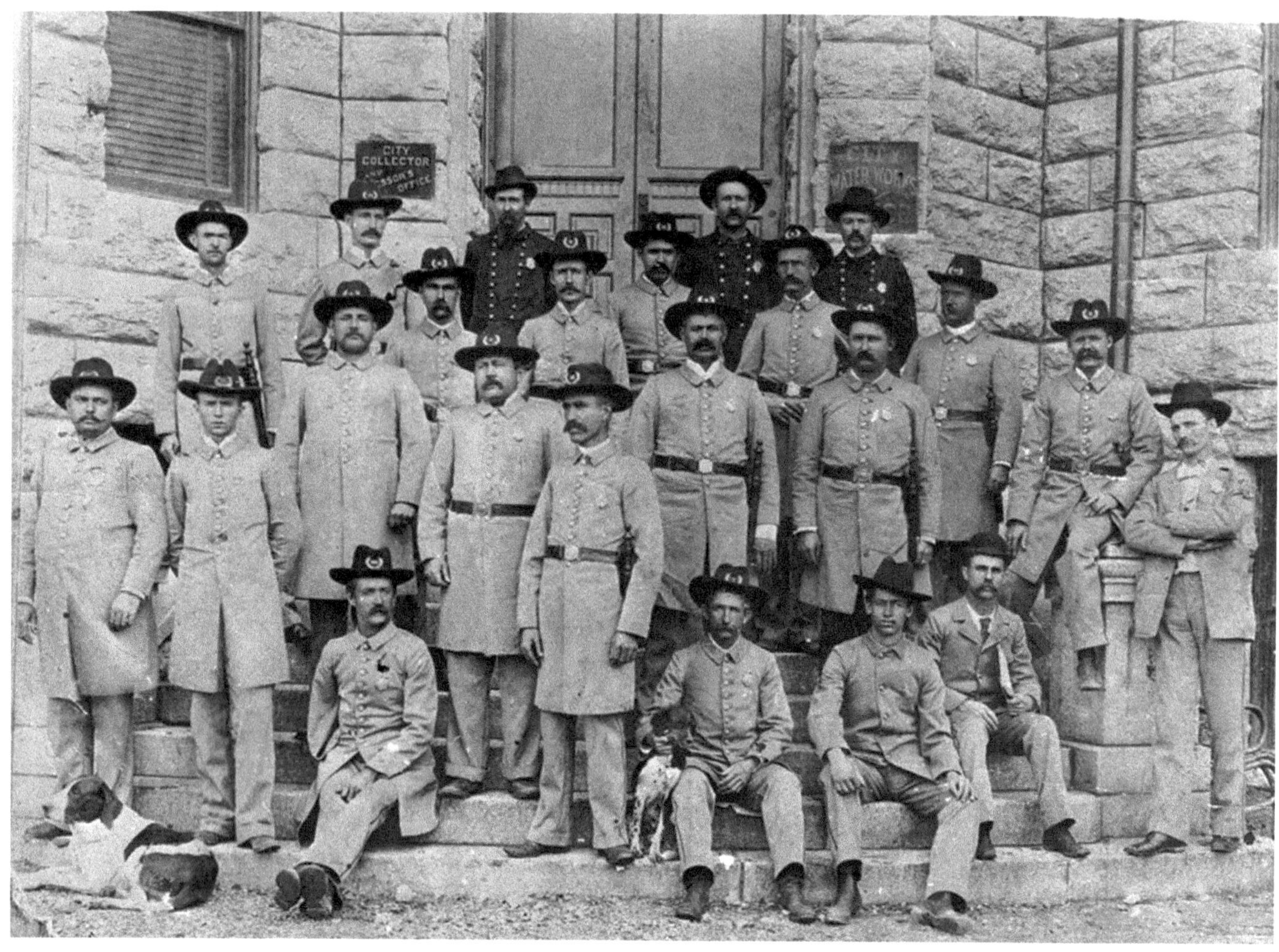


Fort Worth authorized its first police force shortly after the city incorporated in 1873, but financial constraints forced the small department to disband within a month. Before becoming a permanent city department in 1887, the police operated for a few years under the direction of town marshals, including, from 1876 to 1879, Jim Courtright, who would later die in a famous gunfight with gambler Luke Short. Here, several members of the force, including legendary officer George Craig, seated at left, pose in their summer (gray) and winter (blue) uniforms about 1895 in front of city hall at Throckmorton and 10th.

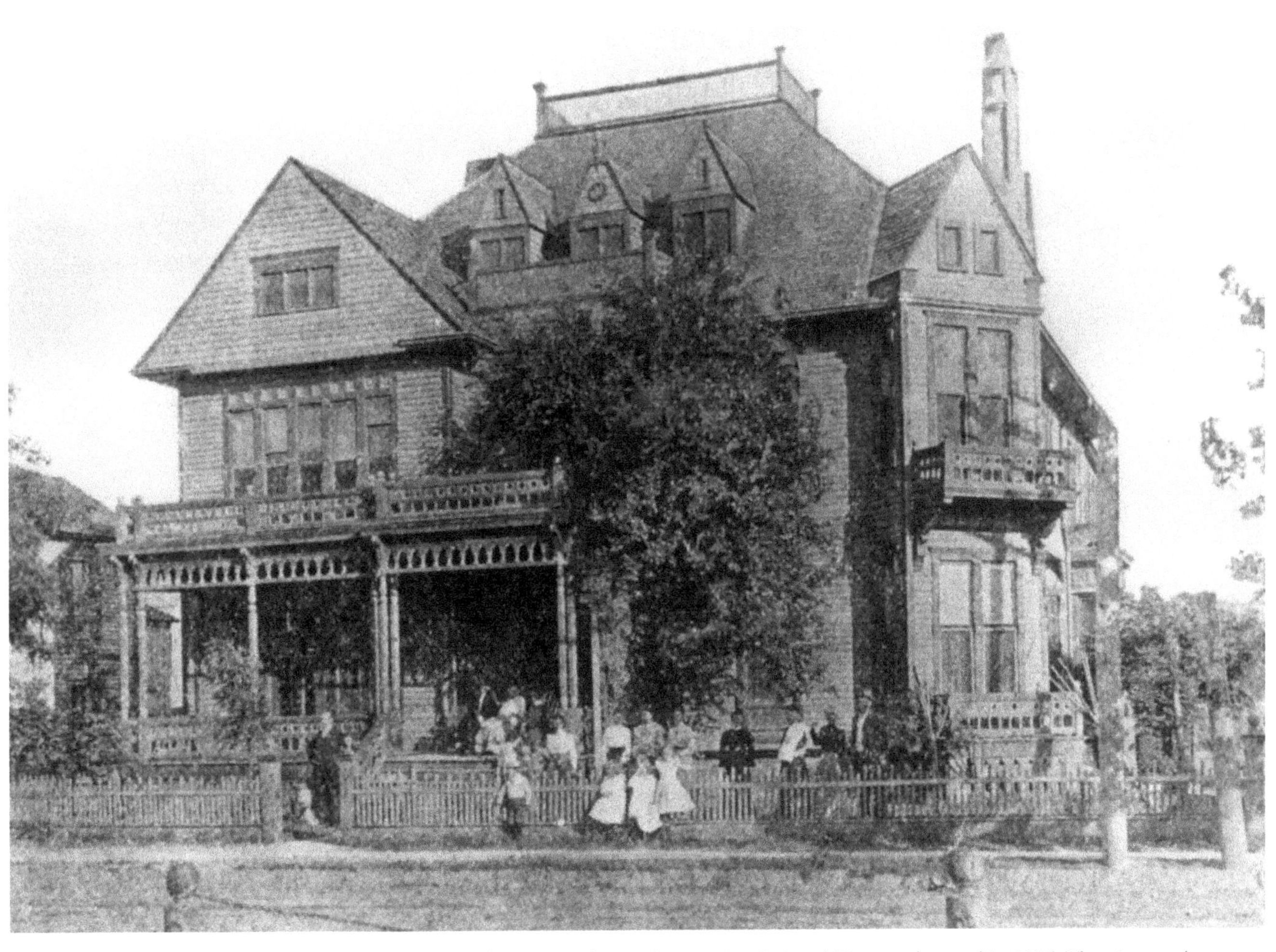

Fort Worth Lodge, number 124, of the Benevolent and Protective Order of Elks was chartered in 1906. The nineteenth-century residence shown in this photograph is identified as the fraternity's first lodge building in town, but its location remains unknown. In 1910 the Elks built a magnificent building at 7th and Lamar Streets downtown, replacing it in 1928 with a newer clubhouse that today houses the Young Women's Christian Association.

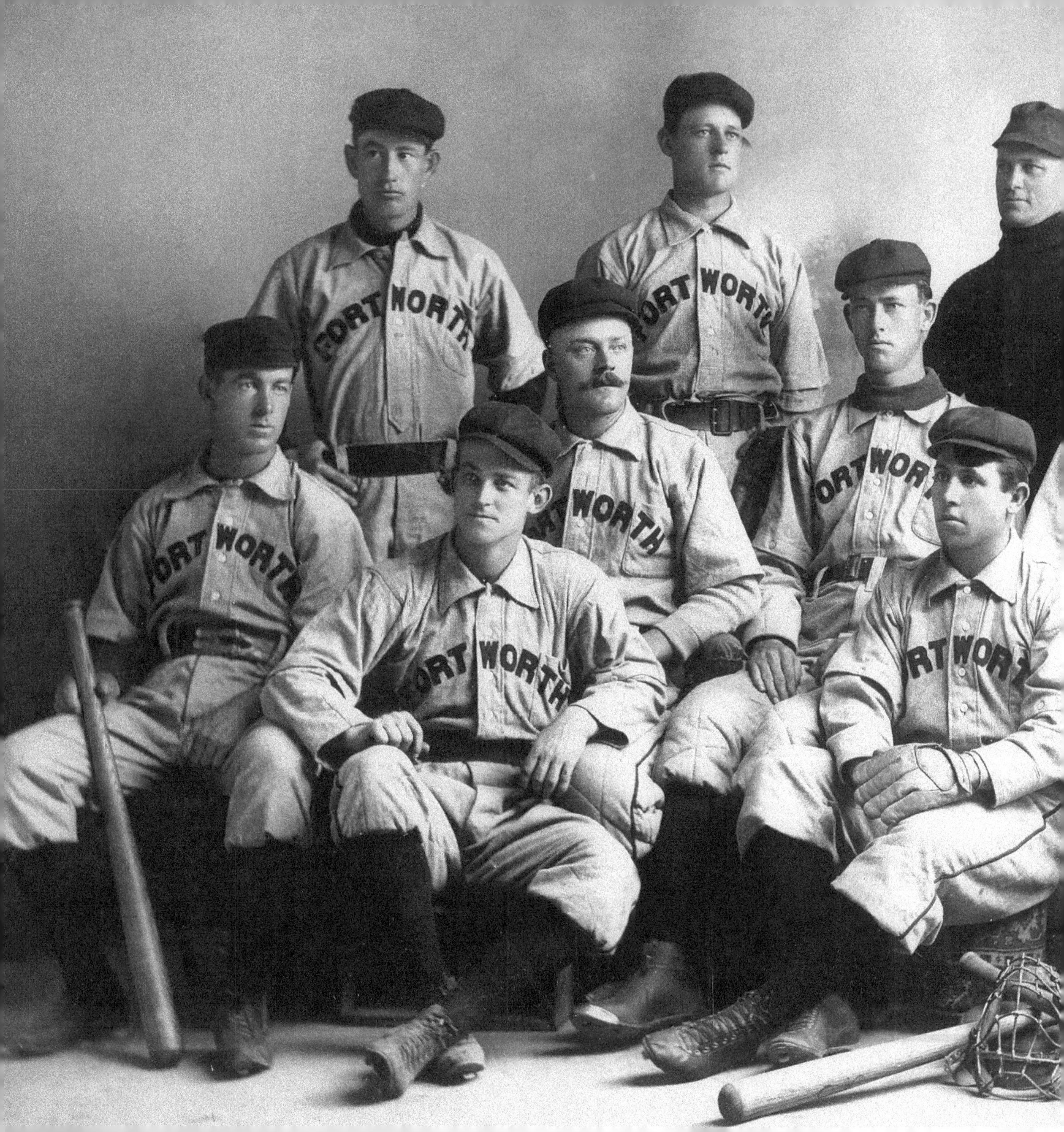
FORT WORTH
FORT WORTH

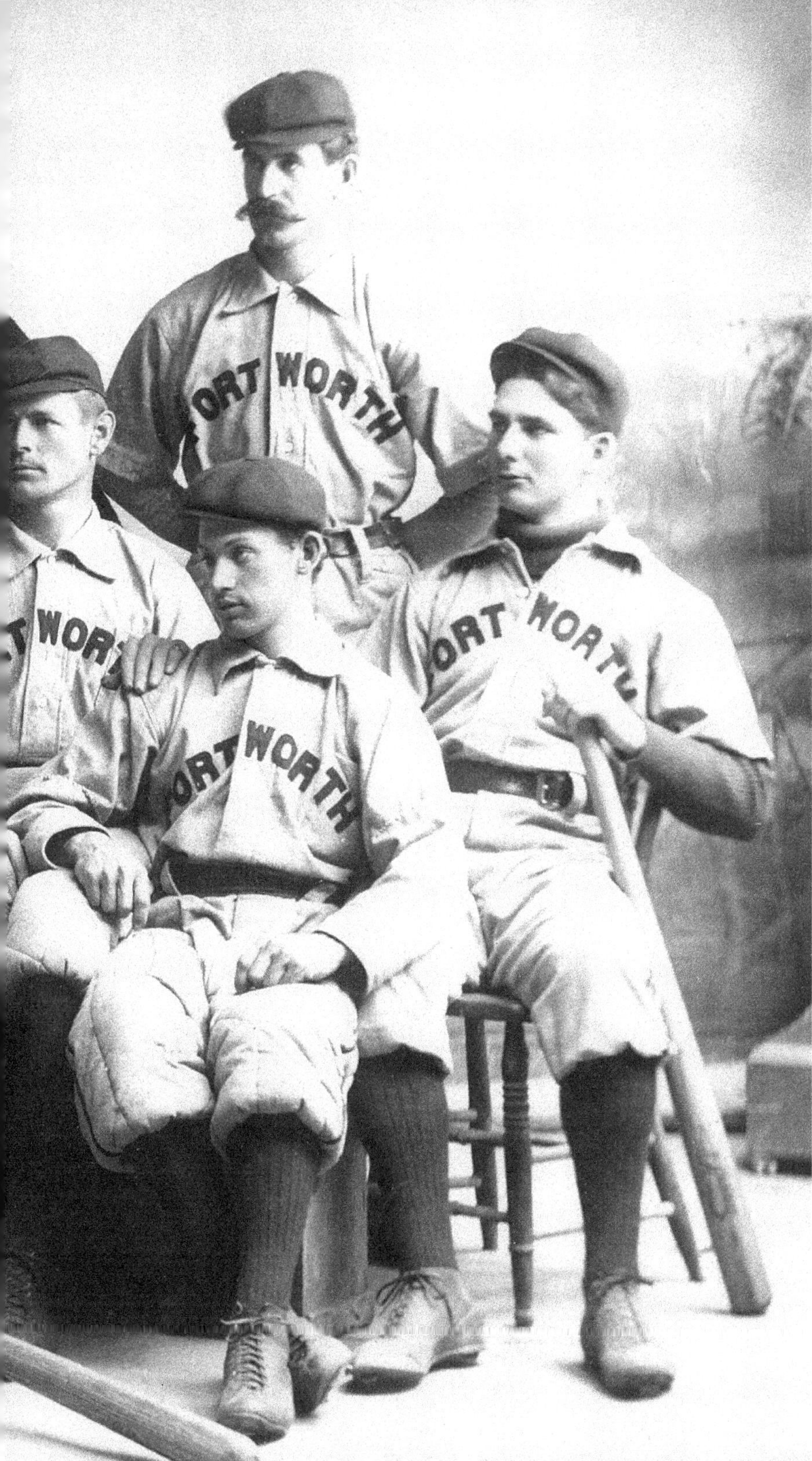


Fort Worth's love affair with baseball began in the 1870s, and blossomed after the 1887 creation of a Texas League comprising cities from across the state. The local team took its name from the town's famous mascot, the panther. This picture was taken in 1895, the year the team won its first championship. The Panthers would eventually shorten their name to the "Cats" and reach legendary status in the 1920s and 1940s. They played their final games in 1964. A new Fort Worth Cats minor league team revived the memories of its famous predecessors and began play at a rebuilt LaGrave Field in 2002.

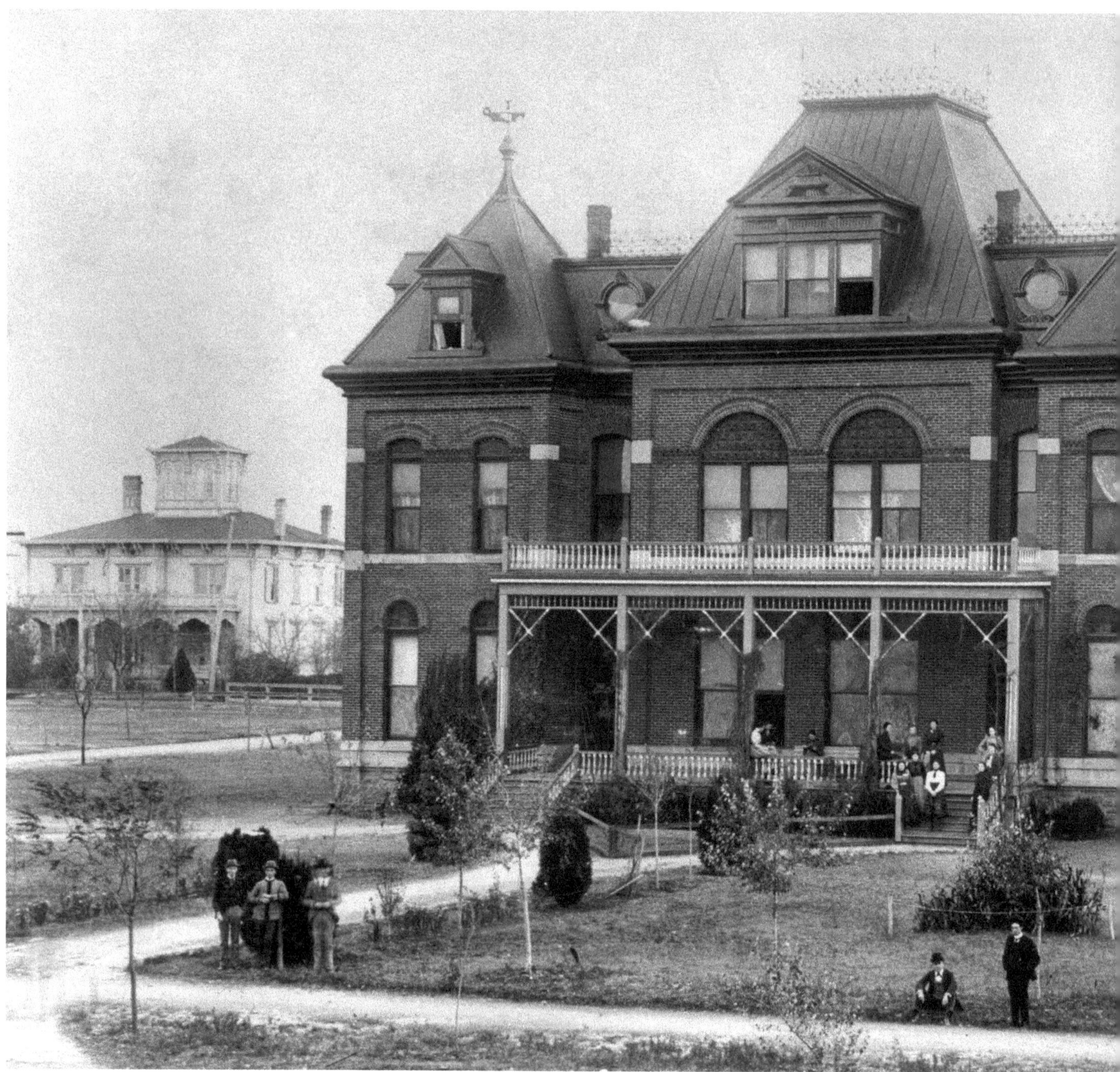

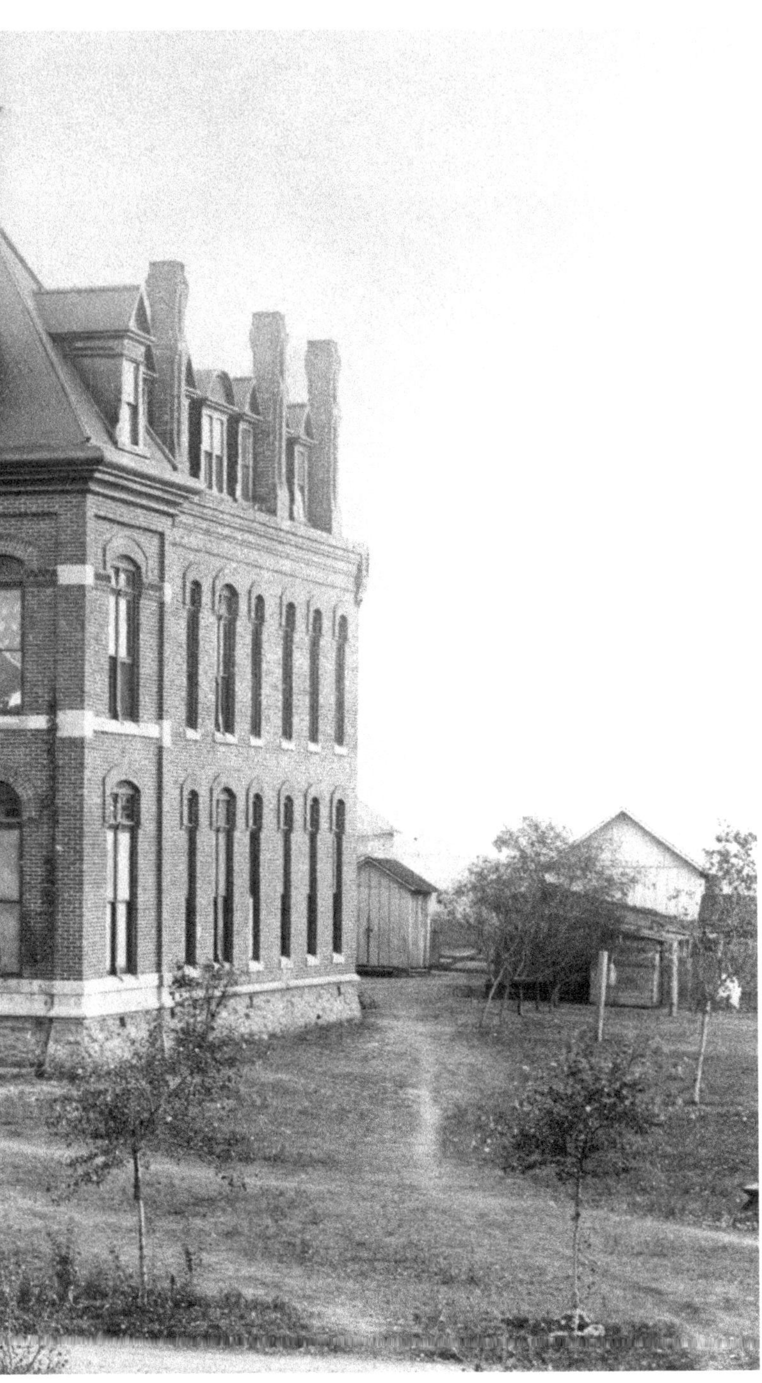

Higher education expanded in Fort Worth in 1881 when the Methodist Episcopal Church opened Texas Wesleyan College. Outgrowing its original downtown facilities, the institution relocated in 1886 to a new site just outside the city limits, initially erecting four buildings, including University Hall, shown here. Green B. Trimble Technical High School occupies the College Avenue site of the old college, which was renamed Fort Worth University in 1889 and grew to include both law and medical schools before closing its doors in 1910. Texas Wesleyan College was not associated with today's Texas Wesleyan University.

The city's first "skyscraper" was the seven-story Hurley Building on the northwest corner of 7th and Main. Construction began in 1889 by the Fort Worth Loan and Construction Co., the firm chartered to build the Texas Spring Palace. Company president George L. Hurley helped transform the intersection of 7th and Main into the financial center of the city by leasing the ground floor to the newly established Farmers and Mechanics Bank, a location the bank would maintain until its acquisition by the Fort Worth National Bank in 1927.

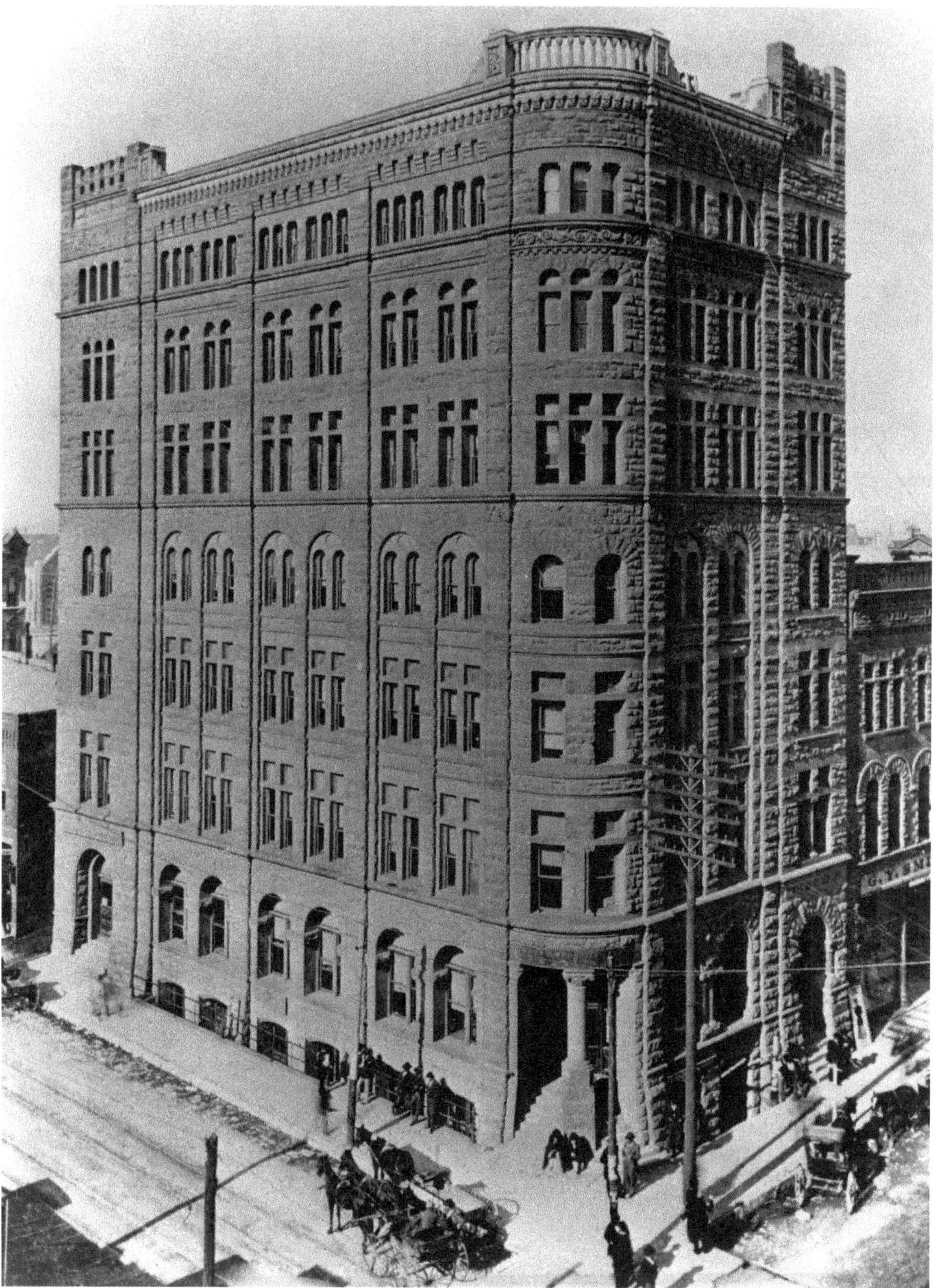

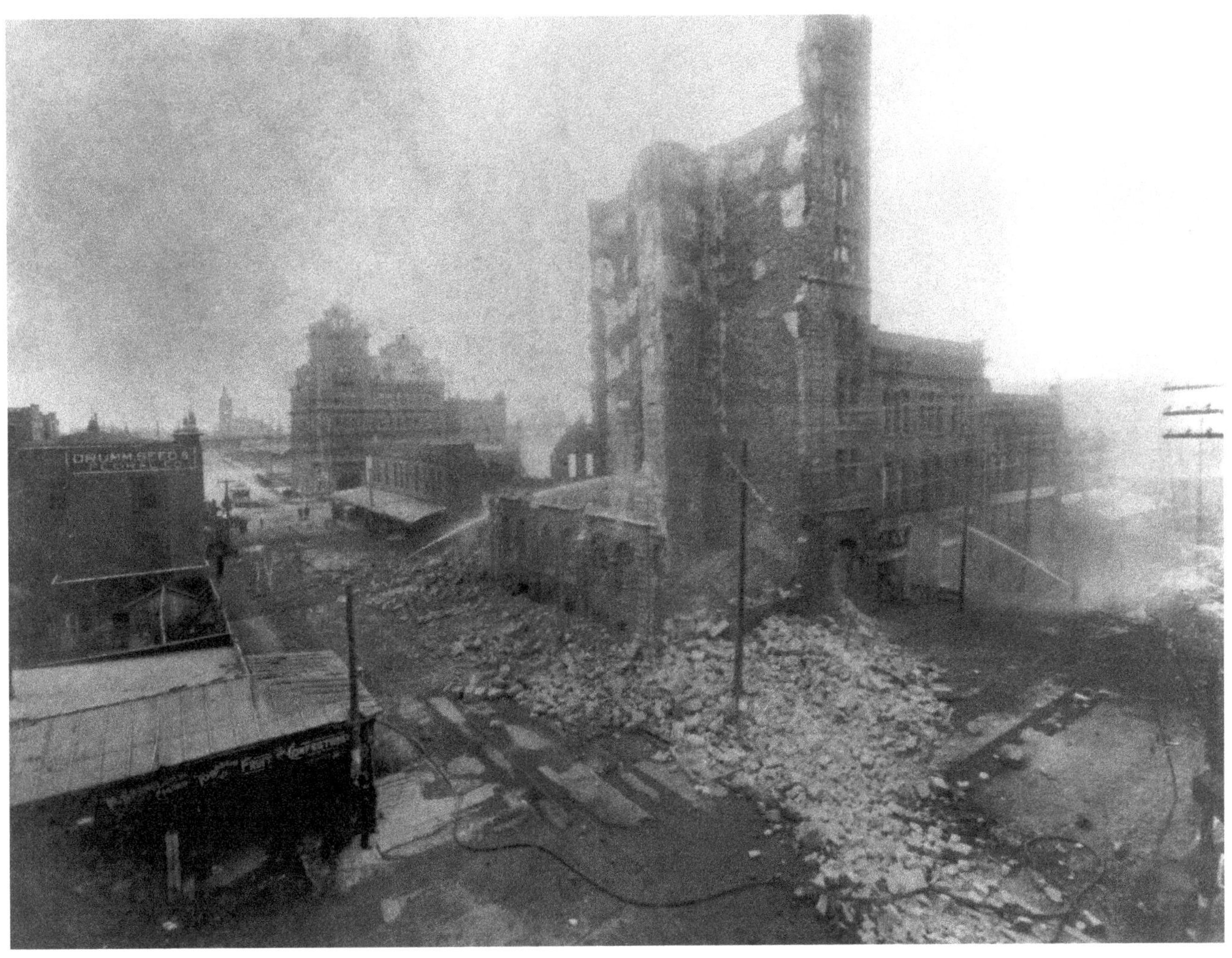

The Hurley Building enjoyed its status as the city's tallest office building for less than a decade; it burned in 1898, spreading debris across Main Street. The remaining structure was dynamited to clear the way for the 1899 construction of the more modest five-story Hoxie Building, the new home to the Farmers and Mechanics Bank. To the left is the 1889 Board of Trade building on Houston Street and the steeple of St. Paul's Methodist Episcopal Church at 7th and Lamar.

This simple brick building on the northeast corner of 7th and Houston streets was home to Lee Whitsitt's Drug Store about 1898. A sign on the utility pole invites people to wait for the streetcar inside at the soda stand. In 1900, the First National Bank bought the lot and replaced the drug store with an imposing two-story structure. That building was demolished in 1910 to make way for the bank's new home, a skyscraper designed by the city's leading architectural firm of Sanguinet and Staats. The bank building was restored in 2006 by XTO Energy, Inc., and renamed for company chairman and CEO Bob R. Simpson.

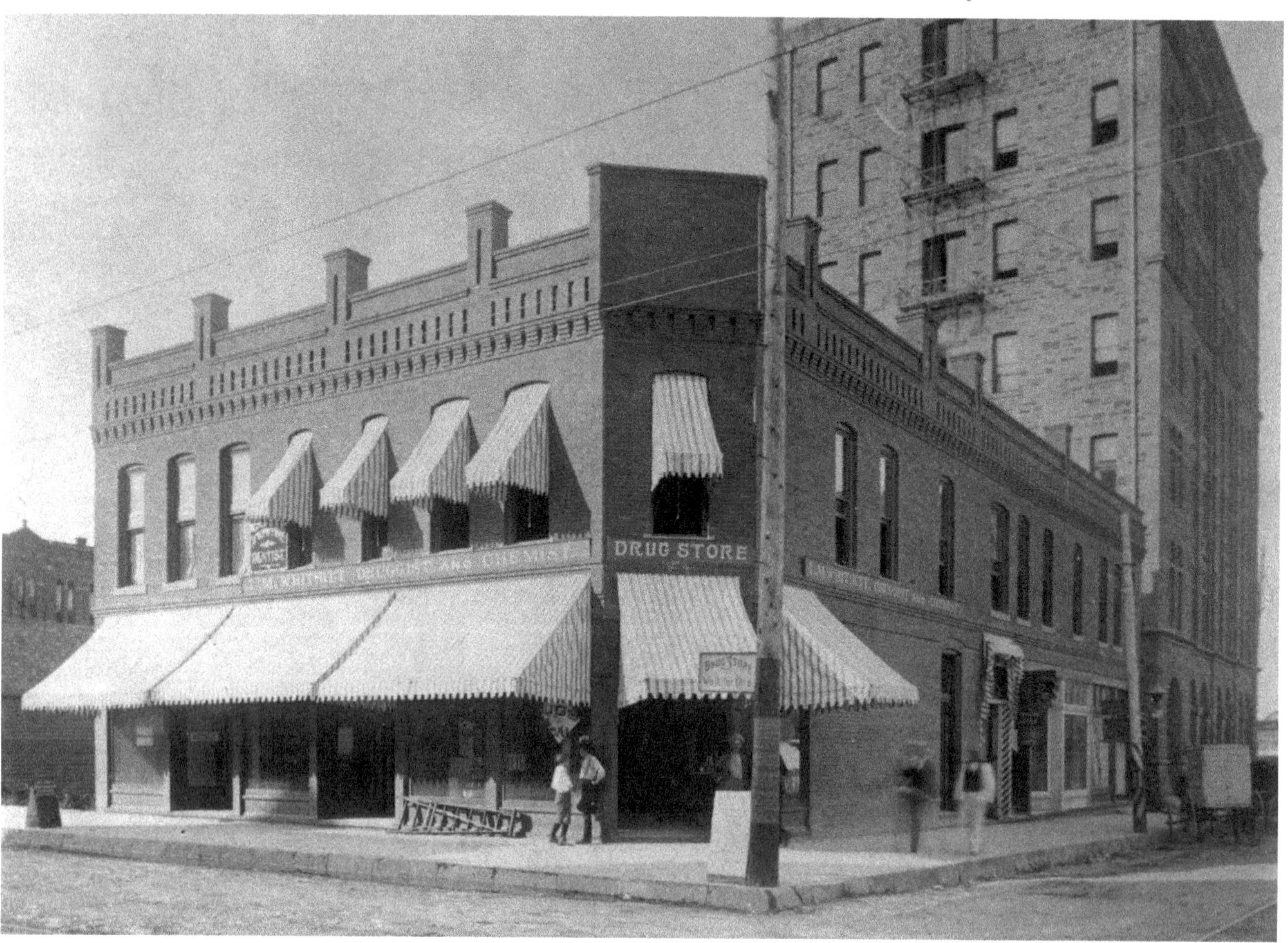

# A New Century Brings New Industry

## 1900–1910

By 1900, 25,000 people called Fort Worth home. Many fortunes had already been made as the livestock industry continued to grow and develop. As early as the arrival of the railroad in 1876, Fort Worth hoped to become more than a mere pass-through for stock headed to other cities for processing and packing. After a few attempts to establish a home-grown industry during the 1890s, the city enticed two of the largest packing concerns in the country, Armour and Swift, to set up side-by-side plants near the stockyards, beginning in 1902. Within a decade, Fort Worth's population nearly tripled to 75,000. For the next forty years, the plants and the stockyards reigned as the area's largest employers.

With the rapid growth came an expansion of services as streetcar lines fanned out across the city, opening new areas for development. Modern skyscrapers as high as seven stories began to dominate the skyline and a group of determined local women decided to bring the city into the modern age by building a library, with the aid of a gift from Andrew Carnegie. Thousands of excited spectators cheered President Theodore Roosevelt when he came to town to meet with cattlemen who were then working in partnership with Comanche Chief Quanah Parker.

Through floods, fires and droughts, Fort Worth pressed on through the first decade of the twentieth century. The stockyards expanded along with the National Feeders and Breeders Show, forerunner of today's Southwestern Exposition and Livestock Show. The city became a major rail center with lines extending in all directions, and educational opportunity expanded with the opening of a seminary and the return of Texas Christian University, which had been forced to leave its original downtown campus years earlier by the growth of Hell's Half Acre. The first planes that awed a crowd gathered at the city's racetrack, near the end of the century's first decade, sparked Fort Worth's love affair with aviation that continues today.

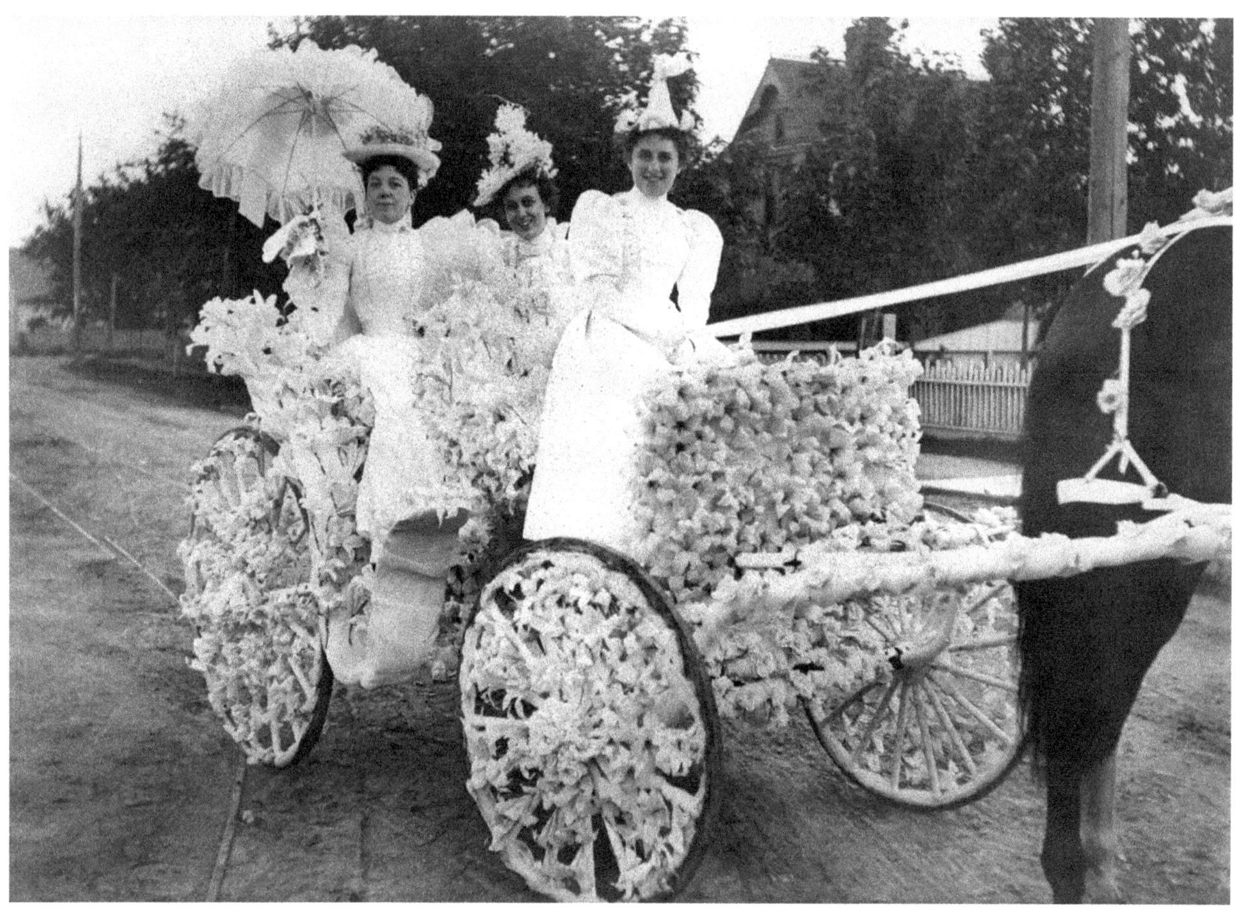

Fort Worth welcomed spring with garden parties, dances, and parades. During the city's version of New York's Easter Parade, carriages and passengers were decorated in their finest. Here, a group of young women proudly pose for the camera. The street might be Belknap or Weatherford, once the heart of a fine residential neighborhood around 1900.

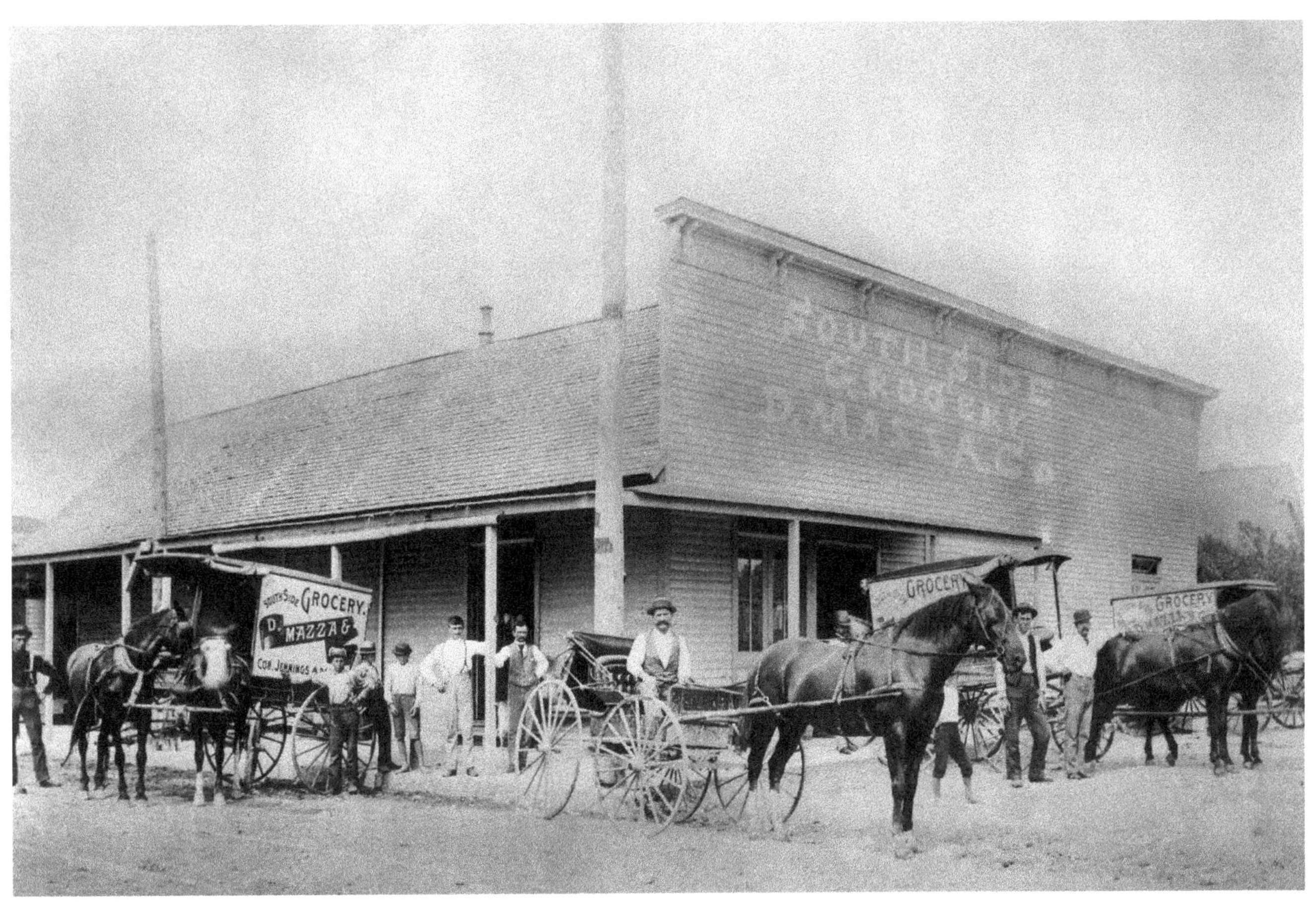


As Fort Worth grew to the south, following the arrival of the Texas & Pacific Railroad in 1876, new businesses followed. D. Mazza opened the first grocery store south of the railroad tracks. By 1900 the business, located at Jennings and West Daggett, was successful enough for the Mazza family to electrify their home around the corner from the store and become the first family on the south side to manage the Texas summer with the aid of an electric fan.

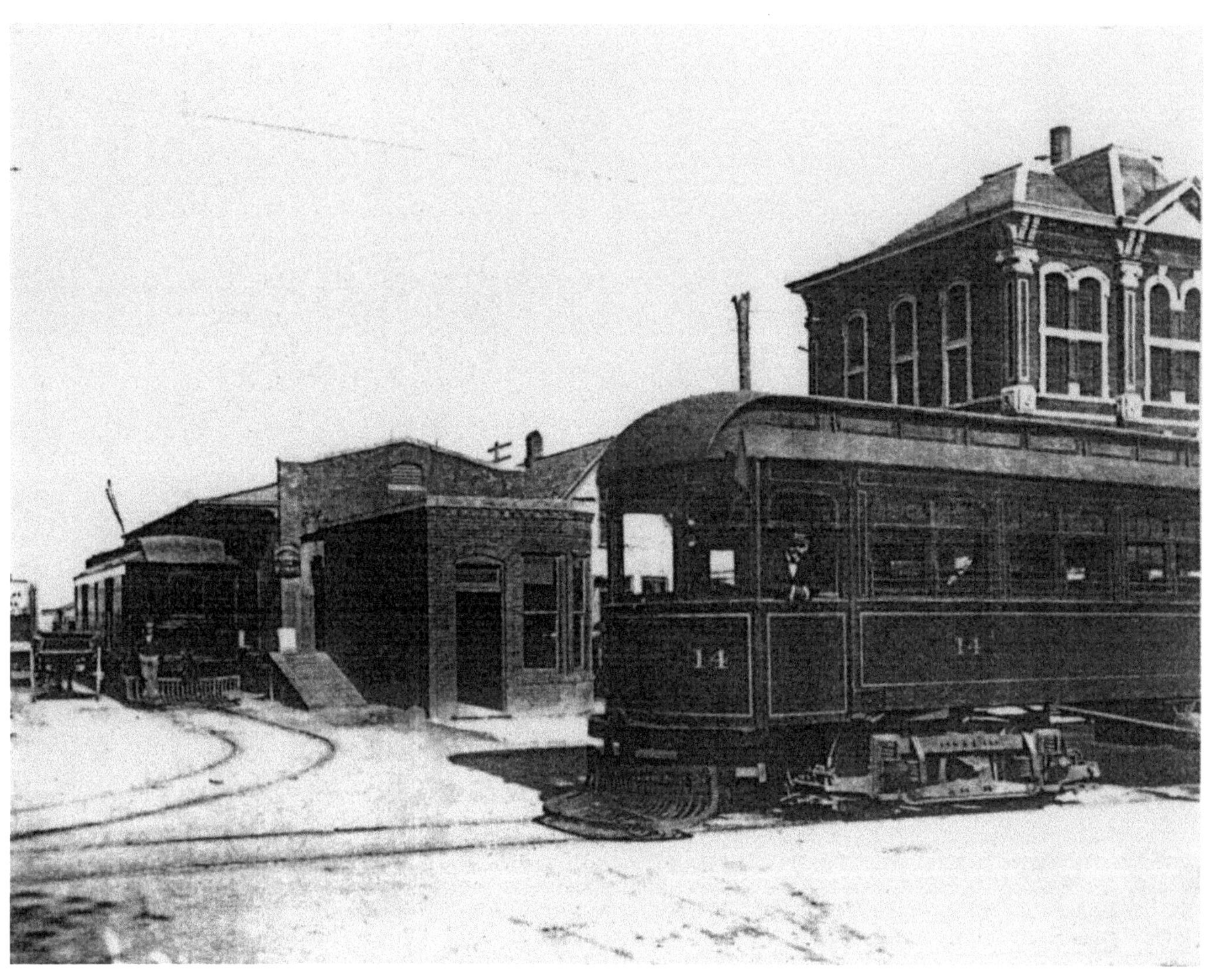

The downtown yard of the Northern Texas Traction Company at Houston and Belknap Streets. The NTTC began operations in 1902, building on a tradition that dated back to 1876, when the first mule-drawn cars moved passengers along Main Street. More than twenty transit companies operated in Fort Worth in the early years, most of them eventually consolidated under the NTTC banner.

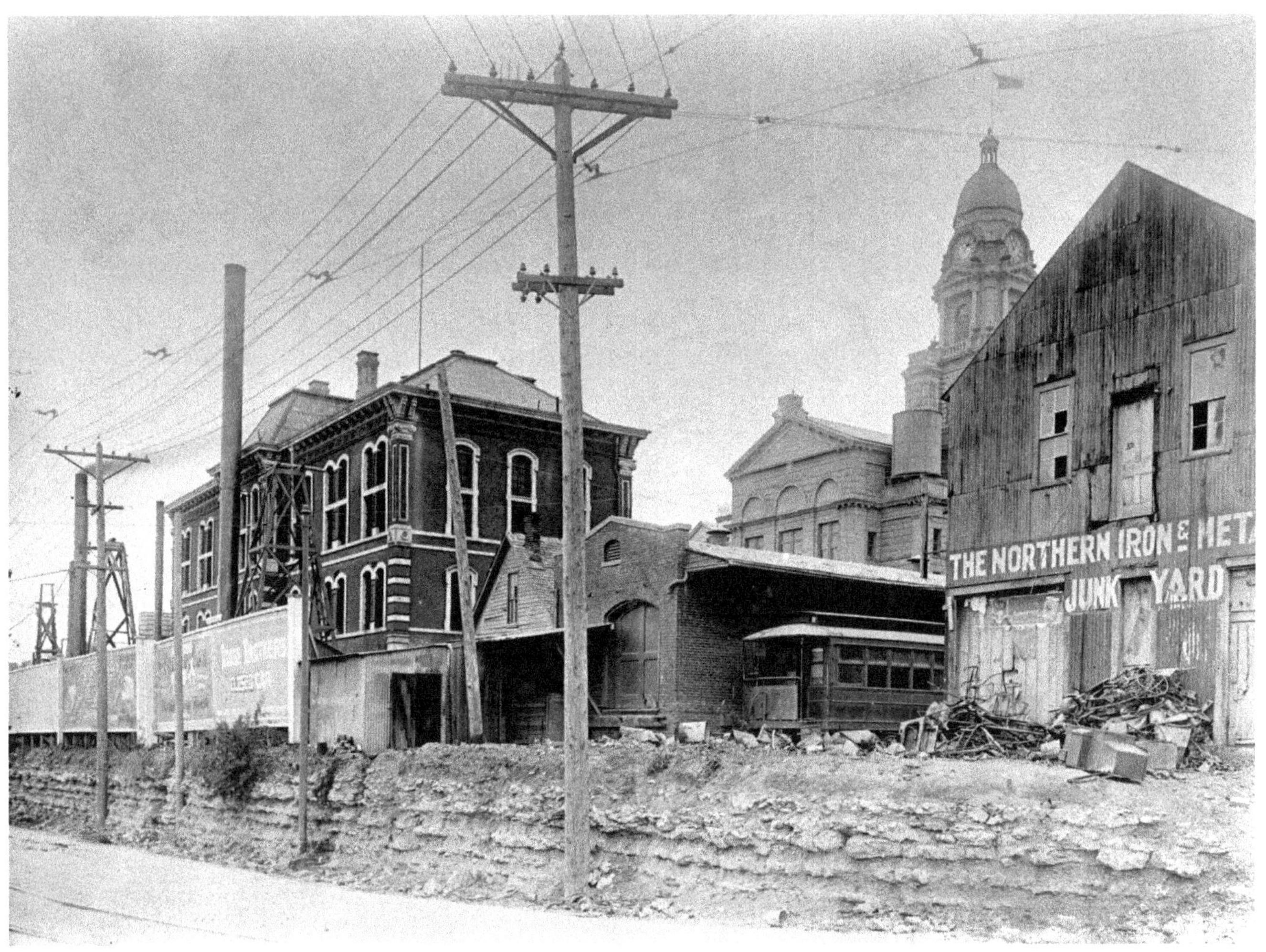


Adjacent to the streetcar barns was the three-story, brick, 1883 Tarrant County jail, designed by Houston architect Eugene Heiner. The image here shows the original street grading at Houston and Bluff streets for the first Main Street Bridge across the Trinity River, completed in 1890. Between billboards and salvage materials, the view greeting visitors coming into downtown from North Fort Worth seems less than inviting.

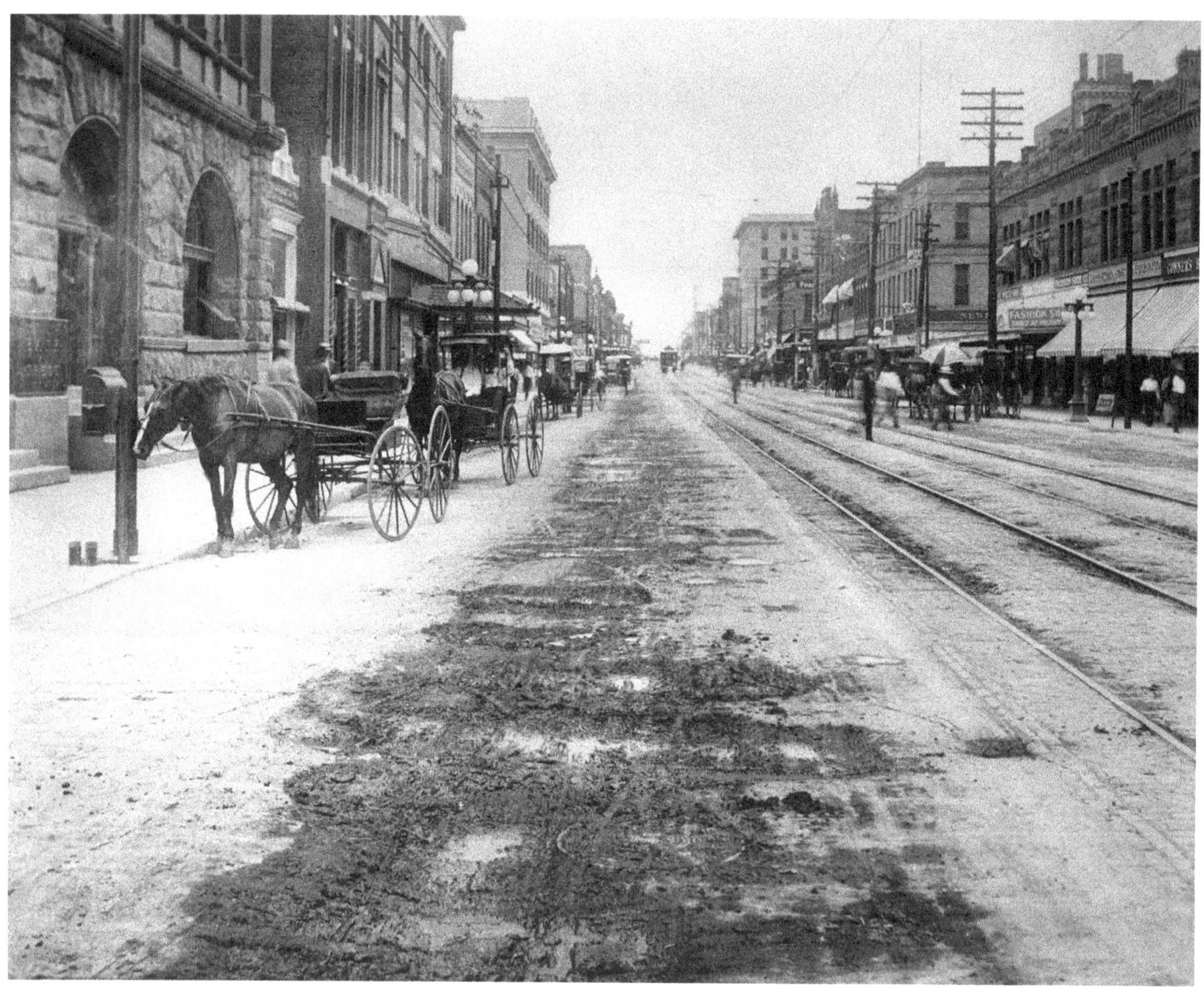

This scene from the intersection of Houston Street and 7th looking north about 1900 shows a growing and bustling city, with pedestrians dodging animals, manure and streetcars to cross to the other side. The city's population at the time was about 25,000, but it would soon nearly triple as the economy boomed following the 1902 opening of the meat-packing operations in the Stockyards.

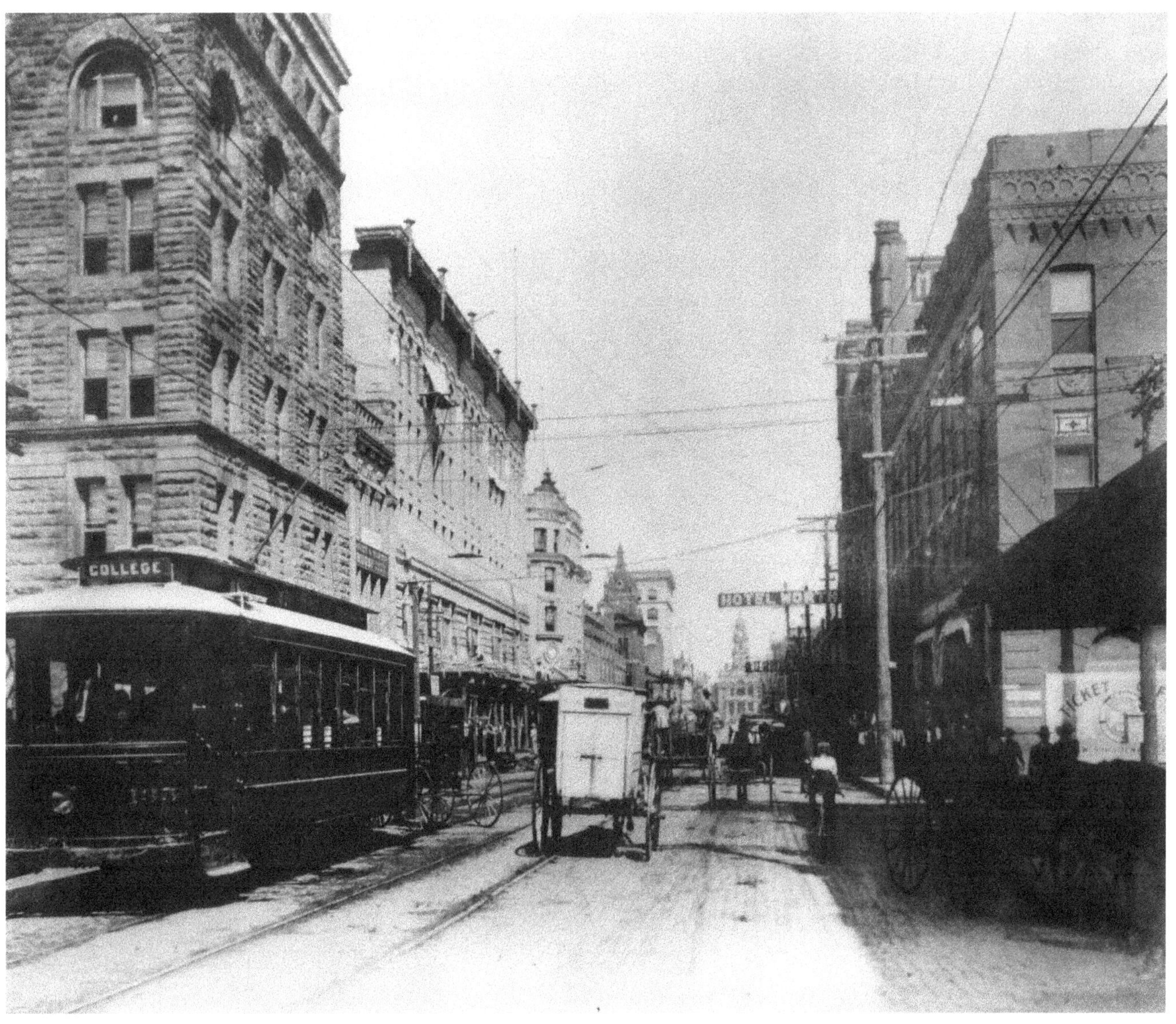


Main Street was equally busy as seen in this view north from 8th. The College Avenue streetcar heads south to Fort Worth University and the growing Fairmount neighborhood beyond. Behind the car is the 1890-era Wheat Building, whose limestone foundations, as well as portions of its former basement, are visible to visitors to the modern building on the site. In the next block stands the new, curved-front, 1899 Hoxie Building that replaced the burned Hurley Building.

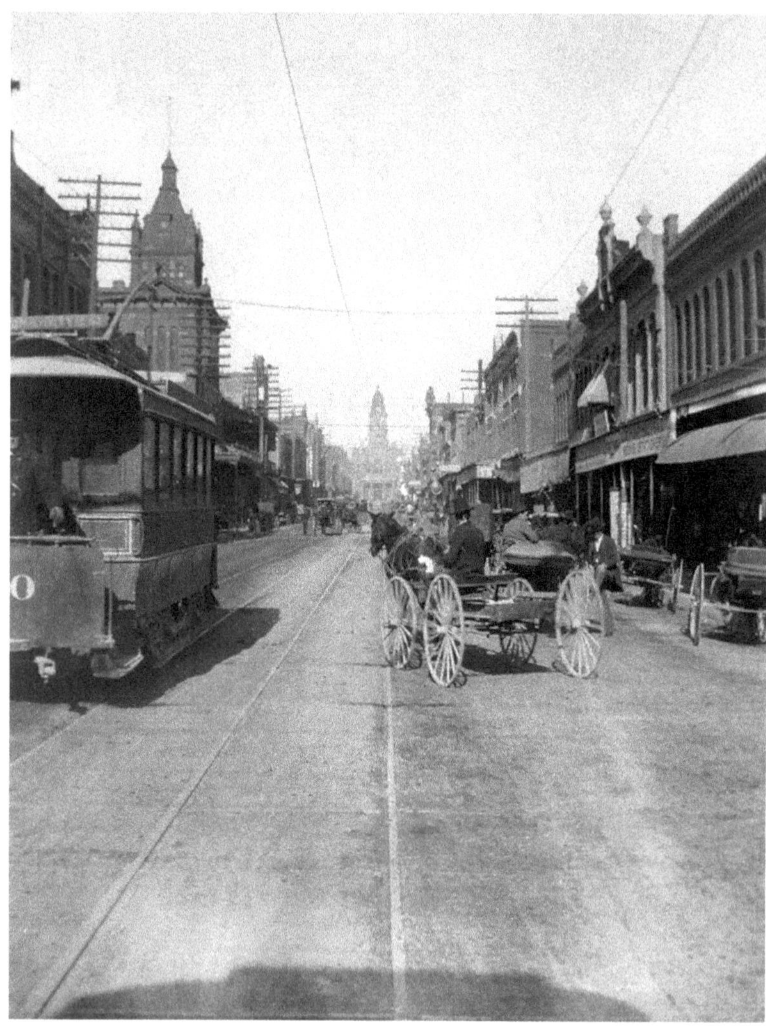

The photographer's view from the front platform of a northbound streetcar captured a frequent frustration for the line's drivers—a buggy pulling out in front. Accidents were frequent, and the streetcars usually won. Ahead and to the left is the tower of the Commercial Club Building at 6th and Main. The Club, founded in 1885 and renamed the Fort Worth Club in 1909, demolished the building in 1915 to construct a new facility that would house the organization until 1926 when it moved to its new home at 7th and Throckmorton.

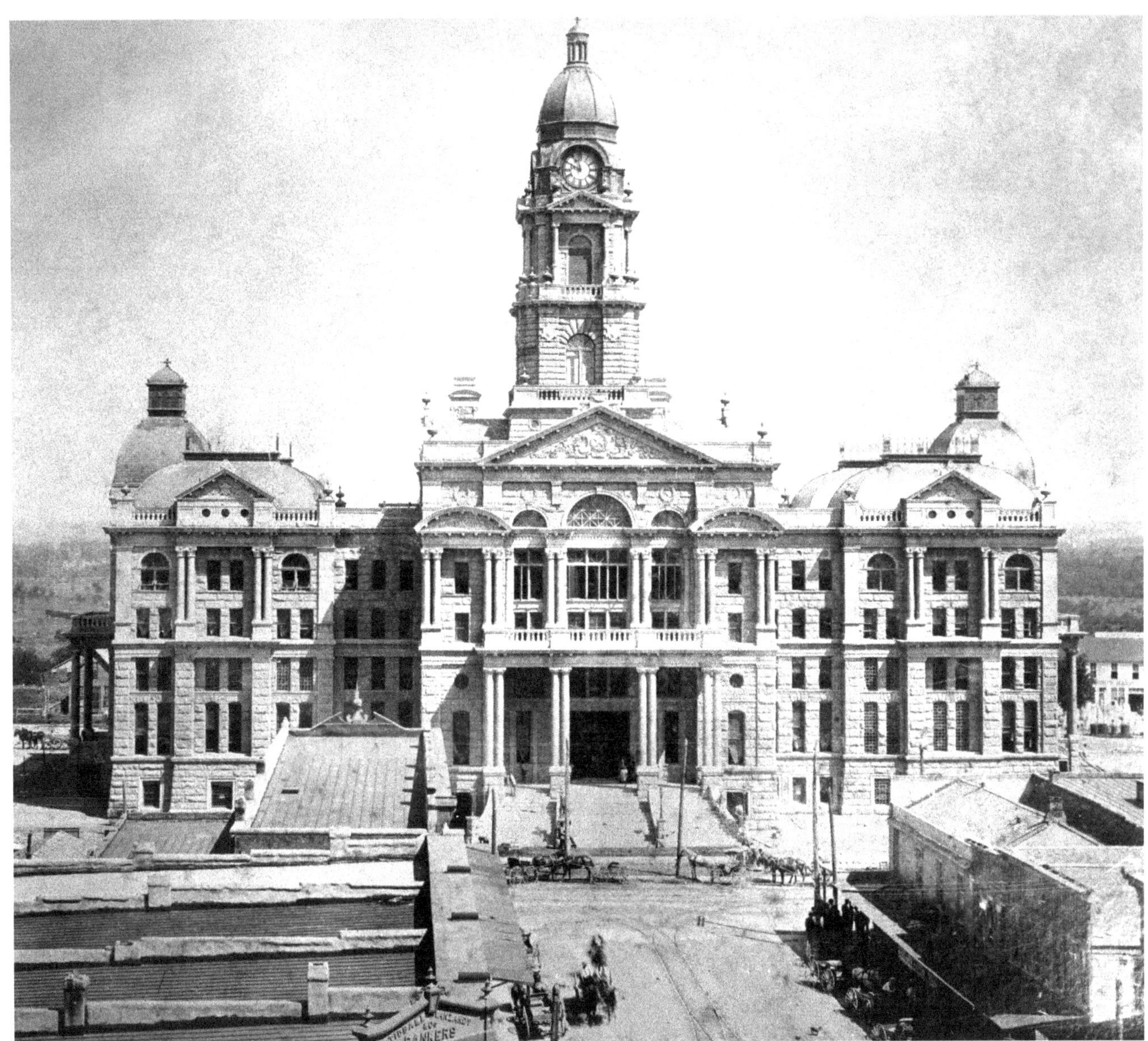


The courthouse dominated the city's skyline as the twentieth century began. The French Renaissance Revival masterpiece, designed by the St. Louis firm of Gunn & Curtiss, is considered by many as the most impressive county courthouse in Texas. In the lower center of this image, the cornice of the building at 1st and Main reads "Tidball, Van Zandt and Company, Bankers." Established in 1873, the private banking operation became the Fort Worth National Bank in 1884. Major K. M. Van Zandt served as president from 1874 until his death in 1930 at age 93.

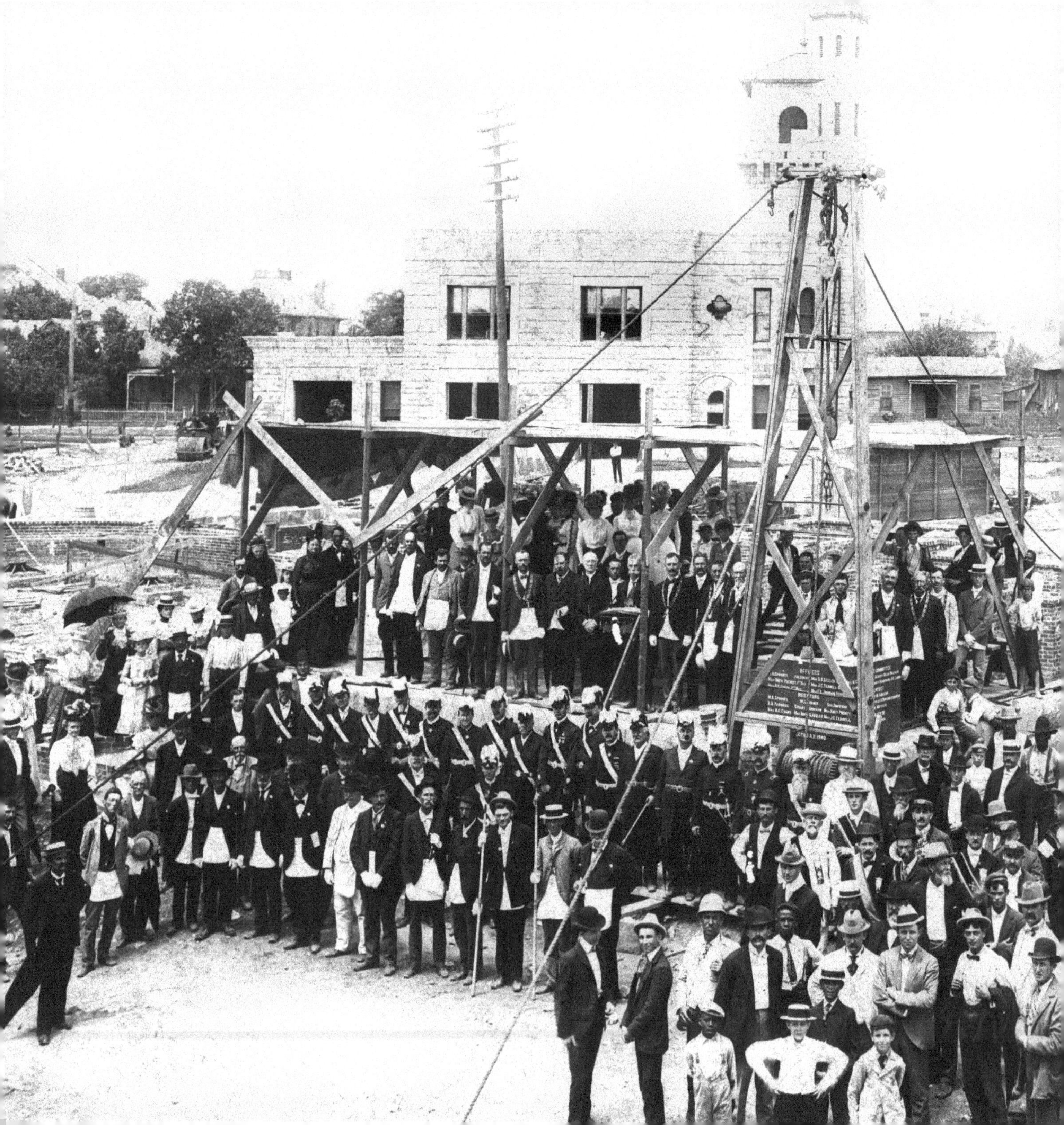

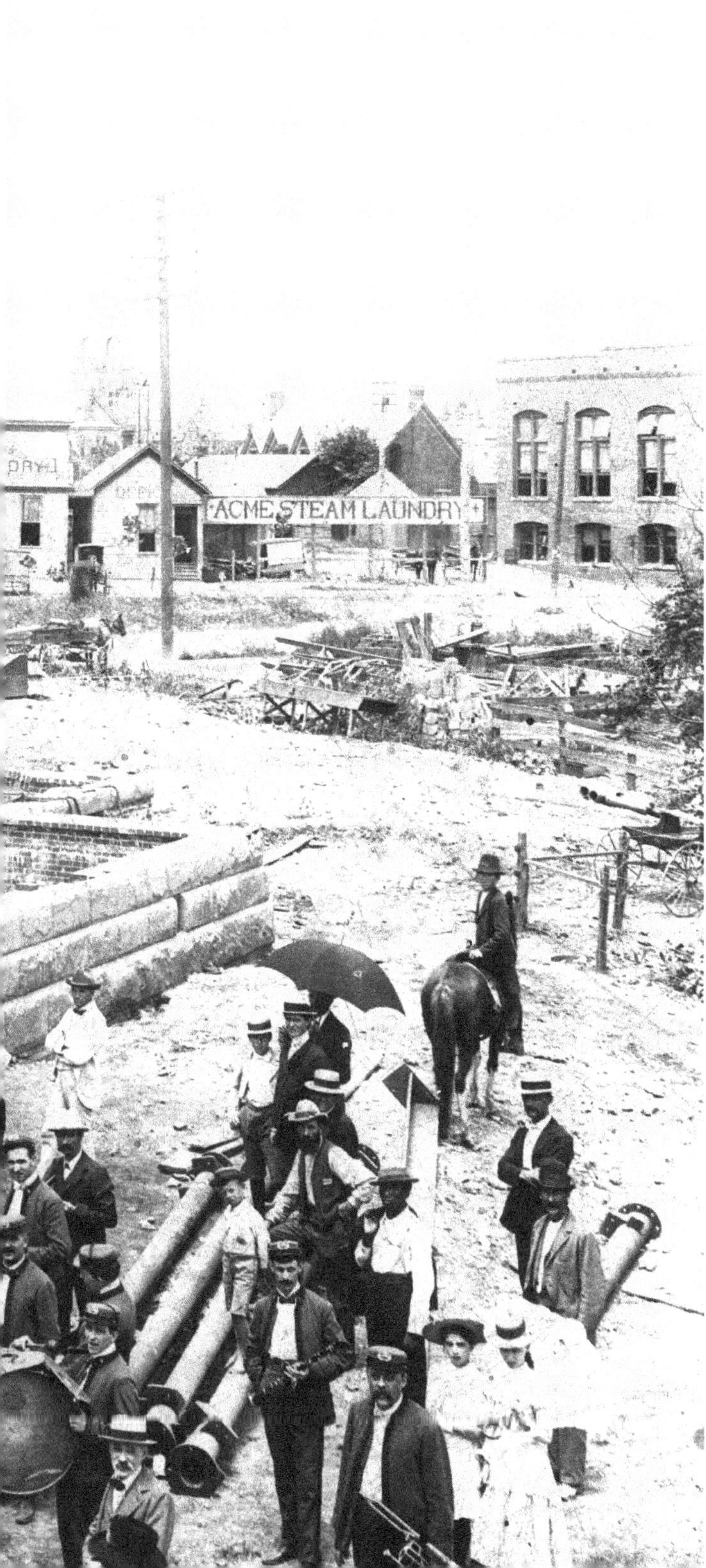


A determined group of Fort Worth women established the Fort Worth Public Library Association in 1892. Struggling to raise funds through the lean years after the Panic of 1893, the group, led by Jennie Scheuber and Delphine Keeler, launched a campaign asking local men to donate the price of a good cigar. Sending the same solicitation to philanthropist Andrew Carnegie, Mrs. Keeler was rewarded with a $50,000 gift. The leveling of the cornerstone took place on October 17, 1901, attended by masons, musicians and the beaming members of the Association.

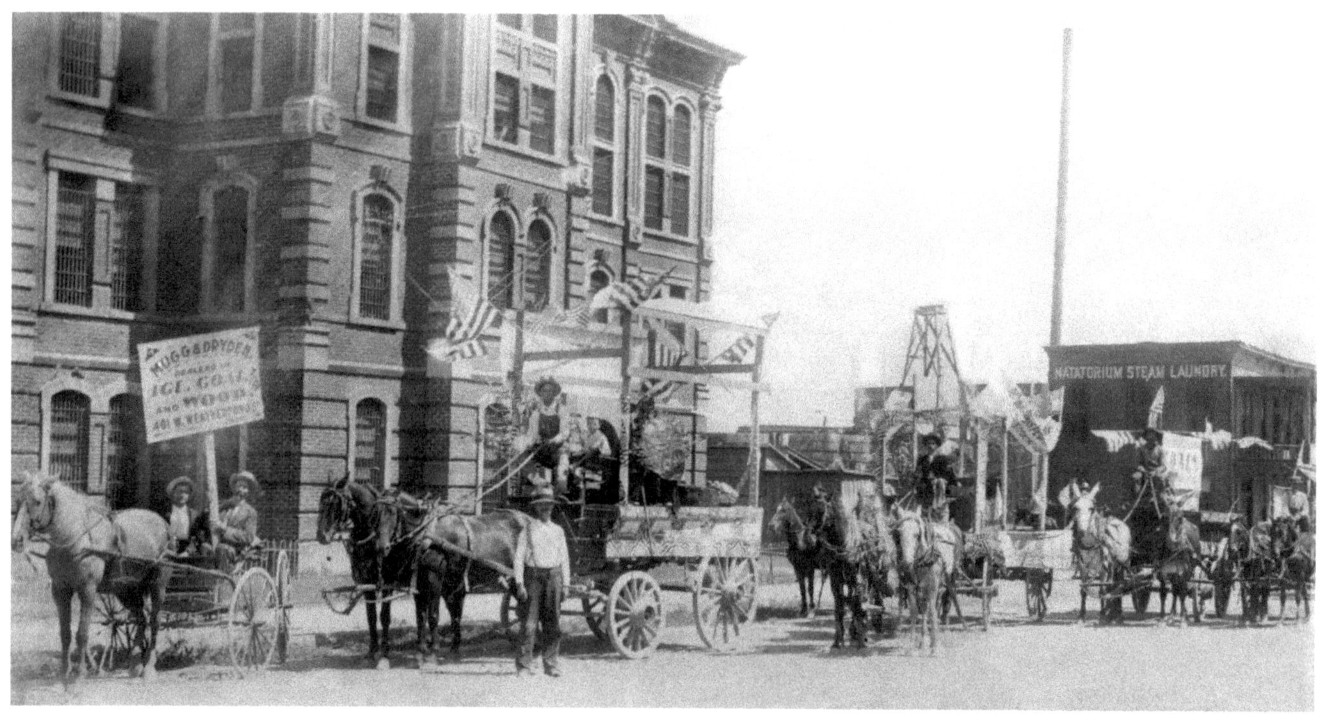


Wagons and teams gather for a parade in front of the old Tarrant County jail on Belknap Street around the turn of the century. Seated at left in the buggy at the head of the line is John A. Mugg, Jr., partner in the ice, coal and wood supply business of Mugg and Dryden, so artfully advertised on the sign held by his seatmate. Mugg came by his mercantile abilities naturally, being the grandson of Archibald Leonard who, with partner Henry Daggett in 1849, opened the first civilian store to serve the soldiers and settlers of Fort Worth.

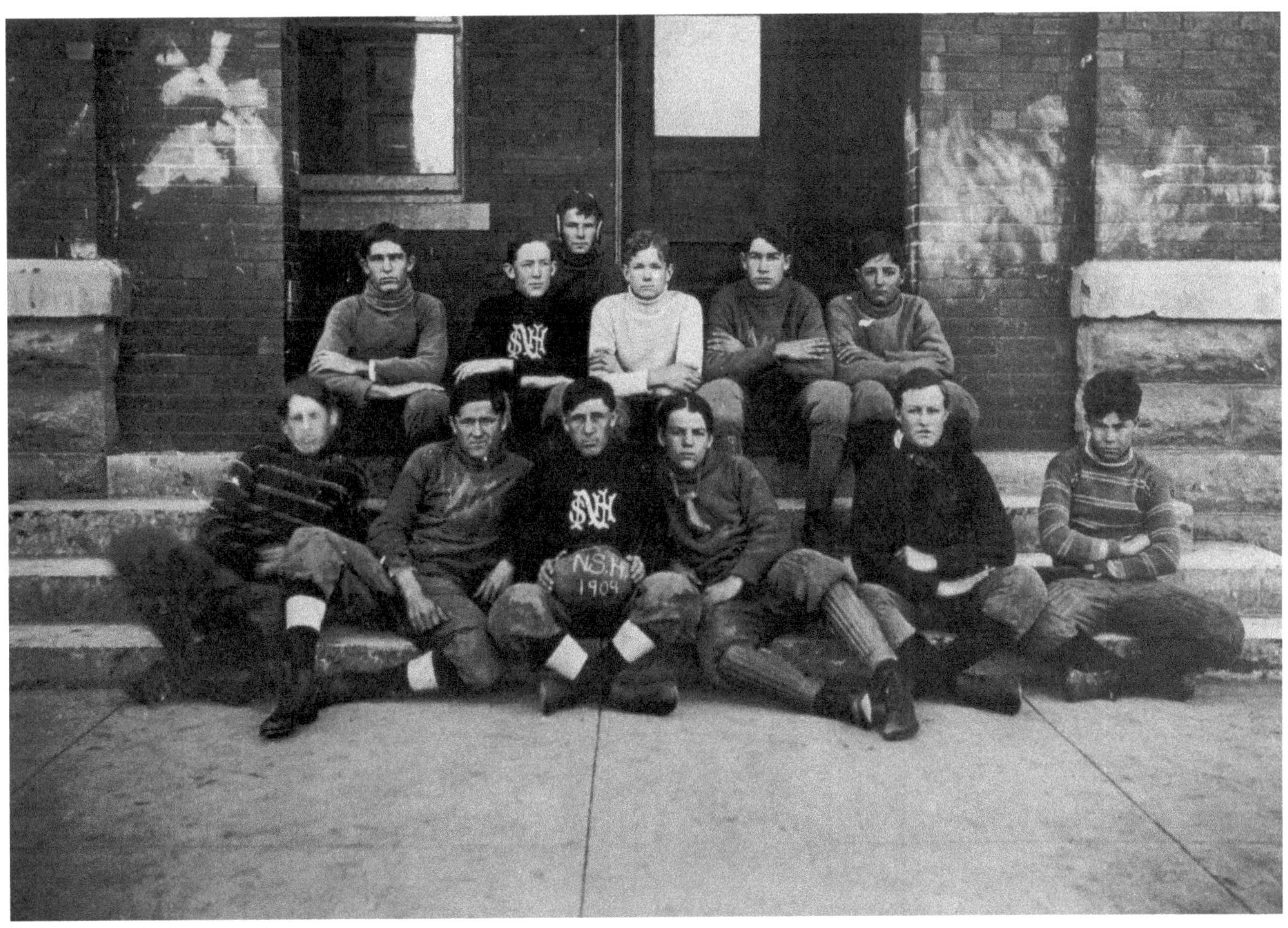


North Fort Worth High School was renamed North Side High School in 1909, the year Fort Worth annexed the City of North Fort Worth. With no athletic program at the school, senior Wenzel "Runt" Stangel, center with ball, put a football team together and played the second teams of Central High School, Fort Worth University and Polytechnic College, launching a school tradition of great football and legendary players. Stangel convinced all of his teammates shown here to join him on the new baseball team the next year.

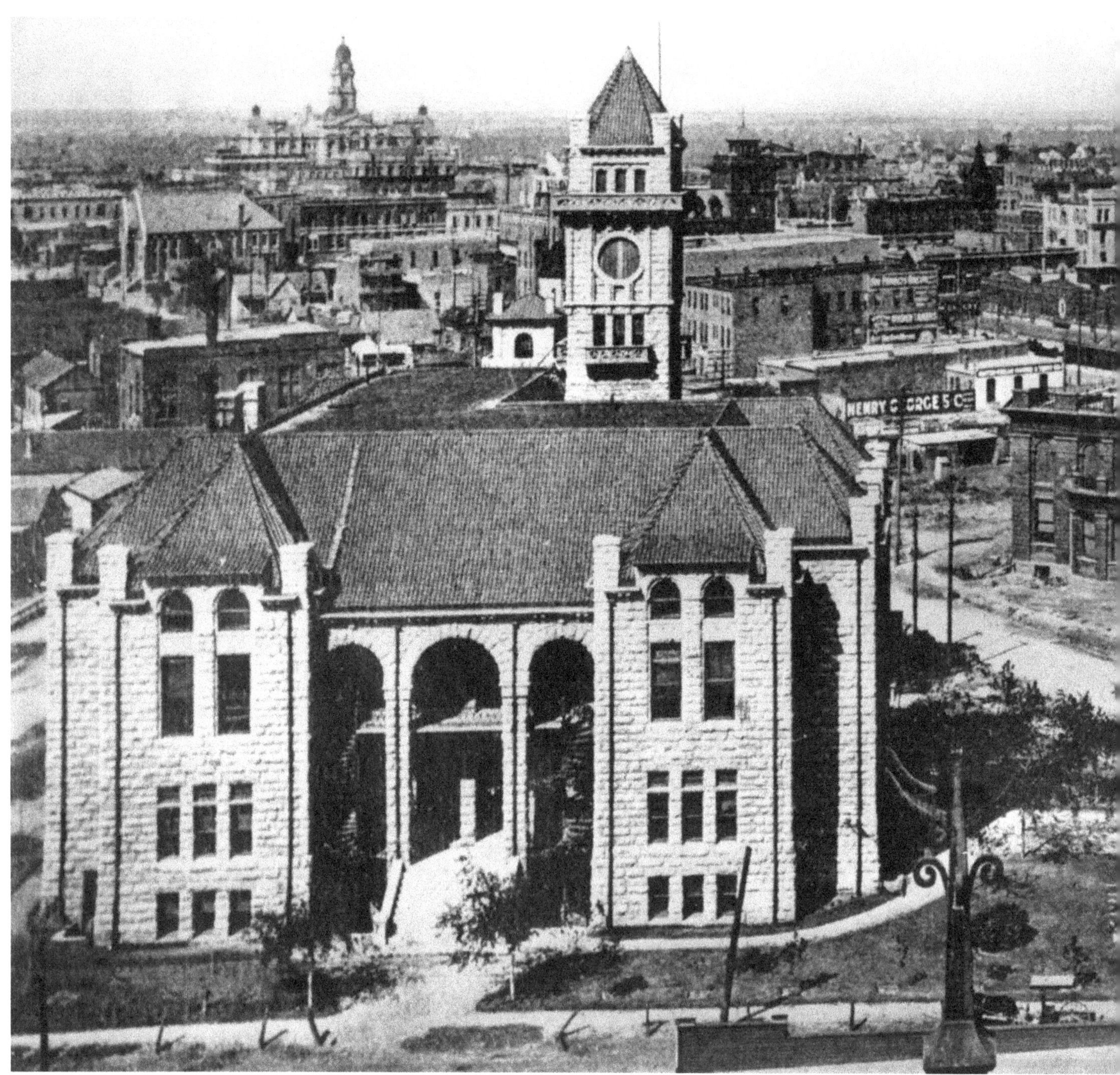

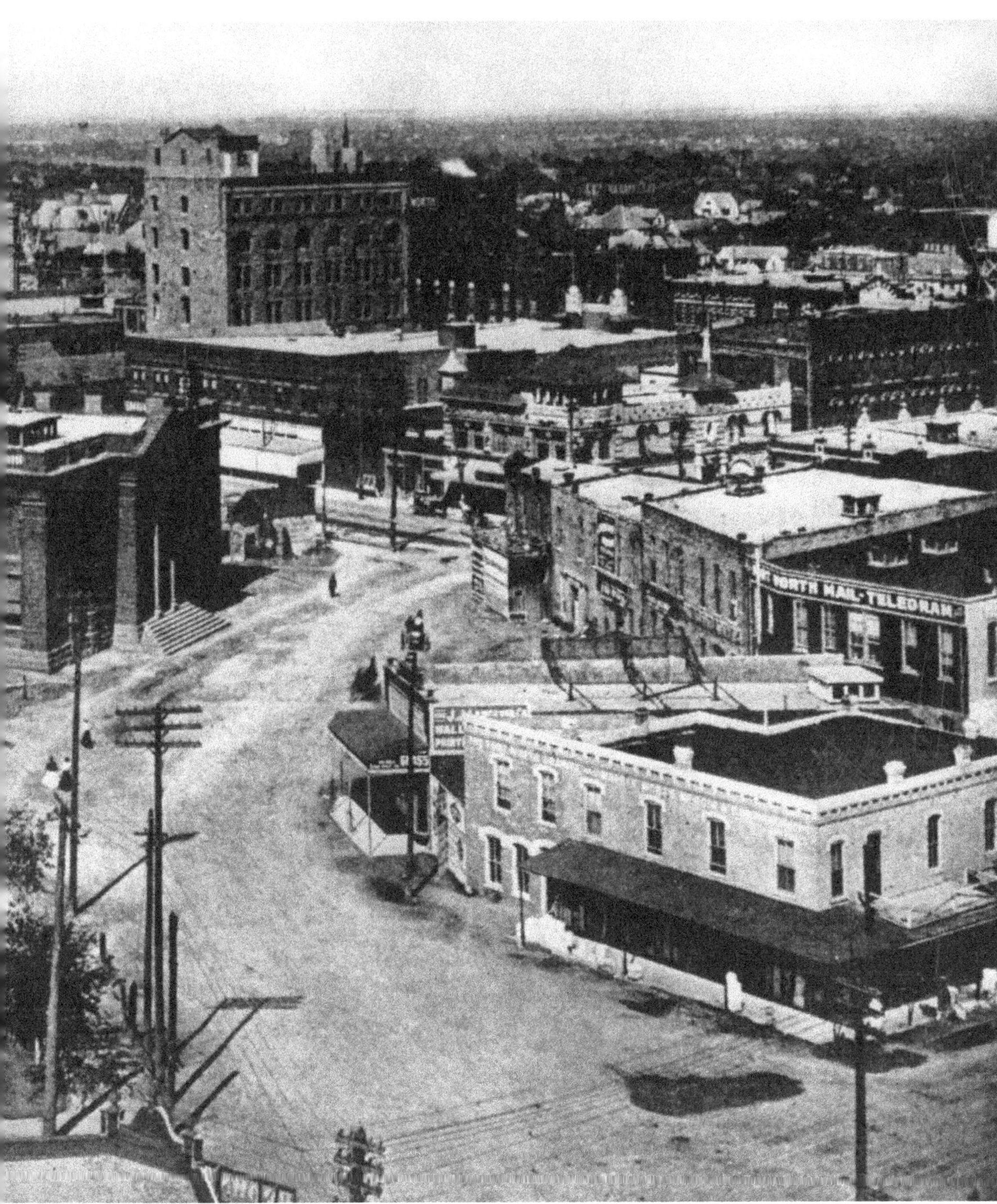


After the 1896 construction of the Federal Building on Jennings Avenue, its rooftop observation deck became a favorite spot for local photographers. This birds-eye view of the business district was probably taken in 1902, shortly after the completion of the Carnegie Library, center. The towers of the 1893 city hall, foreground, and the 1895 courthouse, top left, dominate the skyline of a city on the verge of a population explosion. In the decade following the opening of the packing plants on the North Side in 1902, Fort Worth tripled in size.

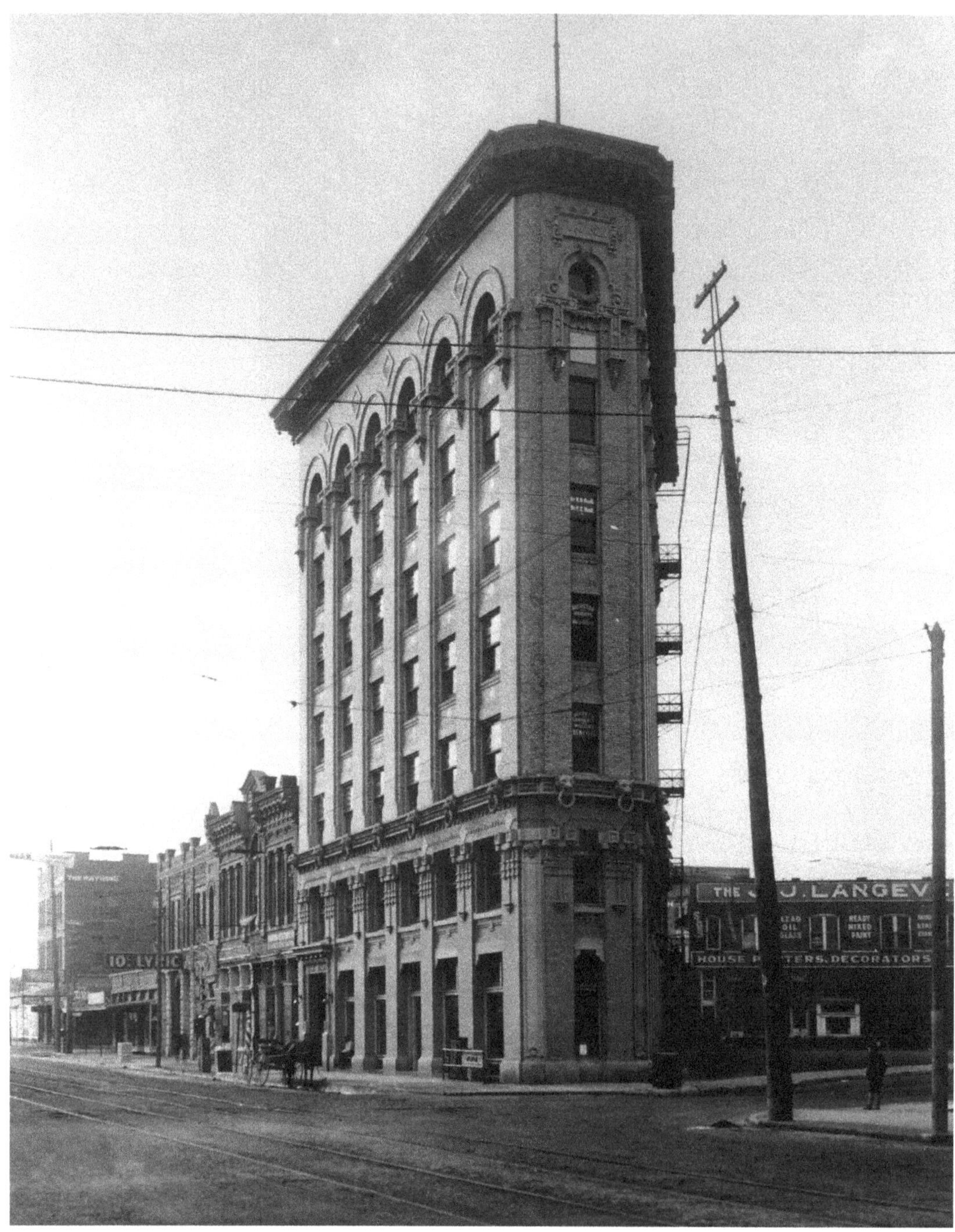


In 1910, the Flatiron Building still ranked among the city's tallest. Built in 1907 by Dr. Bacon Saunders, Dean of the Fort Worth University Medical School, the unique structure allowed local architects Sanguinet and Staats to bring a touch of New York and Chicago to Texas. Carved panther heads around the frieze memorialize the 1873 legend of a panther sleeping undisturbed on Main Street during an economic depression, the source of Fort Worth's nickname, "Panther City."

The Flatiron is at far right in this bird's-eye view taken about 1910 from the roof of the Federal Building at Jennings and 11th streets. In the foreground at left is the 1893 Fort Worth City Hall, with the Tarrant County Courthouse looming behind it on the horizon. To the right of the city hall clock tower is the new First National Bank, designed by Sanguinet and Staats, and reigning, for a brief four-year period, as the tallest building in the city.

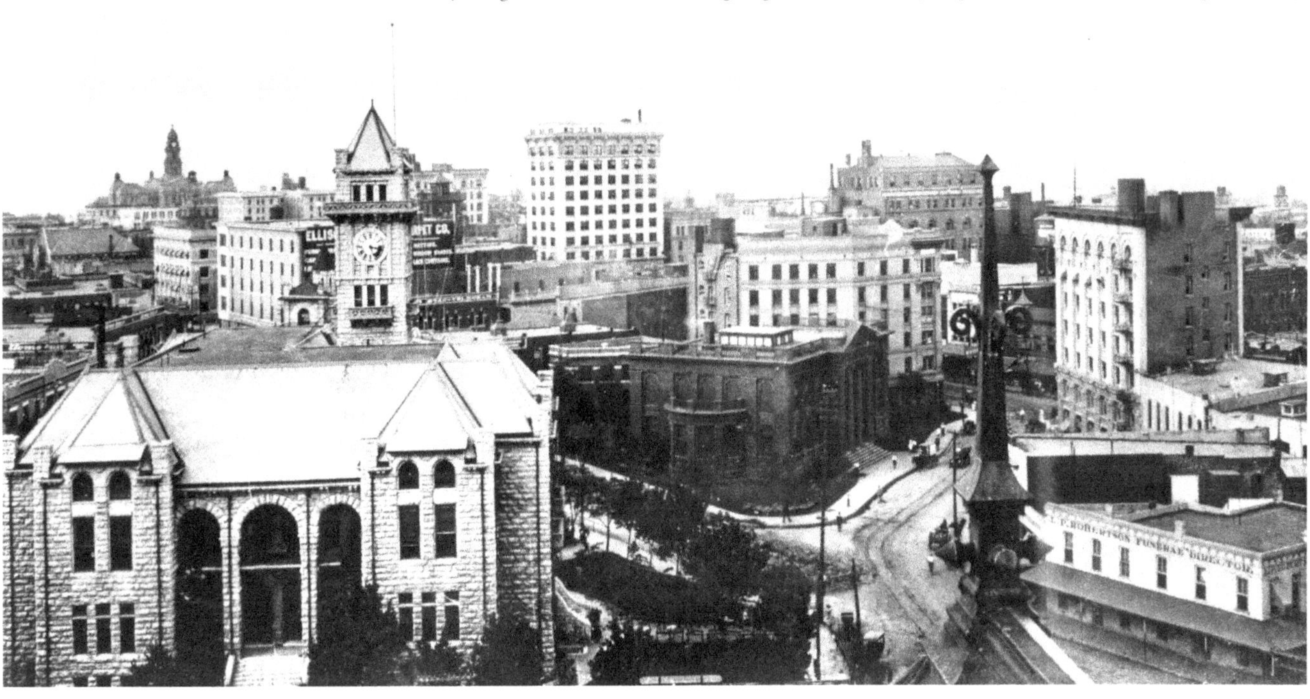

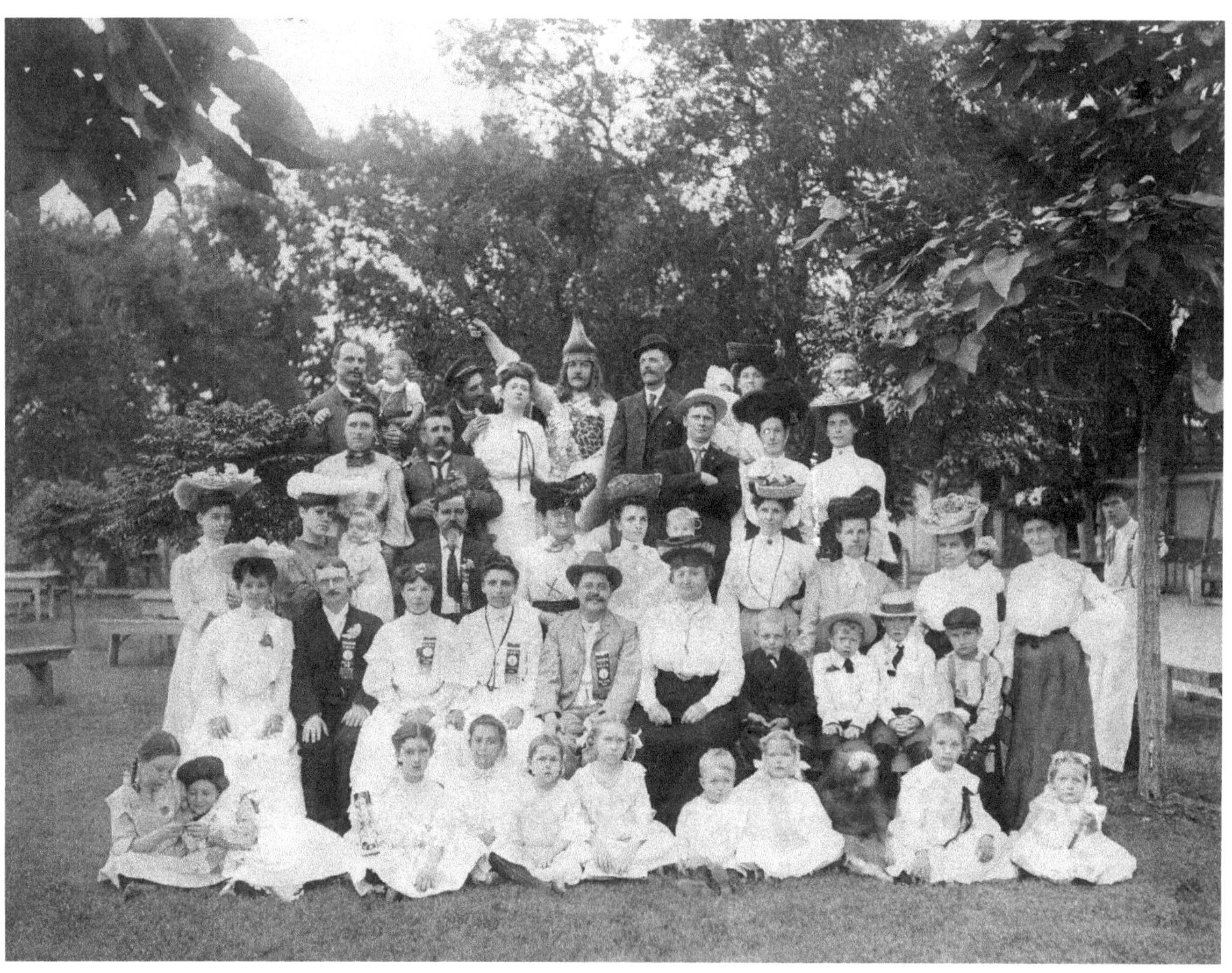

One of the more popular places in town at the turn of the century was the Sons of Hermann Park and Beer Garden located just across the river from the courthouse at the foot of the Main Street viaduct. Summer dances at the open air pavilion were a highlight of the season, although events were scheduled year round. Here, members and guests of the German Verein gather at the park for an evening's entertainment. Damaged during the Flood of 1908, the park site was selected for the location of a new North Main electric generating plant built by Fort Worth Power and Light in 1912.

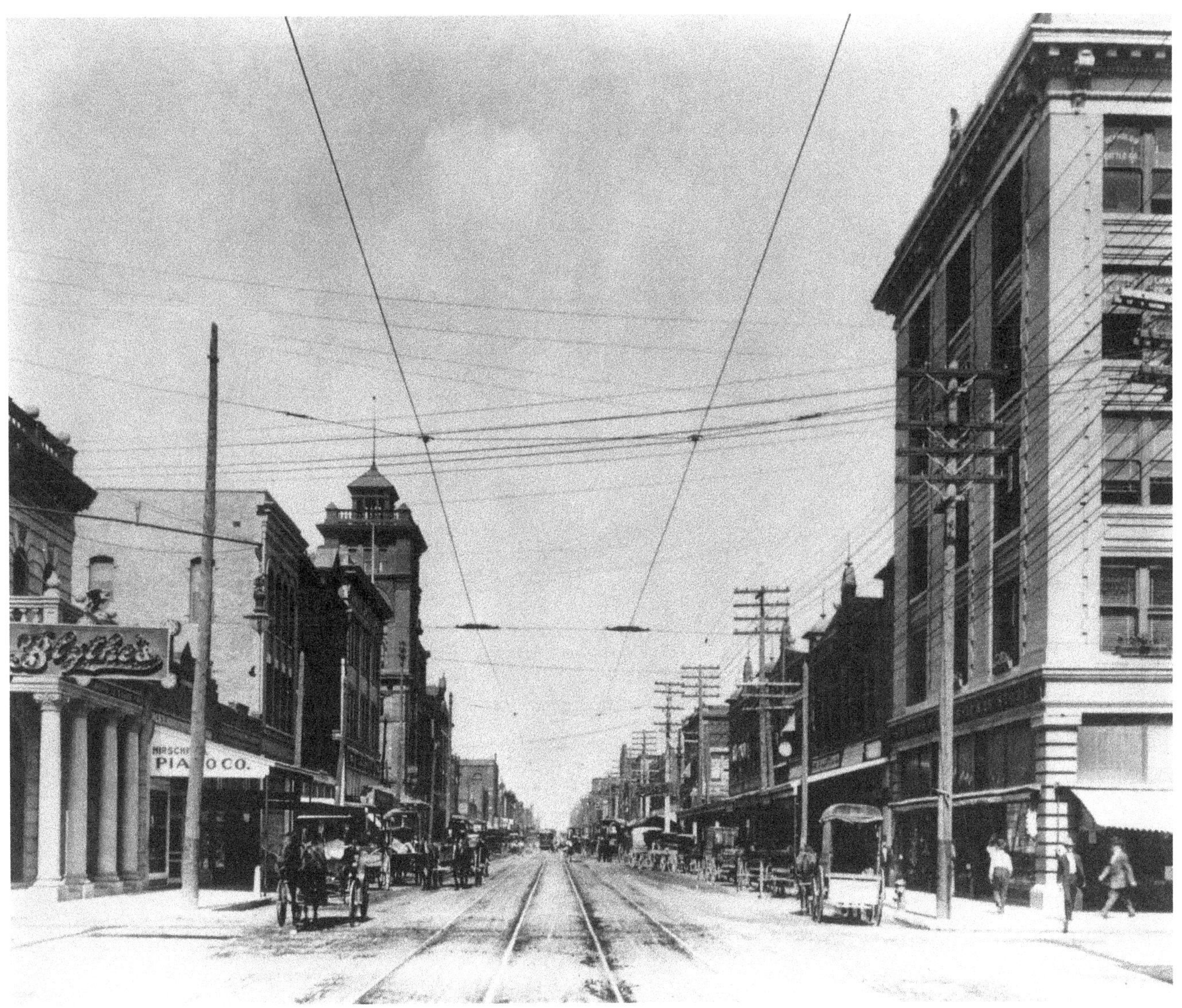


Two buildings opposite each other on Houston Street at 8th represented the influence on the city of the cattle industry and the families who made their fortunes in it. The ornate, columned building at left was home to the Waggoner Bank and Trust, established in 1901 by W. T. Waggoner, owner of one of the largest ranching operations in the history of the United States. At right is one of the Reynolds Buildings, owned by G. T. and W. D. Reynolds, founders of the legendary Reynolds Cattle Company. One block away on the left in this image taken about 1905 is the 1889 Board of Trade Building.

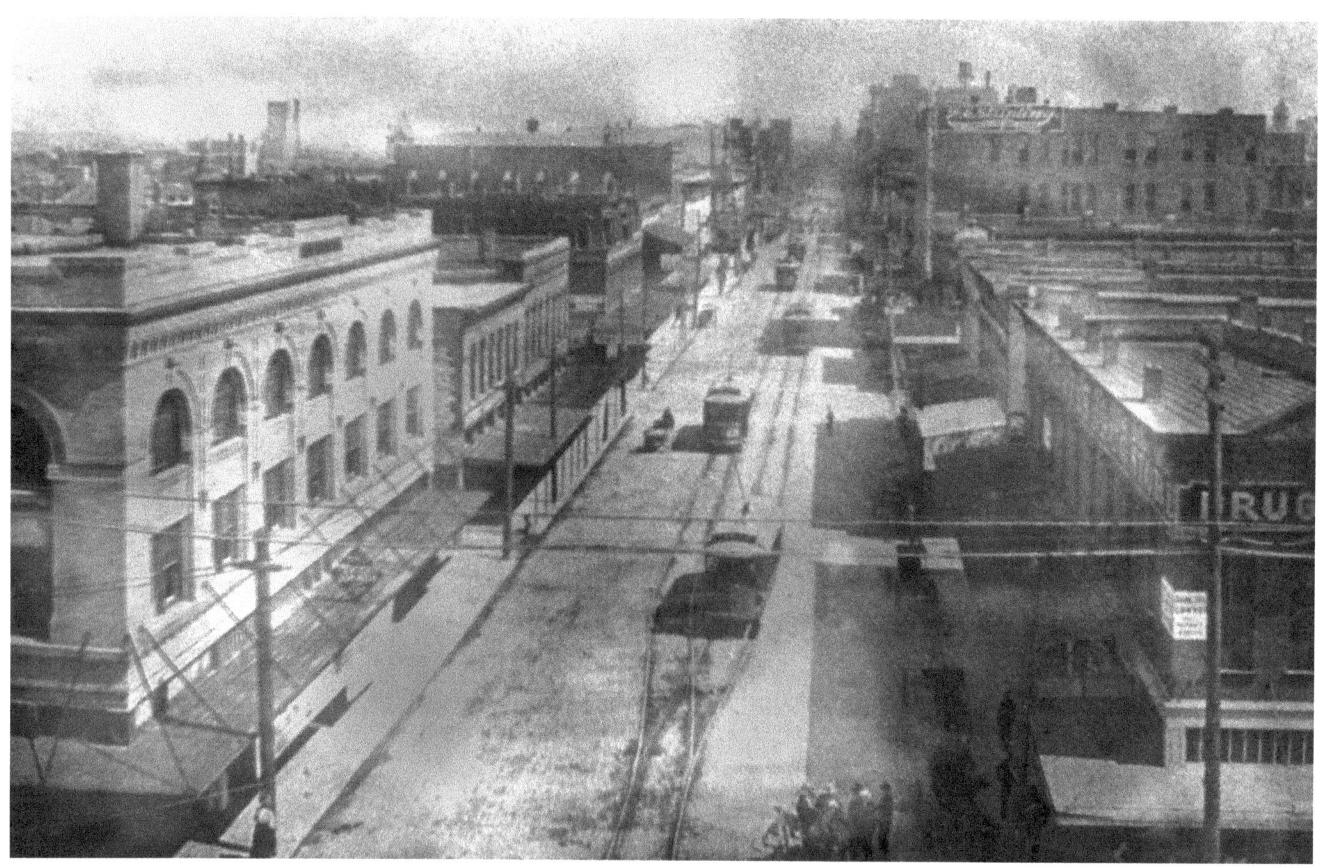


Looking south on Main Street from the top of the courthouse. Seventeen blocks away is the tower of the Texas & Pacific Passenger Station. At left, at the corner of Weatherford and Main, is the 1906 T. B. Ellison Building, designed by Sanguinet and Staats and considered one of the most architecturally significant buildings in Fort Worth before its demolition to make room for the Tarrant County Administration Building.

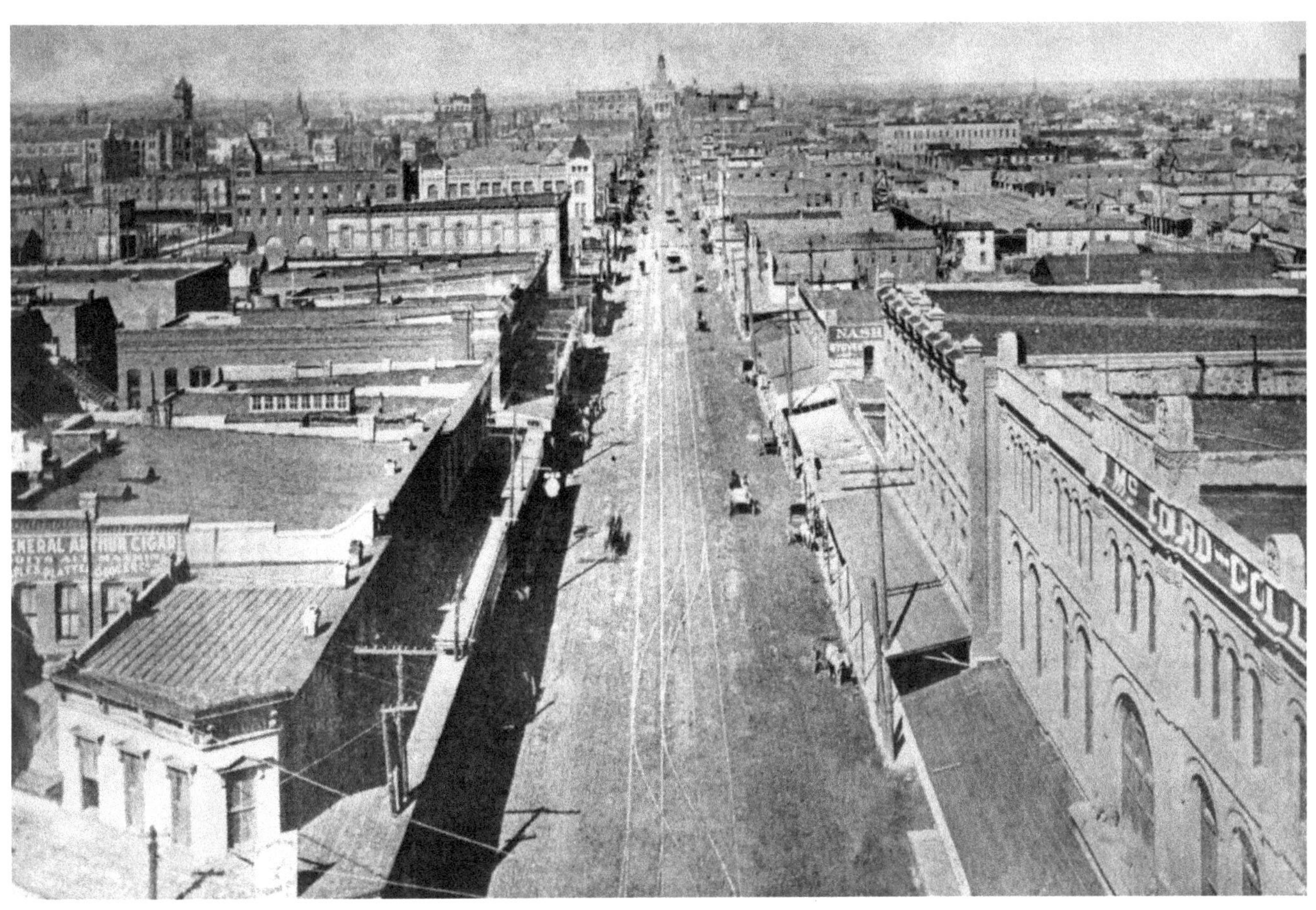


Main Street looking north from the tower of the Texas & Pacific Station around 1904. Virtually every structure along Main, from the 1886 McCord Collins Building at lower right to the Wheat Building at 8th Street, seen just left of the courthouse, was demolished for the Convention Center and Water Gardens. In the top left corner are St Patrick's Cathedral and the tower of the 1893 city hall at 10th and Throckmorton.

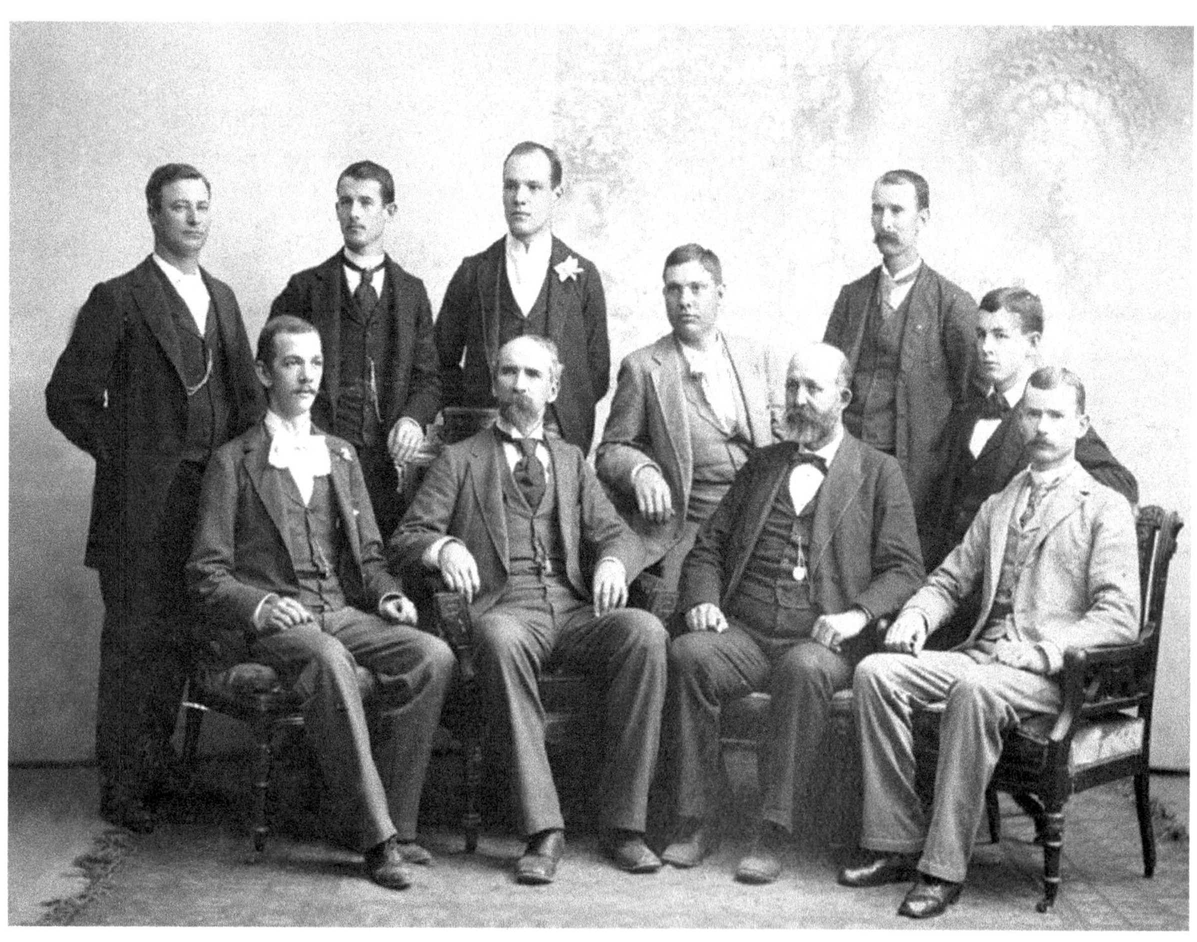

Captain M. B. Loyd, a Confederate veteran and native of Kentucky, arrived in Fort Worth in 1870, establishing an exchange office and becoming the city's first banker. In 1877, he received the ninth national bank charter issued in Texas and founded the First National Bank of Fort Worth, serving as its president until his death in 1912. Seated second from left, Capt. Loyd poses here with officers and employees of the bank about 1900.

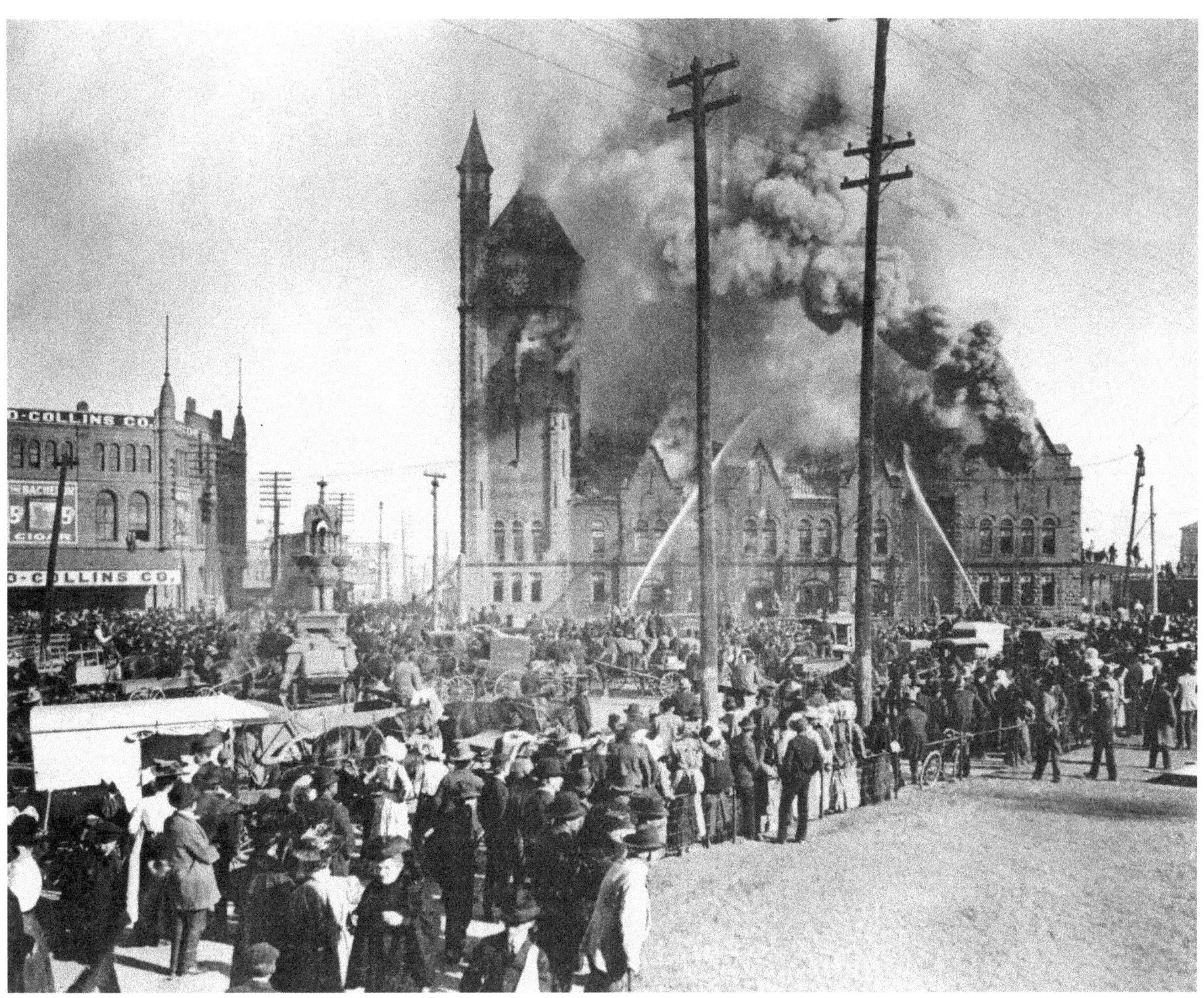


The T&P terminal burned in December 1904, drawing spectators from all over the city, including an enterprising photographer who climbed a telephone pole (far right) to capture the perfect shot. The station was rebuilt and used until it was replaced in 1929 by the modern art deco terminal still in use today. The left center of the photograph shows the monument and horse fountain dedicated in 1893 to the memory of Al Hayne, the hero and lone casualty of the Spring Palace fire of 1890. The fountain still stands on Lancaster, the sole survivor of this scene.

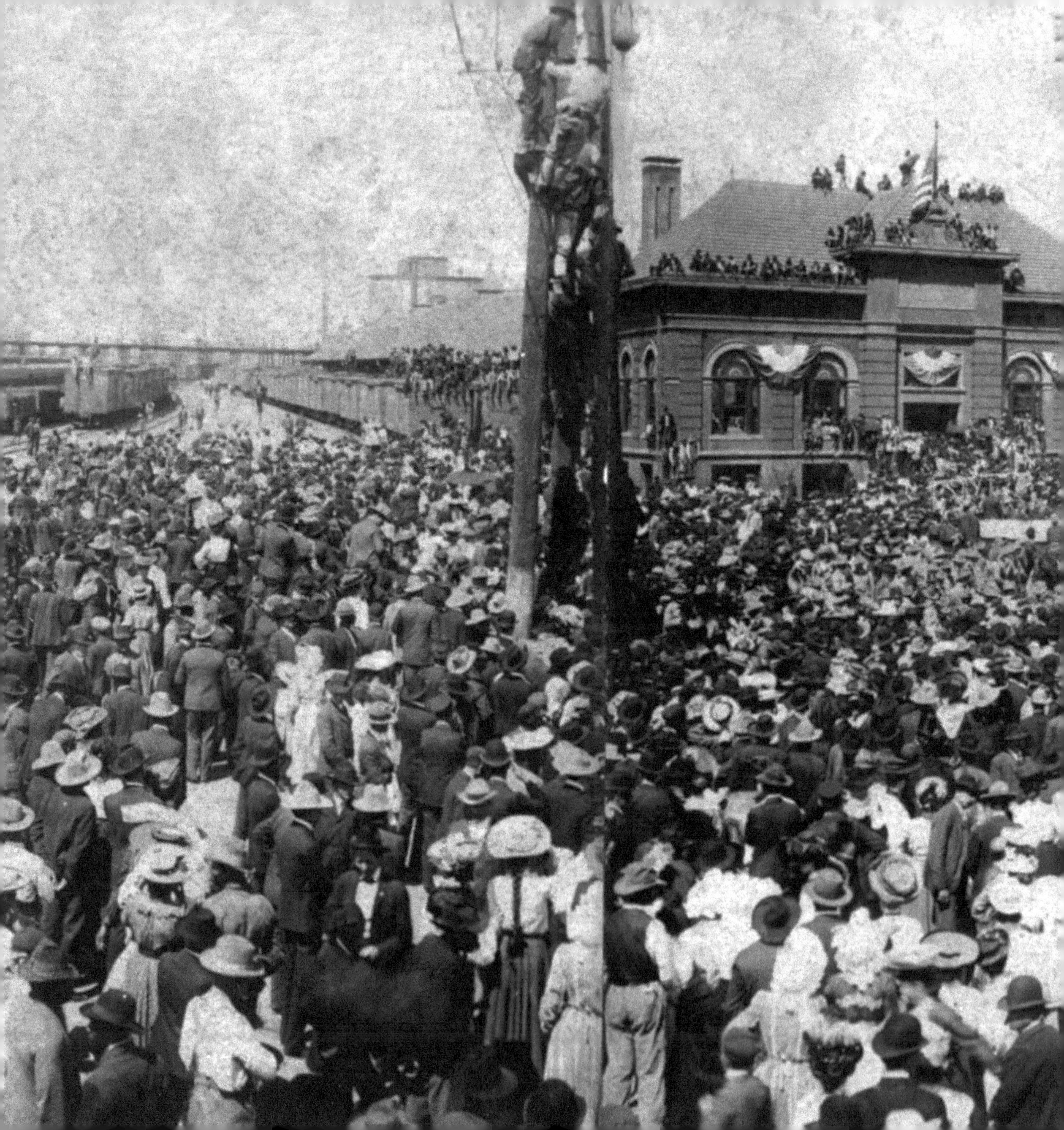

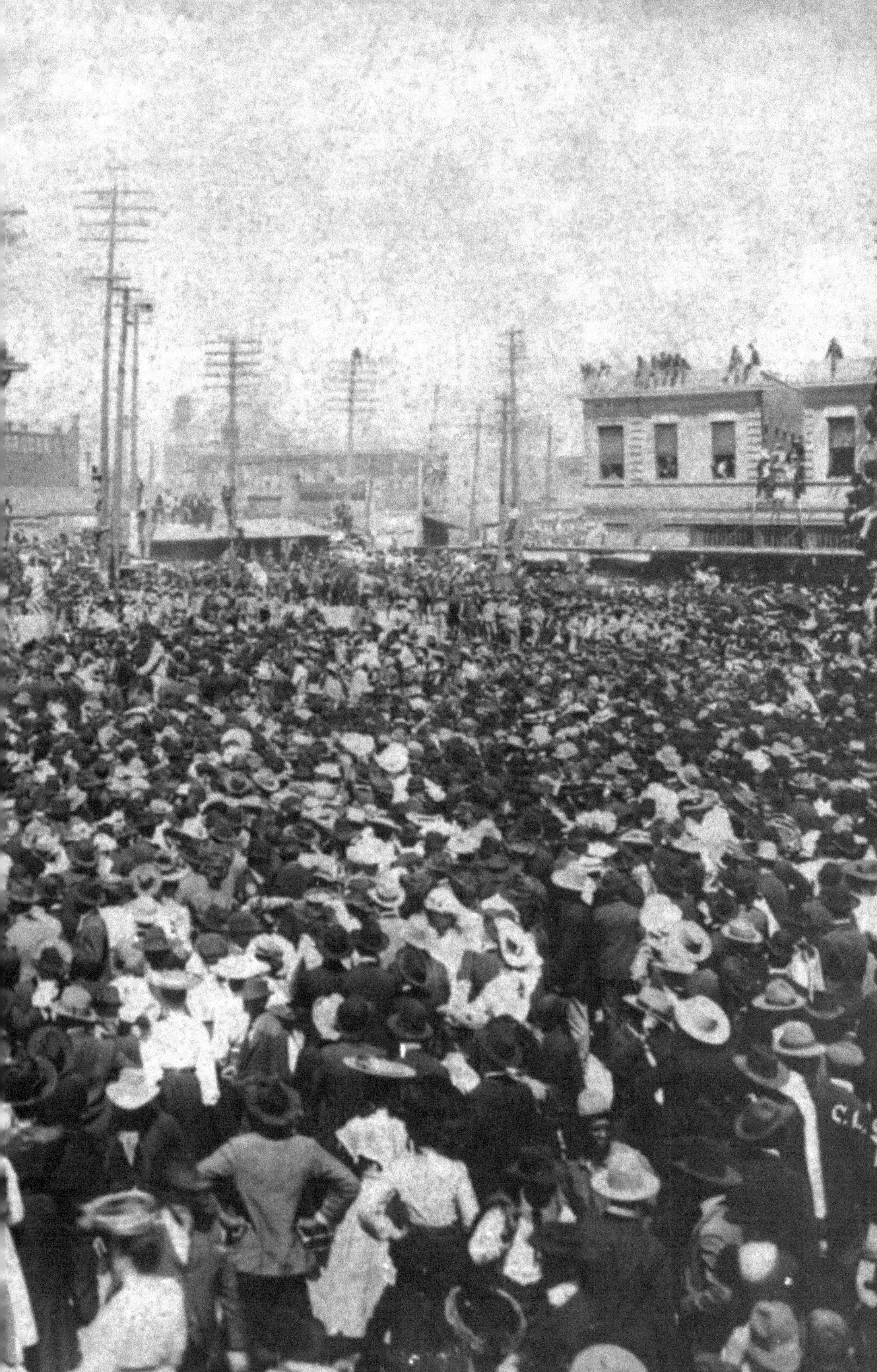

President Theodore Roosevelt visited Fort Worth on April 8, 1905, the first sitting president to venture to the city. Scheduled to speak at the recently burned T&P Passenger Station, the president's platform was moved to the front of the railroad's freight building across the street. Several thousand greeted TR, whose visit included meeting with Burk Burnett and Tom Waggoner to discuss grazing leases on tribal lands in Indian Territory and a wolf hunt hosted by the cattlemen.

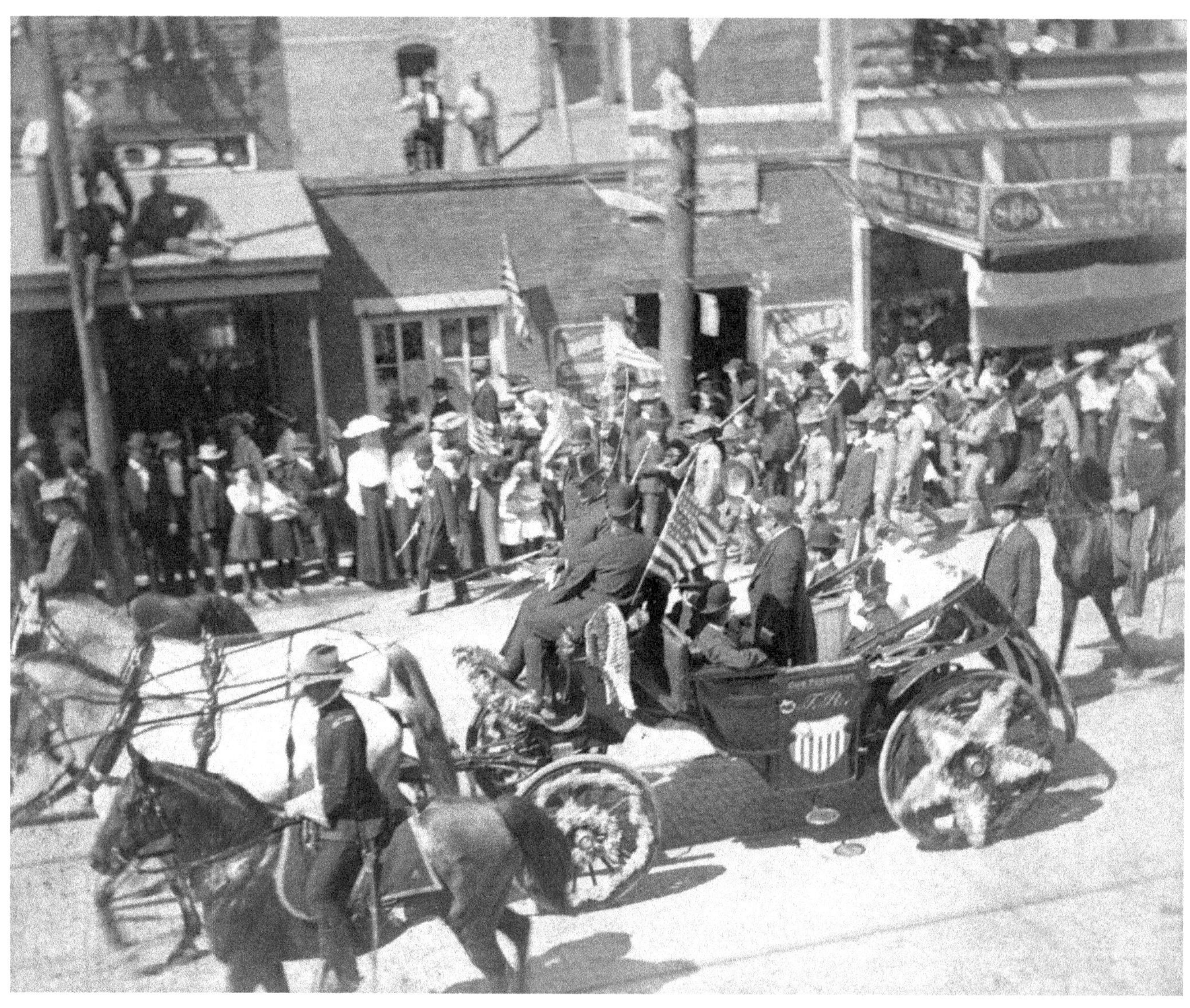

President Roosevelt paraded through town accompanied by veterans and cheered by crowds lining the streets and viewing from rooftops. In fact, one roof collapsed under the weight of fifty people straining to see the procession. No one was hurt, and the president continued to his next official duty, planting a tree in front of the Carnegie Library. Roosevelt visited the city again in 1911, speaking to a crowd in the North Side Coliseum.

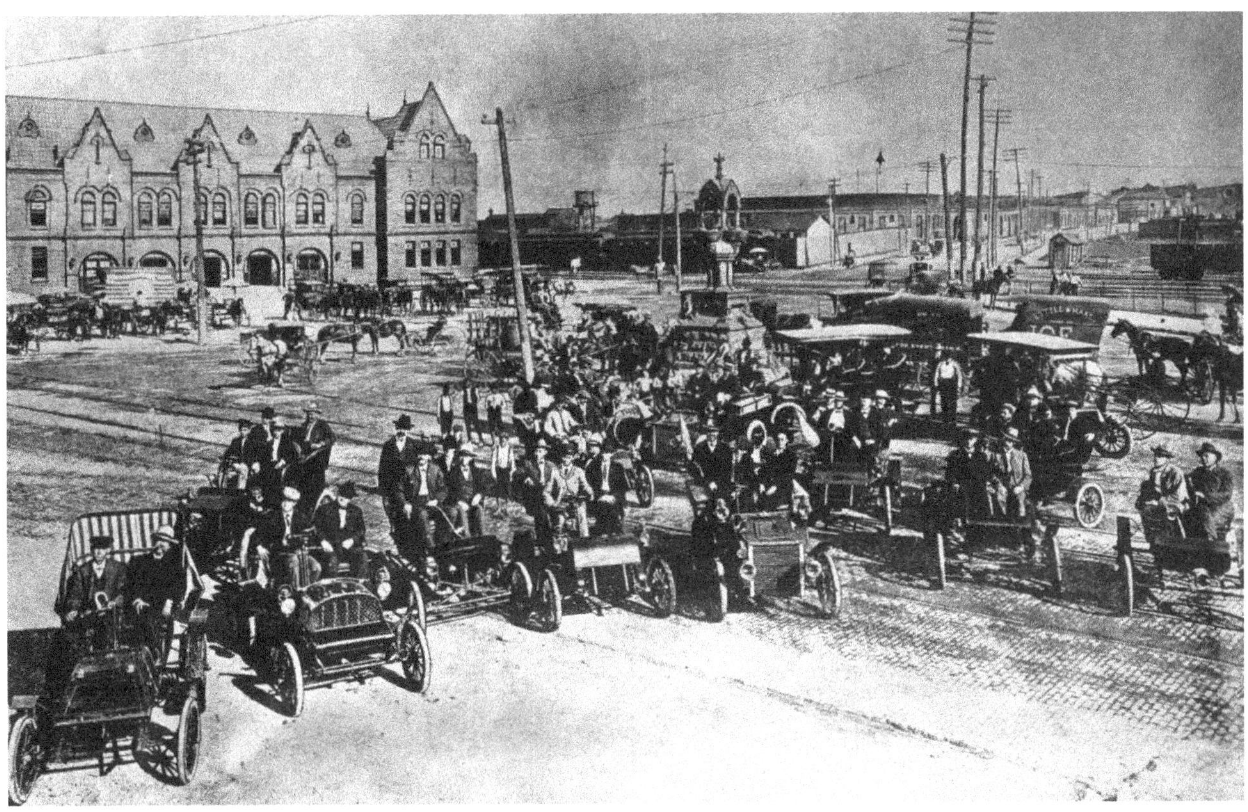

In 1902, Fort Worth bicycle shop owner H. E. Cromer brought the first automobile to the city. While early motorists were cursed, shot at, threatened with flying beer bottles and generally accused of disturbing the natural order of things, cars were here to stay. By 1904, there were fifteen of them in town, including a Winton touring car owned by A. B. Wharton, new husband of Tom Waggoner's daughter, Electra, and proprietor of the first auto dealership in Fort Worth. All fifteen proud owners gathered near the Al Hayne monument in the T&P Plaza for a portrait.

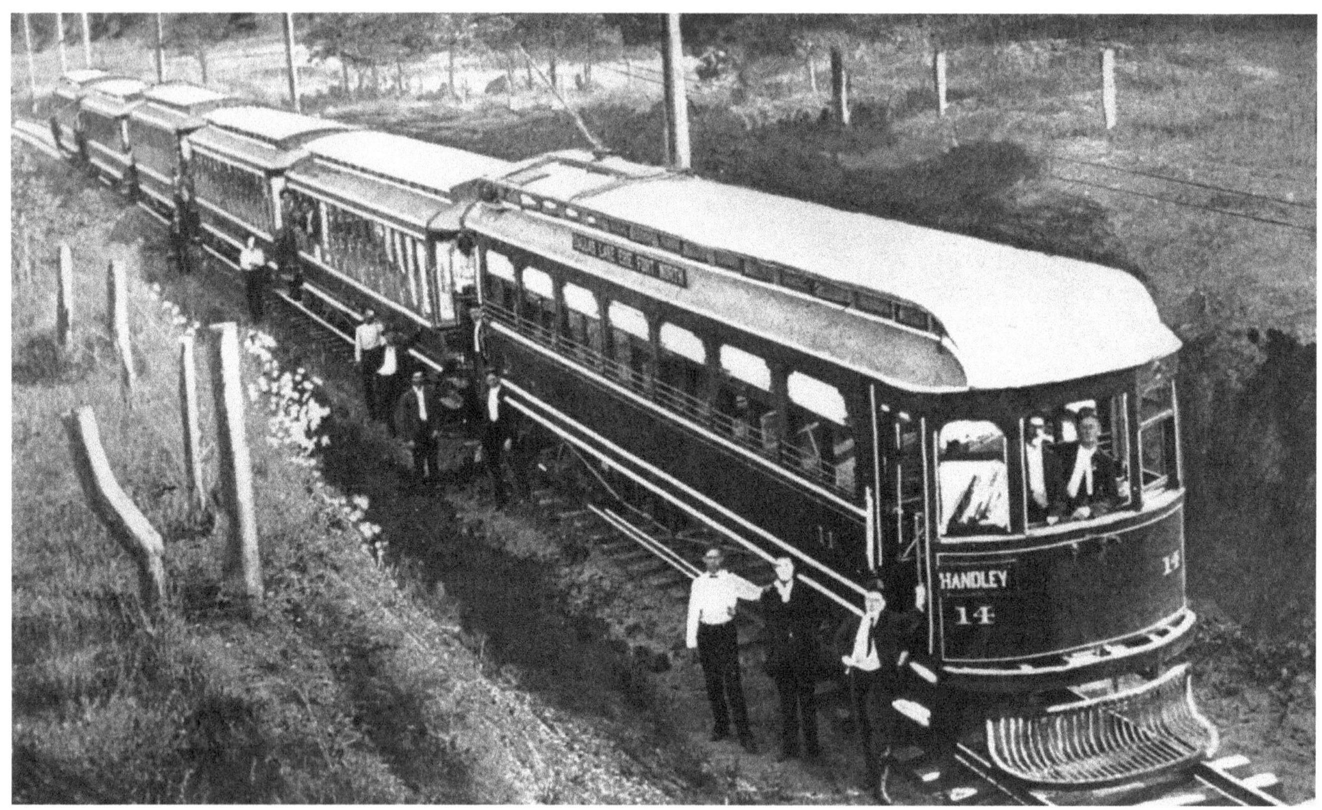


The Boston investors who chartered the Northern Texas Traction Company in 1901 saw the great potential sparked by the growth of Fort Worth and Dallas. In 1902, the company inaugurated interurban service connecting the two cities. To power the electric streetcar line, NTTC built a new generating plant in the small town of Handley, six miles east of Fort Worth. The Interurban served the region until 1938, when the rail system gave way to buses. A restored car, similar to the ones photographed here in 1904, is on display at the Intermodal Transportation Center in Downtown Fort Worth.

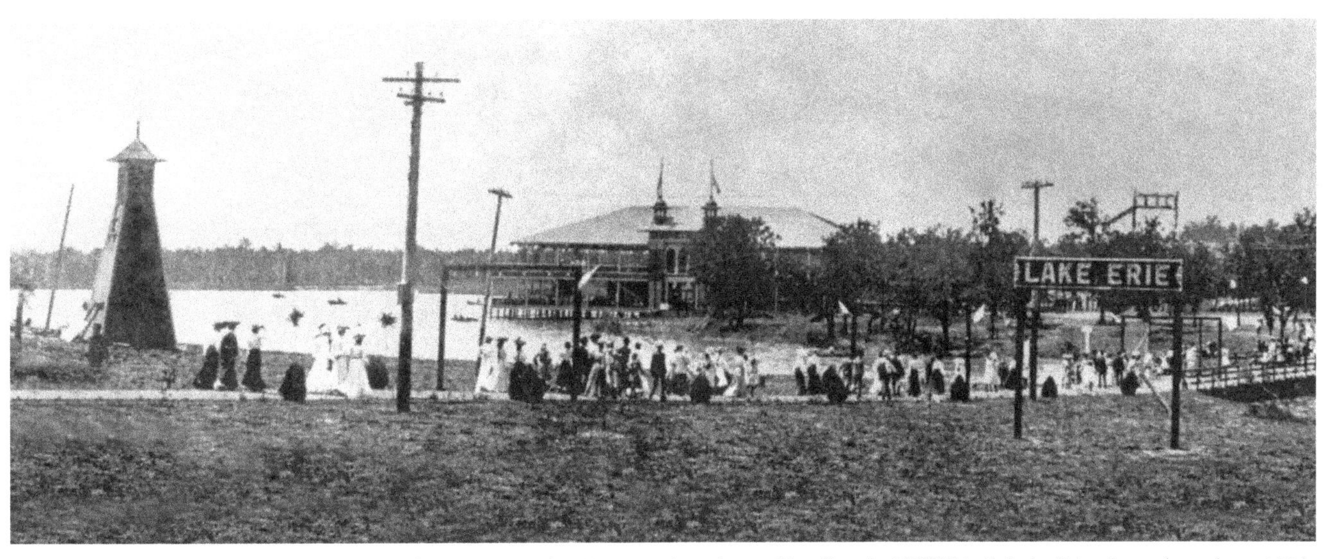


To provide water to its electric generation plant at Handley, the NTTC built Lake Erie, shown here about 1904. In an effort to attract riders to the Interurban, the company developed a pavilion and resort at the lake, offering summer concerts, boat rentals and picnics to a local population unaccustomed to large bodies of water except when the Trinity River flooded. The developers of Arlington Heights had built Lake Como in 1890 for similar purposes. Both resorts remained popular through World War I.

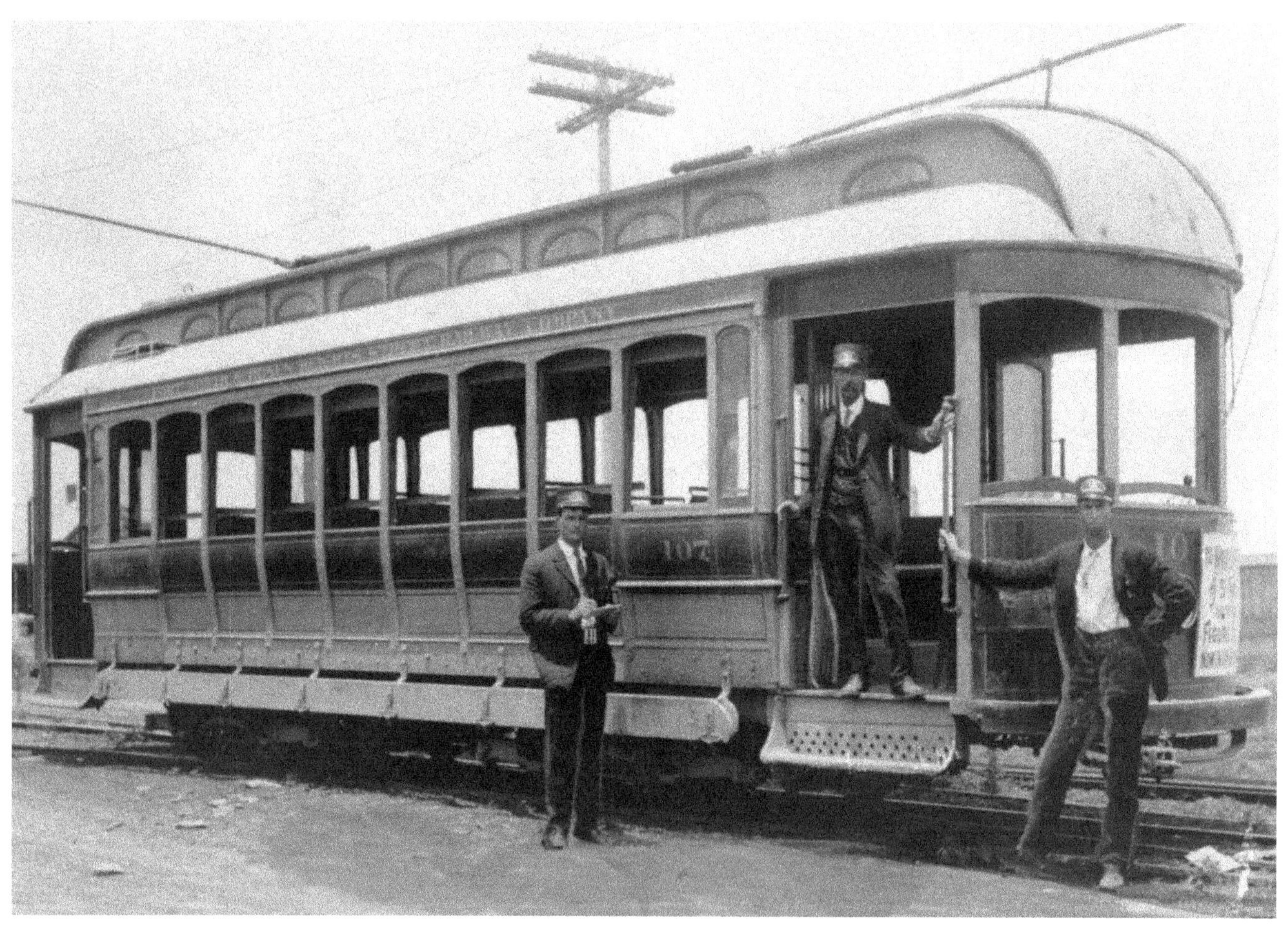


When Sam Rosen began to develop land near the growing stockyards in 1901, he assumed he would be able to work a deal with the Northern Texas Traction Company to provide rail access to his property. When NTTC declined, Rosen built his own line, running from the T&P station, across a new bridge over the river and out to North Fort Worth. The line required the construction of a crossing of the NTTC tracks that Rosen ingeniously accomplished in one night during a snowstorm in 1905, surprising his competitor the next morning and assuring the success of Rosen Heights.

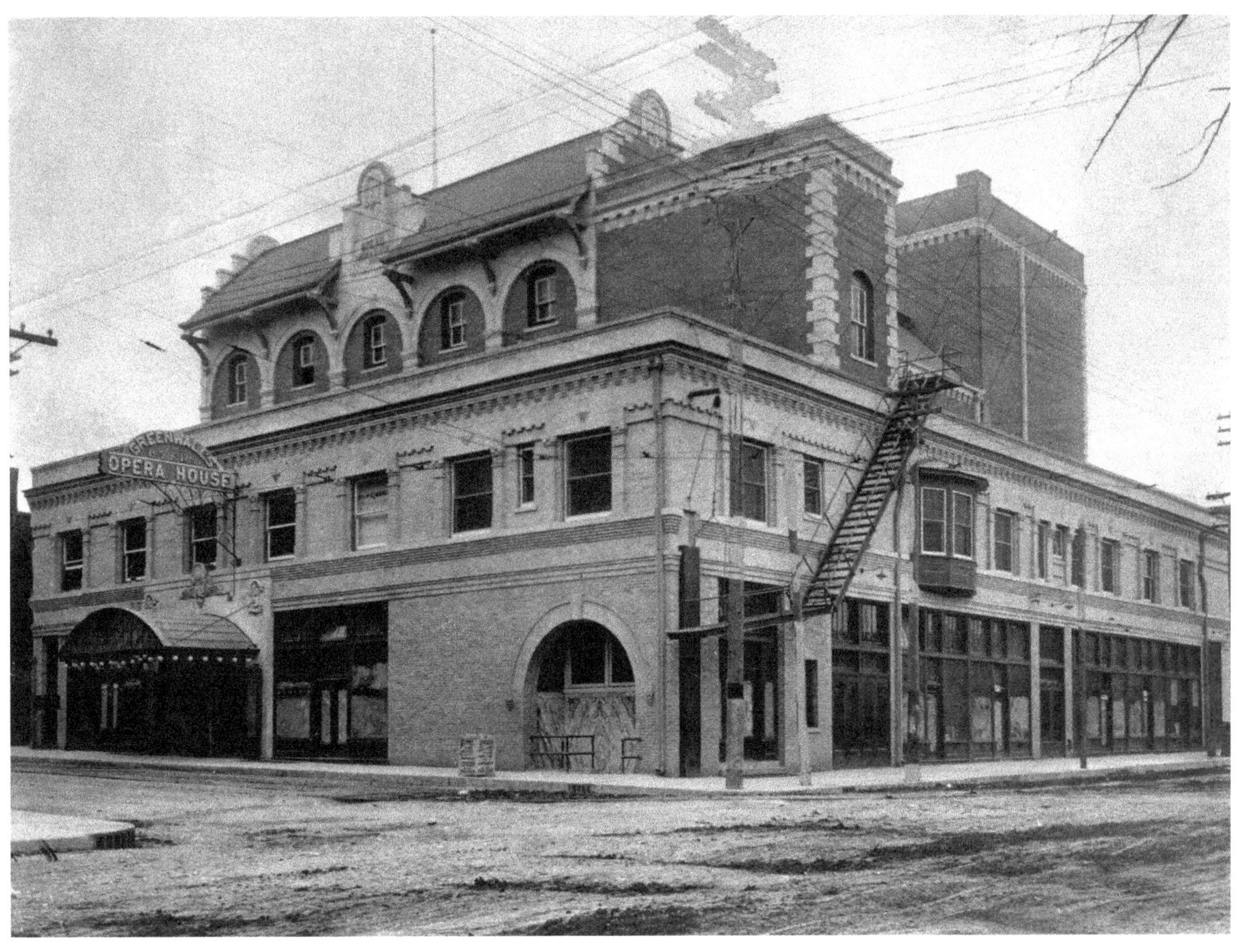


When storm damage in early 1908 closed the 1883 Opera House at Third and Rusk (now Commerce), theater manager Phil Greenwall worked with local developer A. T. Byers to build a larger Opera House at 7th and Rusk. Designed by Sanguinet and Staats, the new facility opened for the fall season and quickly became one of the premier performance venues in the region. By 1919, the name had changed to the Palace and movies replaced live productions. The building was demolished in 1977.

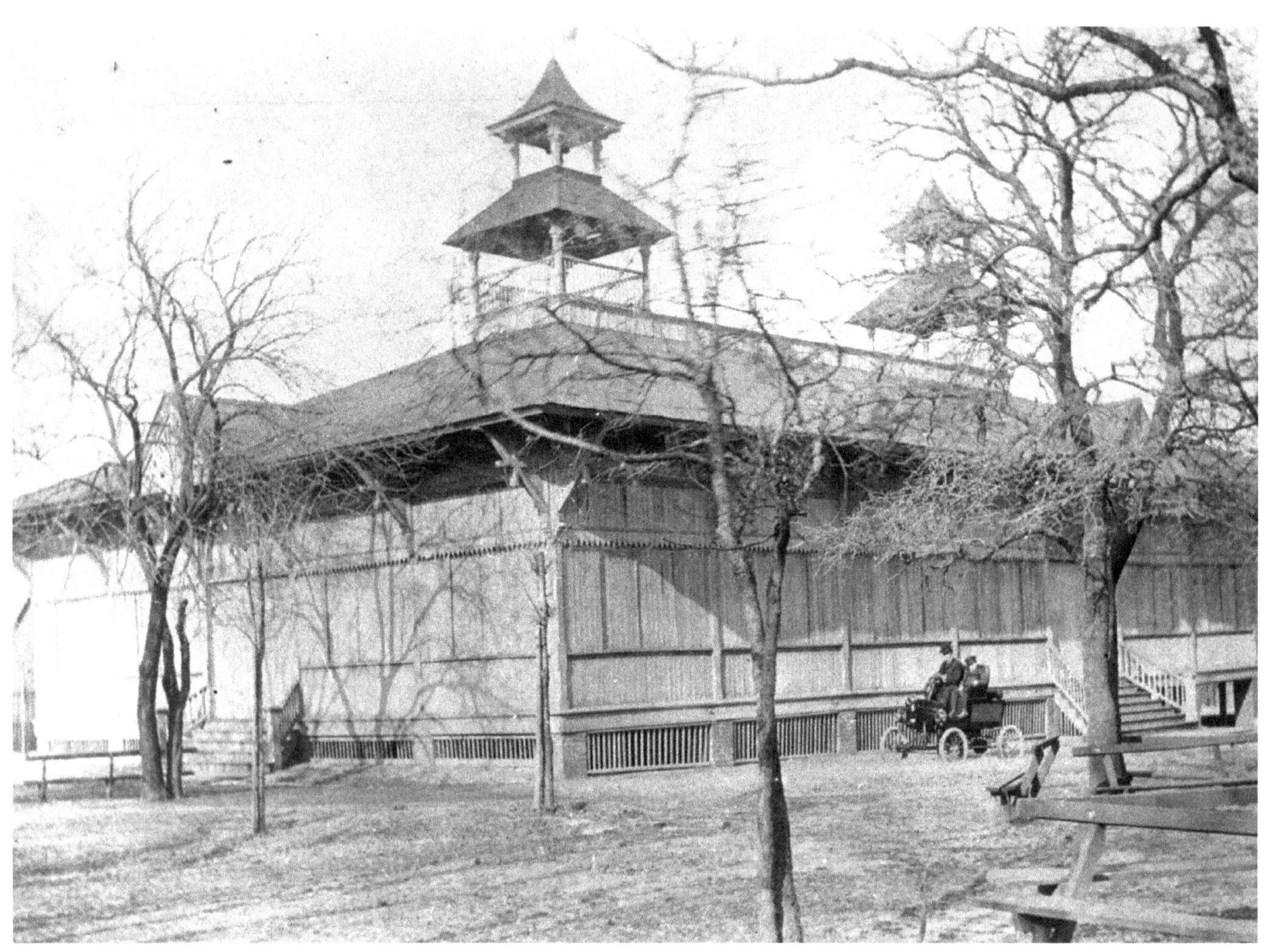

Outdoor entertainment also had a long tradition in Fort Worth, beginning with picnics at the Cold Springs north of the old fort. By 1885, the north end of Samuels Avenue had become the primary recreation area for the city, complete with a racetrack and driving park. Adjacent to the track, Peter Gruenwald opened a *biergarten* (beer garden) and the pavilion shown here. With its removable shutters and observation towers with commanding views of the river valley below, Gruenwald's Pavilion was a major attraction until it closed about 1910.

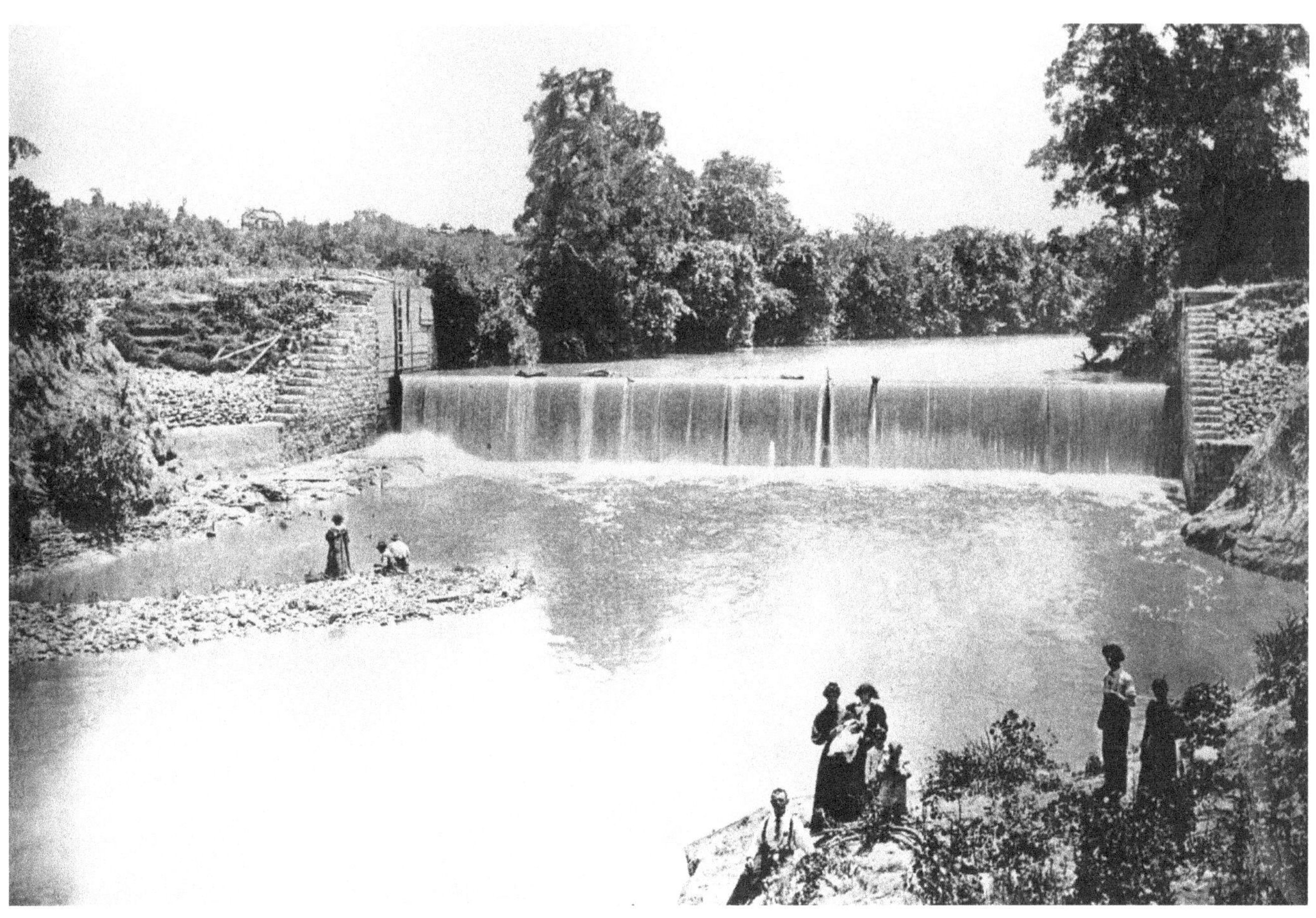

Fort Worth's City Park was laid out in 1892 along the stretch of the Trinity River between today's 7th Street and Lancaster Avenue bridges on the west side of Downtown. This image, from about 1905, views the park dam from a small bridge that crossed the river. Long a favorite spot for picnics and fishing, the dam and park were removed in the 1930s when the river channel was straightened and the Lancaster Bridge was built over the site.

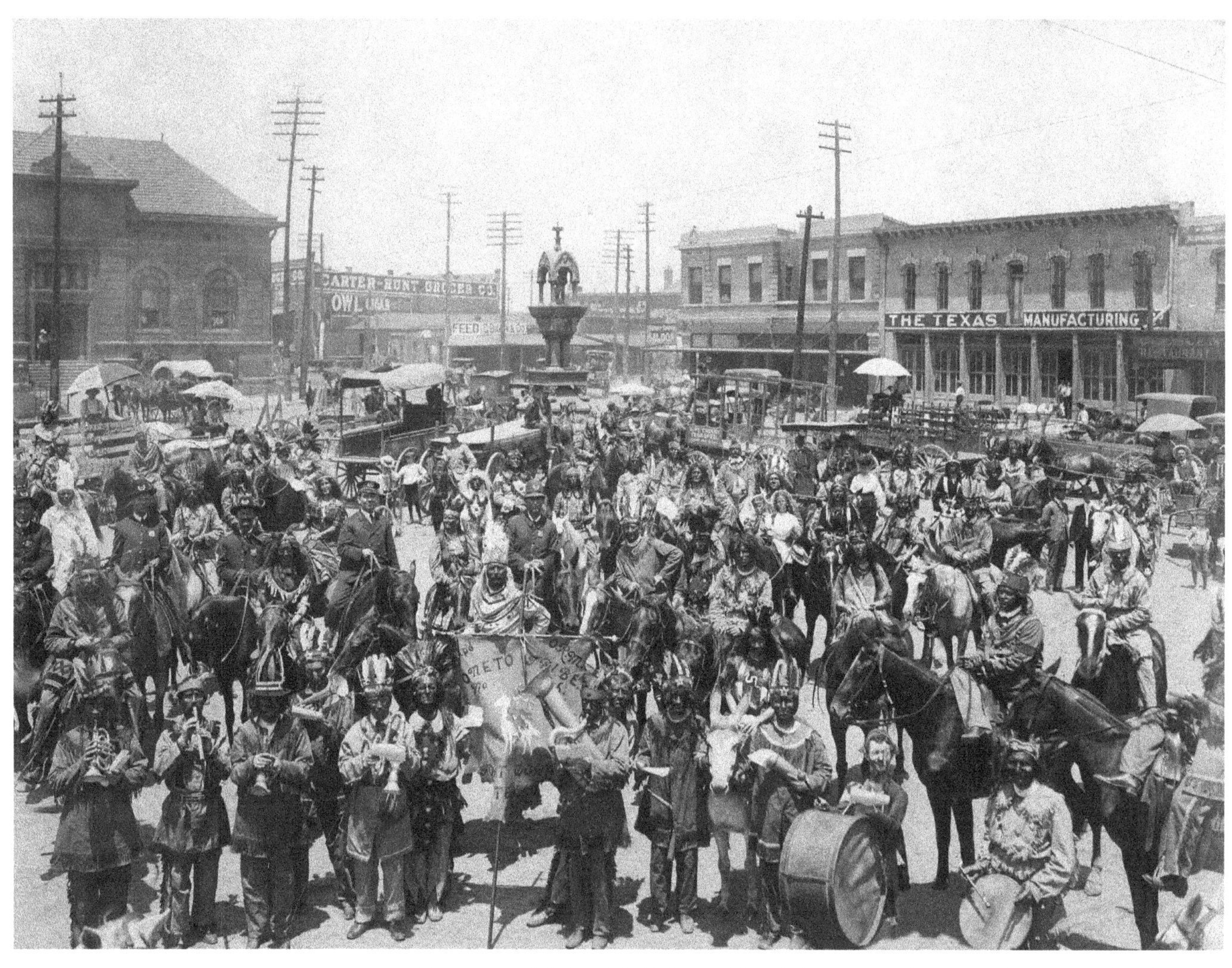


The Improved Order of Red Men established chapters, or tribes, across the country throughout the nineteenth century. In 1907, its Fort Worth members gathered in full regalia around the Hayne Monument near the T&P Station. The organization's roots date to secret societies established prior to the American Revolution, including the Sons Of Liberty who poured British tea into Boston harbor. It continues its promotion of Freedom, Friendship and Charity today.

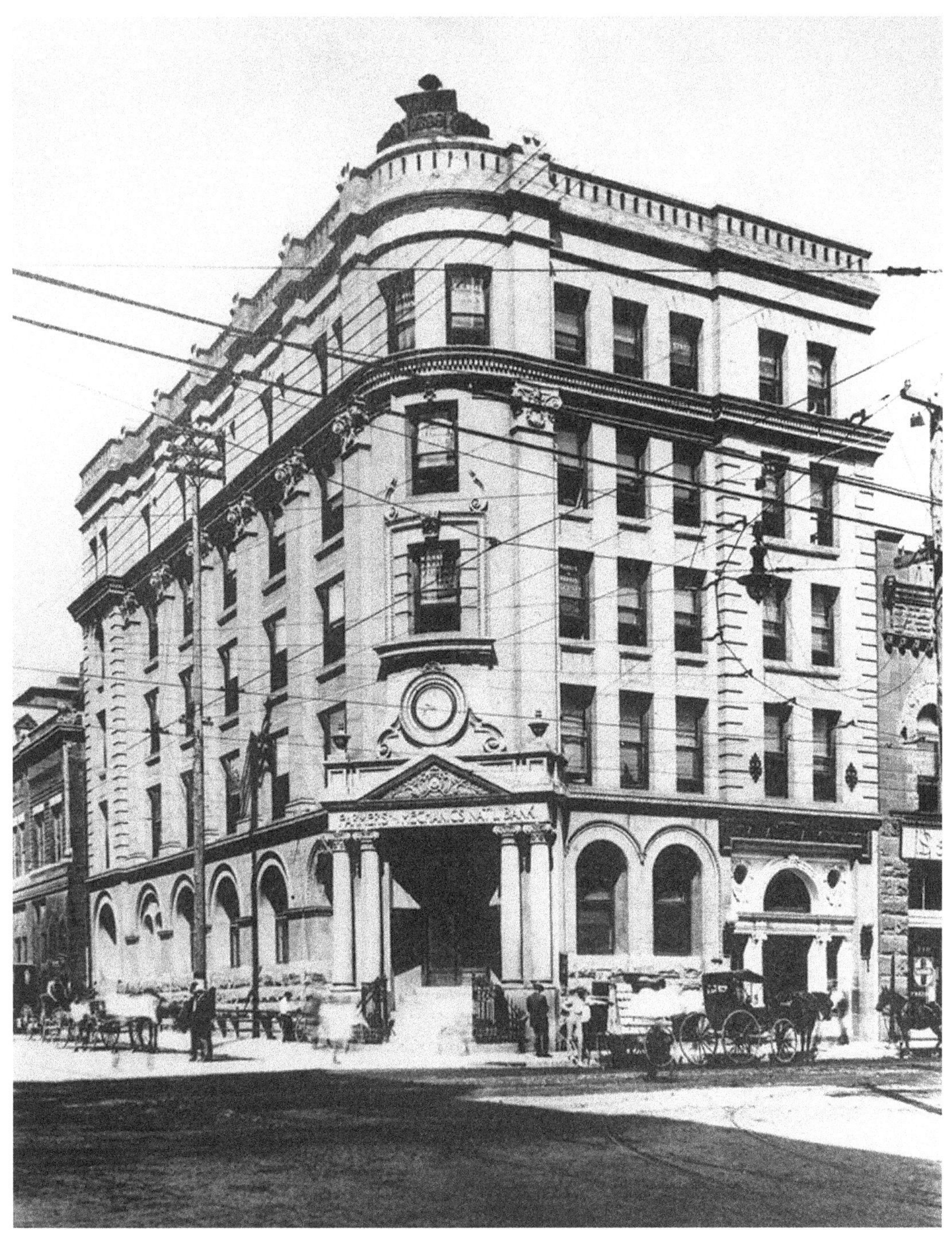


A year after the 1898 fire that destroyed the Hurley Building at 7th and Main, Chicago businessman John R. Hoxie constructed a new building on the important corner. Among the building's early tenants was the law firm of Harris and Harris. Brothers W. D. and M. B. Harris both served as Tarrant County Judge, and W. D., elected mayor of Fort Worth in 1906, served during the South Side fire in 1909. The Hoxie Building's primary tenant, the Farmers and Mechanics Bank, acquired the property and demolished the building in 1920 to build a 24 story Sanguinet and Staats-designed skyscraper, then the tallest structure in the southwest.

On 7th Street, at the intersection with Taylor, the local congregation of the Methodist Episcopal Church, South, built a new sanctuary in 1908, having outgrown their old home at 4th and Jones. The new building would serve the First Methodist Church until it built a newer sanctuary on 5th Street in 1931. Behind the fence at left was the full block of the A. J. Roe Lumber Yard, in operation since 1886. The yard site would become the home of the Fort Worth Club in 1926.

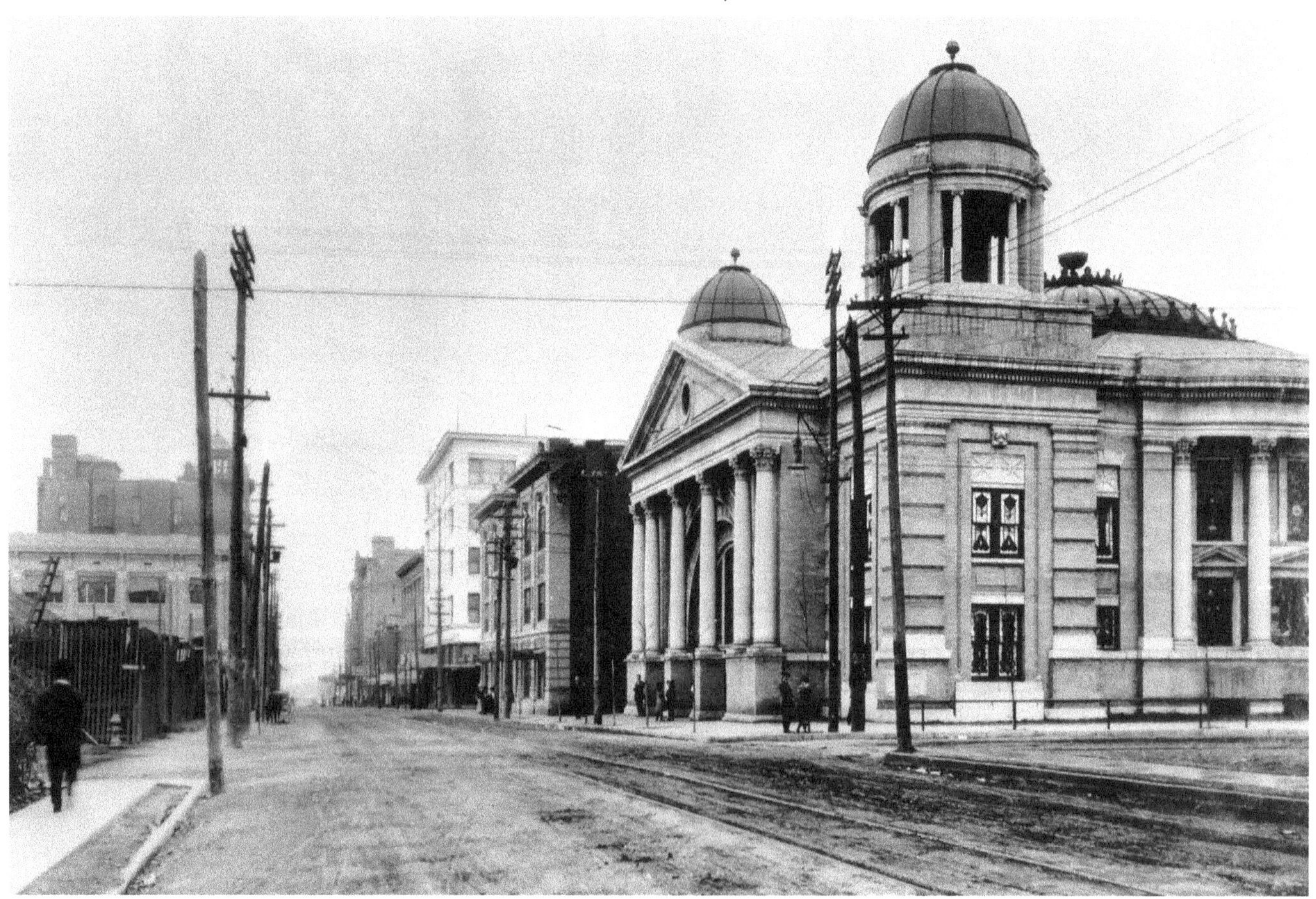

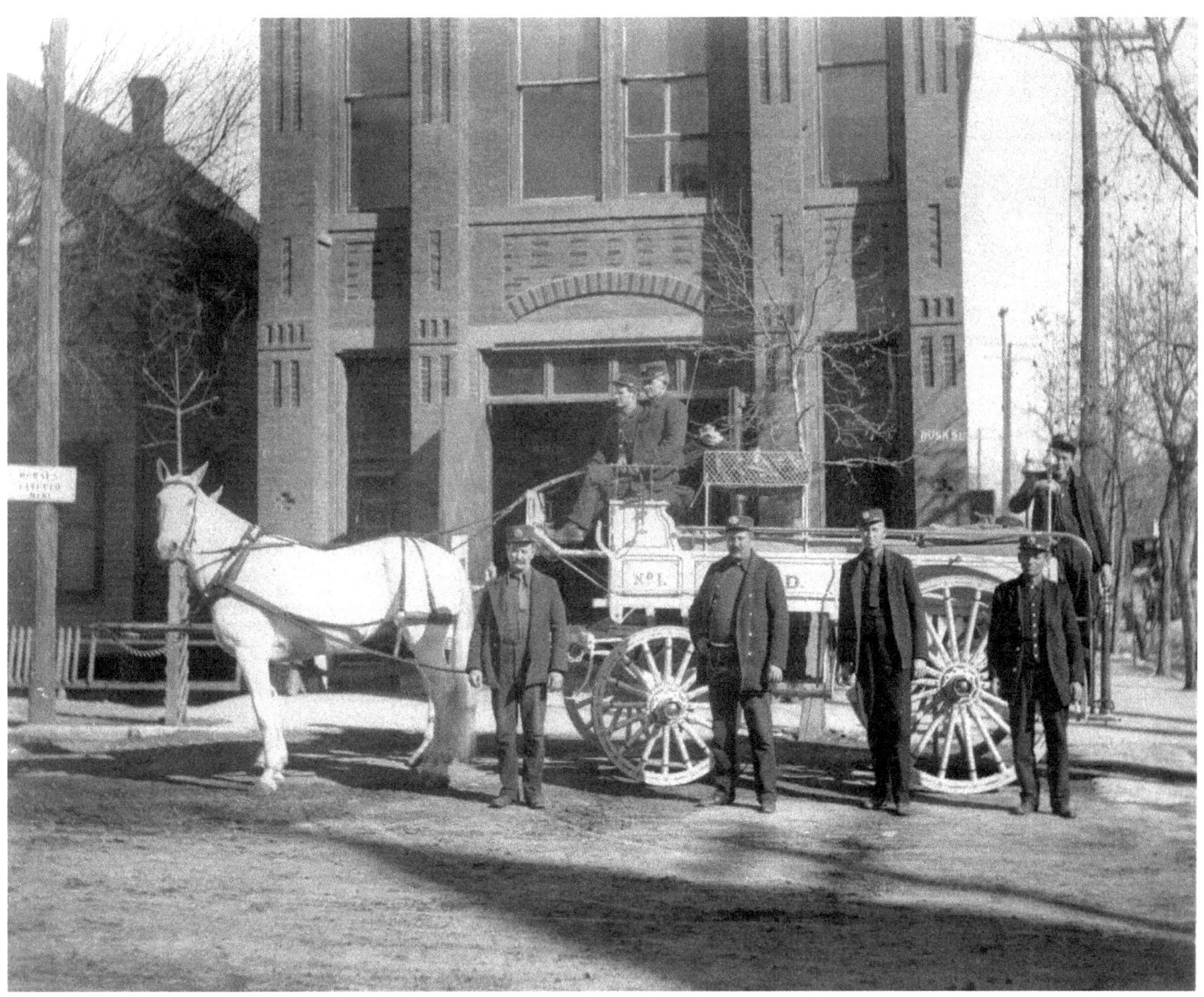

Firefighters from Station No. One at Rusk (now Commerce) and 2nd Streets proudly show off their new wagon and matched team of horses about 1905. The department vehicles got their unique white and gold colors when the men paid to have their entry in the annual State Fair pumper races painted by local buggy shop owner E. E. Lennox, who must have had more white paint on hand than red. The new colors were a hit, and remain part of the city's modern fleet.

Among the many buildings erected by the Stockyards Company was the 1908 Coliseum, shown here a year or so after construction. A group of unidentified dignitaries, perhaps in town for the activities of the annual Feeders and Breeders Show, stopped for the photographer. The Coliseum, completed in less than ninety working days and just in time for the 1908 show, has hosted a wide variety of events over the years, from a performance by Enrico Caruso to the modern weekly reenactments of traditional wild west shows.

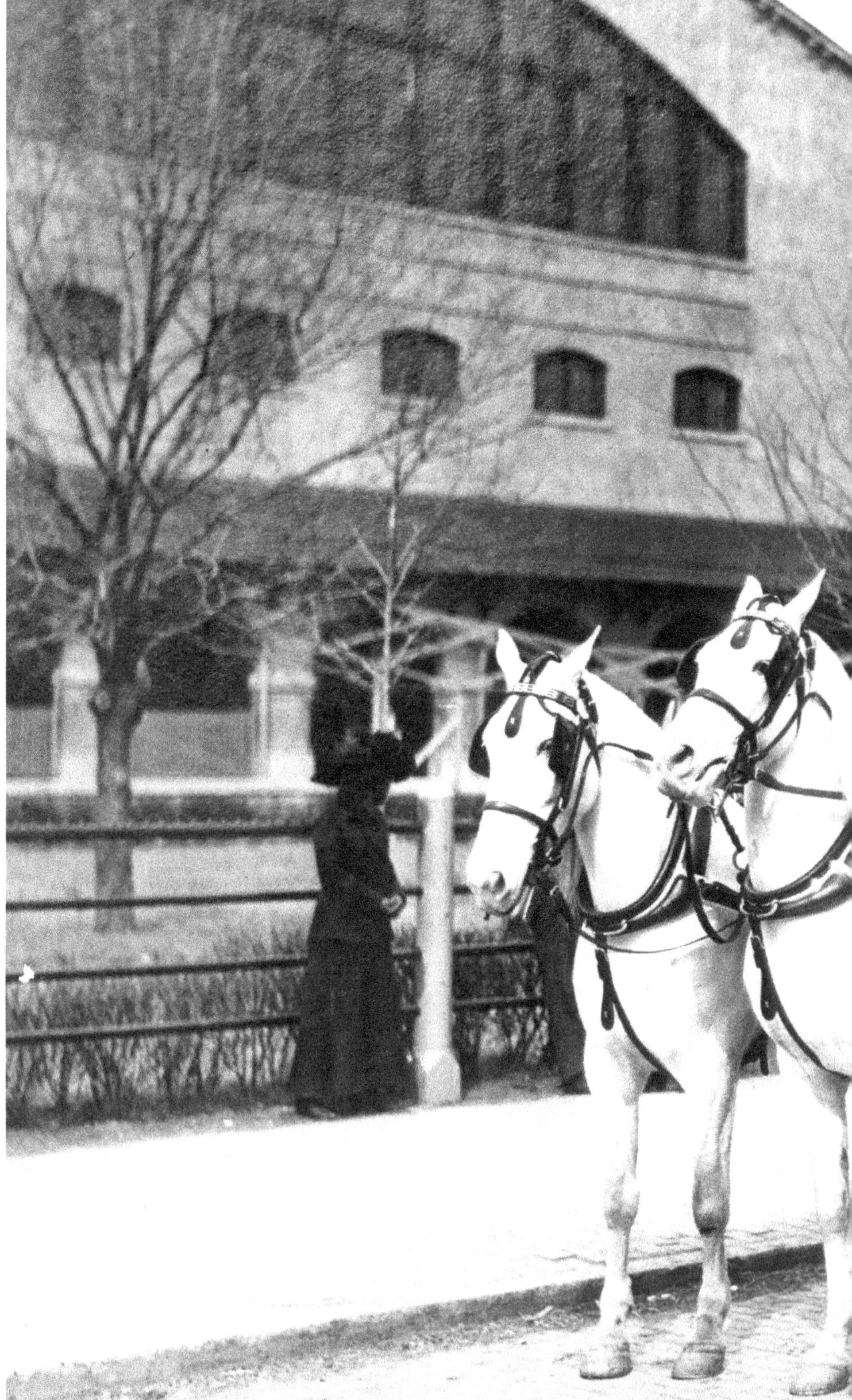

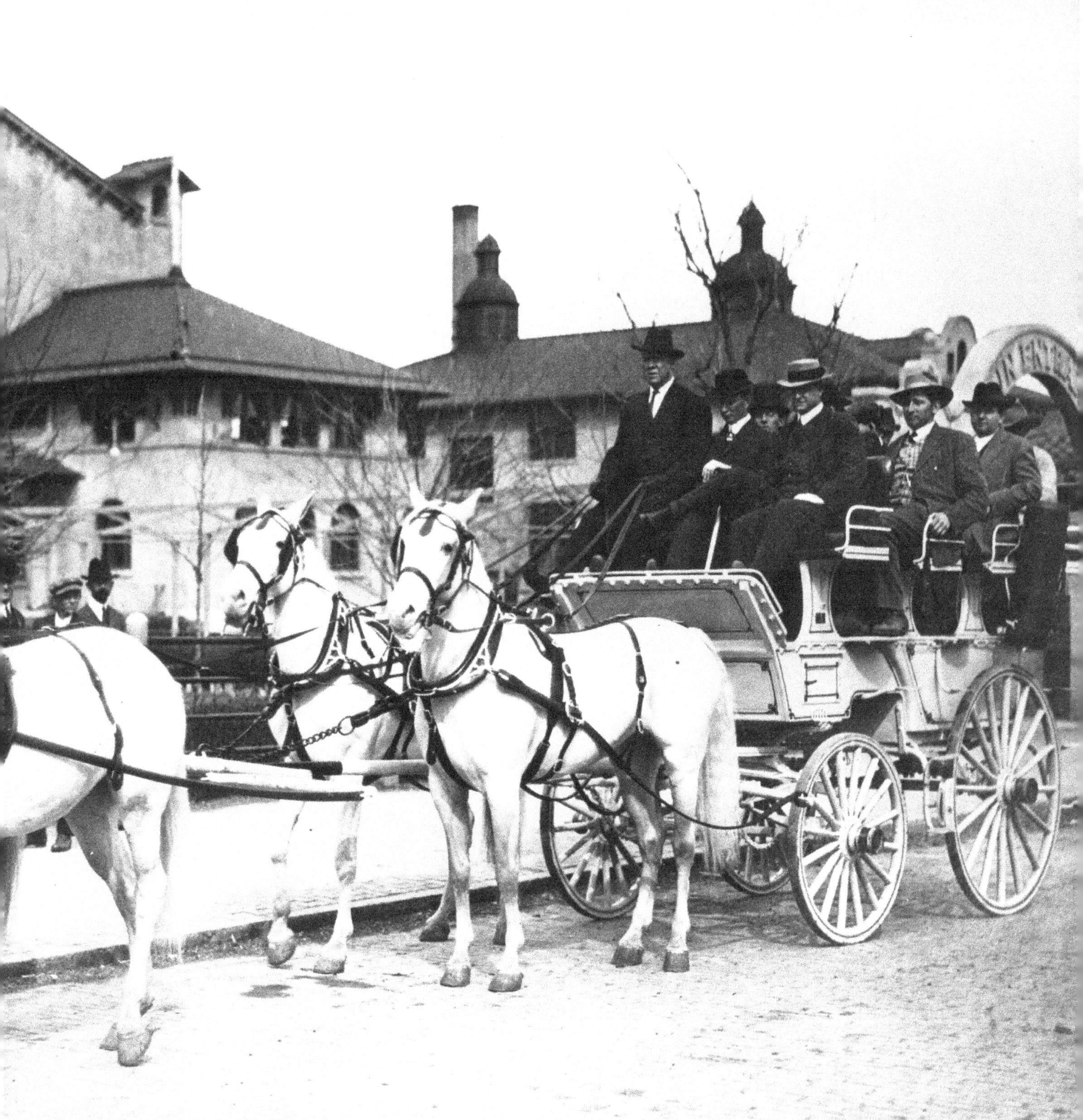

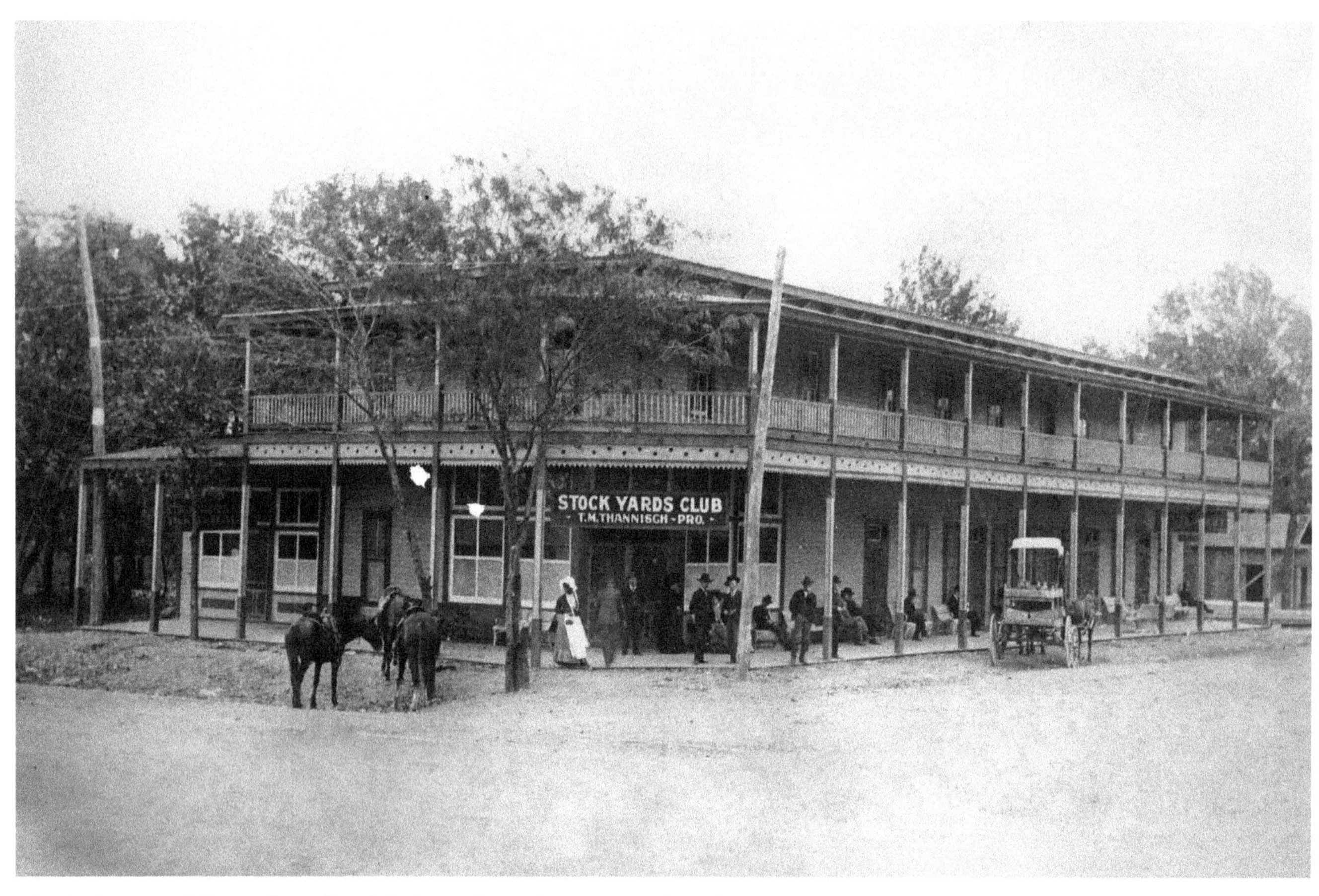


Colonel Thomas M. Thannisch purchased the lot on the northeast corner of North Main and Exchange in 1904 as the Fort Worth Stockyards boomed following the arrival of the Swift and Armour companies. He built his Stock Yards Club Saloon and Billiard Parlor in 1906 and an adjoining brick hotel building in 1907. He later demolished the old club and built a bigger hotel that stands today as the Stockyards Hotel, welcoming visitors to the popular National Historic District.

Fort Worth had two major driving parks at the turn of the 20th century. The oldest was located just off of Samuels Avenue northeast of downtown and near the popular Gruenwald's Pavilion. The other track was just north of West 7th Street and east of the present site of the former Montgomery Ward's building. This image, taken about 1900, has been identified as both at various times, although the advertisement for the Rock Island Line on the grandstand supports the Samuels Avenue site because the rail line ran next to the racetrack.

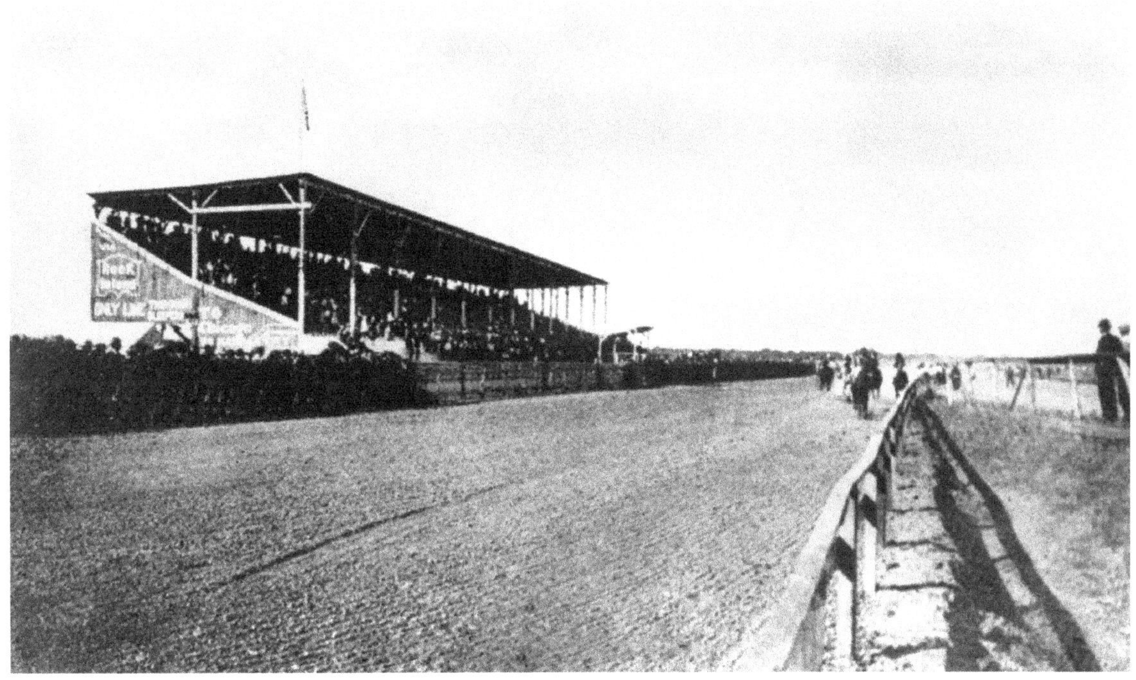

The new seven-story Flatiron Building stands tall at the far left of this view, looking north on Houston from 10th Street about 1907. The Lyric Theatre, at 1010 Houston opened that same year and presented vaudeville performances for ten cents a ticket. It is interesting to note the tangle of telephone and electric wires creating a web over the city streets.

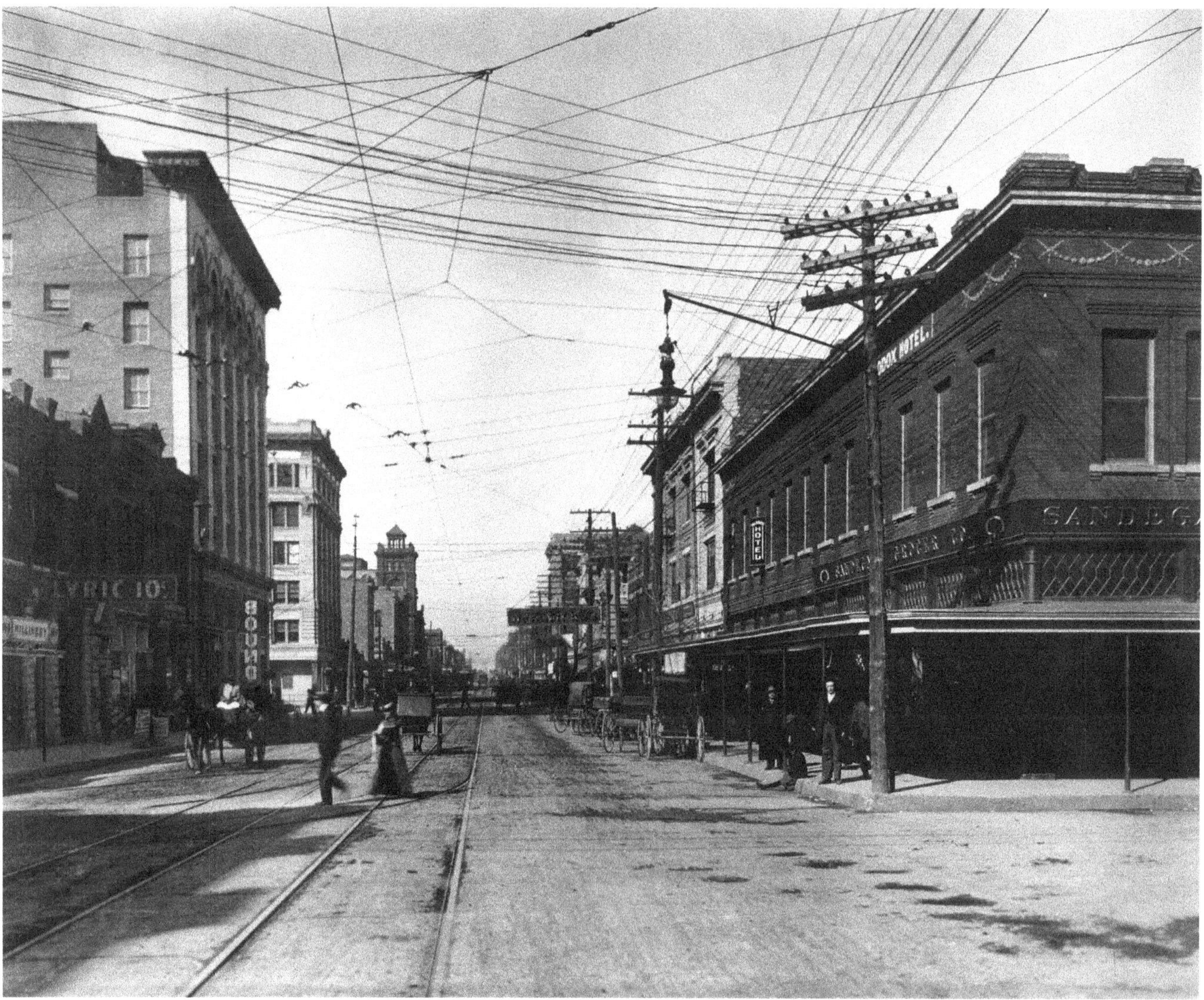

The photographer of the facing view of Houston Street turned his camera for a rare glimpse of 10th Street looking east. The smokestack belonged to the Texas Brewing Company. Its sprawling plant was built in 1890 along Jones, between 9th and 12th streets. This view would change dramatically after 1910 when the new Majestic Theatre opened on the Commerce Street site of the Darnell Lumber Co. The Majestic's owners lined 10th Street with white lights leading to the theater's front door, creating Fort Worth's own "Great White Way."

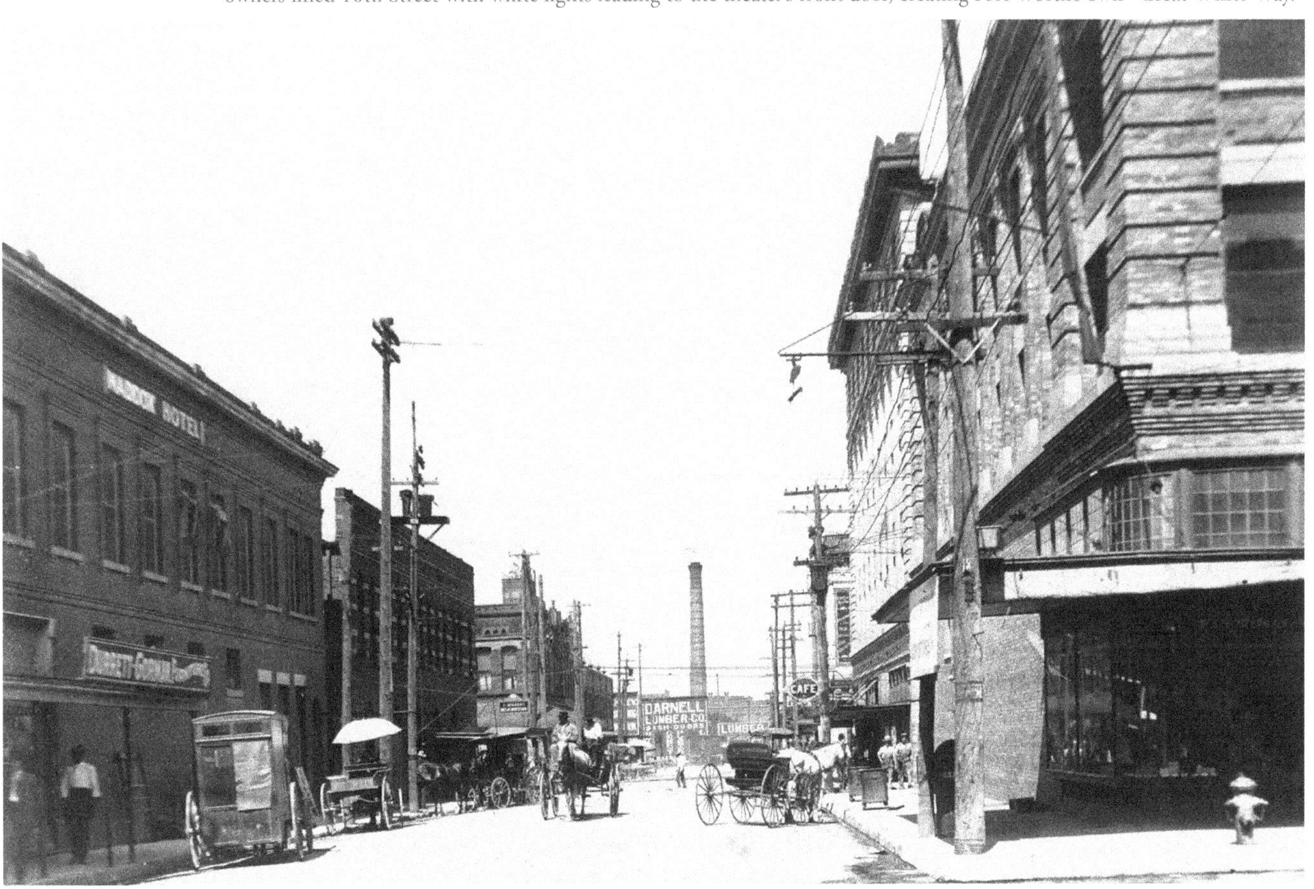

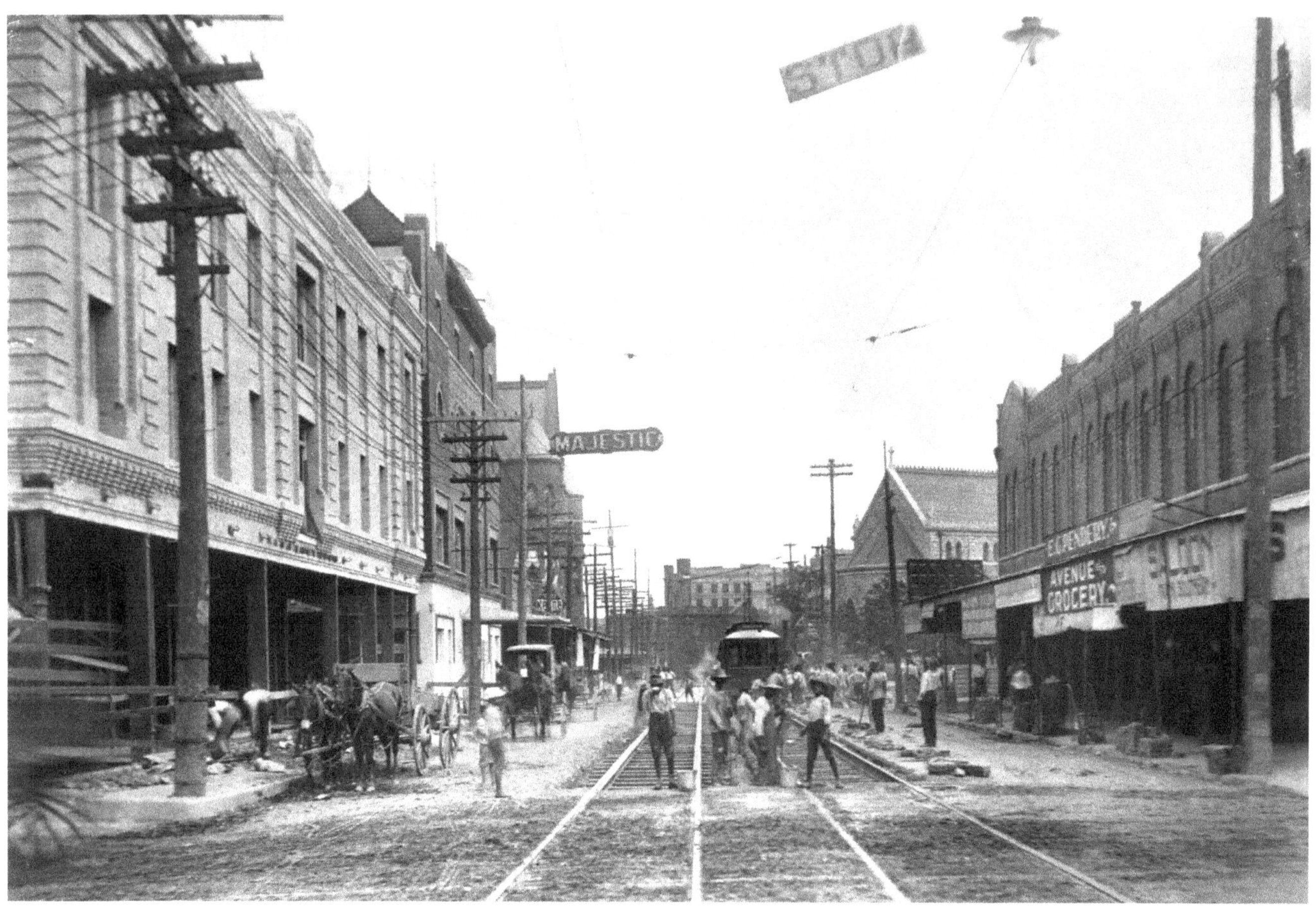


This busy scene of Jennings Avenue looking north from 13th Street about 1910 shows workmen briefly stopping their repair work on the streetcar rails to pose for the photographer. At the head of the street is the Carnegie Library and to its right is St. Patrick Cathedral. The Majestic Theatre, just left of the turreted 1896 Post office, would shortly move from its 1905 home to a new location on Commerce Street. Because 13th Street was one of the major entrances into downtown at the time, this intersection warranted one of the city's first stop signs.

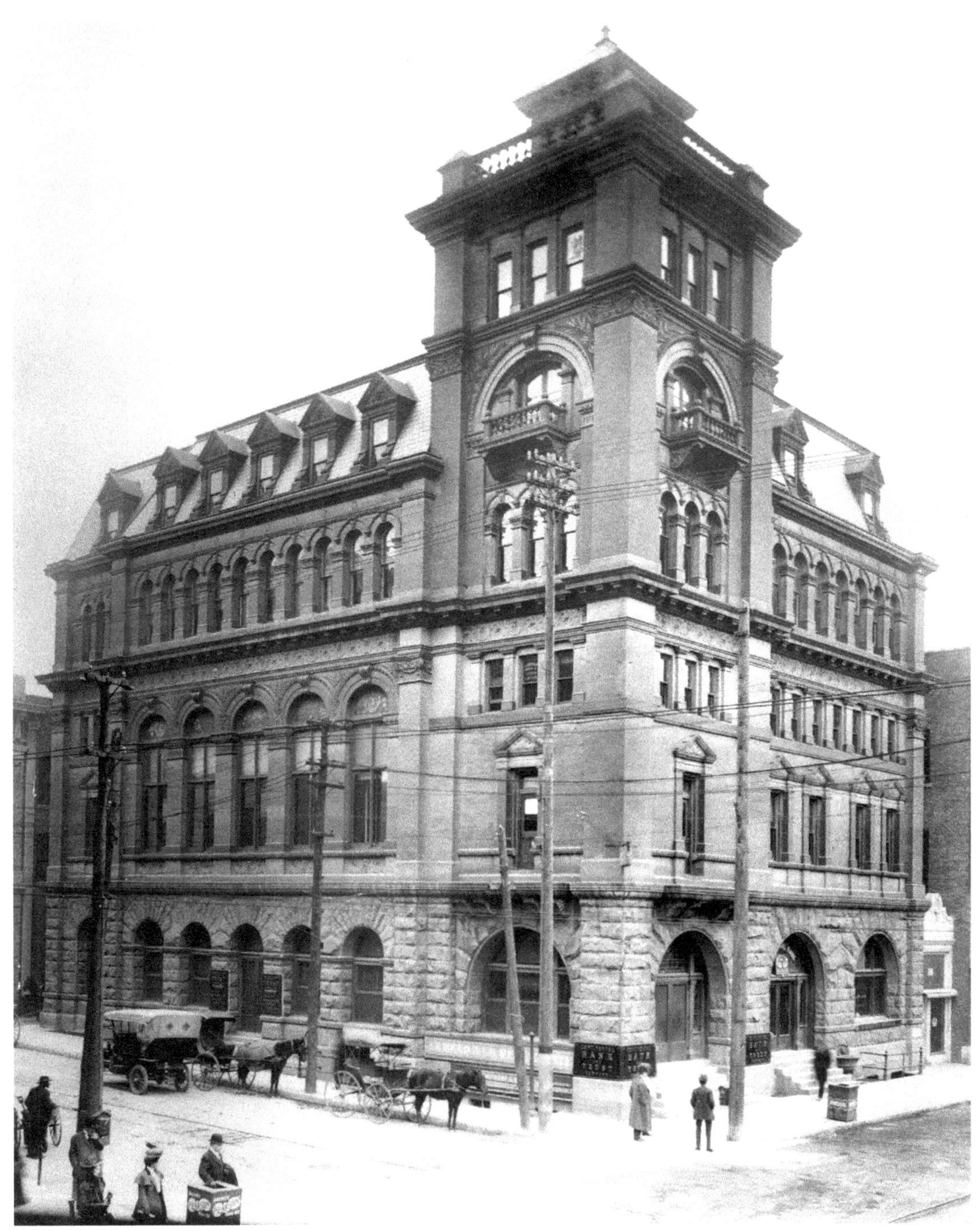

In 1908, the 1889 Board of Trade Building at the northwest corner of 7th and Houston remained one of the city's more elegant structures. The visions for the future that city promoters had touted from the rooftop observation deck had largely come true as Fort Worth was booming from the economic benefits of the stockyards and related businesses. The Continental Bank and Trust Company evolved into Continental National Bank, which demolished the old building in 1949 to make way for a new home for the bank.

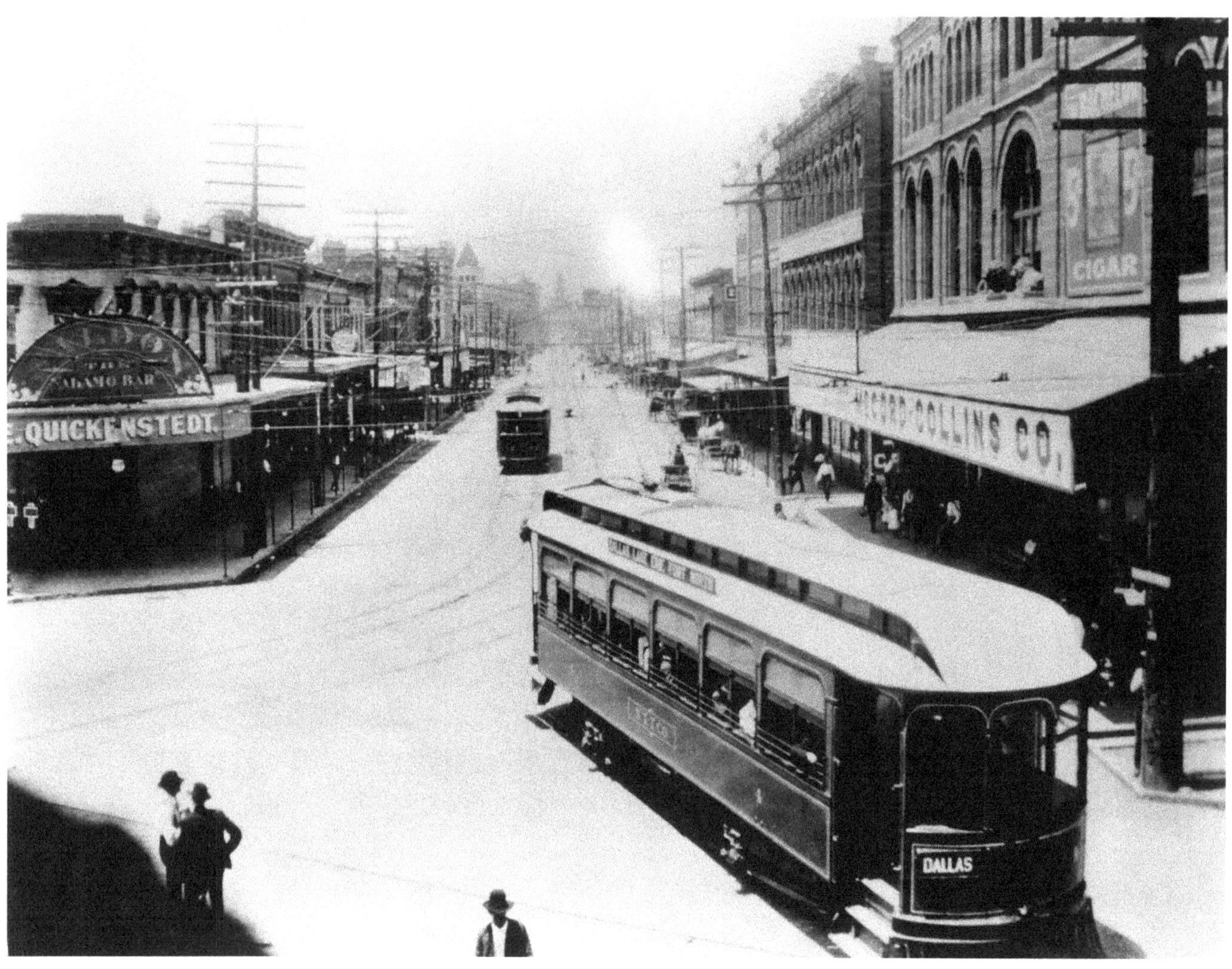


The Dallas-bound Interurban turns onto Front Street about 1909, with the Tarrant County Courthouse seventeen blocks behind. As the streetcar worked its way east toward Dallas, the driver would pick up or unload passengers at several stations, including the sixth stop out of town, and the community that grew up around it, Stop Six. On the northwest corner of this intersection, Ernst Quickenstedt's Alamo Bar occupied a favored location for saloons from the time the railroad arrived in 1876 until Prohibition.

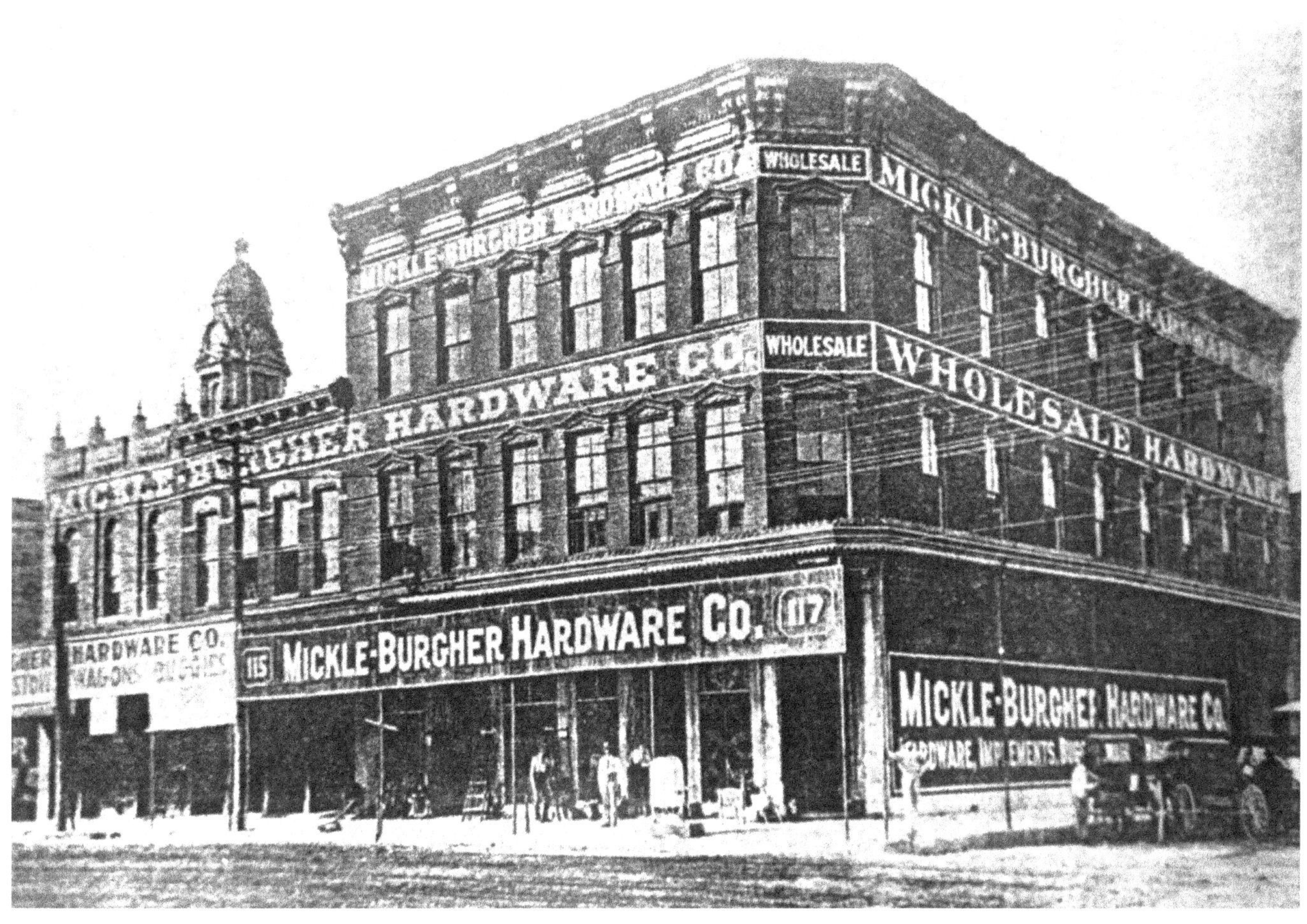


By the turn of the twentieth century, the Mickle-Burgher Hardware Co. had grown into one of the larger businesses in town. Located on the northeast corner of Houston and 1st streets, with the courthouse dome rising in the background, the building had been built in the 1880s by merchant B. C. Evans to replace his smaller building across the street. In 1876, Evans converted part of that former store into Fort Worth's first theater, which moved performances out of the saloons and set the stage for the construction of the Opera House in 1883.

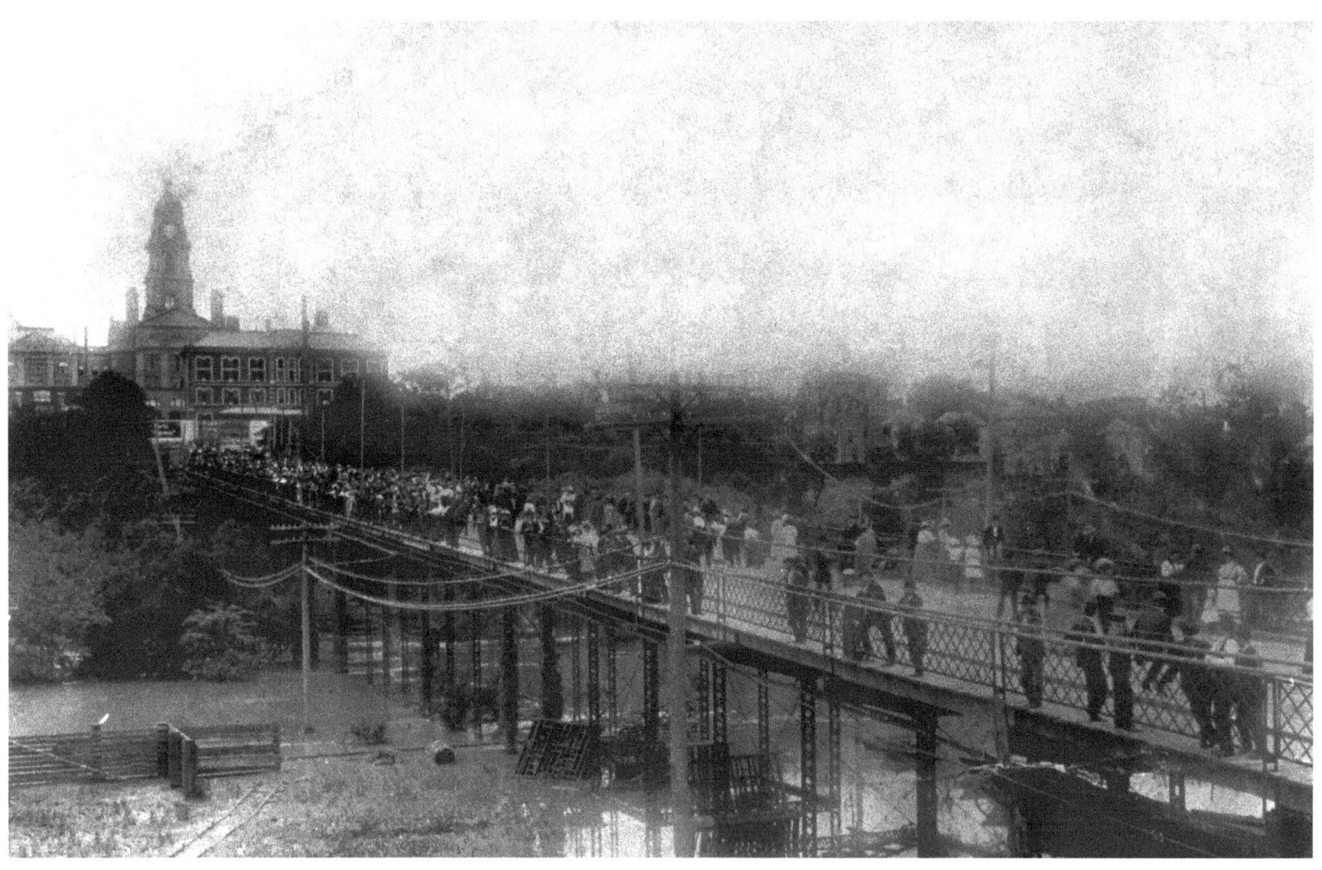

The first bridge to cross the Trinity River and connect Fort Worth with North Fort Worth via Main Street was erected in 1890. Here, crowds have gathered on the bridge to view the devastation of the May 1908 flood, one of the worst in the state's history. The 1883 jail is seen at left in front of the courthouse. To the right of the bridge and tucked into the side of the bluff are the houses of the small community known as La Corte, one of the early Hispanic neighborhoods in the city.

The 1890 Main Street bridge, photographed from the peaceful riverbank looking east toward the bluff and the neighborhood along Samuels Avenue, with the courthouse and jail just out of view on the right. Damage from the 1908 flood led to the decision to replace the old iron bridge with the Paddock viaduct, completed in 1914.

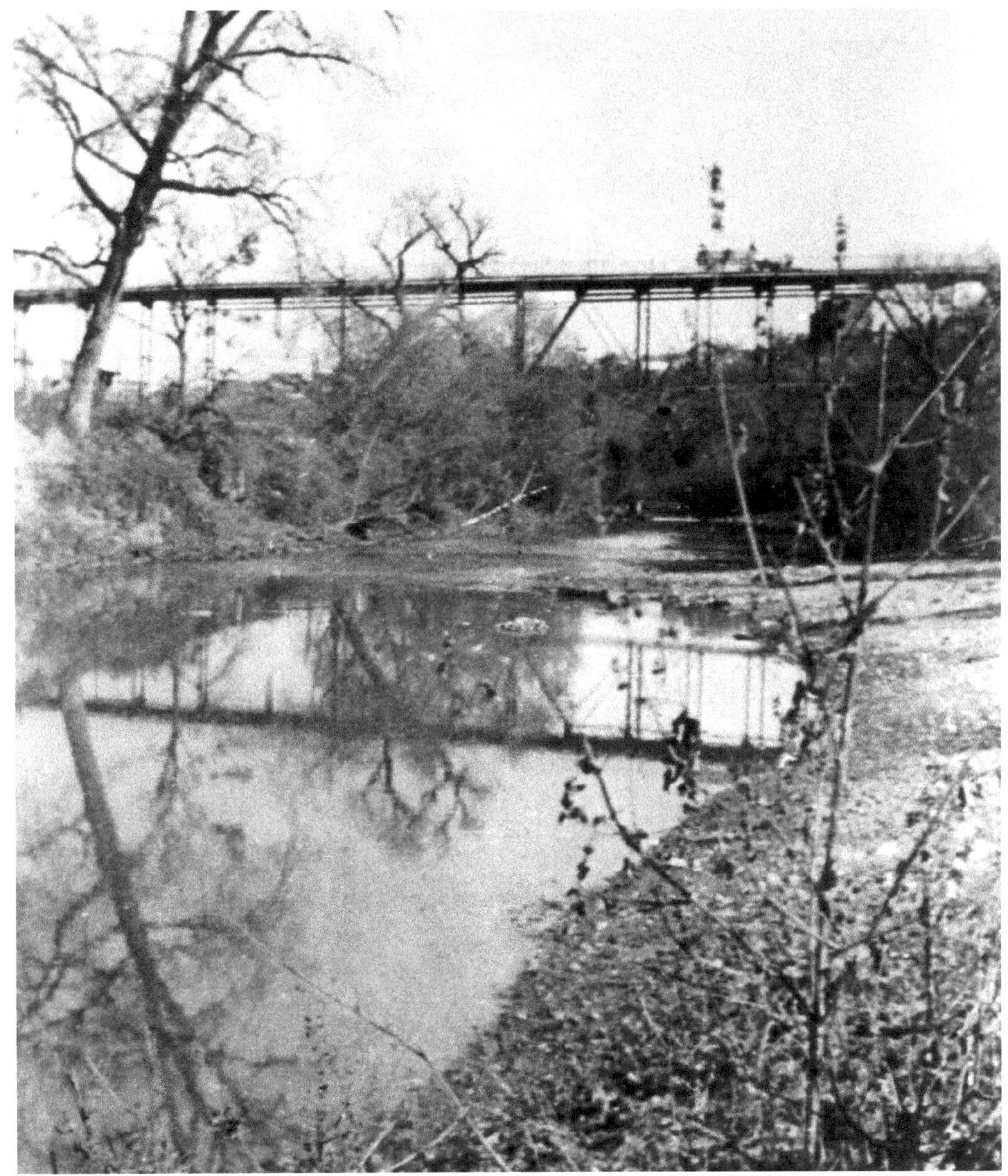

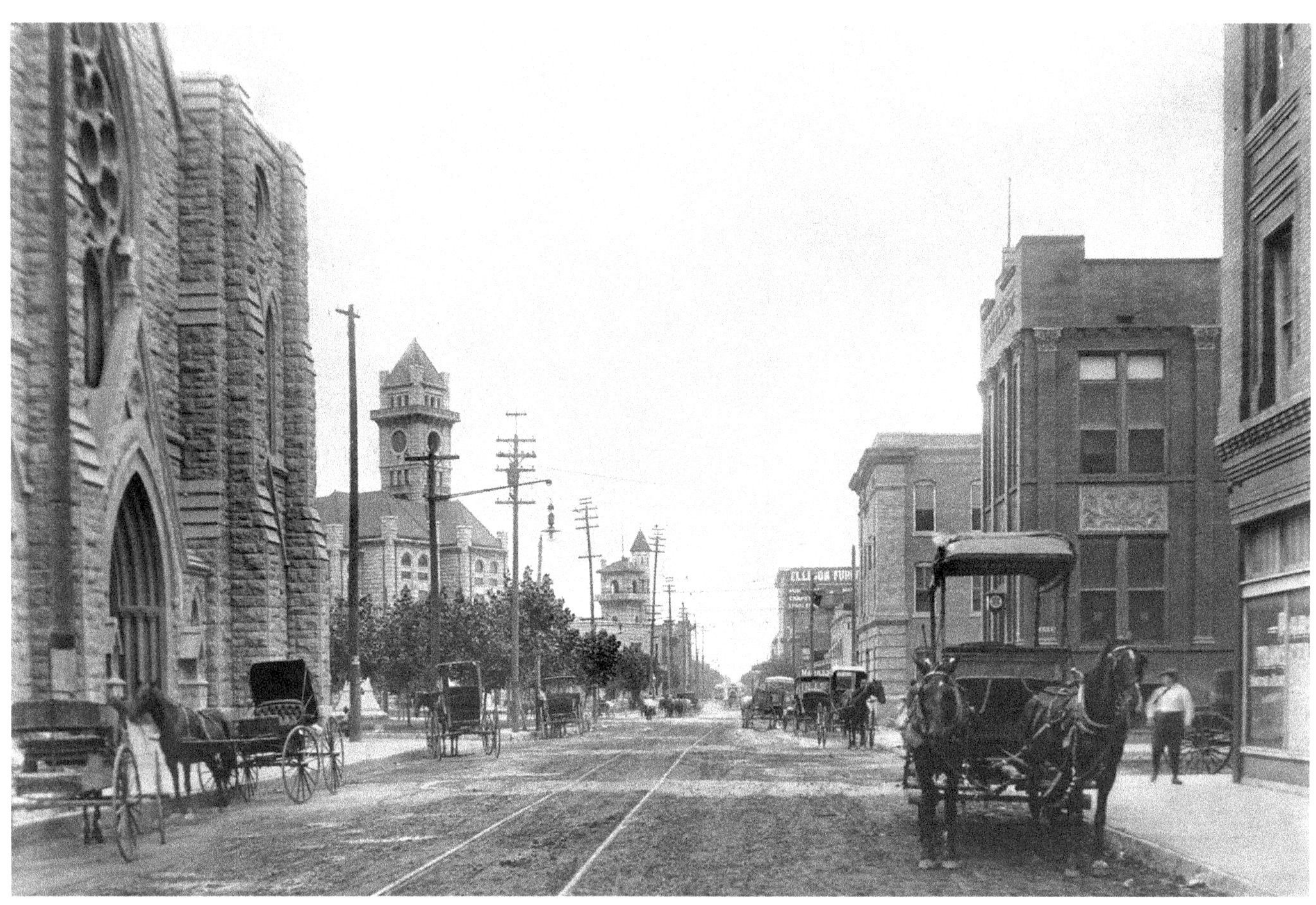

St. Patrick Cathedral, left, completed in 1892, anchored a row of limestone buildings along Throckmorton, shown here looking north from 10th Street. Beyond the church are the 1893 city hall and the 1899 Central Fire Station. At right is the two-story Fort Worth Telephone Company building. Chartered in 1903, the phone company had about a thousand subscribers but could not successfully compete with the larger Southwestern Bell, which acquired the local company and its building in 1916.

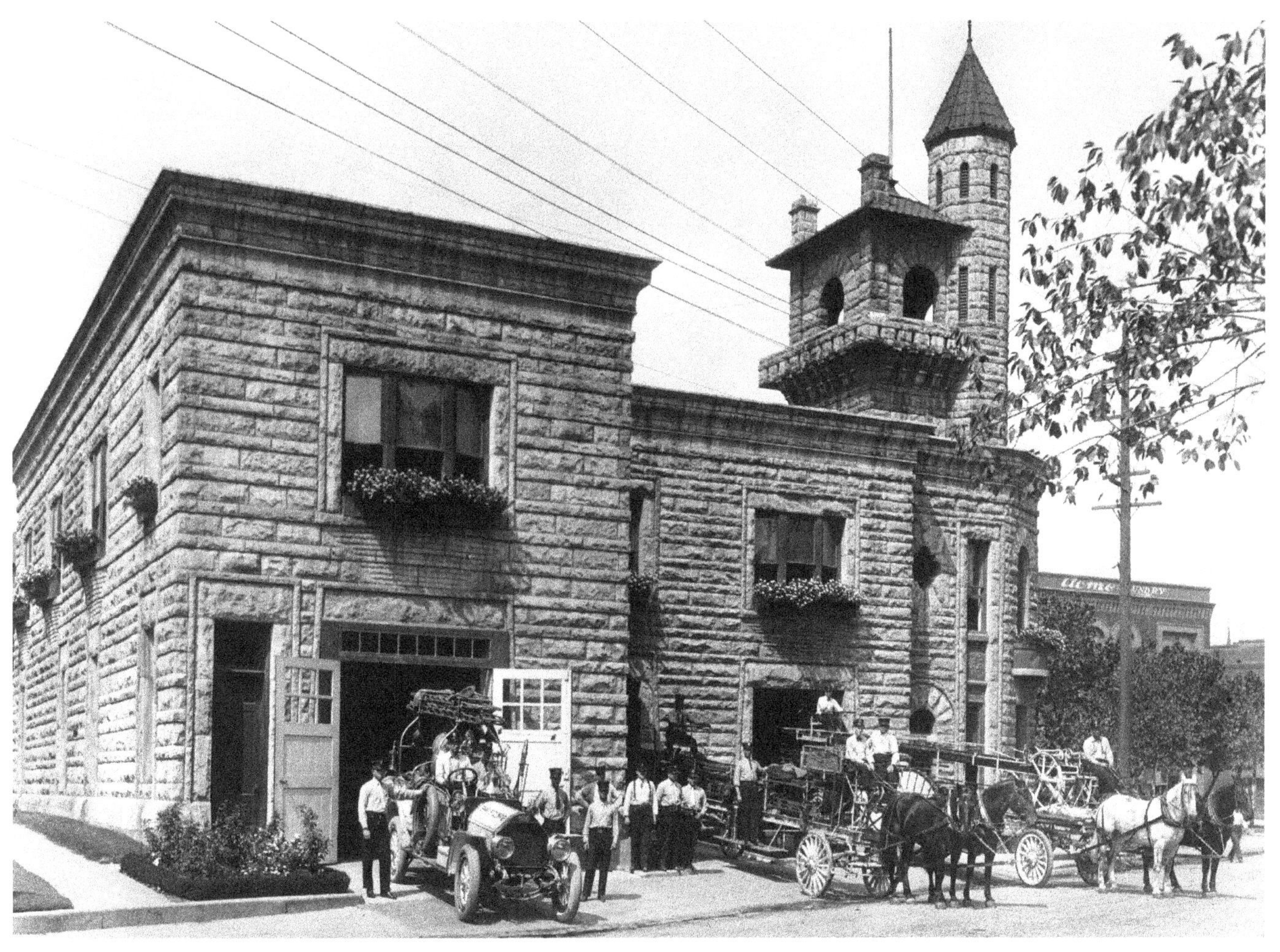

The old and new worked side by side in 1910 as fire horses and the new fire truck posed at the 1899 Central Fire Station on Throckmorton Street. If no fire had been called in by 4 a.m. each day, the horses had to be exercised, and were usually ridden around the station. If the bell rang during this morning routine, an unwary firefighter might well find himself swept off the horse as it raced back to the station and its place in the traces.

Founded in 1855, the First Christian Church congregation is the oldest in Fort Worth. Conducting their early services in a log house that had been part of the 1849 fort and then in the Masonic Lodge, the members built a frame church at Main and 4th Street about 1858. In 1878, under the leadership of Major K. M. Van Zandt, the congregation moved again, this time into its new stone sanctuary on Throckmorton, between 5th and 6th streets. Major Van Zandt would lead the church as Chairman of the Board until his death in 1930.

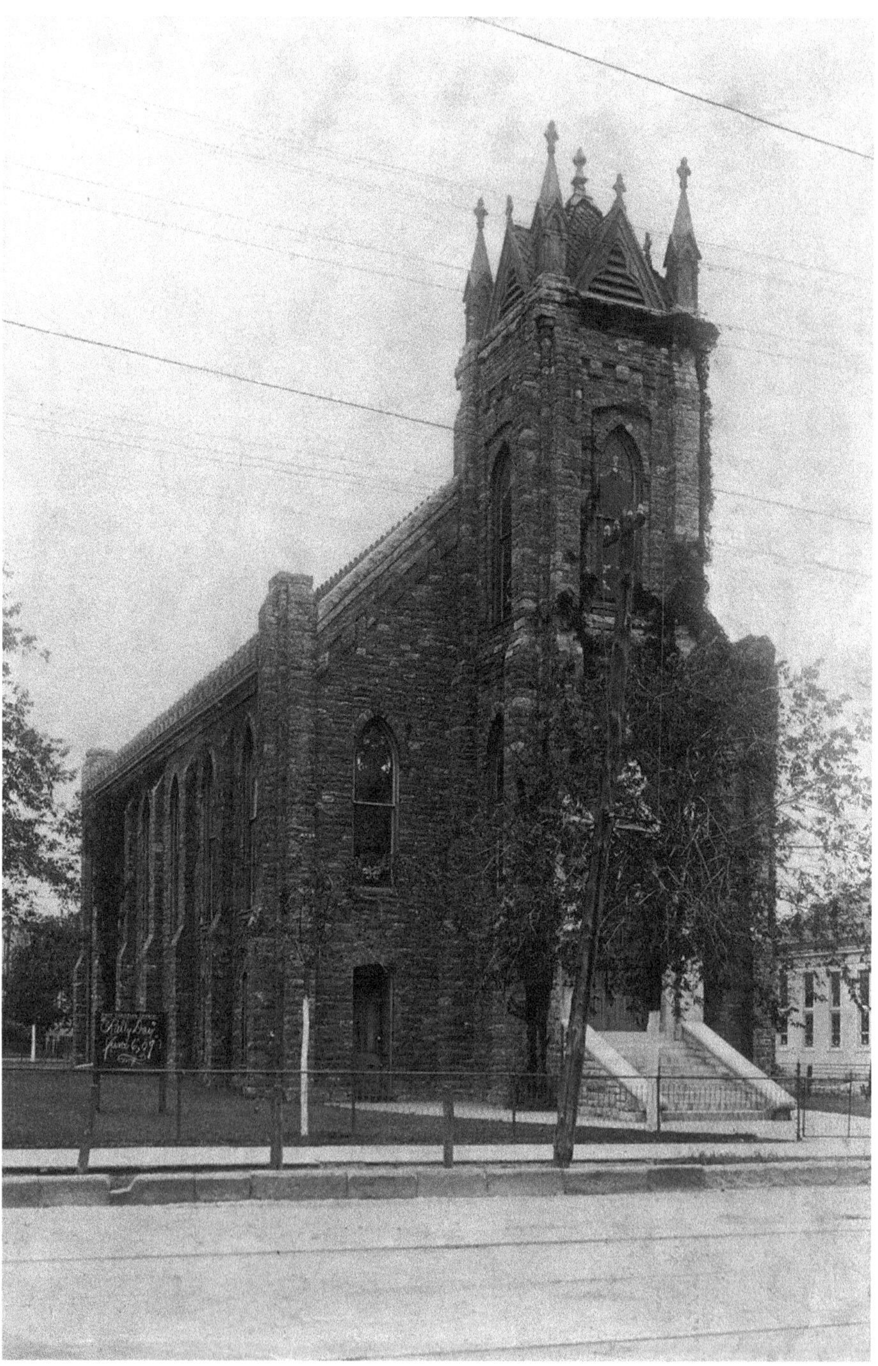

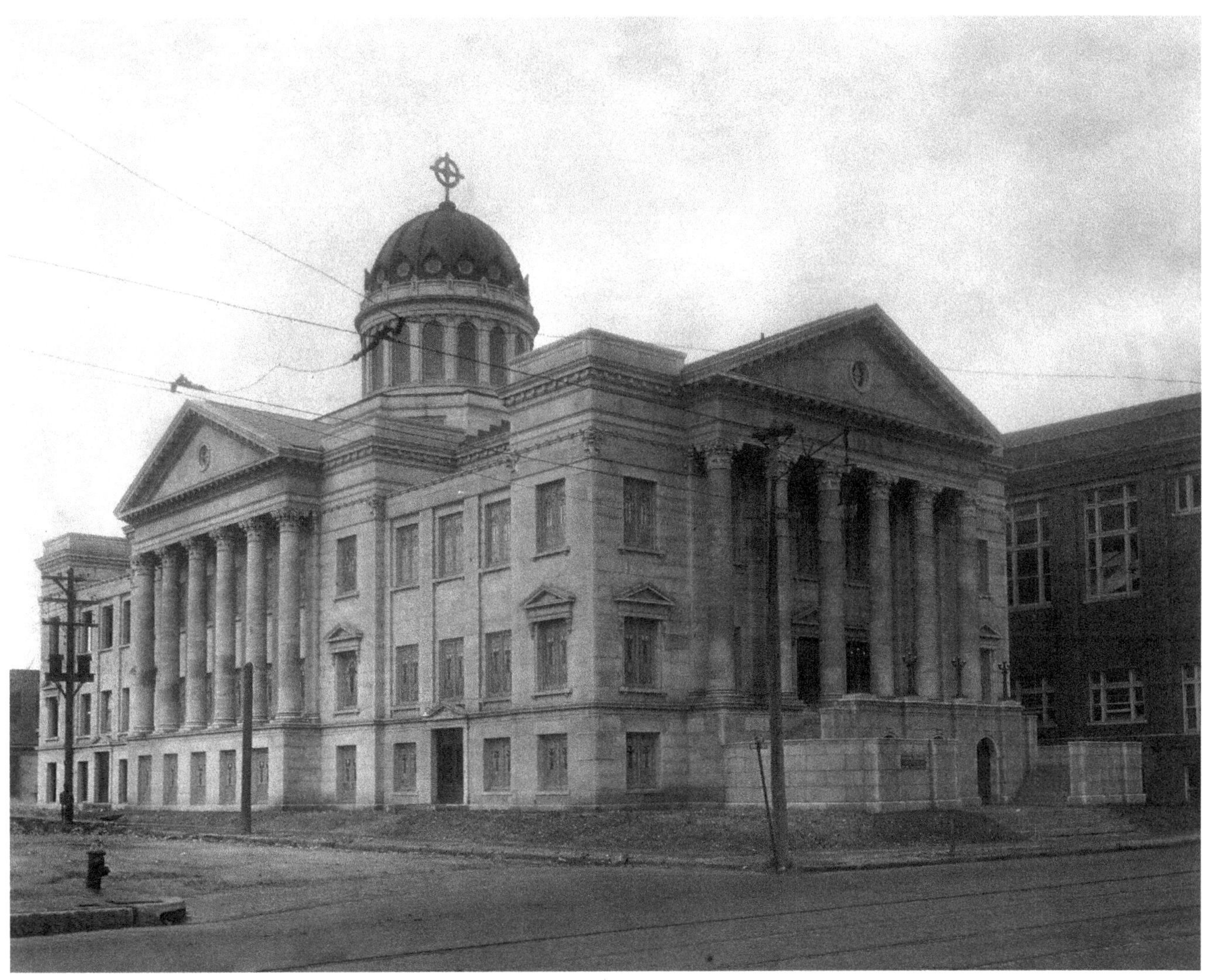

Having grown from about a dozen members to become one of the largest Disciples of Christ congregations in the world, First Christian hired architects Van Slyke and Woodruff to design a new sanctuary to replace the aging facility built in 1878. The new church was completed on the Throckmorton site in 1915. Adjacent to the church, on the right, was the 1,800 seat Chamber of Commerce Auditorium, opened in 1914.

The new miracle of electricity came to Fort Worth in 1885, providing a light on the courthouse tower and scattered streetlights downtown. By the time the North Main Street generating plant opened in 1912, most businesses and a few families had access to power. One of the first to offer modern lights and fixtures was the Bound Electric Company at 1006 Houston Street, just south of the Flatiron Building. The store's showroom seen here appears filled to capacity with choices of every shape, style and size.

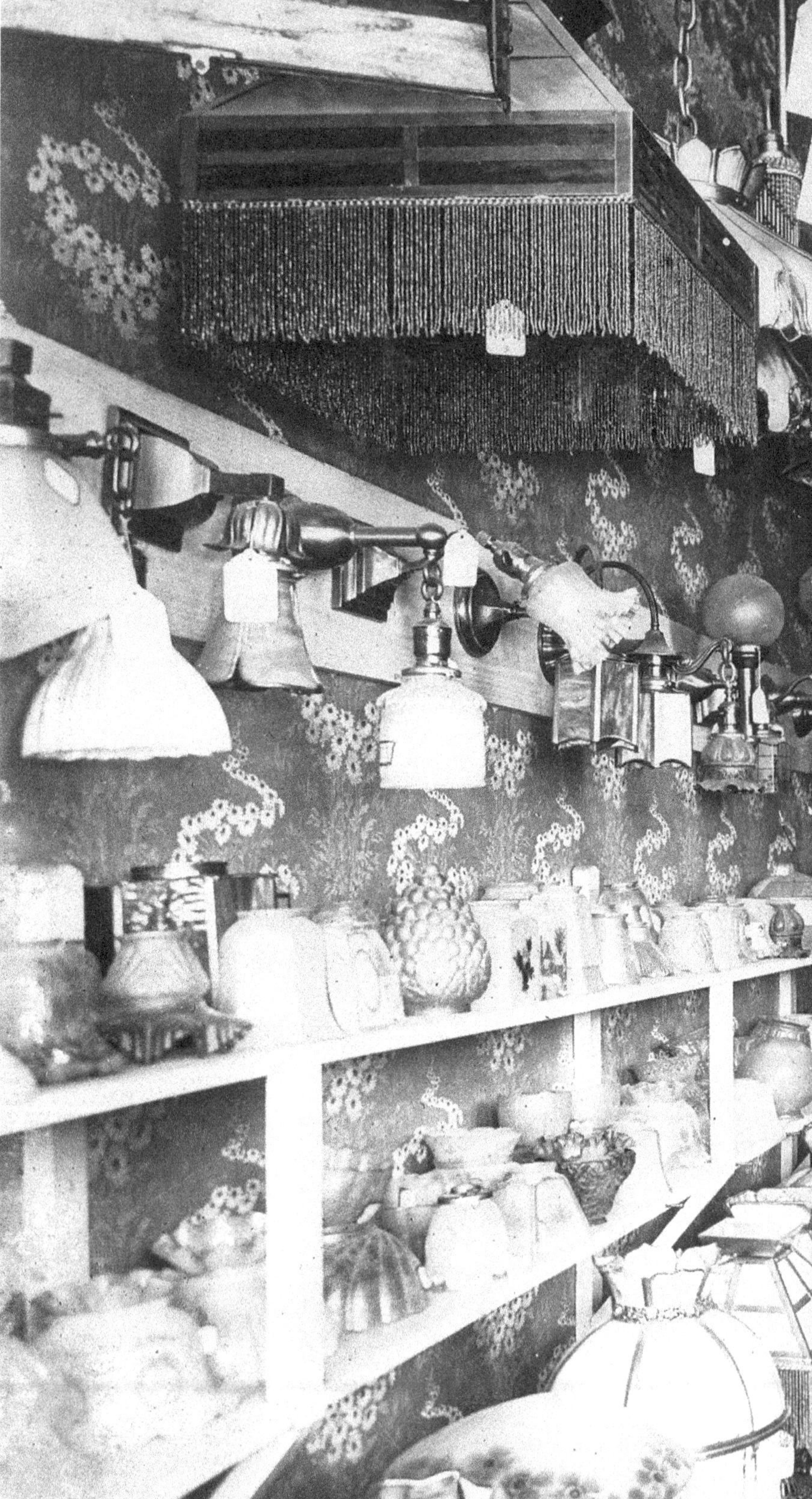

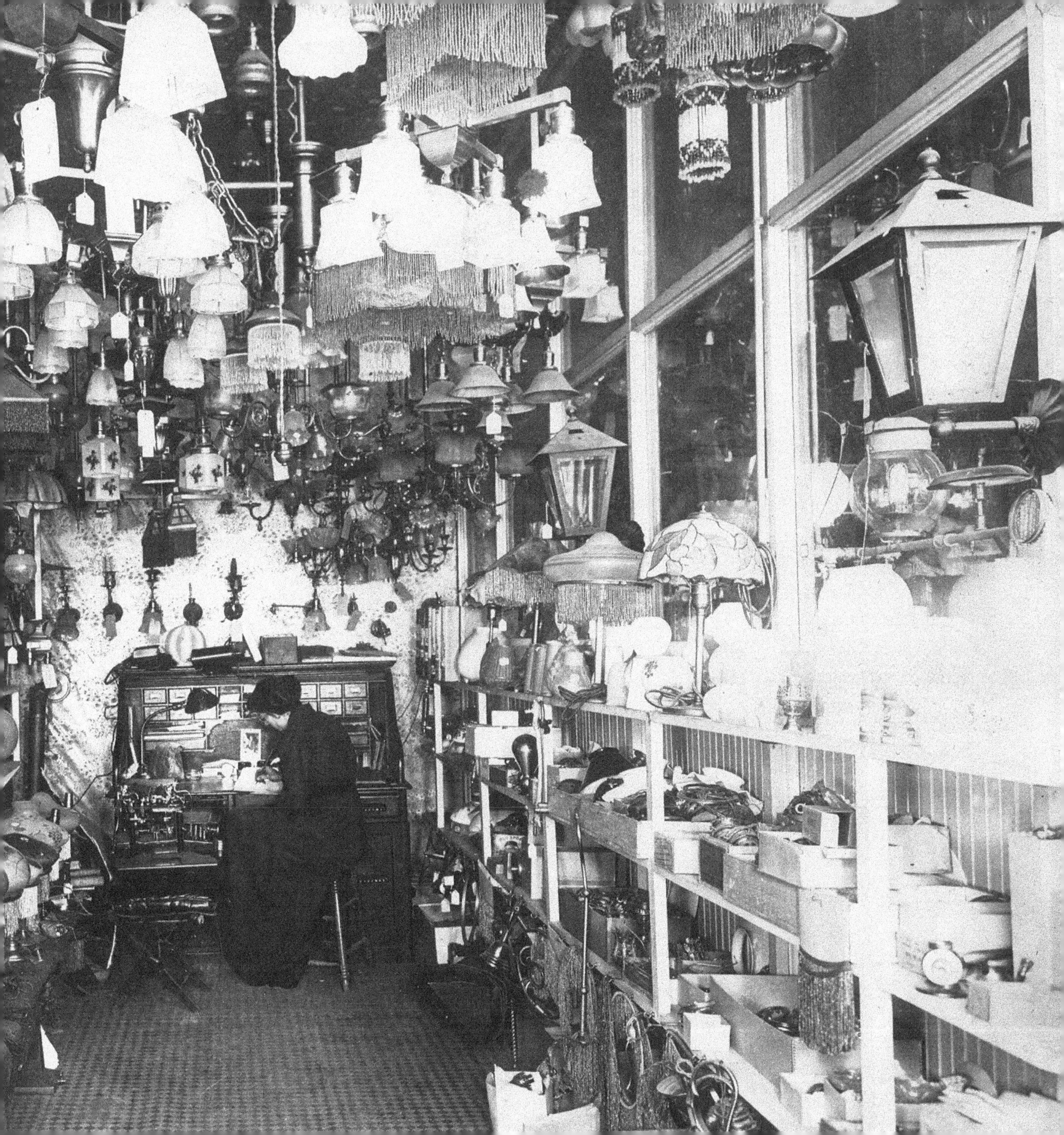

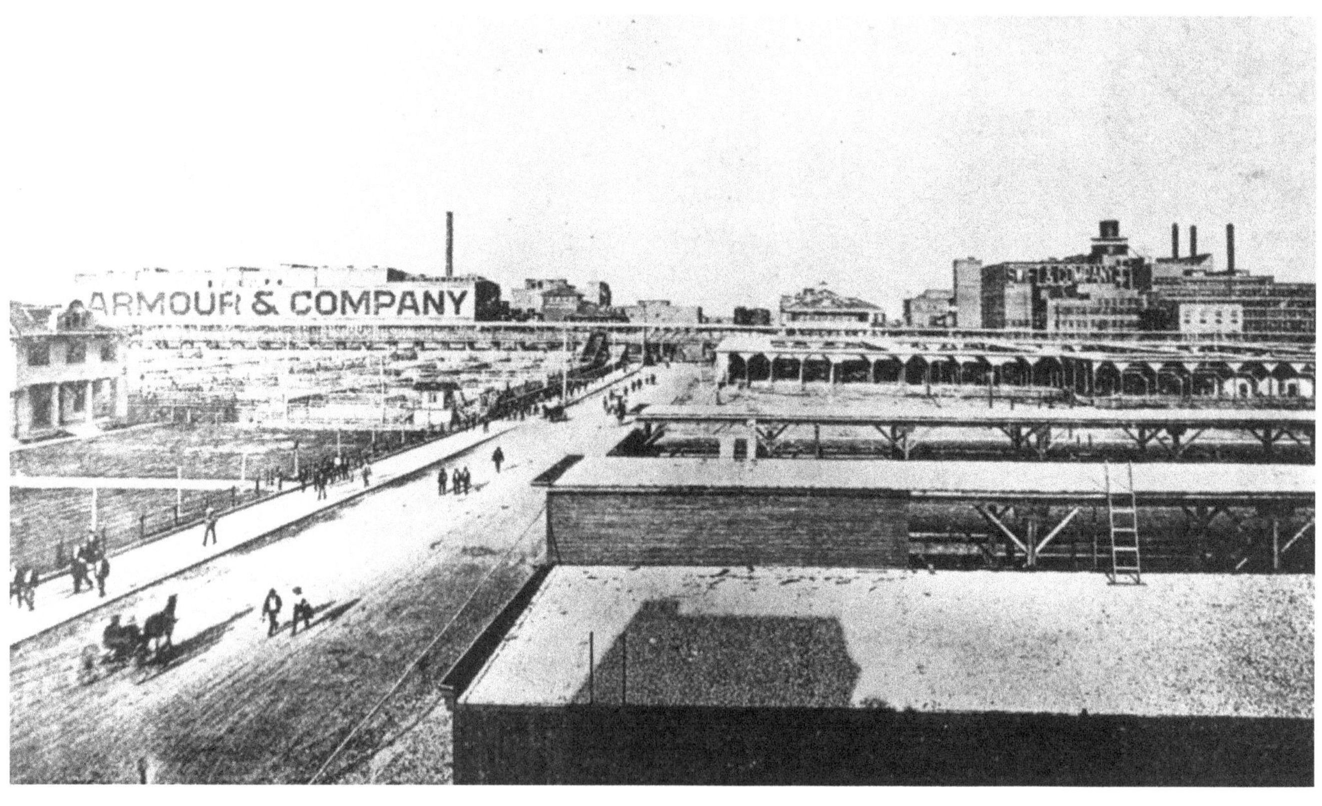


The impetus for much of Fort Worth's success during the early part of the century was the development of the Fort Worth Stockyards. This view east on Exchange Avenue catches the corner of the Livestock Exchange Building at far left, the sprawling facilities of the Armour and Swift packing plants and the extensive livestock pens in between. A devastating fire in 1911 destroyed most of the pens in the right foreground, leading to the construction of the fireproof Horse and Mule Barns still in use today.

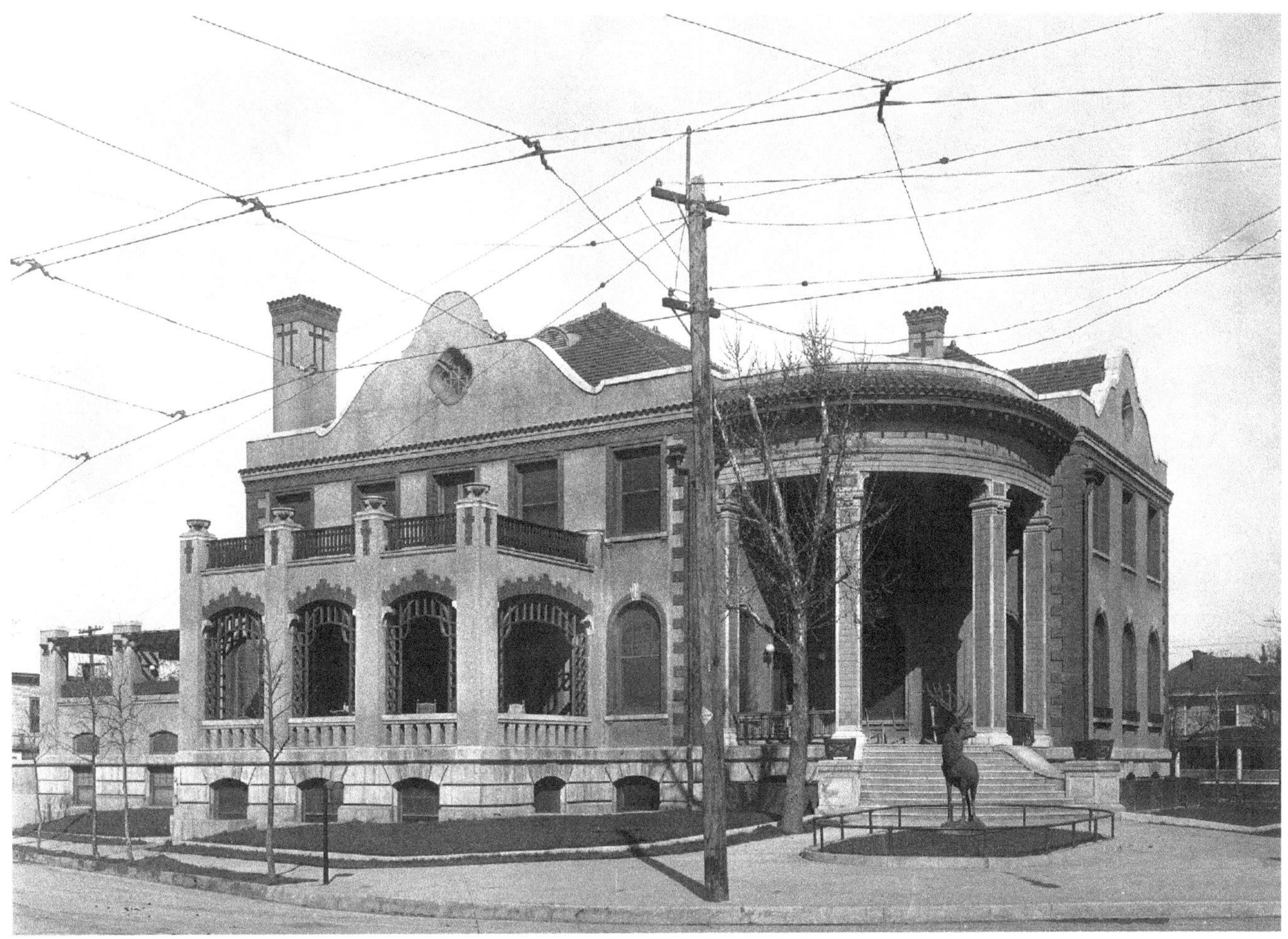

In 1910, the Fort Worth Lodge #124 of the Benevolent and Protective Order of Elks built a magnificent new clubhouse on the northwest corner of 7th and Lamar streets. Architecturally compatible with the neighboring homes of some of the city's wealthiest families, the lodge building served the club until 1928 when the Elks built a new facility at 4th and Lamar. The old clubhouse shown here was demolished about 1934.

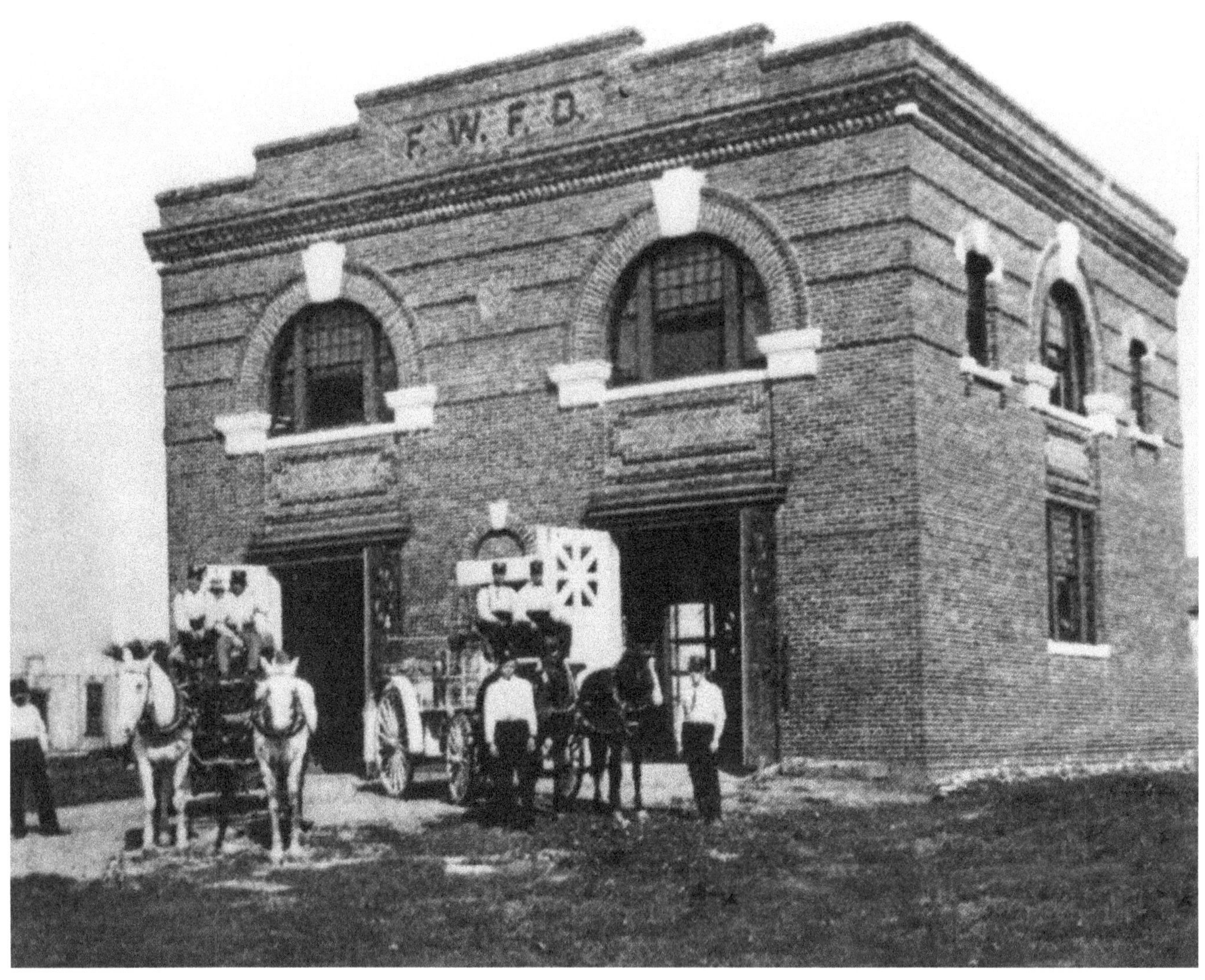


As the full-time, professional fire department grew after its creation in 1893, keeping pace with a rapidly expanding city, new equipment and facilities were added. In this image from about 1907, firefighters at Station No. 8 at 1601 Lipscomb Street display their new engine and hose wagon. Motorized vehicles soon replaced the beloved horses that bore names such as "Six Bits," "Big Enuff," "Dutch" and "Irish."

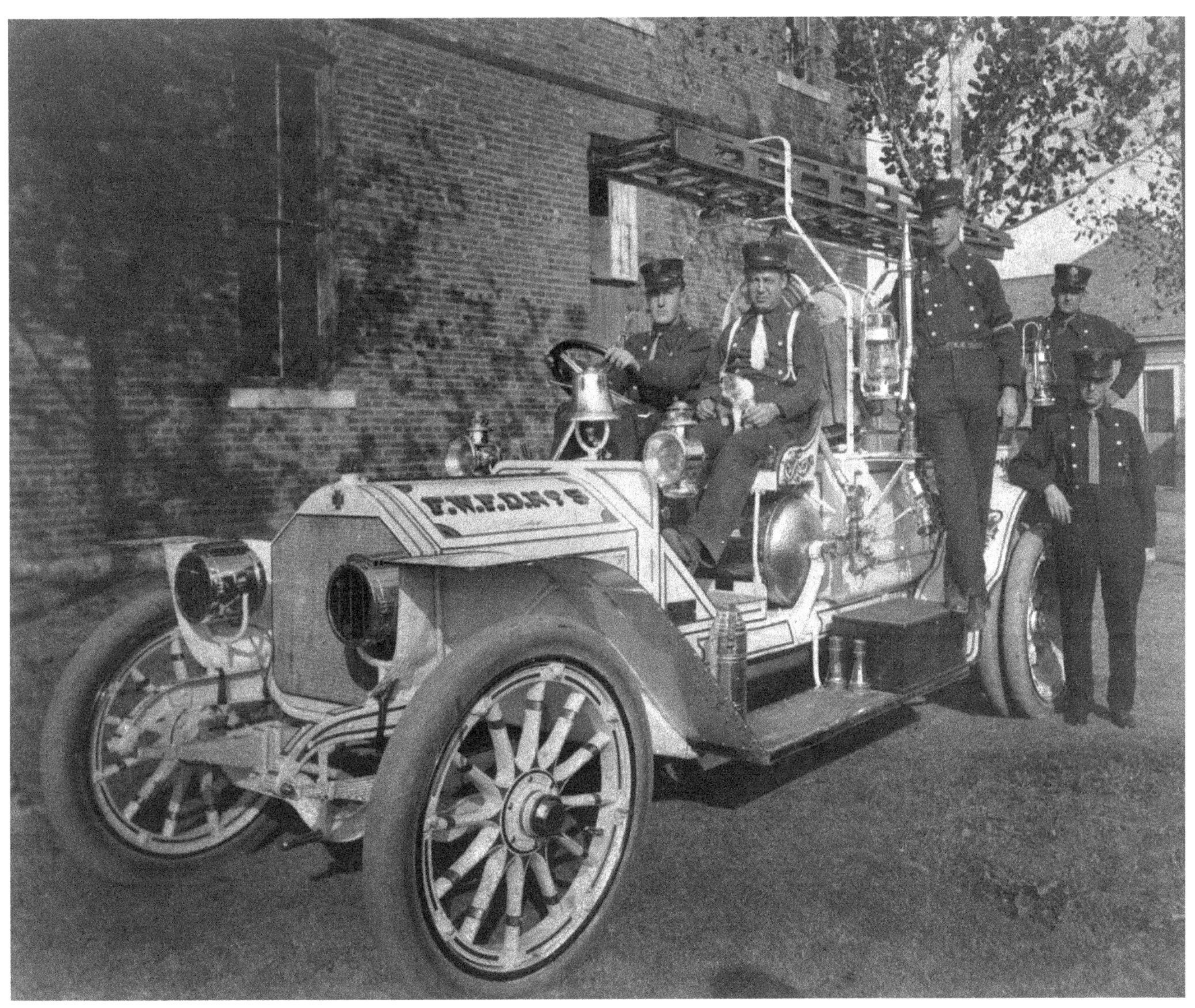


The Fort Worth Fire Department purchased its first motorized vehicle in 1910. That year, the crew of Engine Company No. 5 proudly posed with the new equipment in front of their equally new station near South Main Street. The new firehouse replaced the nearby 1890 W. B. Tucker Hose Company No. 5.

Texas Wesleyan University began its career as Polytechnic College in 1890, a distant four miles east of a raucous downtown Fort Worth. Shown here are members of the Polytechnic Militia practicing in front of the Old Administration Building about 1906. The building was expanded in 1909 and continues to serve the university as the administrative center of the growing, historic campus.

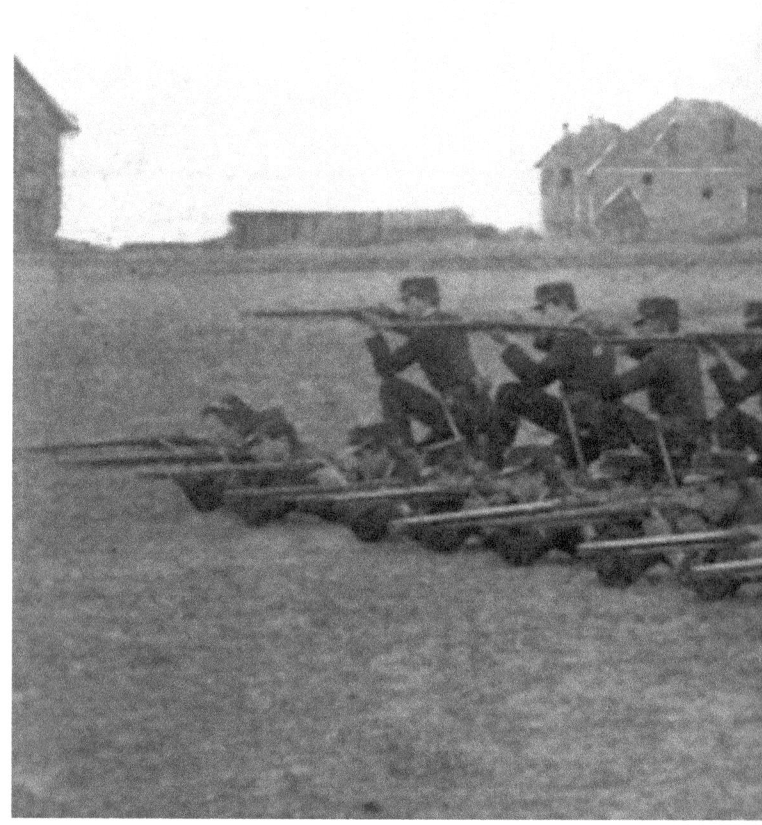

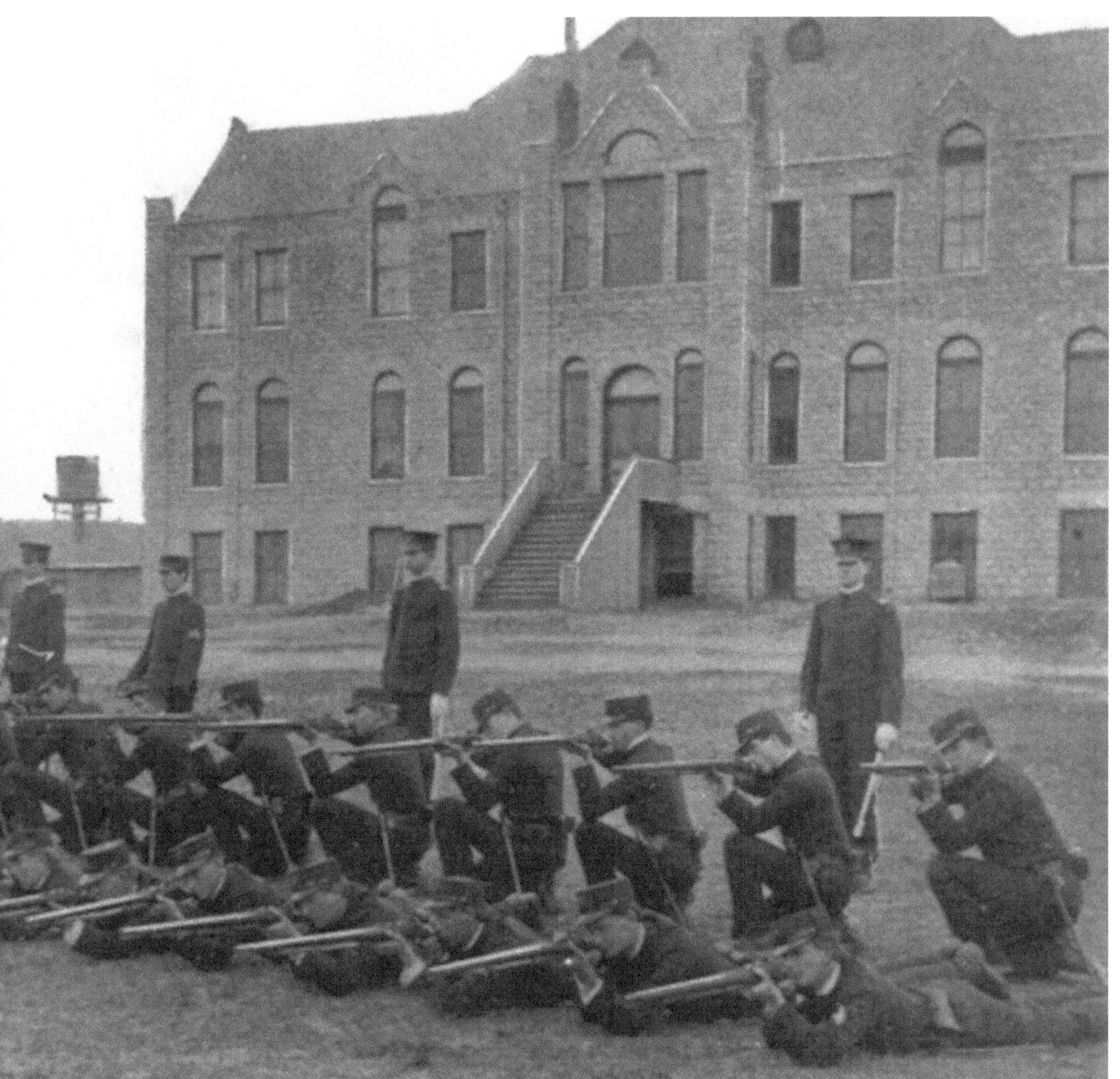

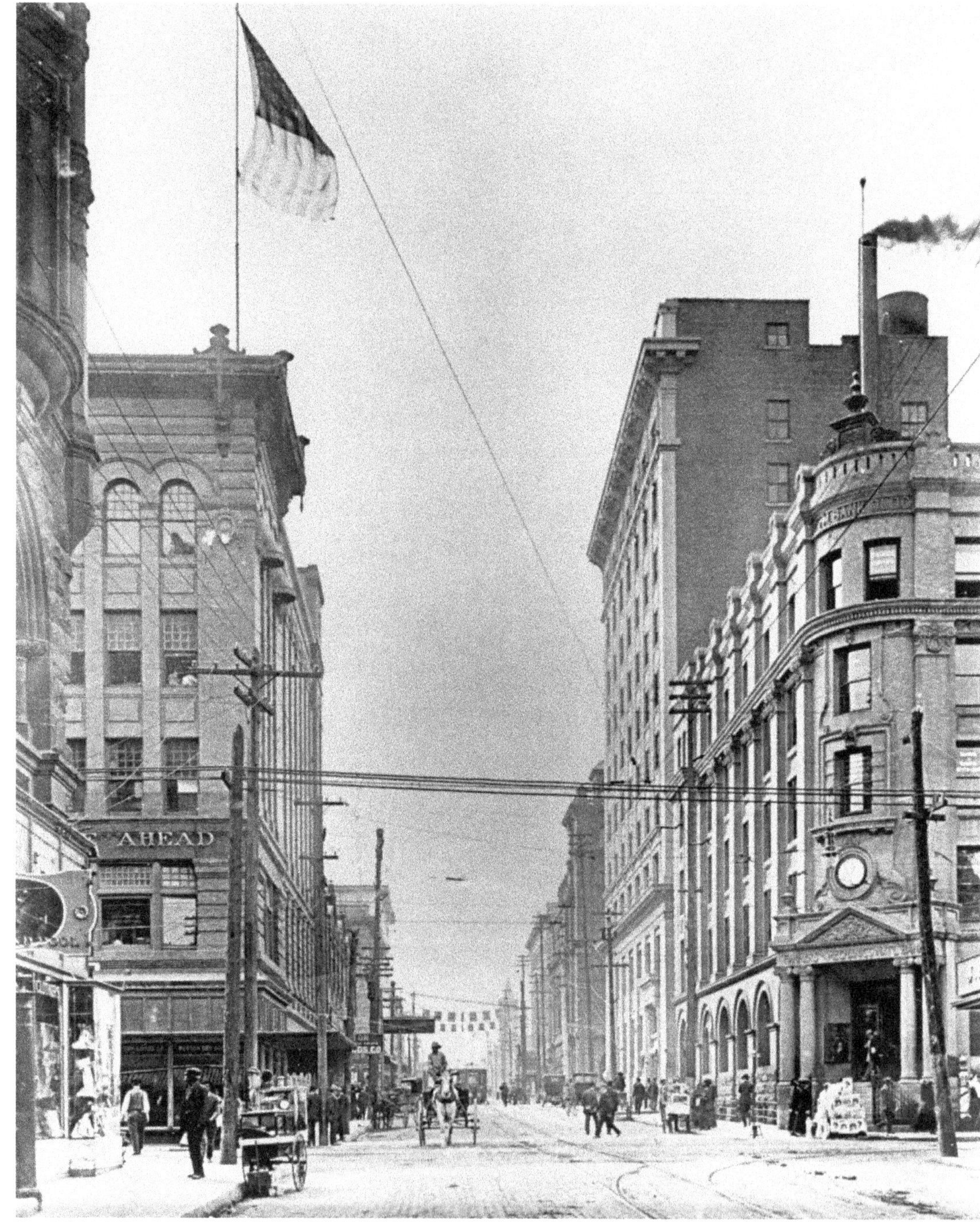


At the busy intersection of 7th and Main, horse-drawn vehicles, automobiles, streetcars, pushcarts, and pedestrians compete for space about 1910. The 1899 Farmers and Mechanics Bank Building, formerly the Hoxie Building, sits at right. Immediately behind it to the west is the newly completed First National Bank Building facing its neighbor across Houston Street, the 1889 Board of Trade Building. At the far end of the view is the steeple of St. Paul's Methodist Episcopal Church. Of all the structures in this image, only the First National Building remains.

# Into the Modern Era

## 1911–1940

With the expansion of the Stockyards and packing companies came a new diversity in Fort Worth as immigrants from Mexico and Europe joined the established Anglo and African American populations. Workers from Greece, Russia, Poland, Czechoslovakia and other eastern and southern European countries established communities in the neighborhoods on the city's north side. Families fleeing Mexico's revolution initially settled in an area east of North Main Street, joining earlier immigrants from Mexico who first came to the city in the 1880s.

As the United States prepared to enter World War I, Fort Worth hosted three major air-training fields as well as the sprawling Camp Bowie, a vast training facility that spread over most of the city's west side and was home to some 100,000 Texas and Oklahoma soldiers of the 36th "Panther" Division. The Army's insistence that the remnants of Hell's Half Acre be shut down as a condition for establishing the camp encouraged the campaigning of a young Baptist minister to clean up a Fort Worth he termed "the modern Sodom." While the illegal activities did shut down in their old downtown haunts, they spread out to other parts of the city, most notoriously along Jacksboro Highway, nicknamed "thunder road." Other, more legitimate, economic opportunities related to war preparations abounded, however, and Fort Worth became the largest horse and mule market in the world as Allied countries sent representatives to Texas to purchase animals.

The discovery of oil in West Texas launched another boom for Fort Worth as the city became a refining and shipping center, making the ranchers on whose land the oil was found even wealthier, and launching a tradition of private philanthropy that continues to shape the city. The city's skyline changed dramatically as new wealth spurred competition for the tallest buildings, biggest houses, and greatest charitable gifts.

Fort Worth weathered the Great Depression perhaps better than many other cities, but its effects did hit home. Federal funding programs helped build new parks, schools and roadways. The city's 1936 Frontier Centennial celebration, with its Casa Manana amphitheater, was a true delight and represented a successful challenge to the official Texas Centennial celebration hosted by the city's long-time rival Dallas.

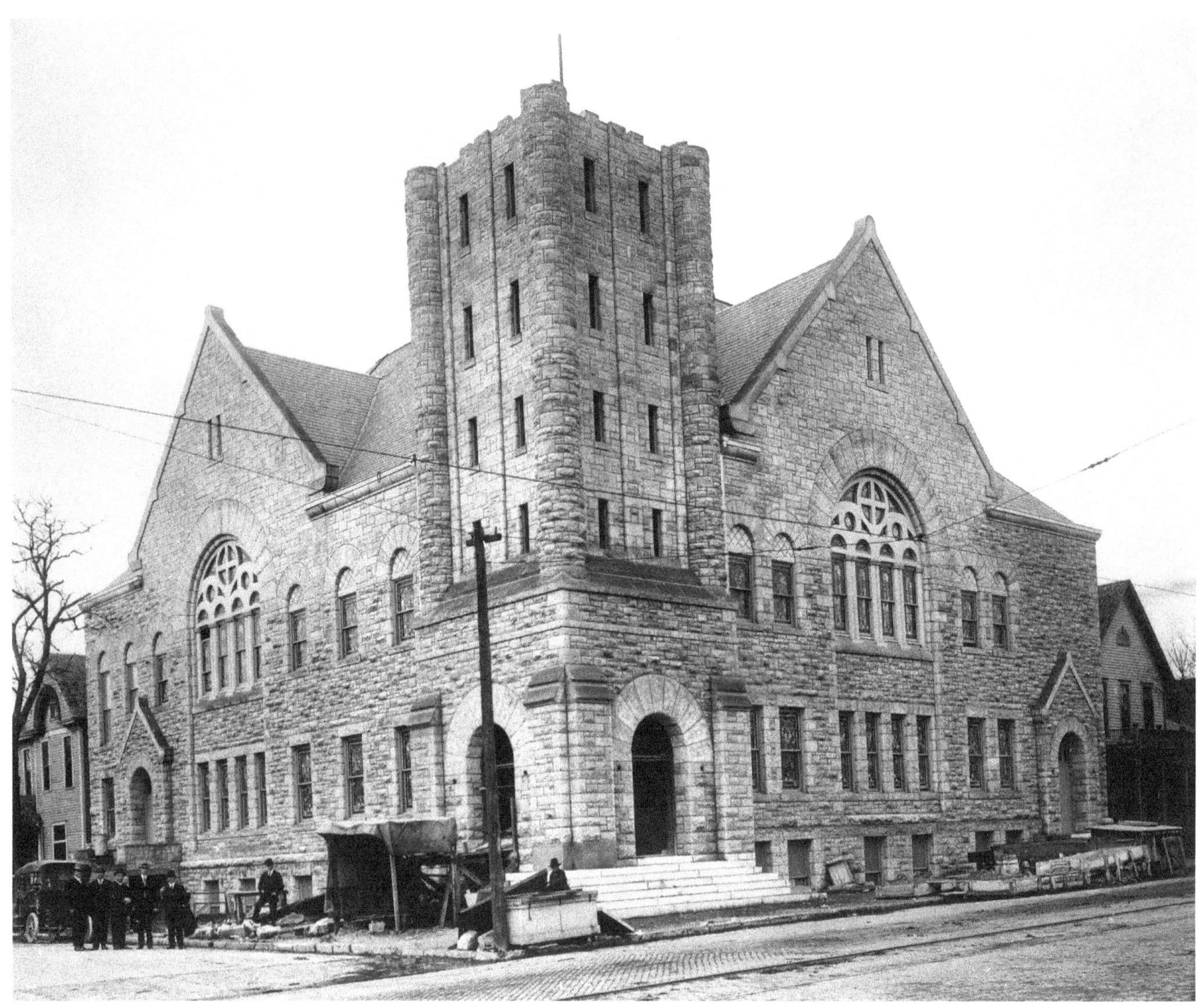

A new First Baptist Church sanctuary nears completion on the southeast corner of Taylor and 4th Streets in 1912. The church's 1886 building a block north on 3rd was destroyed by fire. Its charismatic but controversial young minister, J. Frank Norris, was accused and acquitted of arson. Norris led the church from 1909 until his death in 1952. In his early years, he compared Fort Worth to a modern Sodom and launched campaigns to clean up vice and corruption.

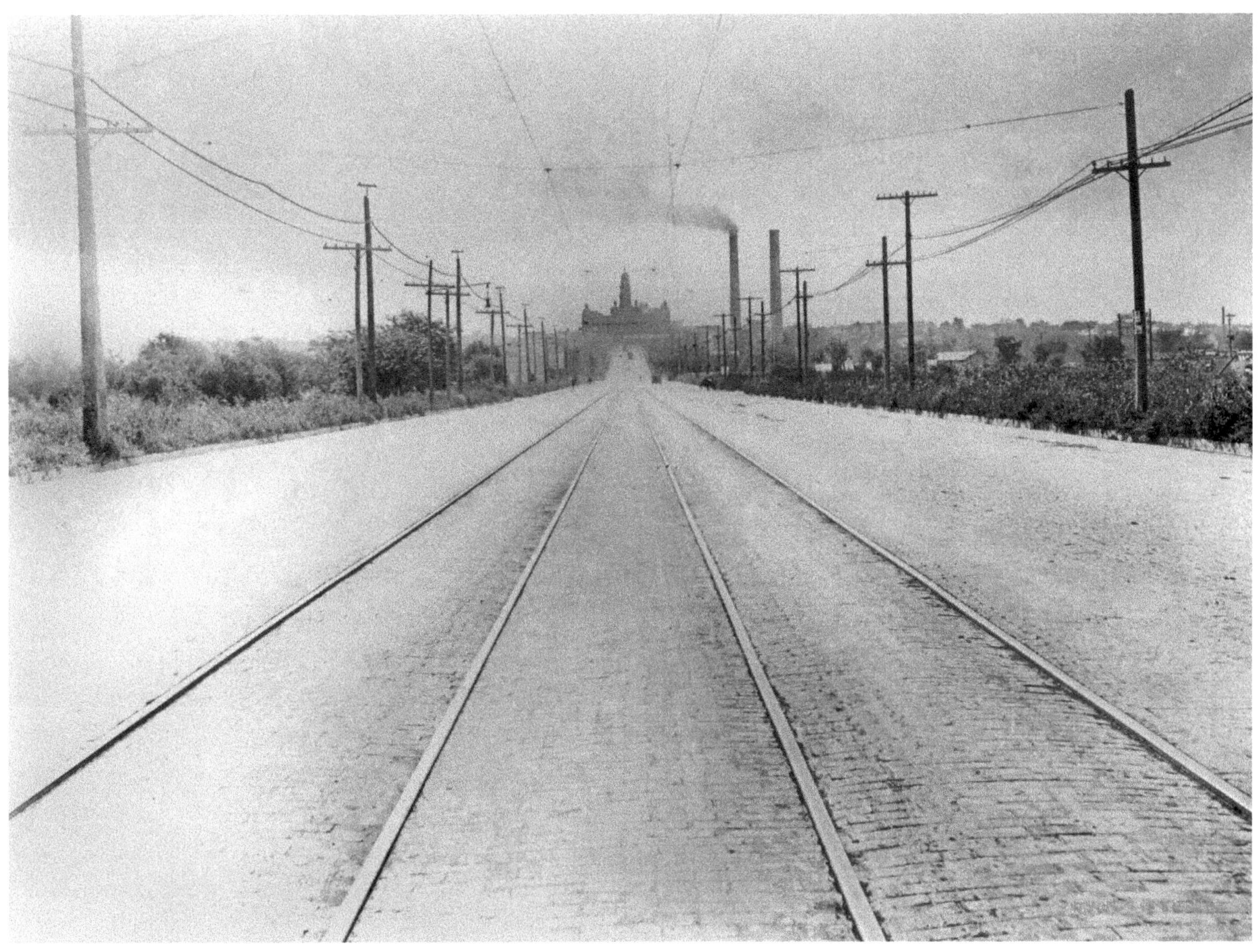

The courthouse and old jail dominate the skyline in this view looking up North Main. This photograph was taken about 1912, just after the Fort Worth Power and Light Company began operations of its coal-fired electricity generation plant.

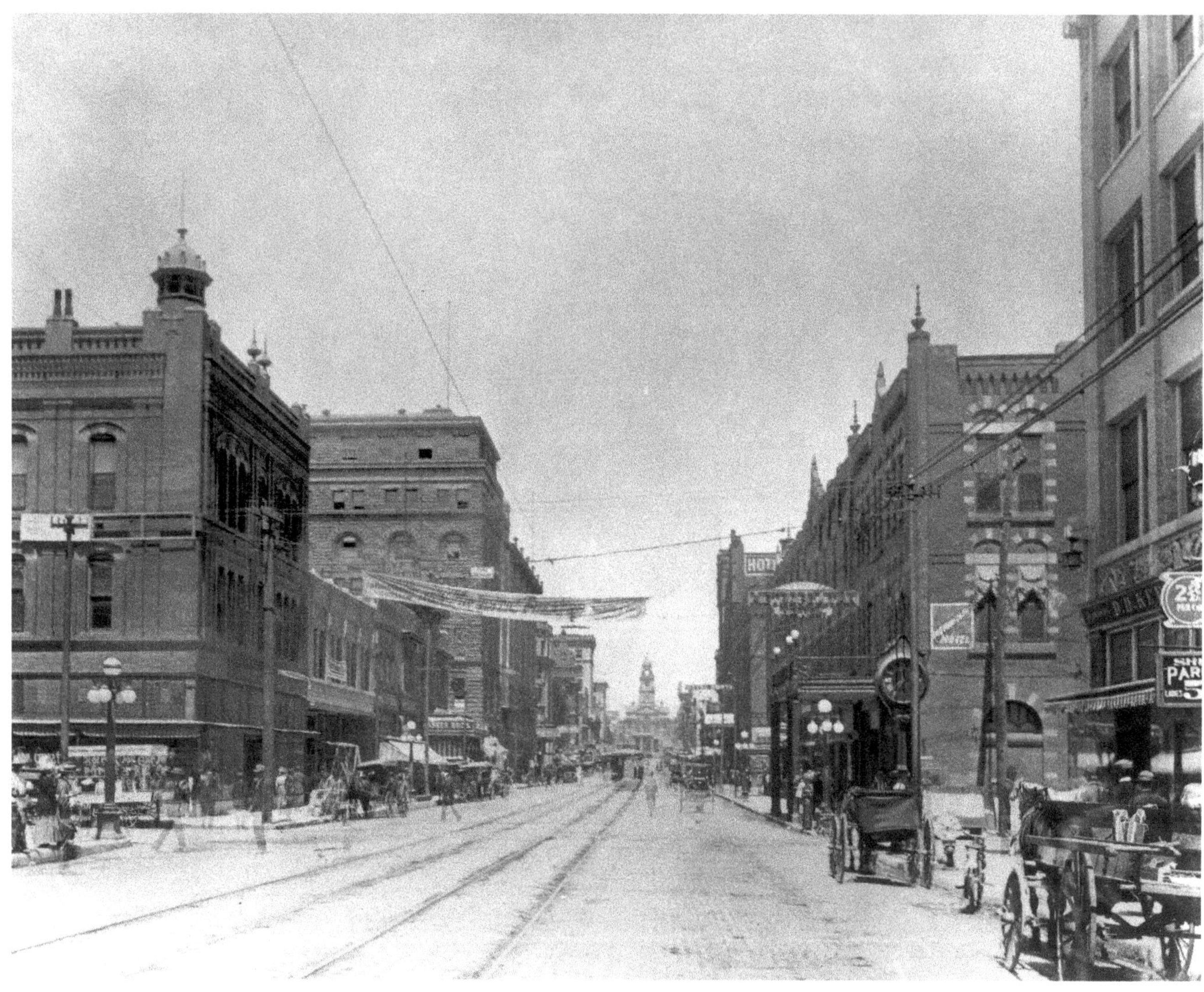

The banner across Main Street dates this photograph to 1911 when a new Majestic Theatre opened on Commerce at 10th, replacing the smaller "old" Majestic built in 1905 on Jennings Avenue. The Majestic ushered in a new era of entertainment for the city, as major performers and traveling road companies took advantage of the opulent facility. It was demolished in 1966.

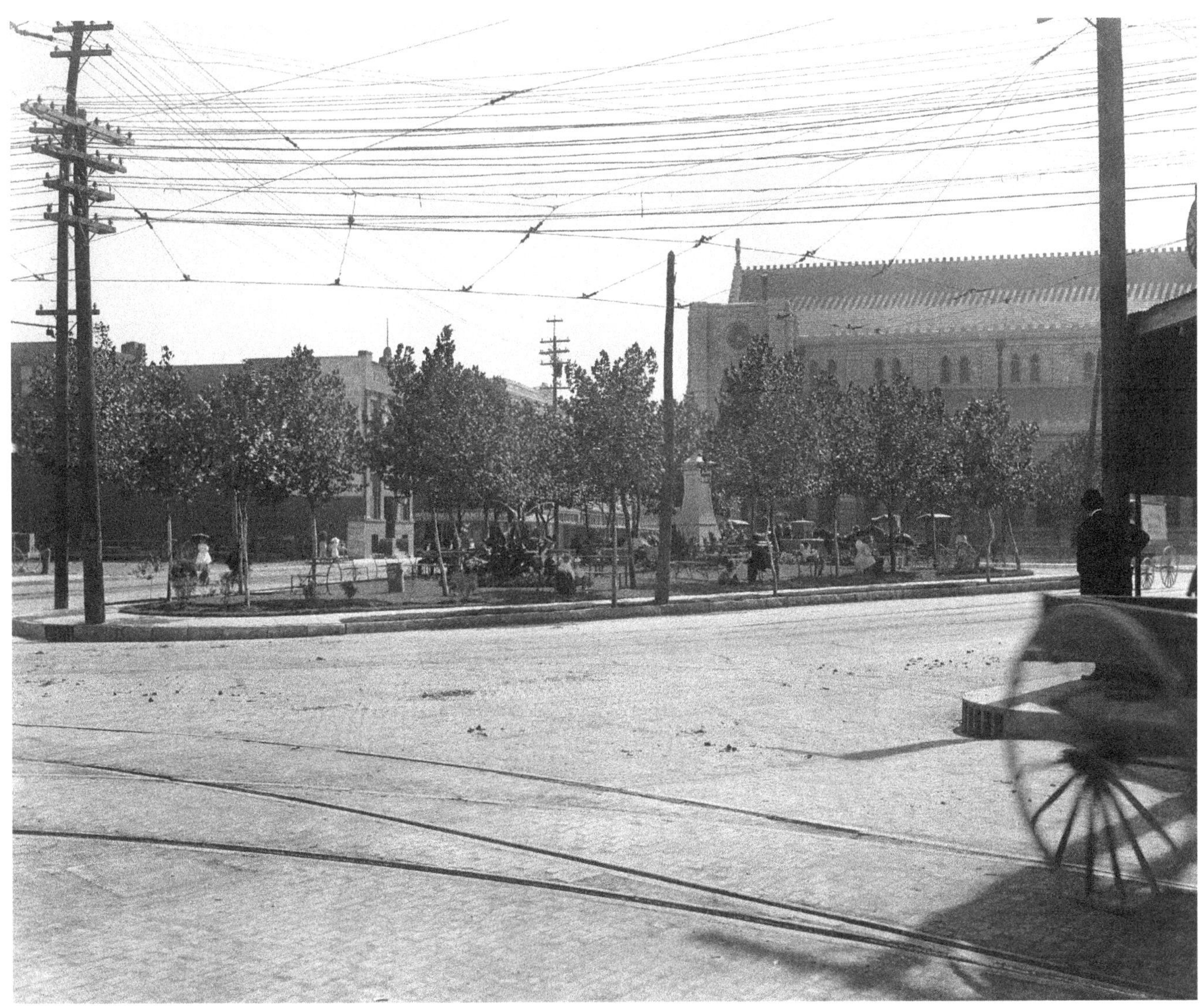

Thirsty horses stop for a drink from the fountain in Peter Smith Park, just north of St. Patrick Cathedral between Jennings and Throckmorton. The small, triangular park was dedicated to Fort Worth pioneer John Peter Smith, called "the father of Fort Worth," shortly after his untimely death in 1901. He arrived in the young city in 1853, taught school, surveyed, practiced law and, while serving as mayor from 1882-85, oversaw major improvements in water supplies, street paving and sanitation that moved Fort Worth into the modern age. He died following a robbery and assault while on a trip to promote the city.

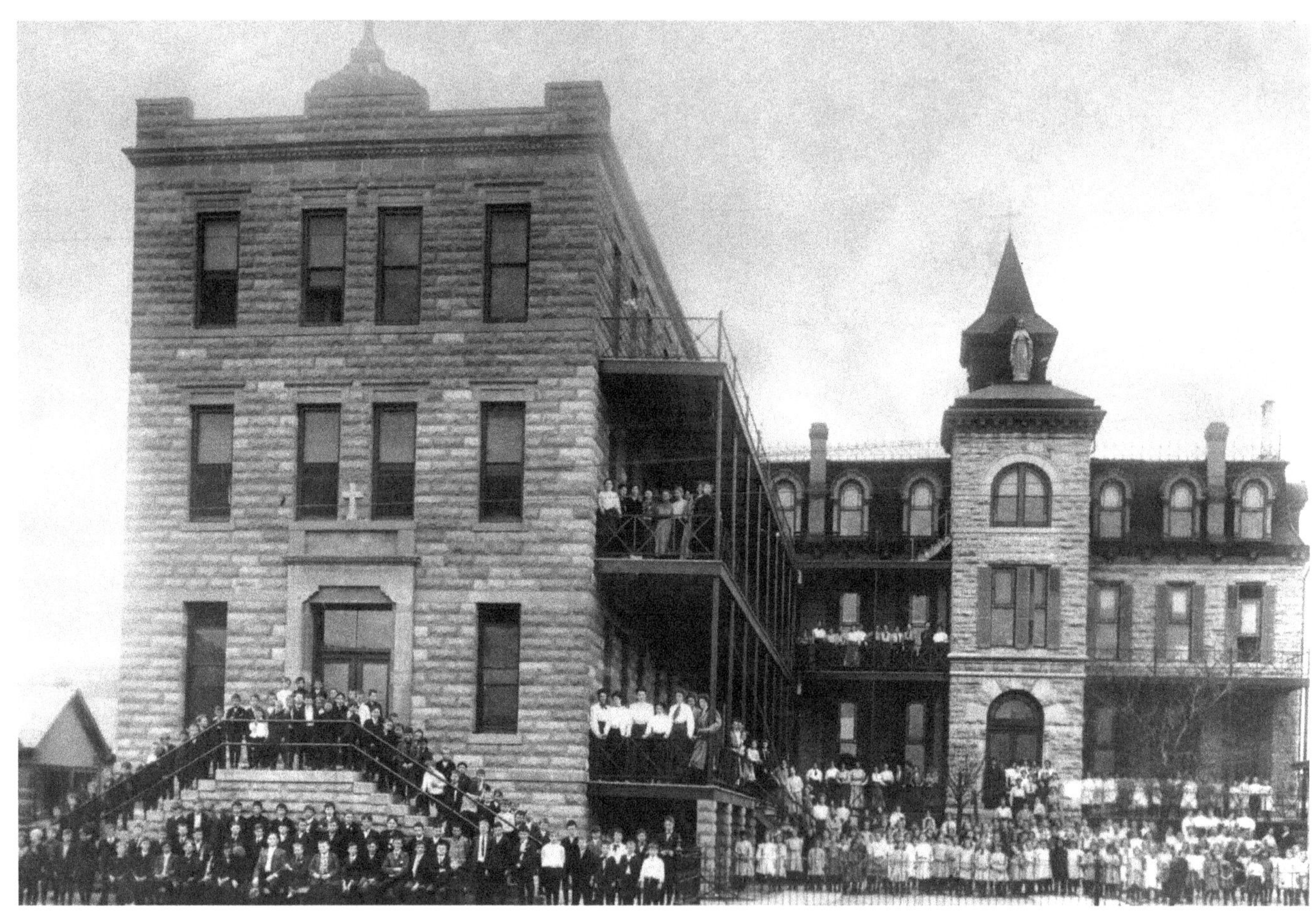

On the opposite side of St. Patrick's stands the 1888 St. Ignatius Academy, chartered in 1885 and operated by the Sisters of St. Mary of Namur. Architect J. J. Kane, who also designed the Cathedral, designed the original Academy building, at right. To accommodate the growing student body, the Sisters built an adjacent classroom building in 1905 that allowed the school to teach over four hundred students, many of them seen here filling the grounds and balconies. The 1905 structure was demolished in 1926 to make way for street expansion.

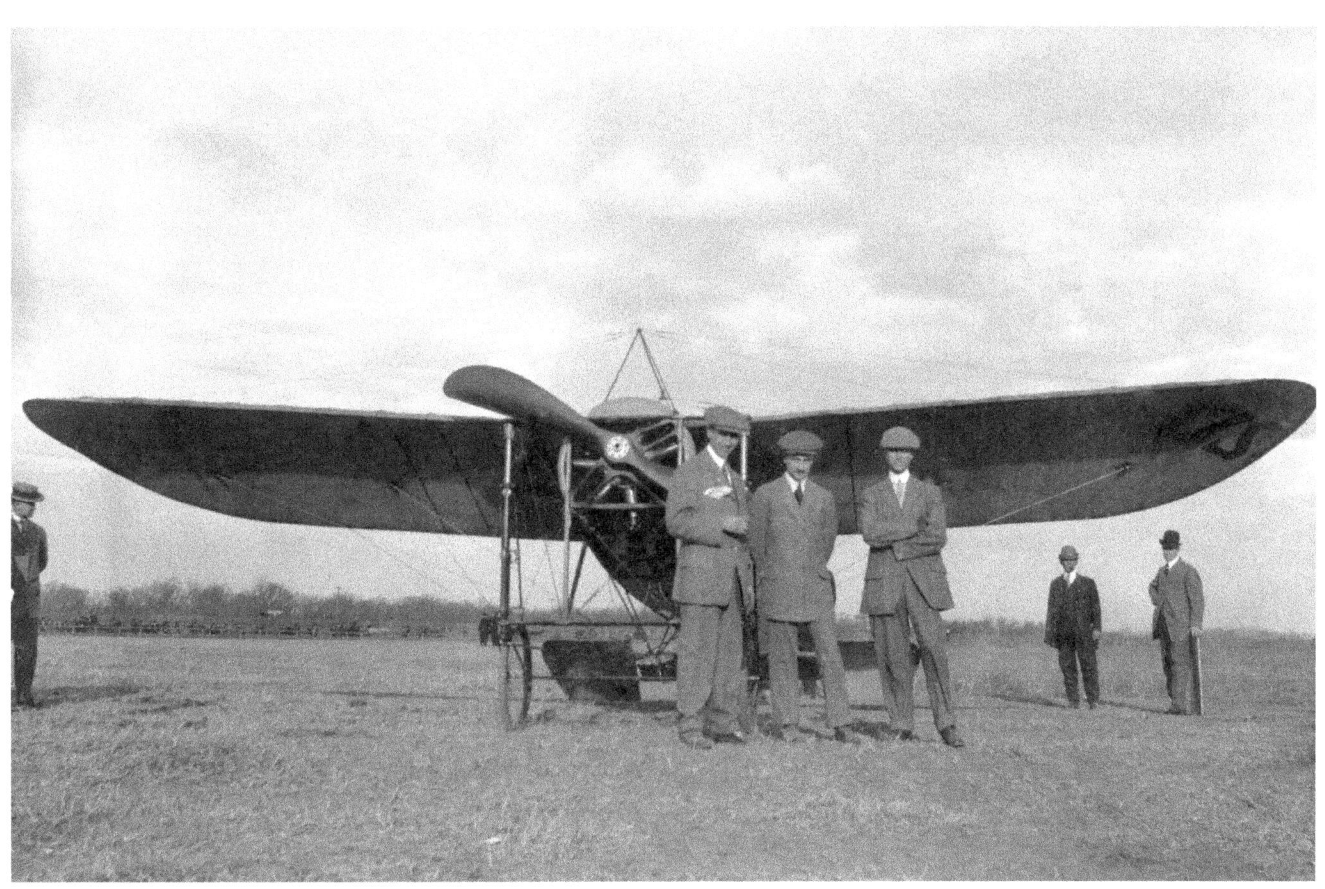

Risking the windy conditions, pioneering French pilot Roland Garros, standing in the middle with moustache, completed the first flight in Fort Worth on January 12, 1911, in his Bleriot monoplane. Thrilling a crowd of more than fifteen thousand spectators gathered at the Driving Park on 7th Street, Garros and other pilots of International Aviators, Inc. spent two days of a national tour igniting Fort Worth's passion for aviation. Garros died in 1918 when his plane was shot down during World War I.

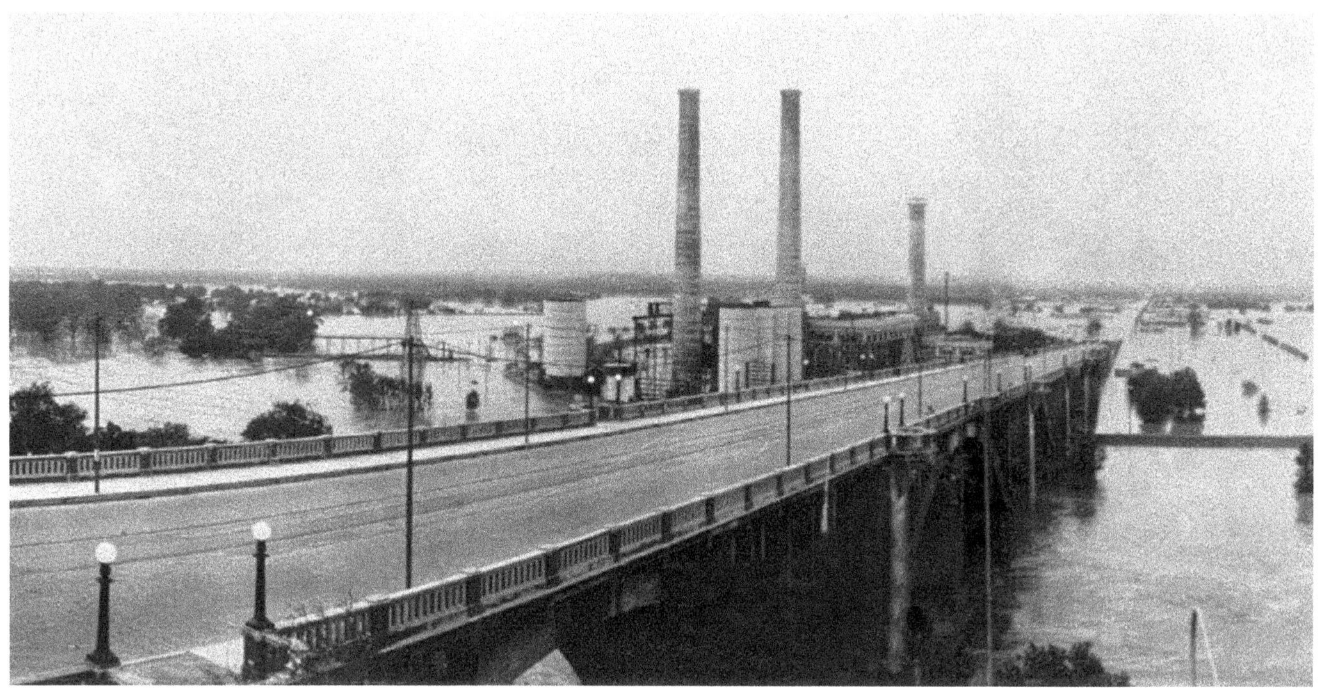

This early view of the Paddock Viaduct connecting North Fort Worth to Downtown was taken during the Trinity River Flood in 1922. Completed in 1914 and named for Fort Worth pioneer and leading promoter of the city B. B. Paddock, the bridge was designed by Brenneke and Fay of St. Louis and was the first in the country to use self-supporting, reinforcing steel. On the west side of the bridge are the smokestacks and electric generating station built in 1912 by the Fort Worth Power and Light Company.

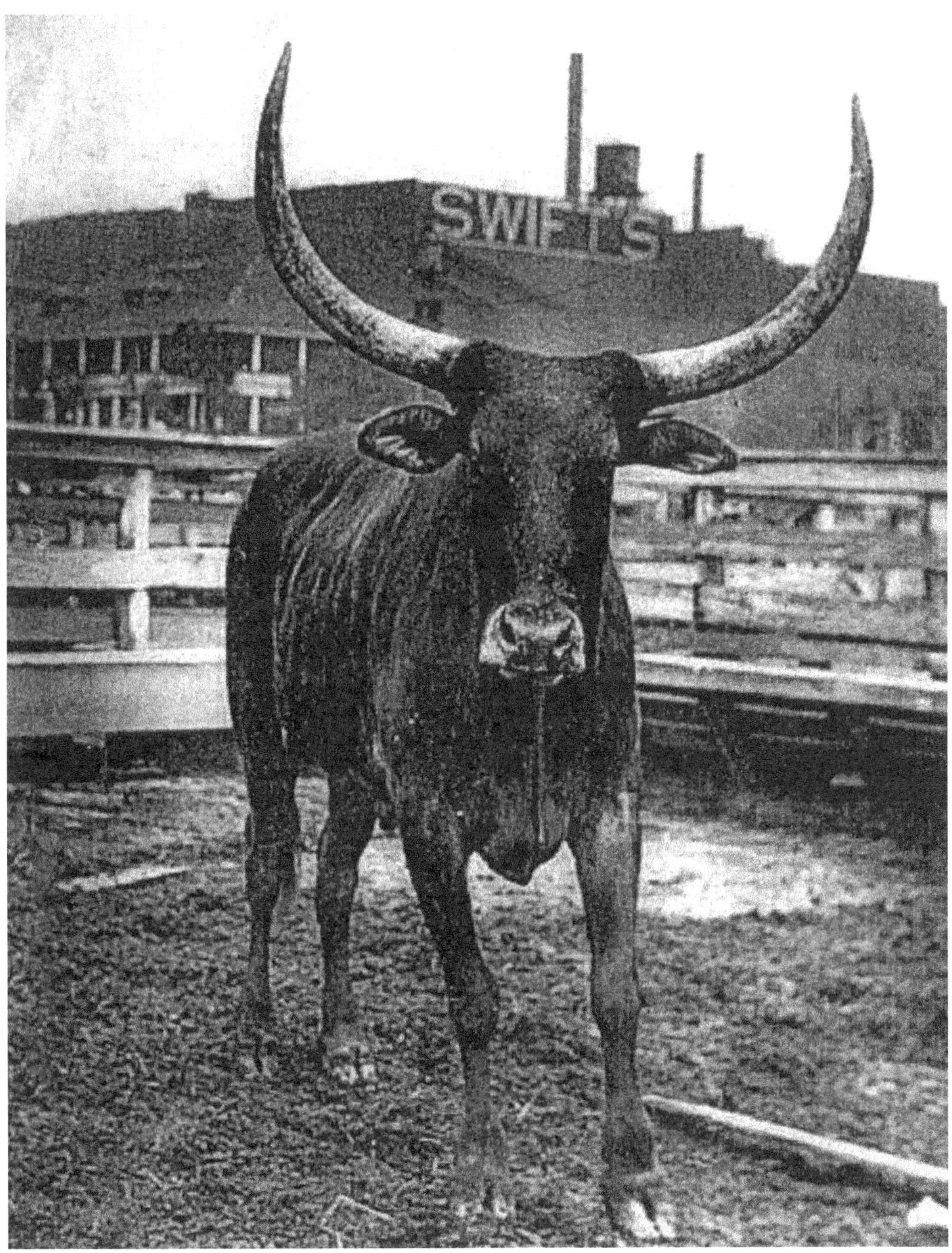


With the first herd of Longhorns that pushed through Fort Worth in 1866, the city staked its future on livestock and agriculture. Over the next twenty years, drovers moved millions of cattle through the town on the way to northern railheads and pastures. When the Swift and Armour Companies established major packing facilities here in 1902, the city became one of the leading livestock processing centers in the country, making the Fort Worth Stockyards the city's largest employer through World War II.

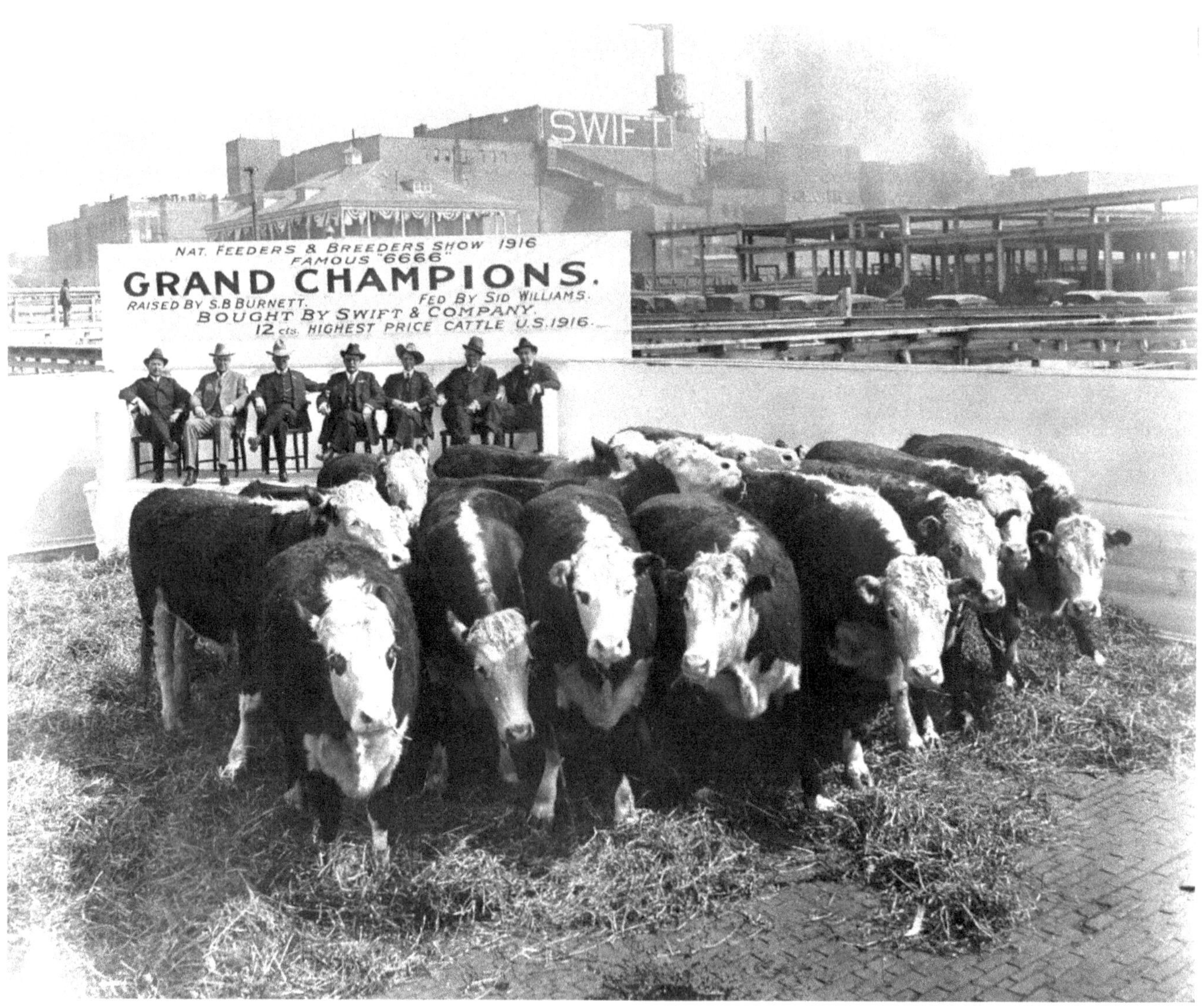


Key to the successful marketing of the Fort Worth facilities was the Annual Feeders and Breeders Show, forerunner of today's Southwestern Exposition and Livestock Show. Tracing its roots to 1896, the show rapidly developed a reputation of introducing some of the finest livestock in the country. In 1916, Captain S. B. Burnett proudly displayed the Grand Champions from his Four Sixes Ranch, the products of careful breeding to enhance the quality of beef available to American consumers.

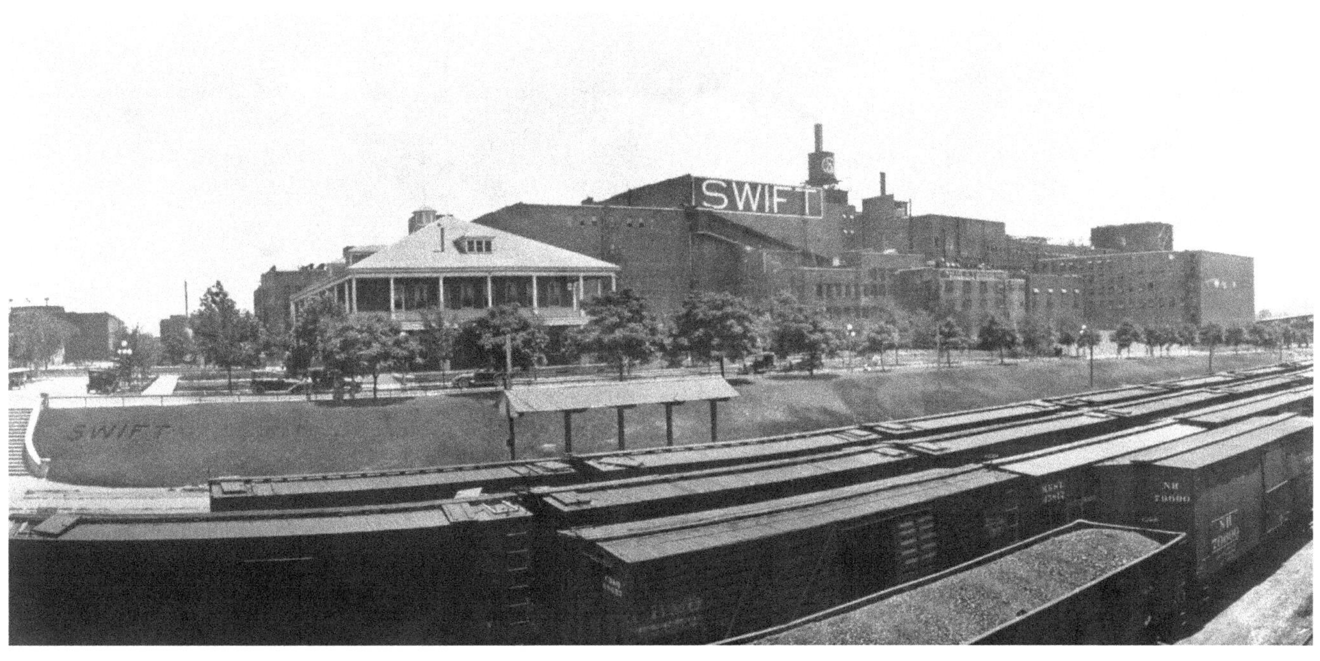


By World War I, the Stockyards had grown into the largest horse and mule market in the world, and competed for the third-largest in terms of general livestock activity in the United States. Here, the Swift & Co. plant, with its columned 1902 headquarters building, rises above Exchange Avenue and rail spurs packed with freight cars.

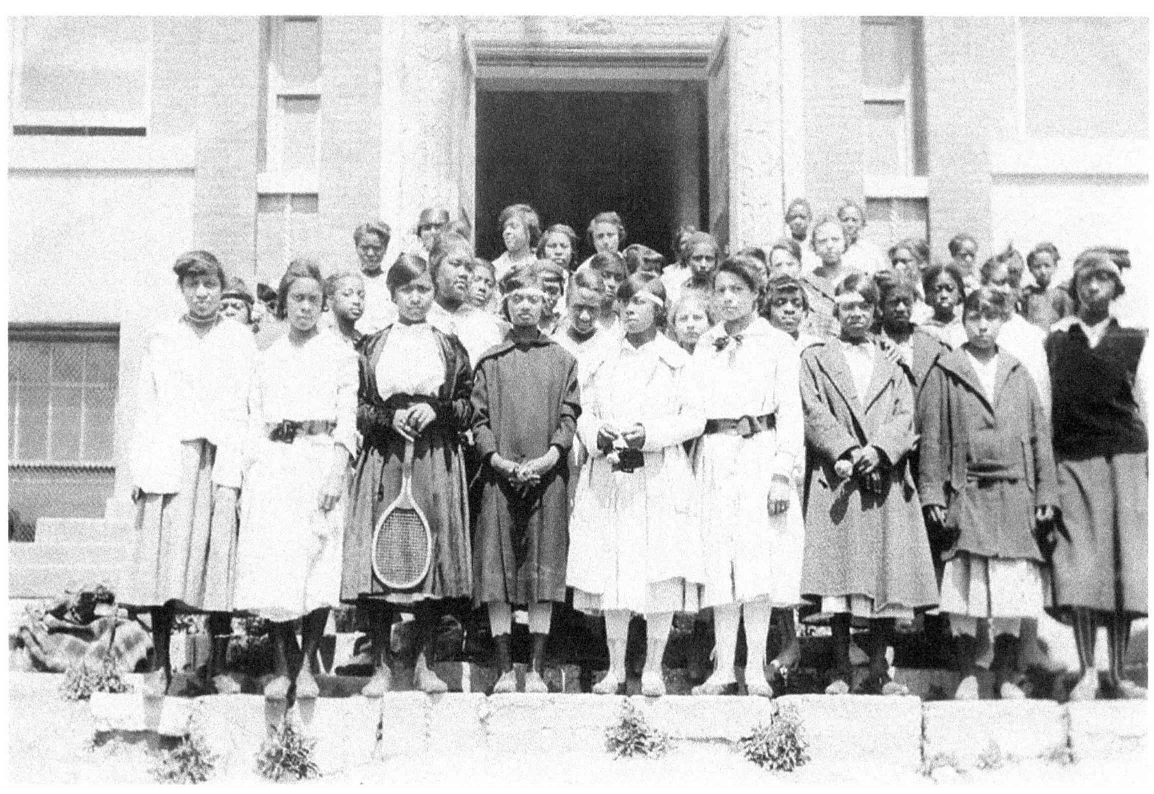

Young women of the Fort Worth Colored High School stood for their group portrait in front of the school in 1918. Three years later, the segregated campus would be renamed for education pioneer Isaiah M. Terrell. Arriving in Fort Worth in 1882, Terrell headed the first public school established in the city for African Americans. By the time he left in 1915 to head what would become Prairie View A&M University, Terrell had established a tradition of teaching and academic excellence that continued for decades under such noted educators as Dr. Hazel Harvey Peace.

Following a merger of his Waggoner Bank & Trust with First National Bank in 1917, cattle and oil man W. T. Waggoner demolished his old bank building at 8th and Houston and hired Sanguinet and Staats to design the tallest building in Fort Worth as a replacement. Waggoner got the better of friend and fellow cattleman S. B. Burnett, who owned what was then the current tallest structure, the 13-story Burk Burnett Building. Waggoner proudly dedicated his 20-story skyscraper in 1919.

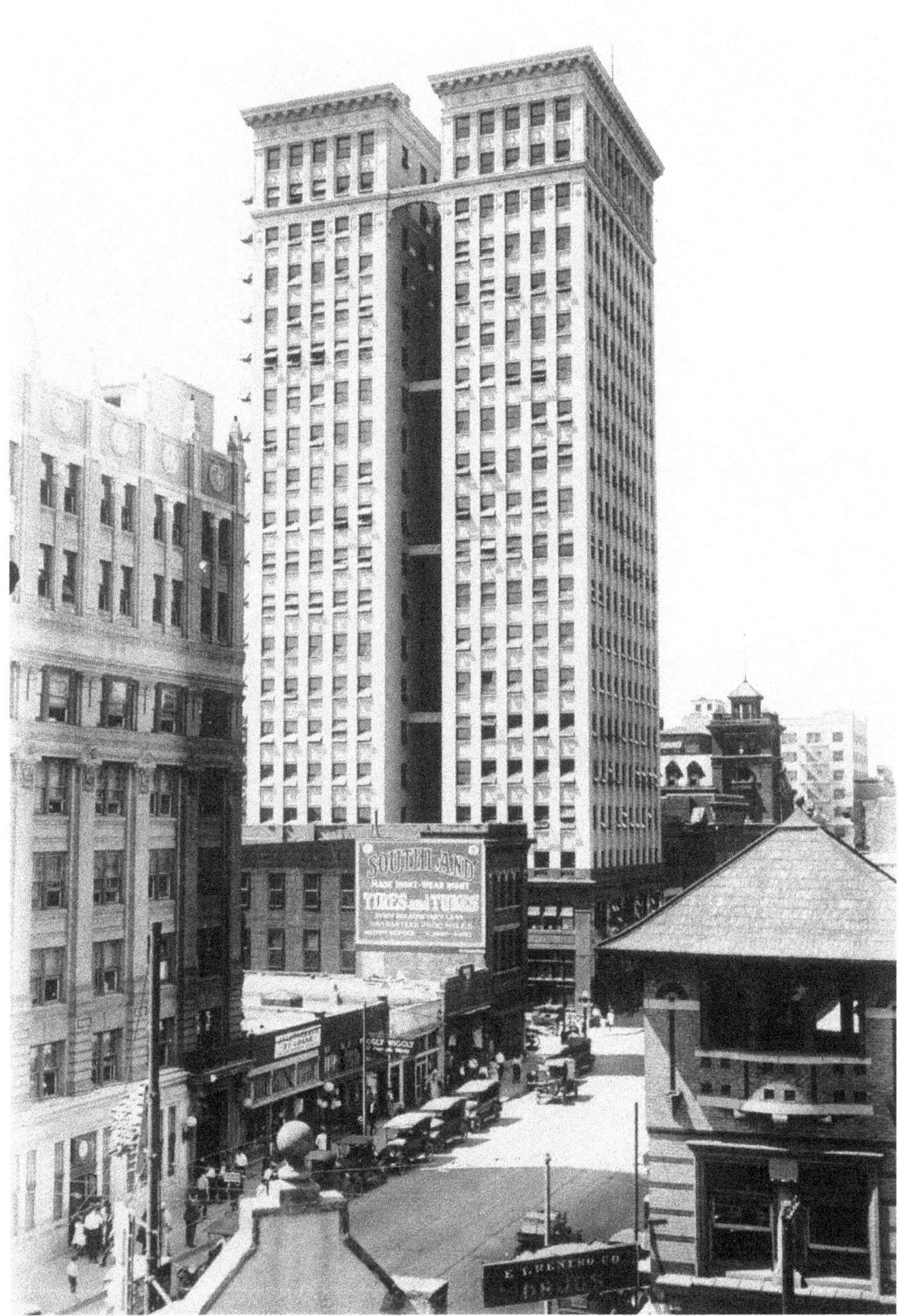

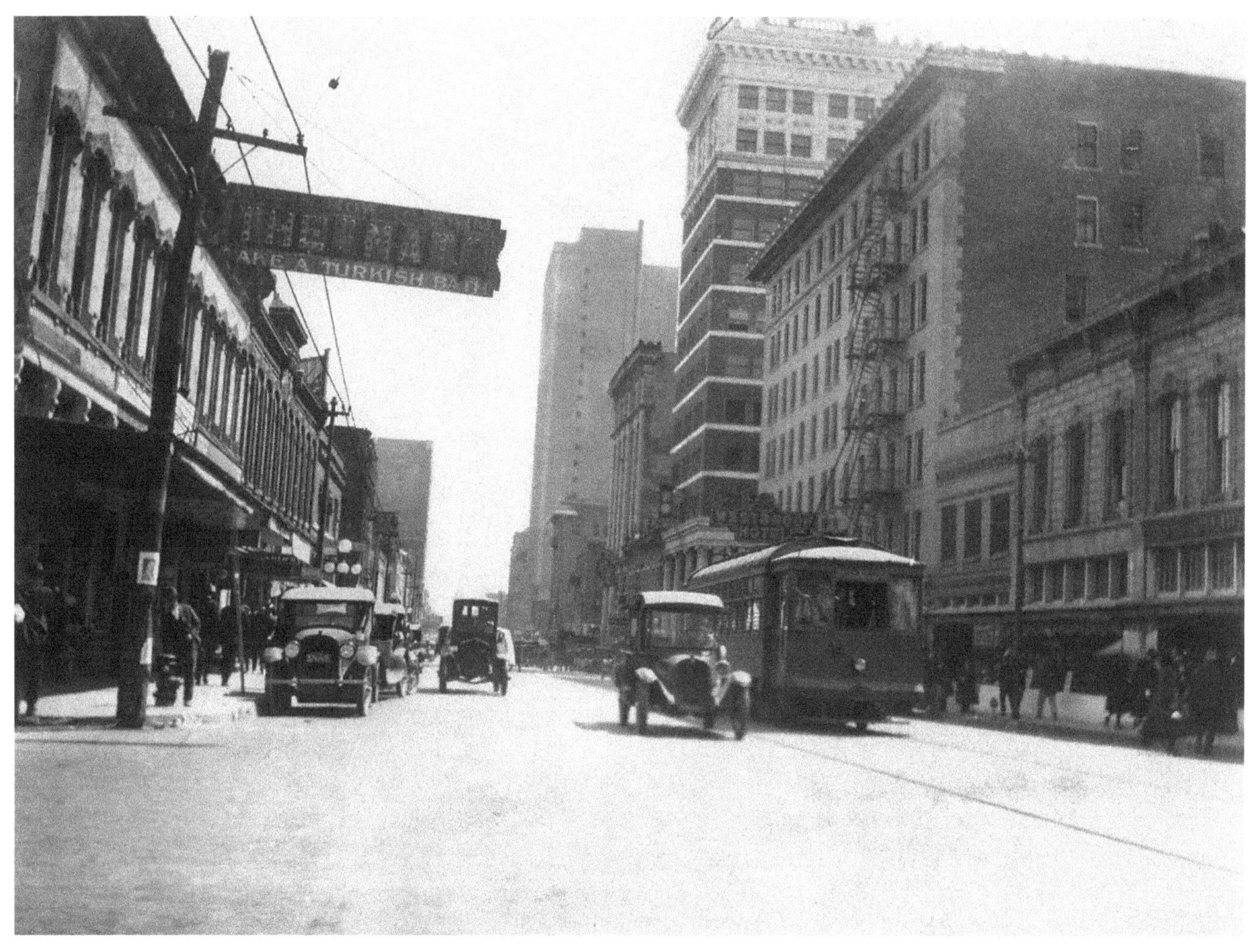


The view south on Main Street from 3rd about 1921 presented an interesting mix of old and new buildings. Beyond the nineteenth century row at left, the just-finished Farmers and Mechanics Bank rises at 7th Street. At twenty-four stories, it was the tallest building in the Southwest. The seven-story Westbrook Hotel stands at right, with the Burk Burnett Building just beyond.

From Main and 3rd, the photographer captured the view north to the courthouse. The 1893 Masonic Lodge stands at right on the corner of 2nd behind the streetcar. The Sanger Brothers expanded their Dallas-based retail store to Fort Worth in 1918, operating briefly from a building on Main Street before building their own facility on Houston Street in 1924.

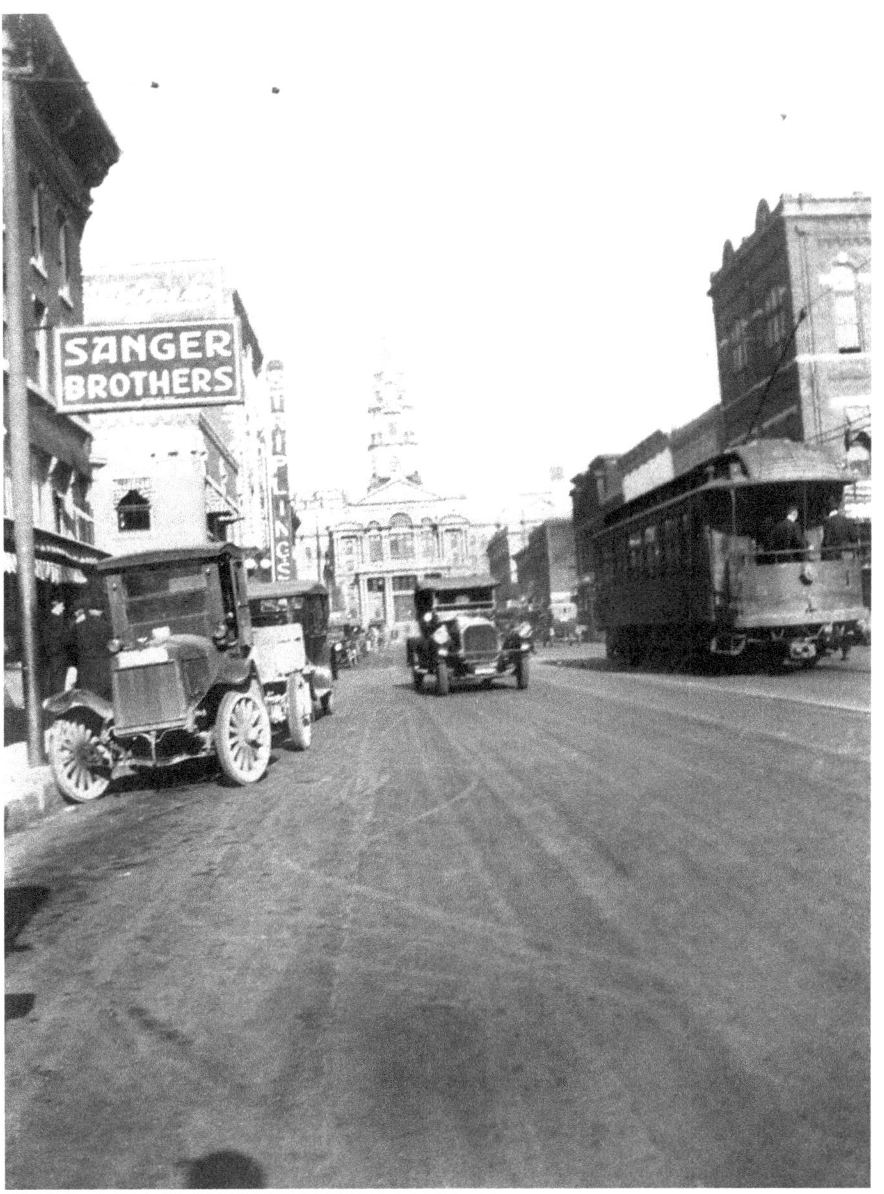

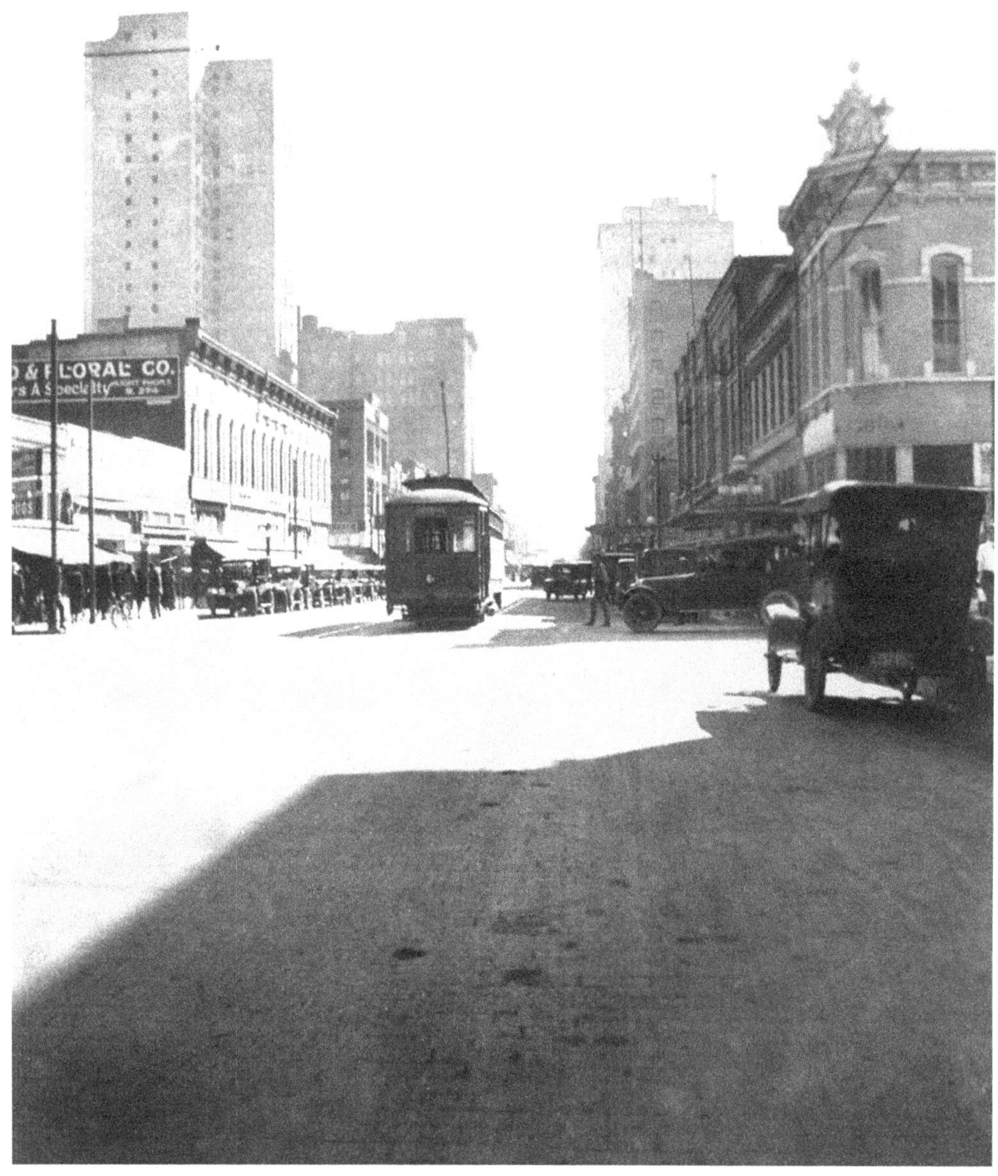


The view of Houston Street looking south from 3rd about 1921 illustrates the tremendous growth around the midtown financial and business center, which was expanding on either side of the 7th Street corridor. The Farmers and Mechanics Bank tower rises at left, with the W. T. Waggoner Building on the west side of the street at 8th. Uptown, closer to the courthouse, remnants of the city's nineteenth-century architecture still dominate the streetscape.

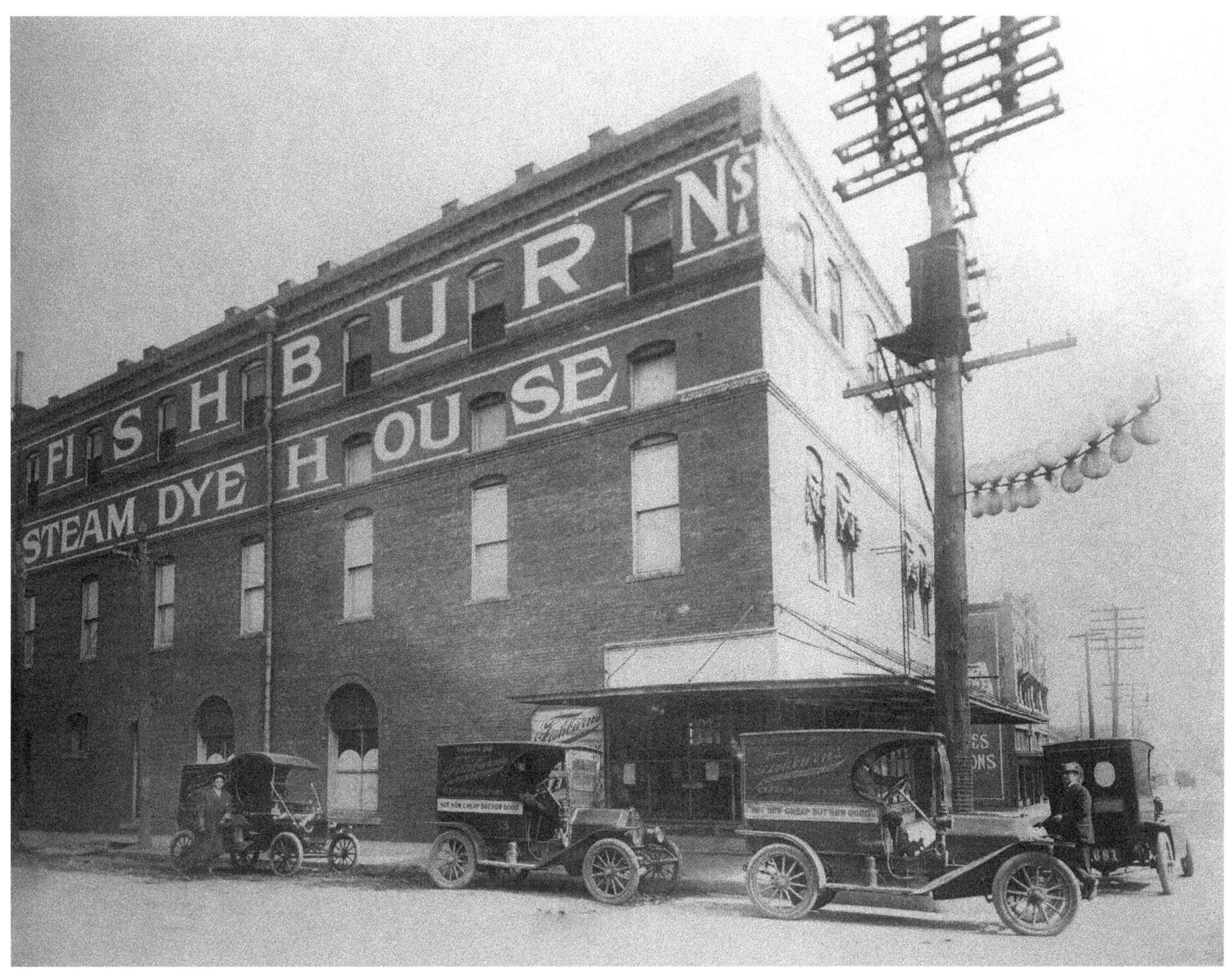


Starting in Dallas in 1901, Fishburn's Steam Laundry expanded to Fort Worth in 1909, opening at 501 Rusk Street, soon to be renamed Commerce Street. Having graduated from horse-drawn delivery wagons, Fishburn's promoted its new automobile delivery with "Service Always in the Lead." The monumental lettering on the building, coupled with internally lighted orbs spelling the company name, extending over the street from the pole at right, allowed the newly established business to promote itself day and night.

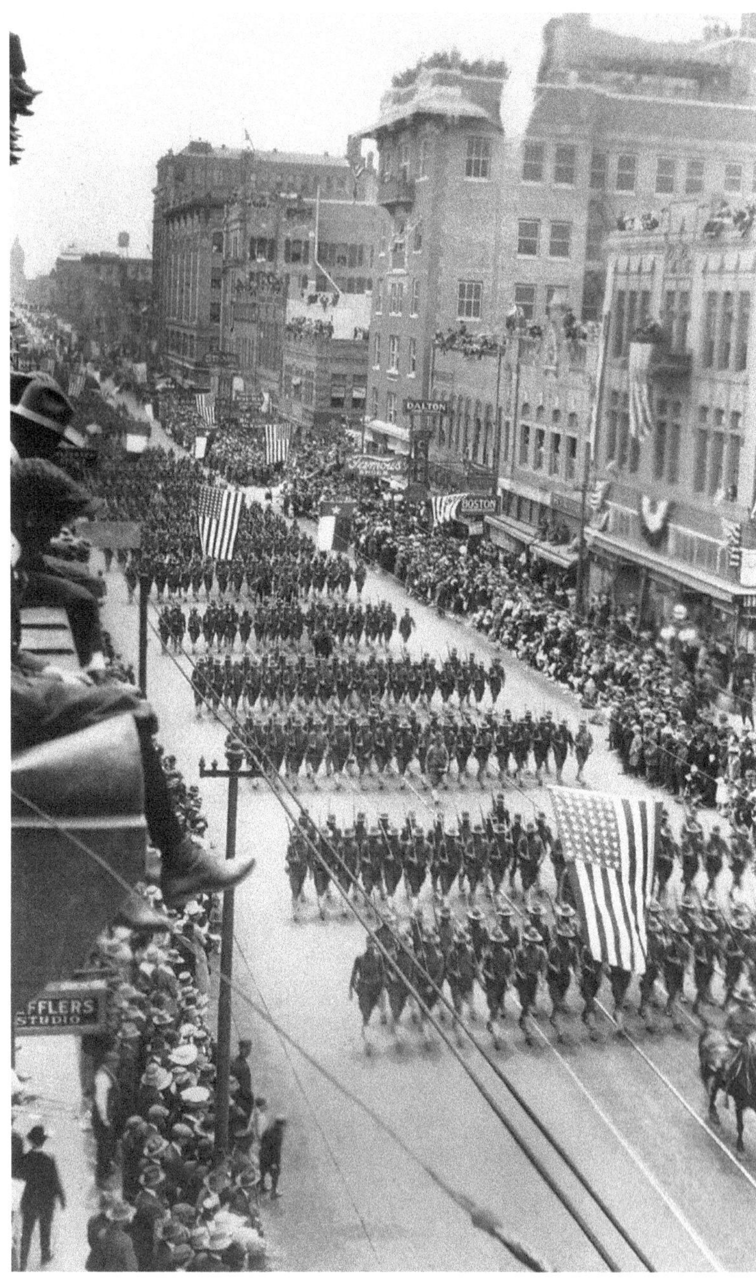


When America entered World War I, Fort Worth rallied to the cause. It was selected in 1917 as the home of Camp Bowie, a sprawling military base built on the city's west side to house and train 100,000 Texas and Oklahoma National Guard soldiers for the 36th Division. Before departing for the war in Europe, the troops staged a massive "Pass in Review" on April 11, 1918. Here, soldiers march up Main Street cheered by a crowd that local accounts say reached 200,000. The 36th became known as the Panther Division, adopted from Fort Worth's nickname, Panther City.

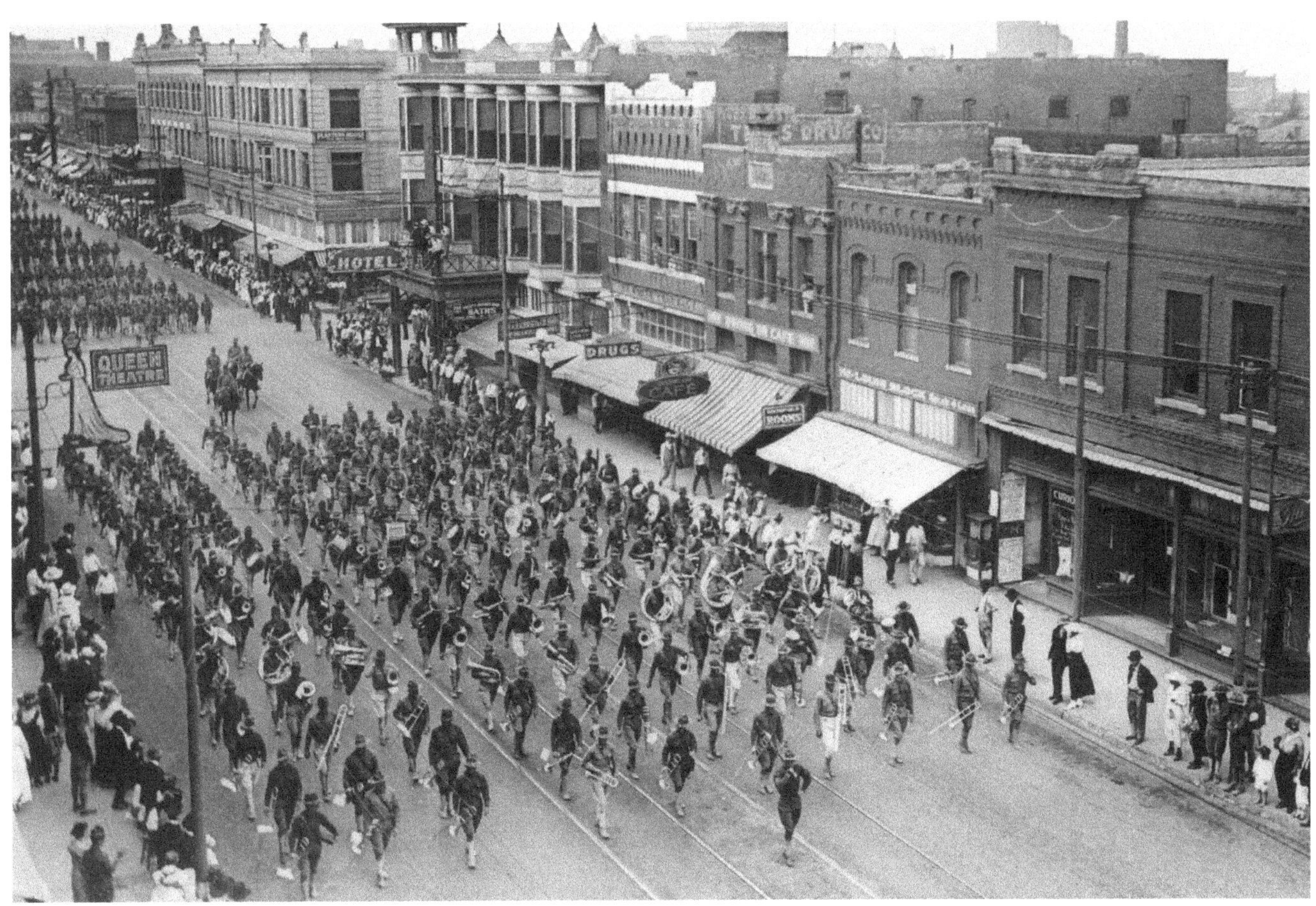


Before Camp Bowie officially closed after World War I, Fort Worth hosted another parade for the troops stationed there. Marching south on lower Main Street in June 1919, the Camp Bowie Band leads the column. The street and other infrastructure improvements made by the Army for the camp served to jump-start development of the west side following the war.

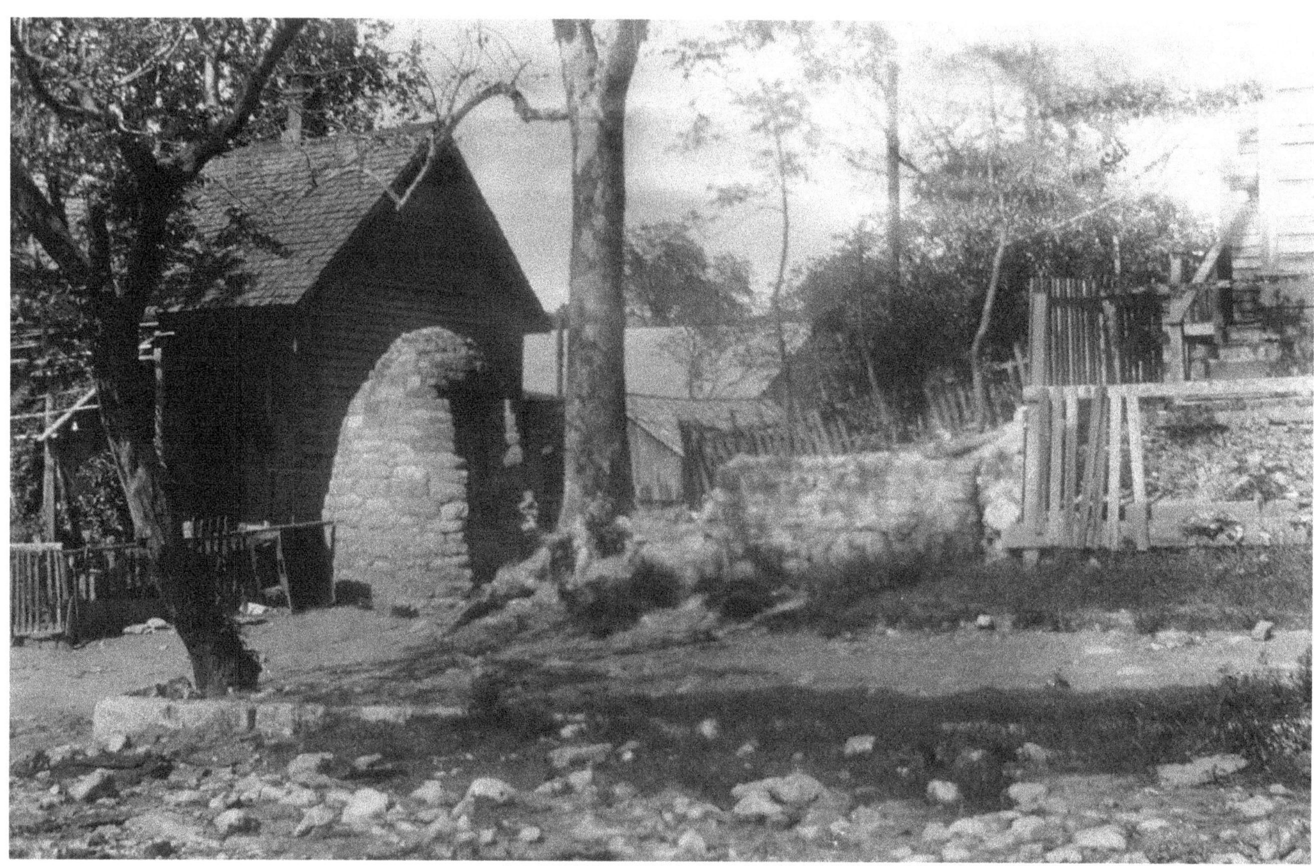

As soon as the soldiers and civilians began to settle in and around the army post in 1849, they dug several wells to provide fresher and safer water than was often available from the Trinity River. The "Frenchman's Well," near the intersection of Bluff and Taylor streets, may have been built by early resident Adolphus Gouhenant, whose talents in art, music and language made him a popular member of the tiny frontier community. Not long after this picture was taken around 1925, the beehive-shaped well was dismantled. It was reconstructed for a time on the courthouse grounds before its stones were moved to a west side residence.

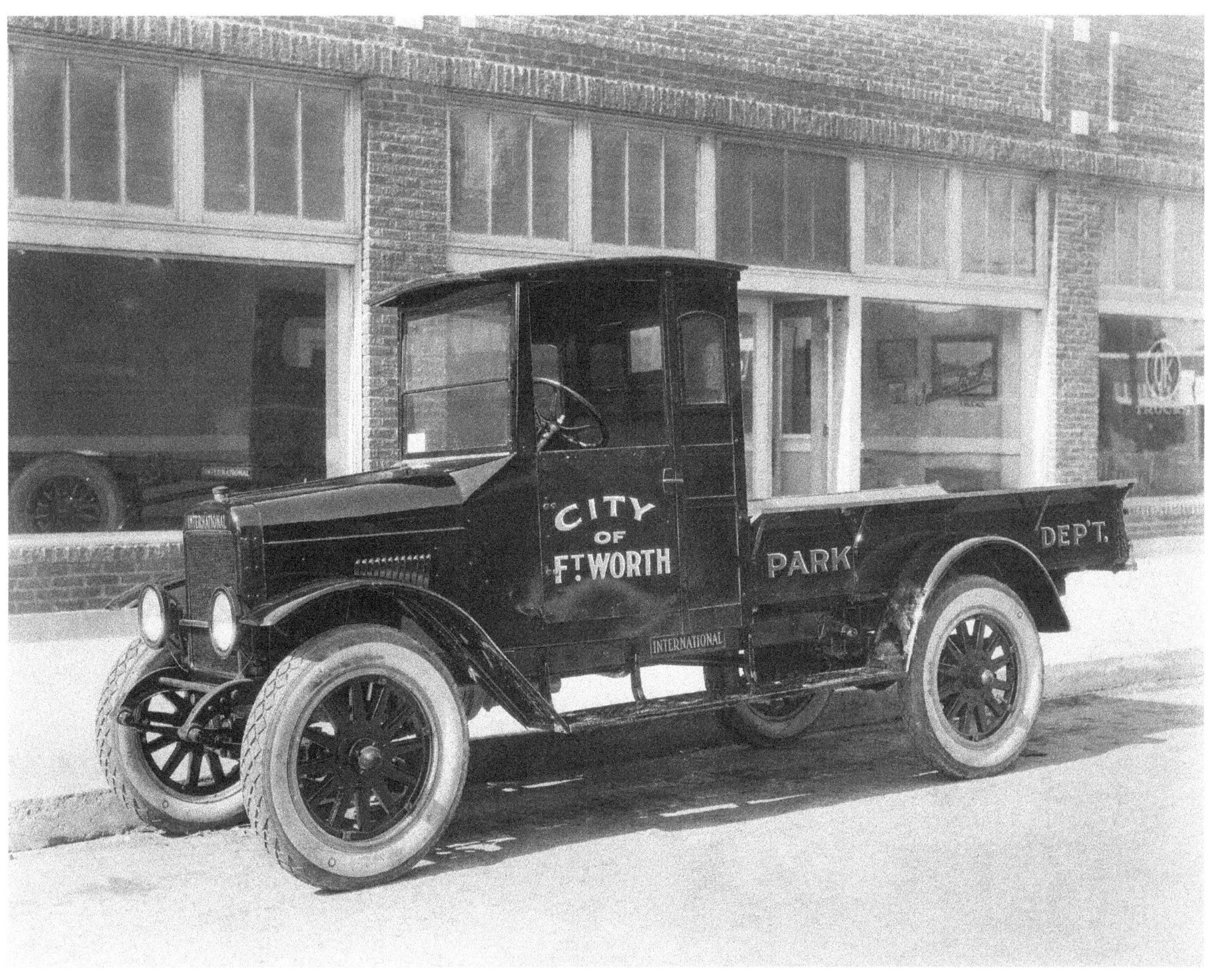


Fort Worth's first Park Board convened in 1907, but struggled for adequate funding during its early years. The local Rotary Club, under the leadership of one of its founders, Harry Adams, raised money to pay for park acquisition and support the development of the Park Department, including purchasing equipment like a new International truck.

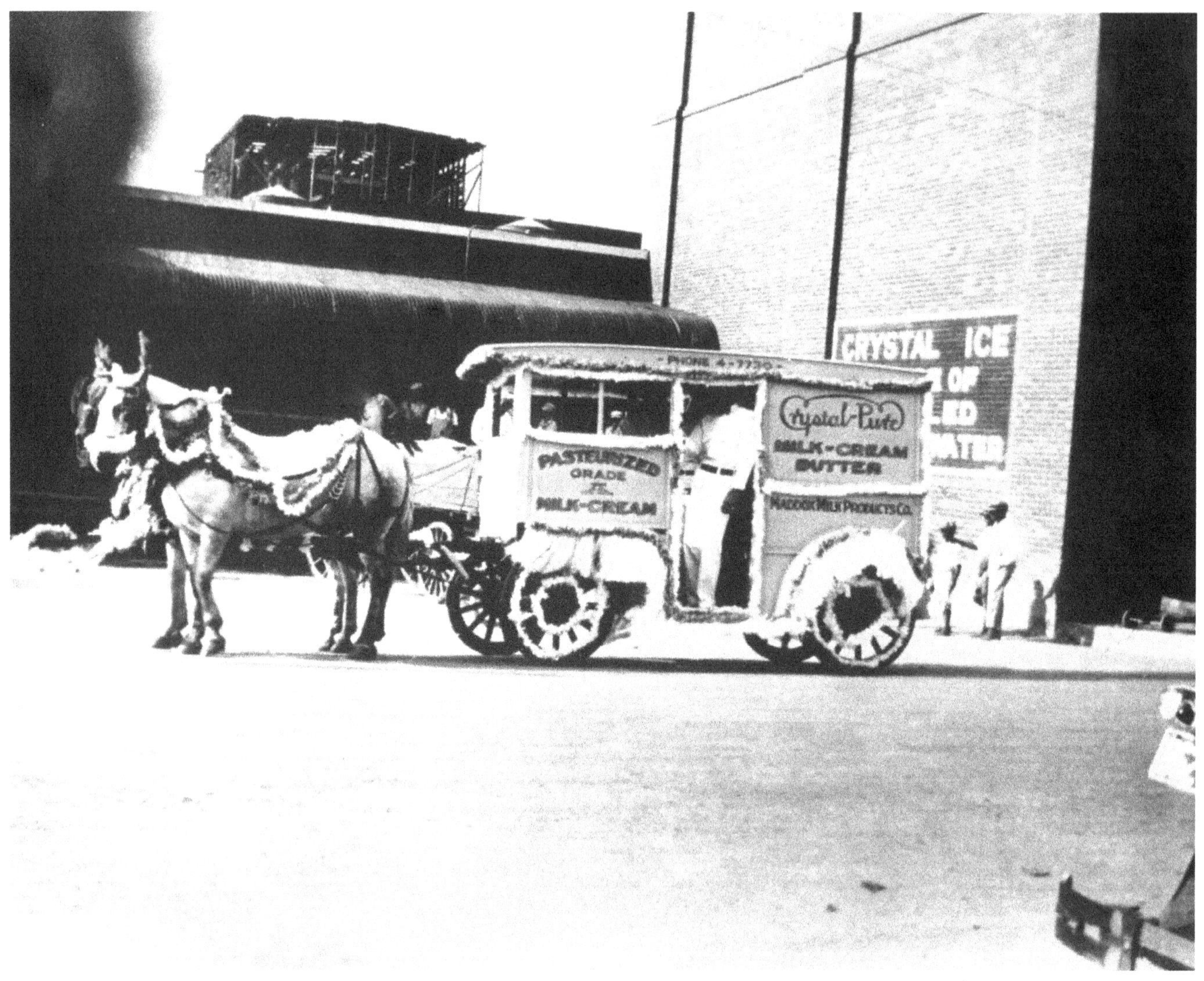


Fort Worth's Crystal-Pure Dairies continued to use horse-drawn delivery wagons well into the 1920s, and then again during the gas-rationed years of World War II. Decorated here for a parade, the wagon may have just picked up its supply of ice from the Crystal Ice Company, one of the first businesses to produce ice for the city, starting in 1887.

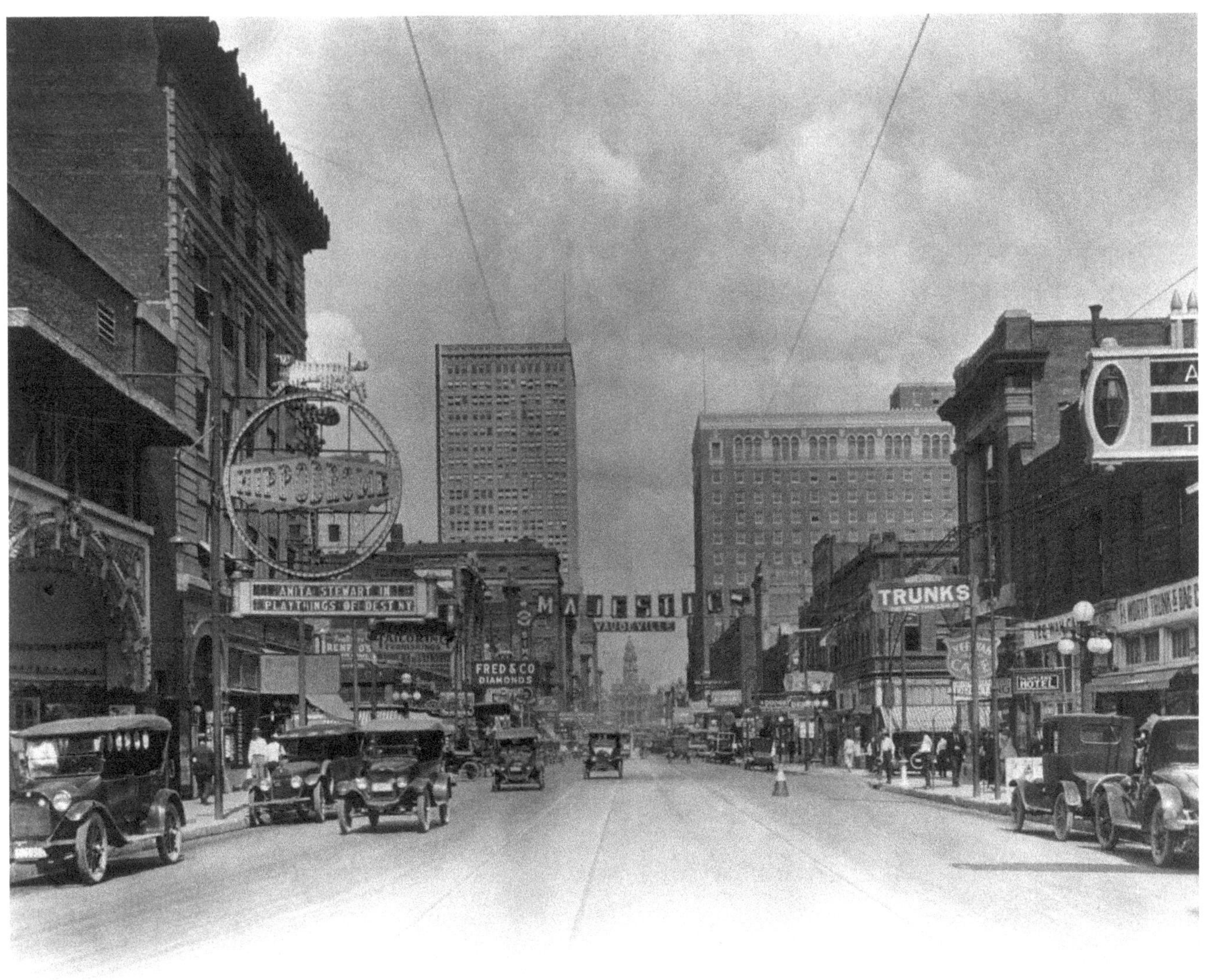


The view north on Main Street from 11th in 1921 illustrates the changing times for local theaters. While the Majestic advertises its vaudeville fair with a huge banner across the street, the Hippodrome, at left, features a first-run silent movie melodrama, "Playthings of Destiny." A decade later, the Majestic itself would be converted to a movie house and end live performances.

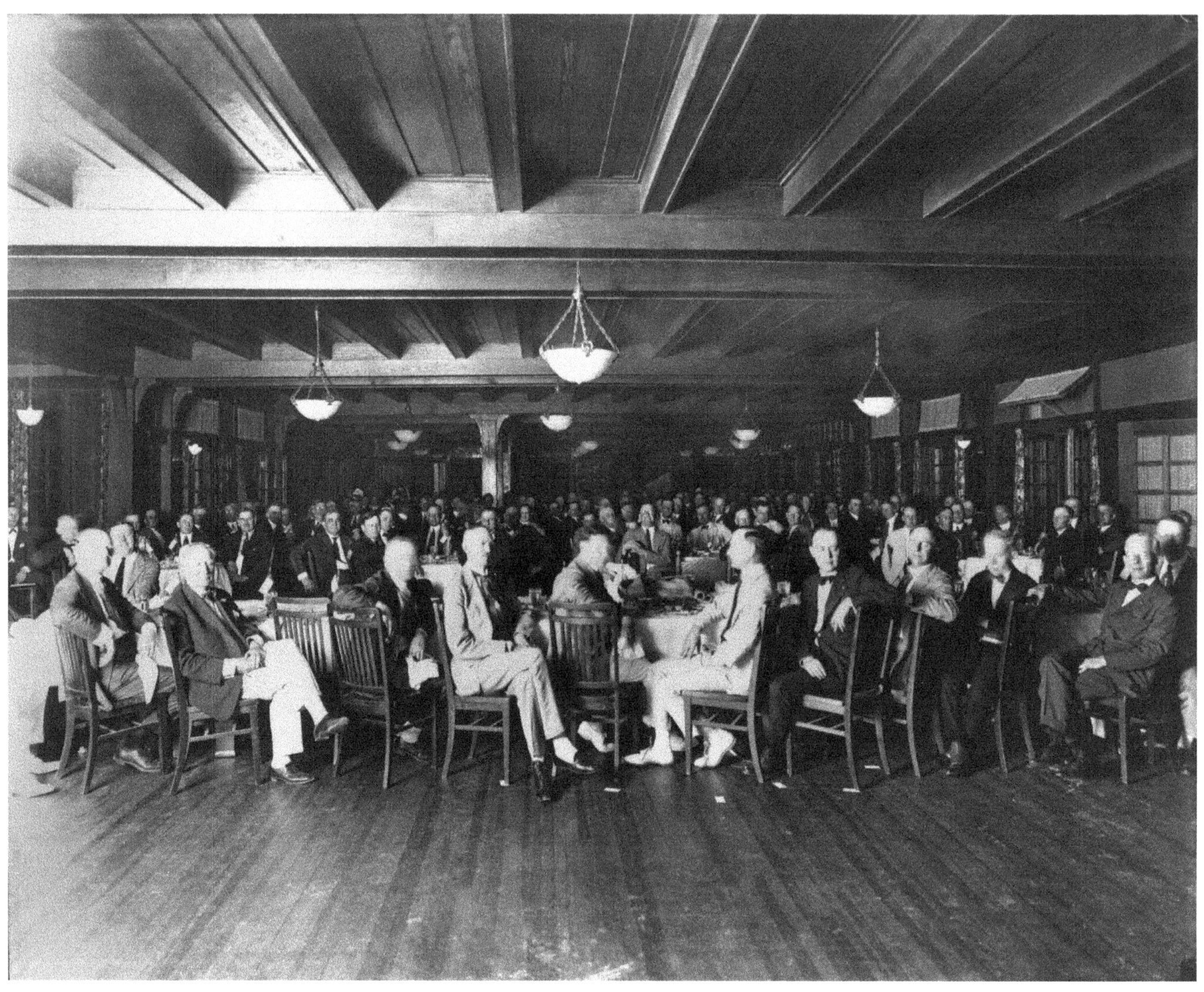

At the time the staff of the Fort Worth *Star-Telegram* sat for this photograph about 1920, the paper served more than eighty Texas counties and proudly boasted on its masthead, "Fort Worth—Where the West Begins." Owner and Publisher Amon G. Carter was one of the most influential local leaders of the twentieth century, promoting his city and all of West Texas to the world.

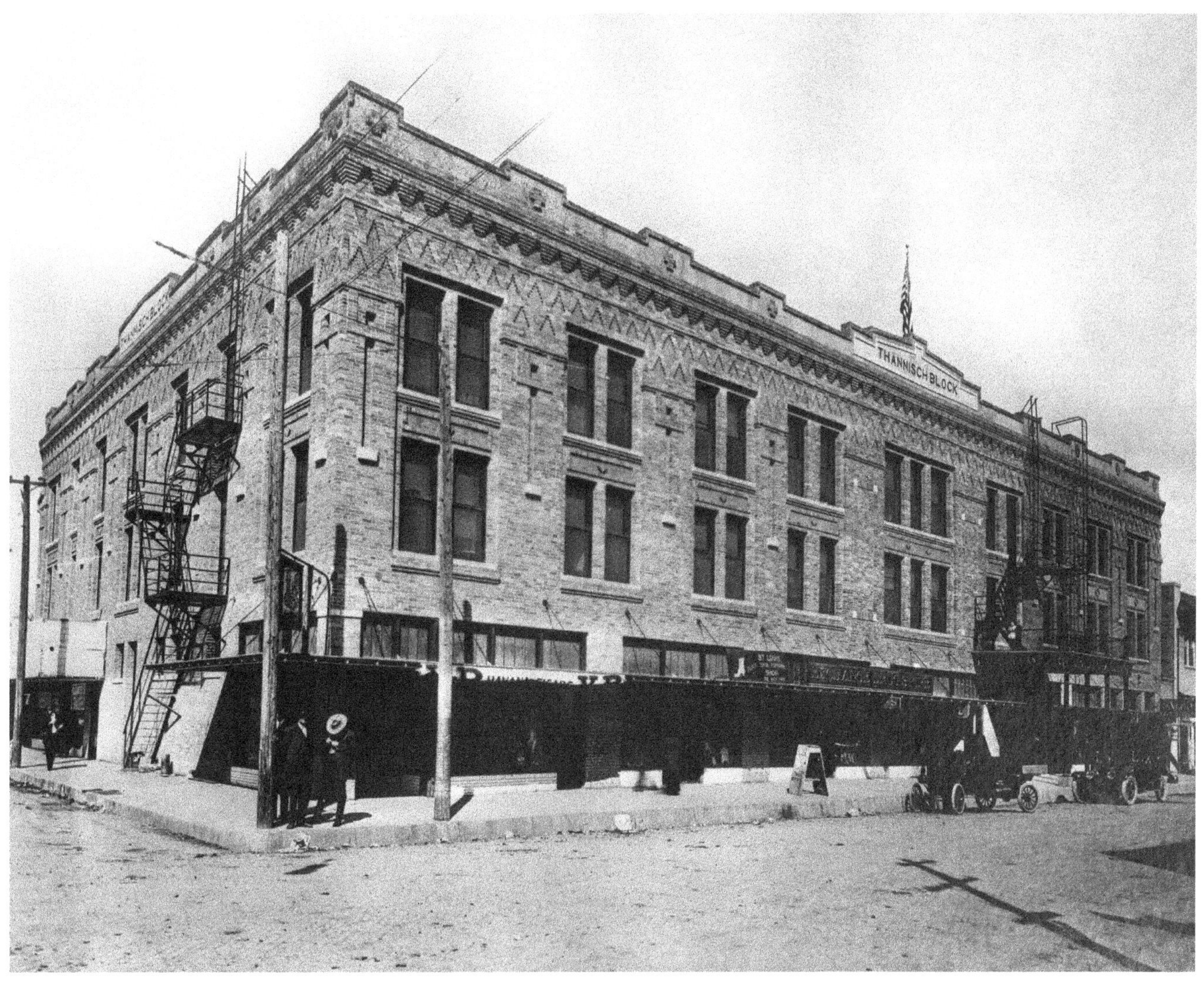


To meet the growing demands for space in the Stockyards following the opening of Swift and Armour, Colonel C. M. Thannisch demolished his Stock Yards Club hotel and office building at North Main and Exchange in 1906 and built the Thannisch Block. It featured expanded lodging rooms and space for new businesses, including the Exchange Drug Store. By the twenties, the building housed the eighty-six room Chandler Hotel.

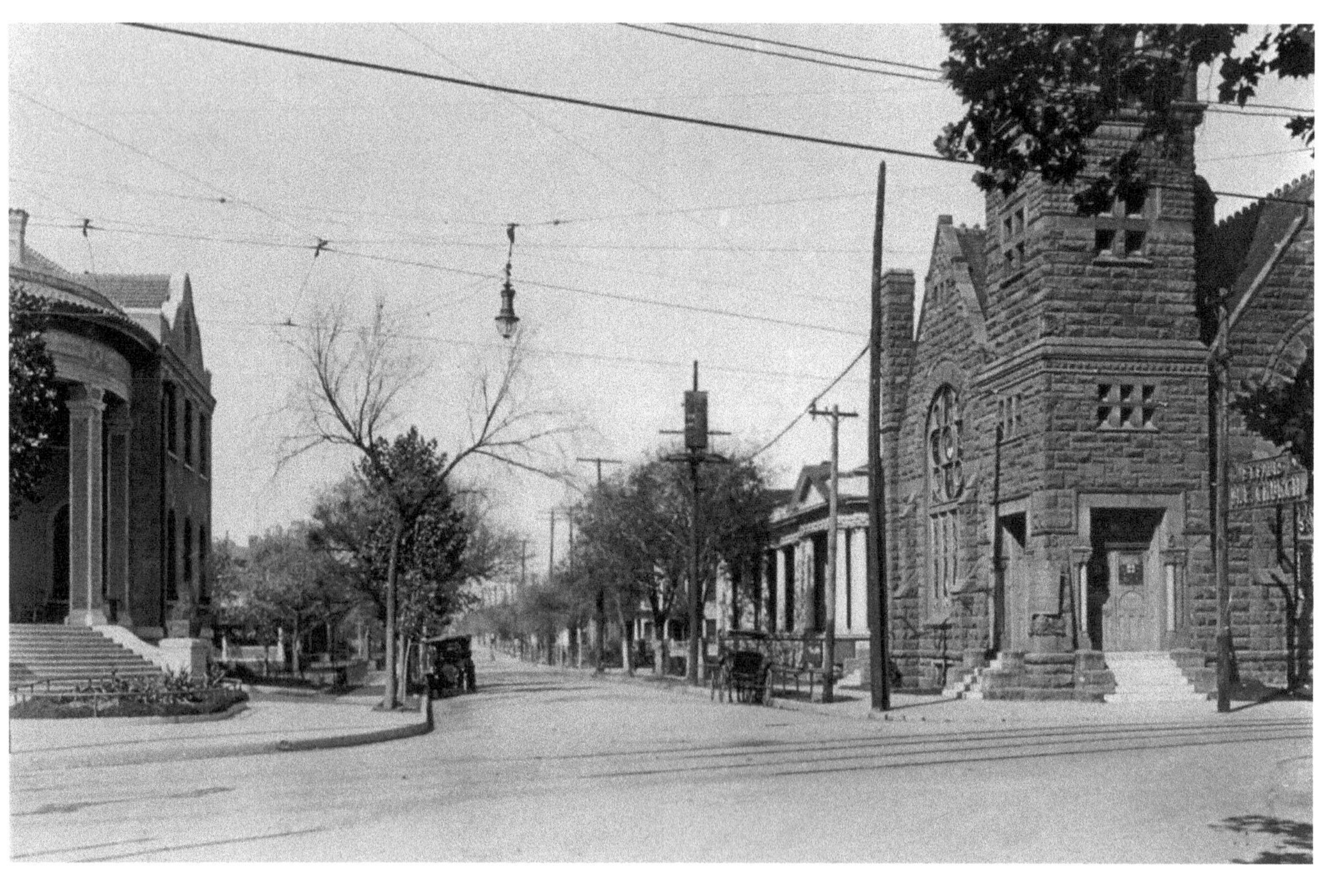

The intersection of 7th and Lamar streets about 1915 marked a neighborhood in transition, as what had been the silk-stocking neighborhood began a shift from residential to commercial use. It was home to some of the city's wealthiest families, including that of Winfield Scott, who owned several of the largest hotels and other buildings in the city. At right is the 1890 sanctuary of the Saint Paul Methodist Episcopal Church, replaced in 1929 by the Electric Building. The 1910 clubhouse of the Fort Worth Elks Lodge stands at left. Between them hangs one of the city's early electric street lights.

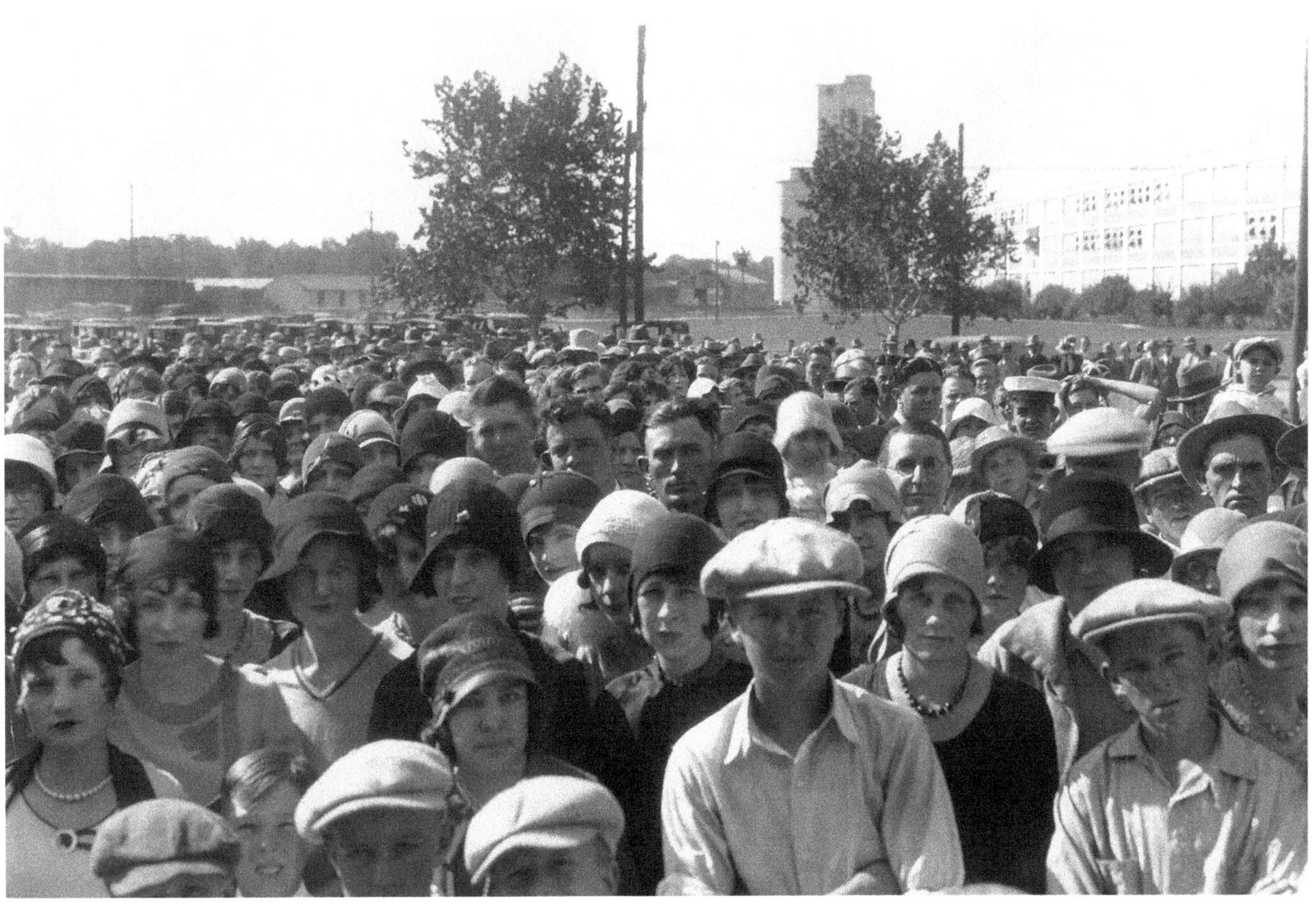

Eager customers crowded the front door of the new Montgomery Ward store on West 7th Street on its first day of business in 1928. In the background, at top right, is the massive assembly plant built and used by Chevrolet from 1915-22, and which Wards occupied until it moved into its new building across the street. Left of the assembly plant was the towering elevator complex of the E. G. Rall Grain Co., built in 1913. Both complexes were demolished in the 1980s.

Montgomery Ward stock boys were issued roller skates to maneuver around the eight-story, 300,000-square-foot warehouse in order to meet demands of its mail-order department. The store closed in 2001, reemerging in 2006 as Montgomery Plaza, a mixed-use development with loft apartments.

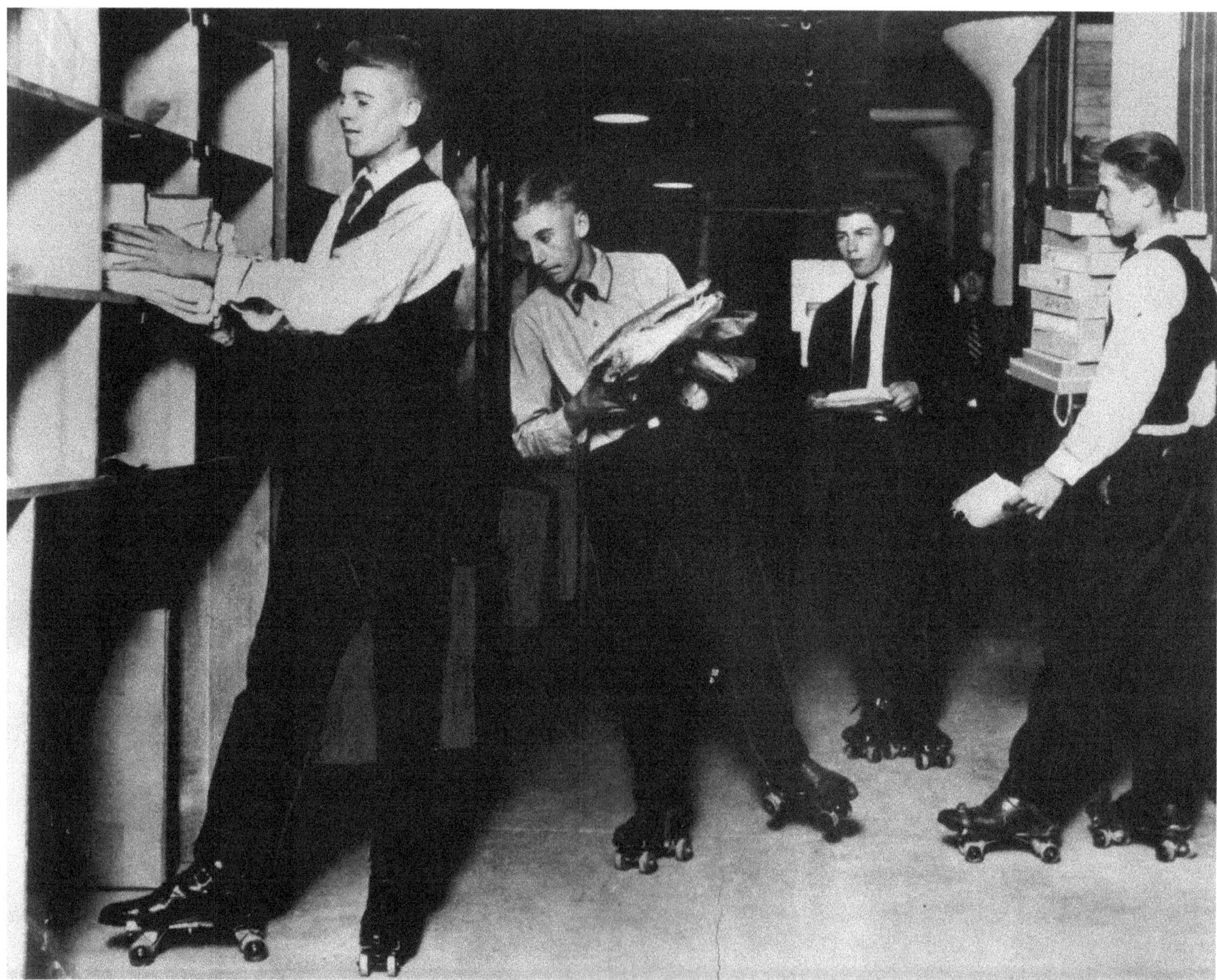

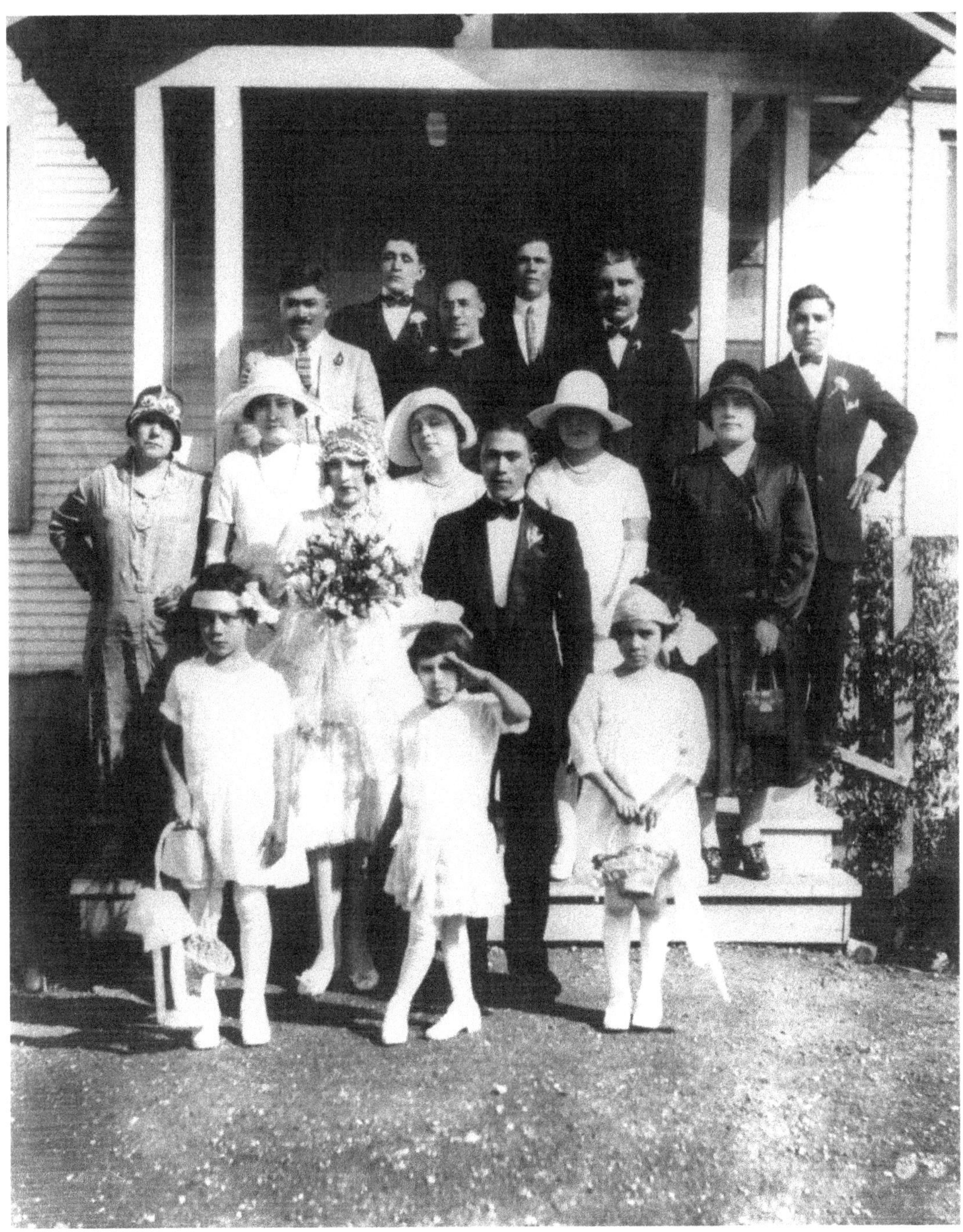

Margarito Padilla left his native San Luis Potosi, Mexico, to escape the dangers of the revolution that began there in 1910. He found work at Swift & Co. in the Stockyards, then the city's largest employer, where he remained until he retired in the 1960s. On November 28, 1926, he married Maria P. Felan, daughter of a South Texas family, at the old San Jose Church on North Calhoun Street. Together they raised a family that continues to help shape the future of the city.

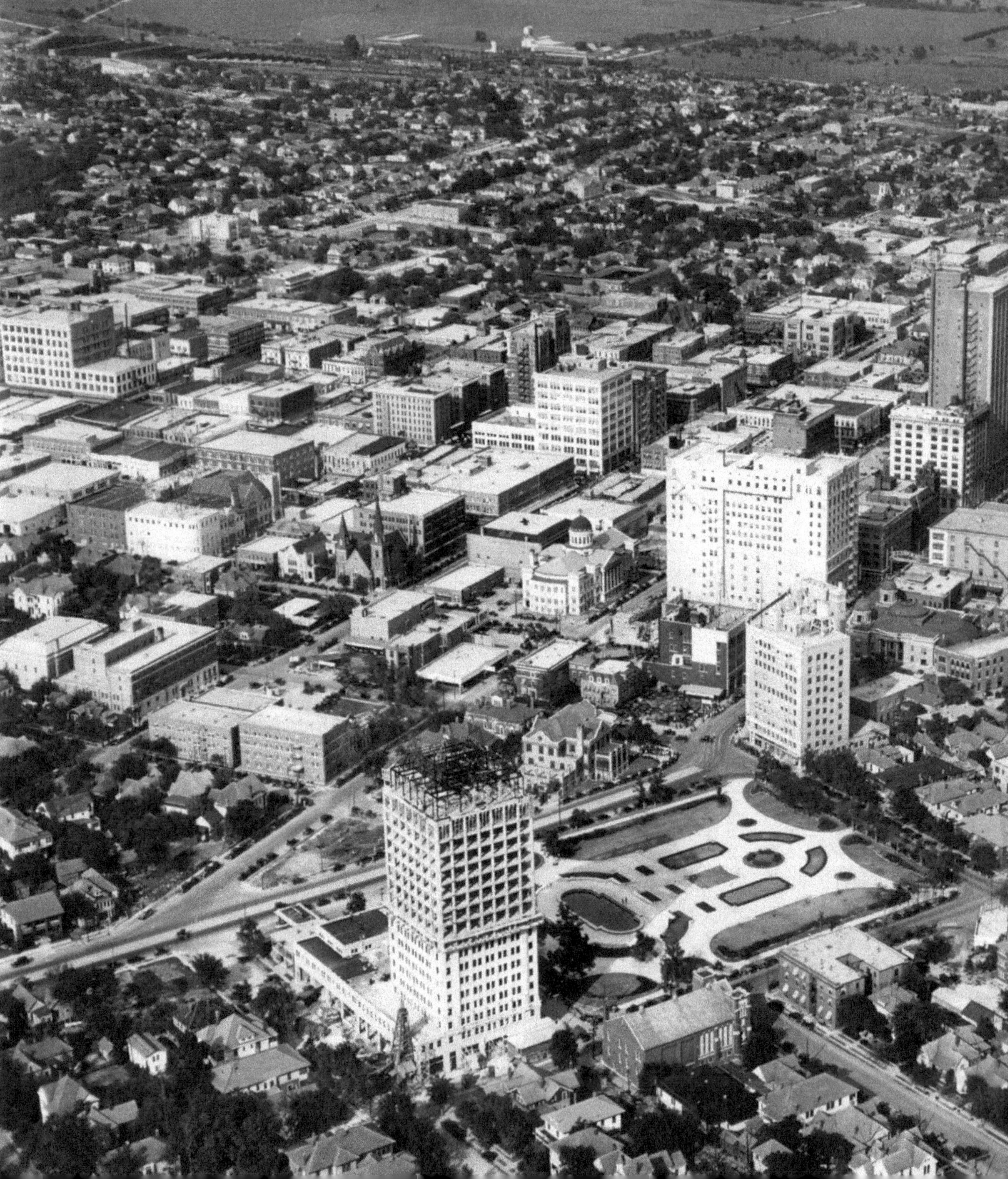

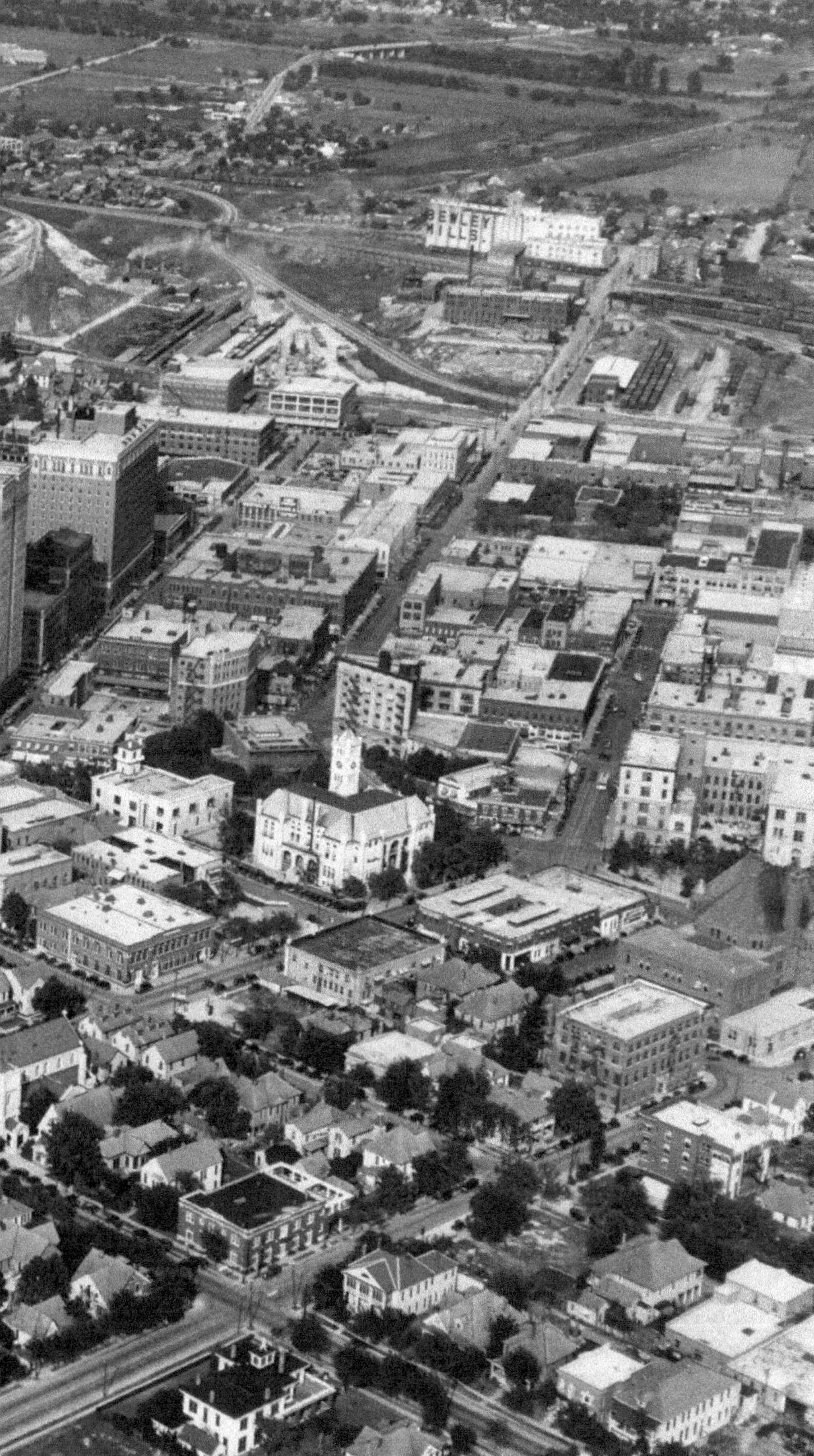


This aerial view of downtown, taken October 6, 1926, shows the Medical Arts Building still under construction at lower left, with residential neighborhoods to its south and west. Just above Burnett Park stands the Elks Lodge and, to its right, the empty lot on which the Electric Building would be built in 1930.

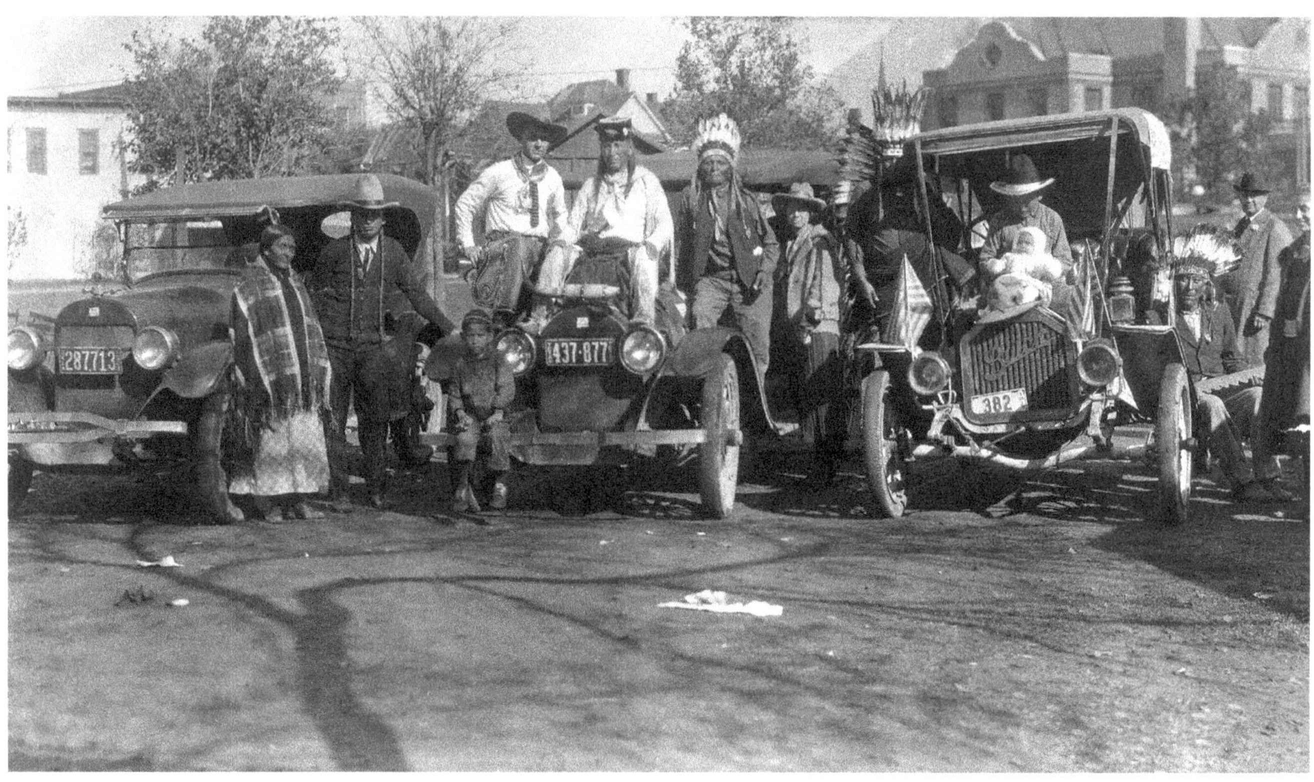

Taken in Burnett Park sometime in the mid-twenties, this photograph by Roy Jernigan is believed to show a group of relatives of Comanche Chief Quanah Parker. They may have been in town to participate in the annual Stock Show Parade. Before Parker's death in 1911, he had been a frequent visitor to Fort Worth. His descendants continue their active involvement in city activities. The Elks Club building, at top right, was on the corner of Lamar and 7th streets.

R. O. Dulaney announced plans for his new office building on the northwest corner of 5th and Main streets just weeks prior to the 1929 stock market crash. Designed by Wiley Clarkson in the zigzag *moderne* style, the Art Deco masterpiece replaced the 1904 Fort Worth National Bank Building. Dulaney secured the Sinclair Oil Company as his major tenant, and the building has carried the Sinclair name ever since. It was restored in 1984.

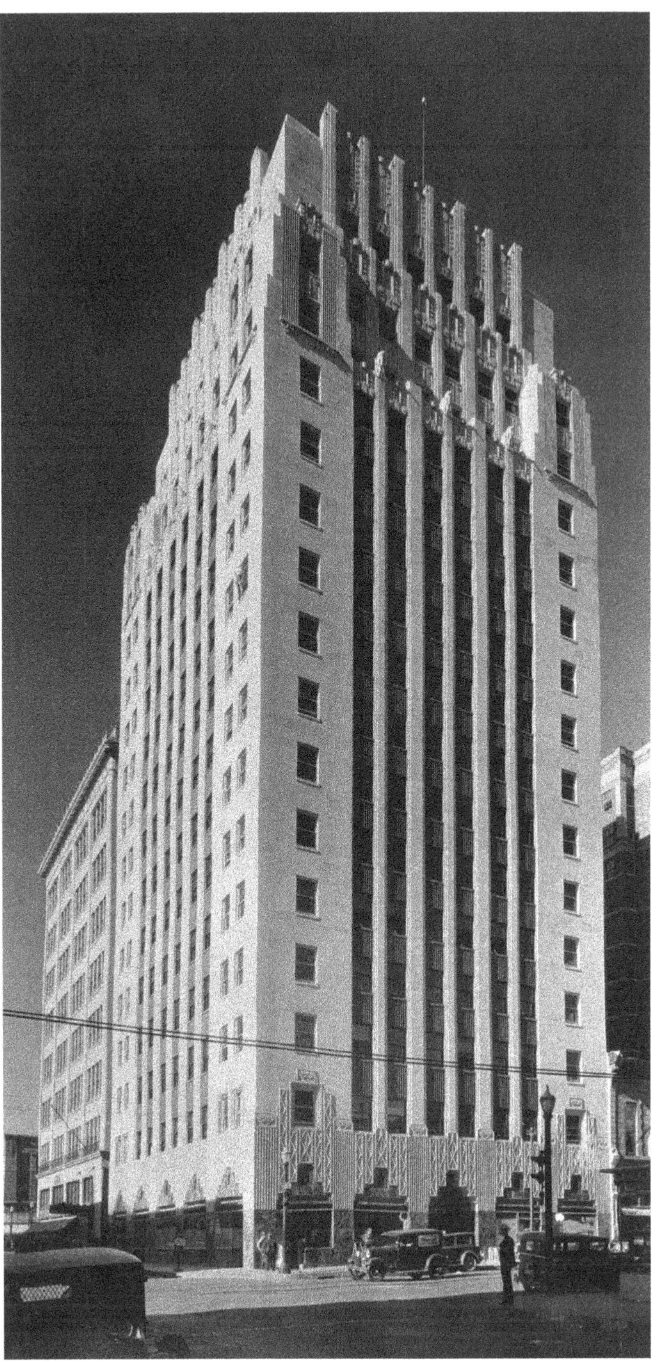

Starting in the late twenties, Fort Worth began a massive street improvement program, working with the T&P Railroad to improve rail crossings at the south end of Downtown before turning attention to other areas. By January 1934, construction was well underway on a new overpass on Belknap Street, east of Downtown, allowing motorists to safely drive over the ever-expanding rail tracks surrounding the city.

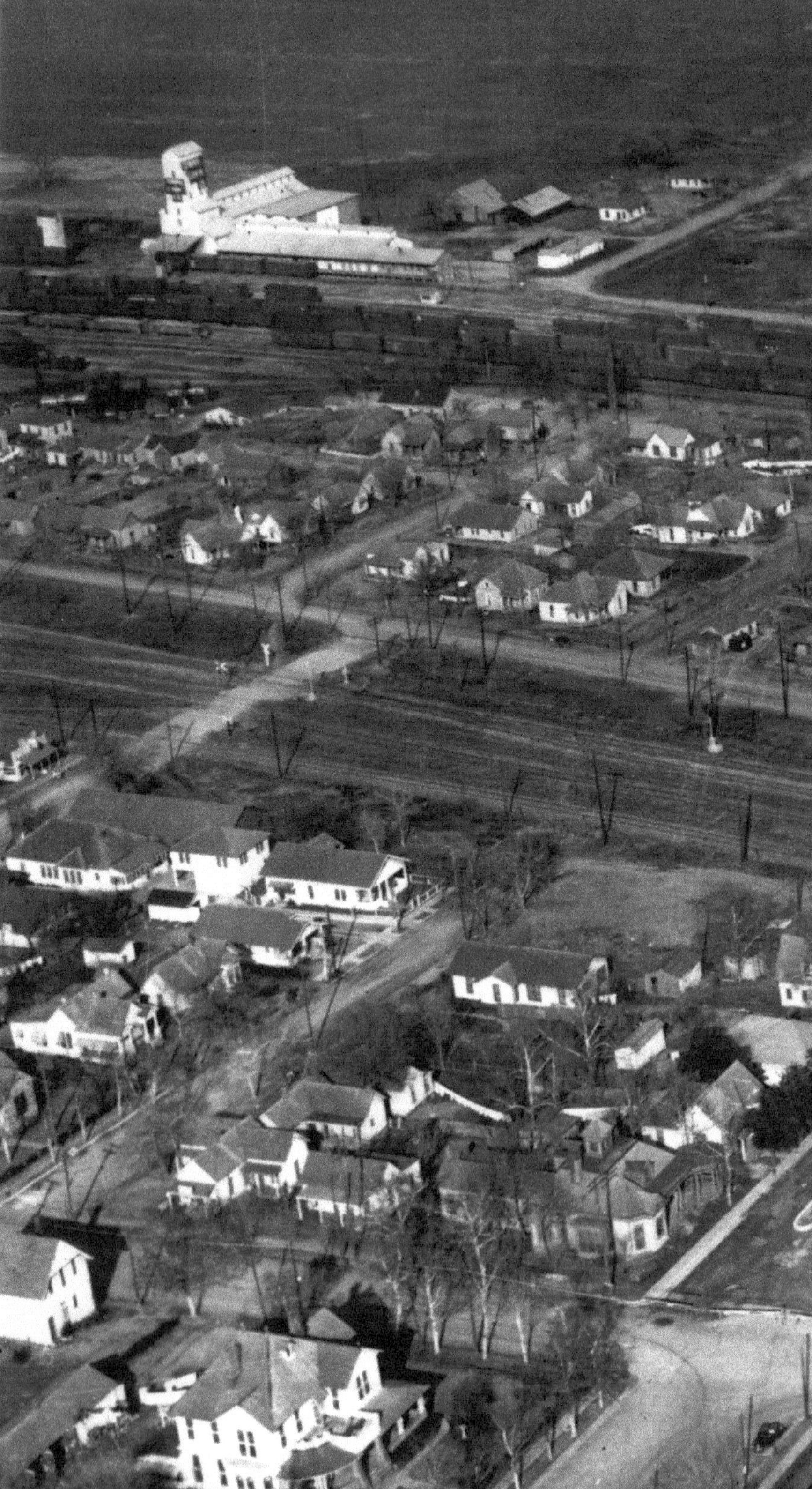

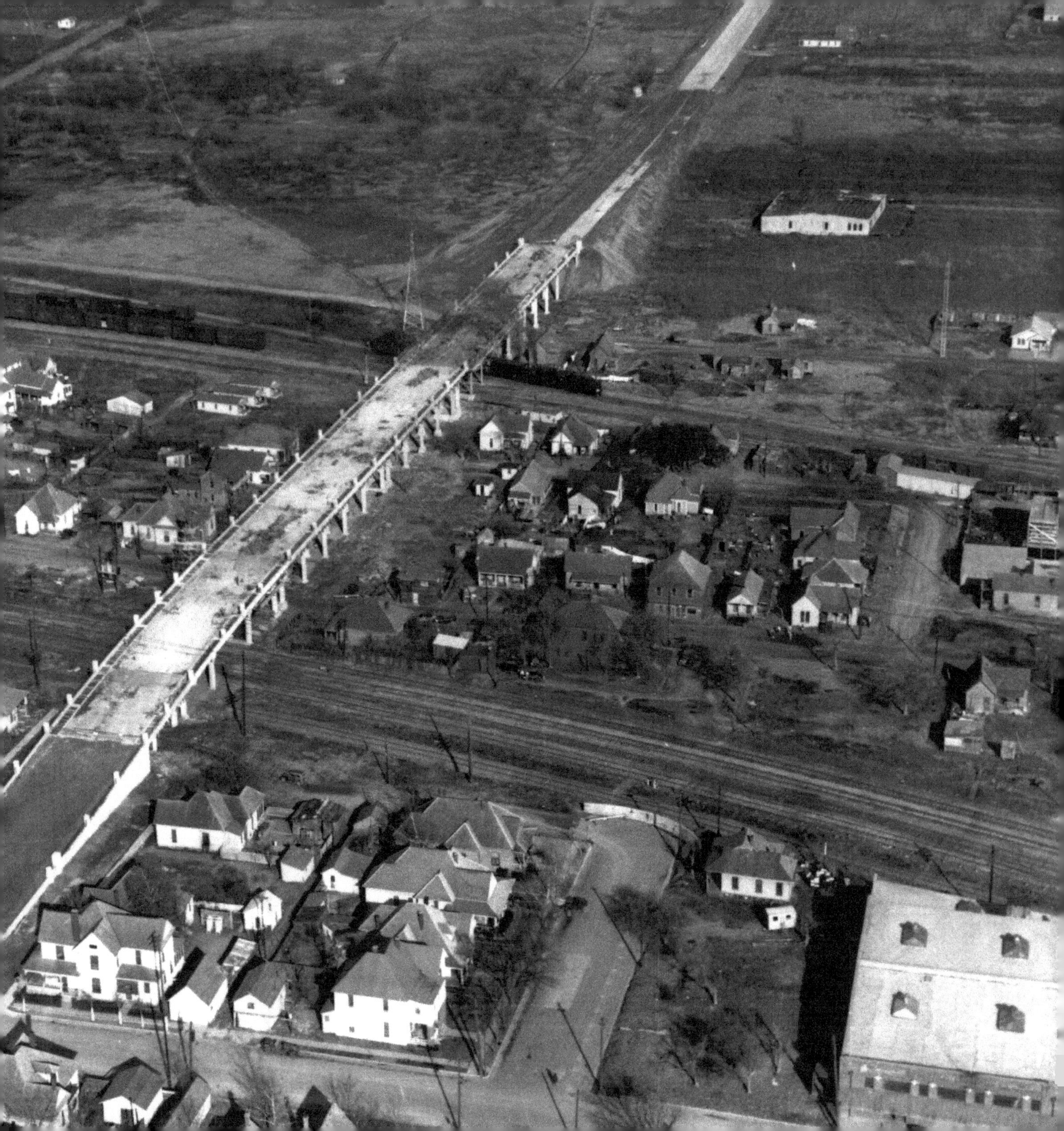

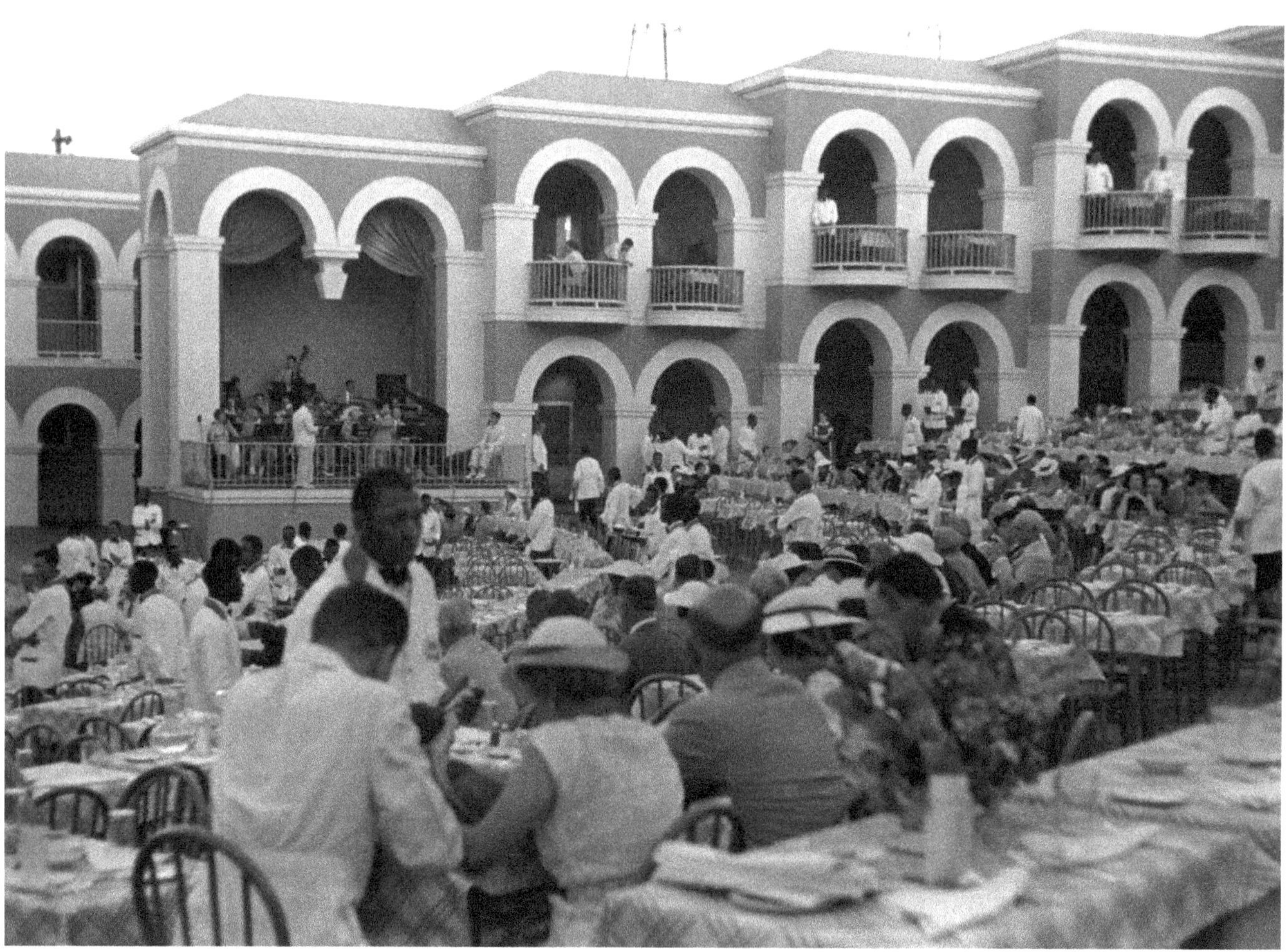

The highlight of 1936 in Fort Worth was the opening of the Casa Manana amphitheater, the star of the Frontier Centennial celebrating Texas's 100th anniversary of independence from Mexico. Through one of the hottest summers on record, people crowded the 4,000 seat open-air theater to enjoy the music of Paul Whiteman and watch a spectacular show produced by Broadway's Billy Rose.

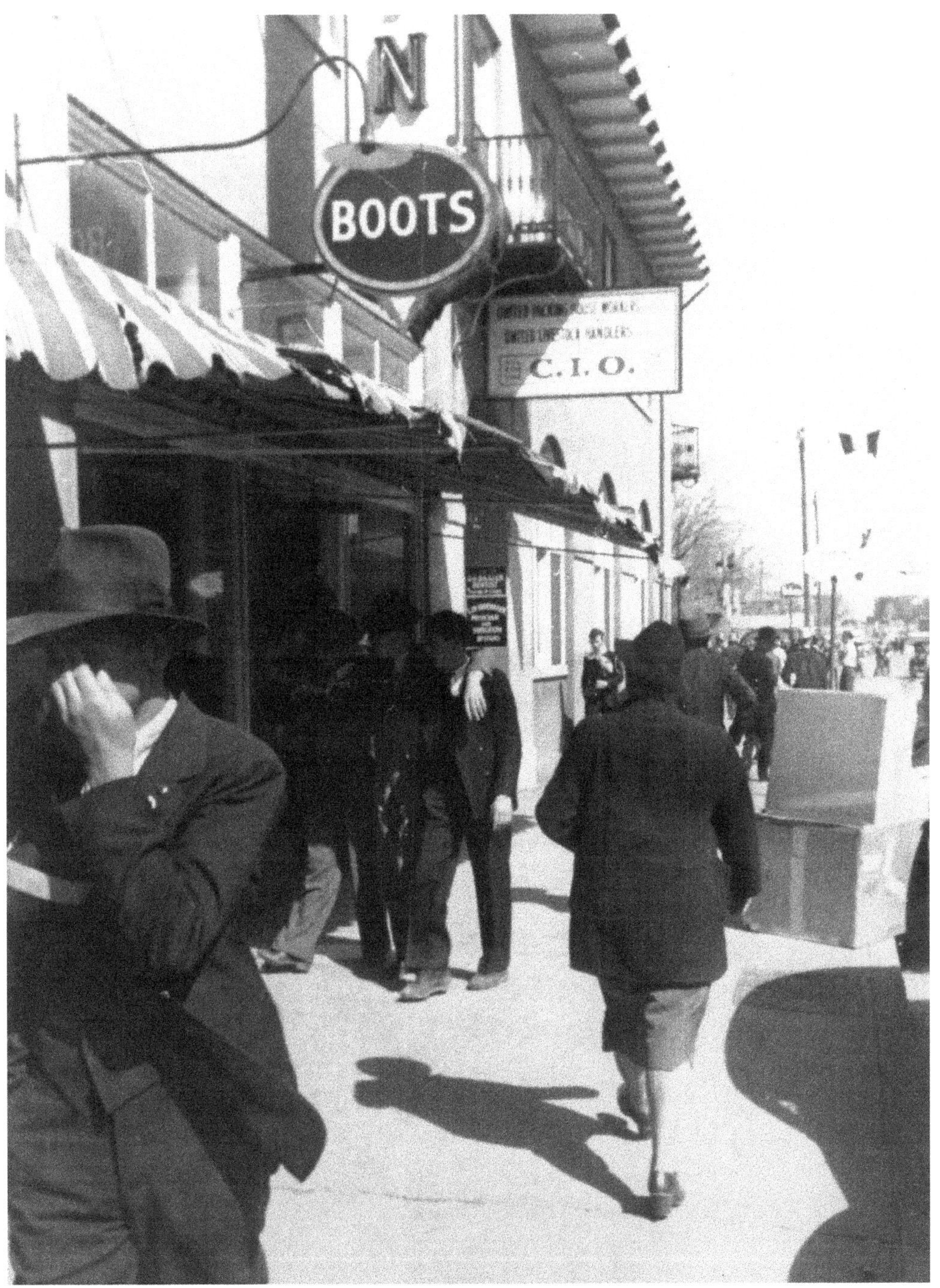


Visitors to the 1936 Stock Show walk past the White Front Store on West Exchange Avenue, around the corner from the Coliseum. The annual show expanded for the Texas Centennial and included more women riders and contestants than ever before. With more than 30,000 spectators crowding into the Stockyards facilities each day, show leaders feared that the North Side location might be getting too small to safely host the event. Some of the show activities were moved to the new Will Rogers complex, but Stockyards promoters figured the show would be back home the following year. They were sorely disappointed when the show made its permanent move to the west side after 1942.

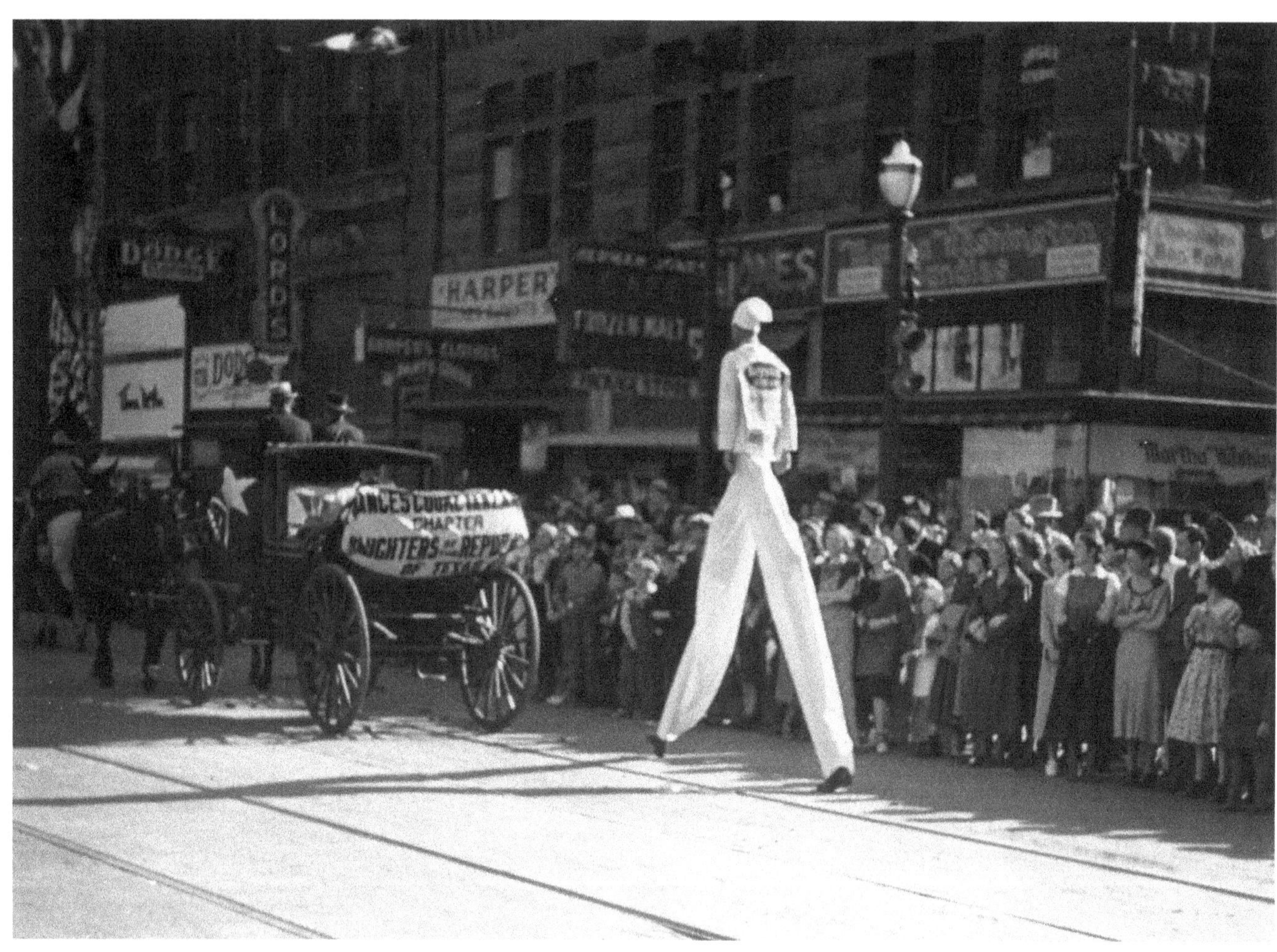


The annual Stock Show parade took on a patriotic theme for the Texas Centennial year and celebrated "the Spirit of the Old West." A few antique automobiles and stilt walkers joined the usual bands and mounted groups on a sunny and warm parade day on March 13, 1936. The year marked the Fort Worth show's recognition by *Time* magazine as the "number three" rodeo in the nation.

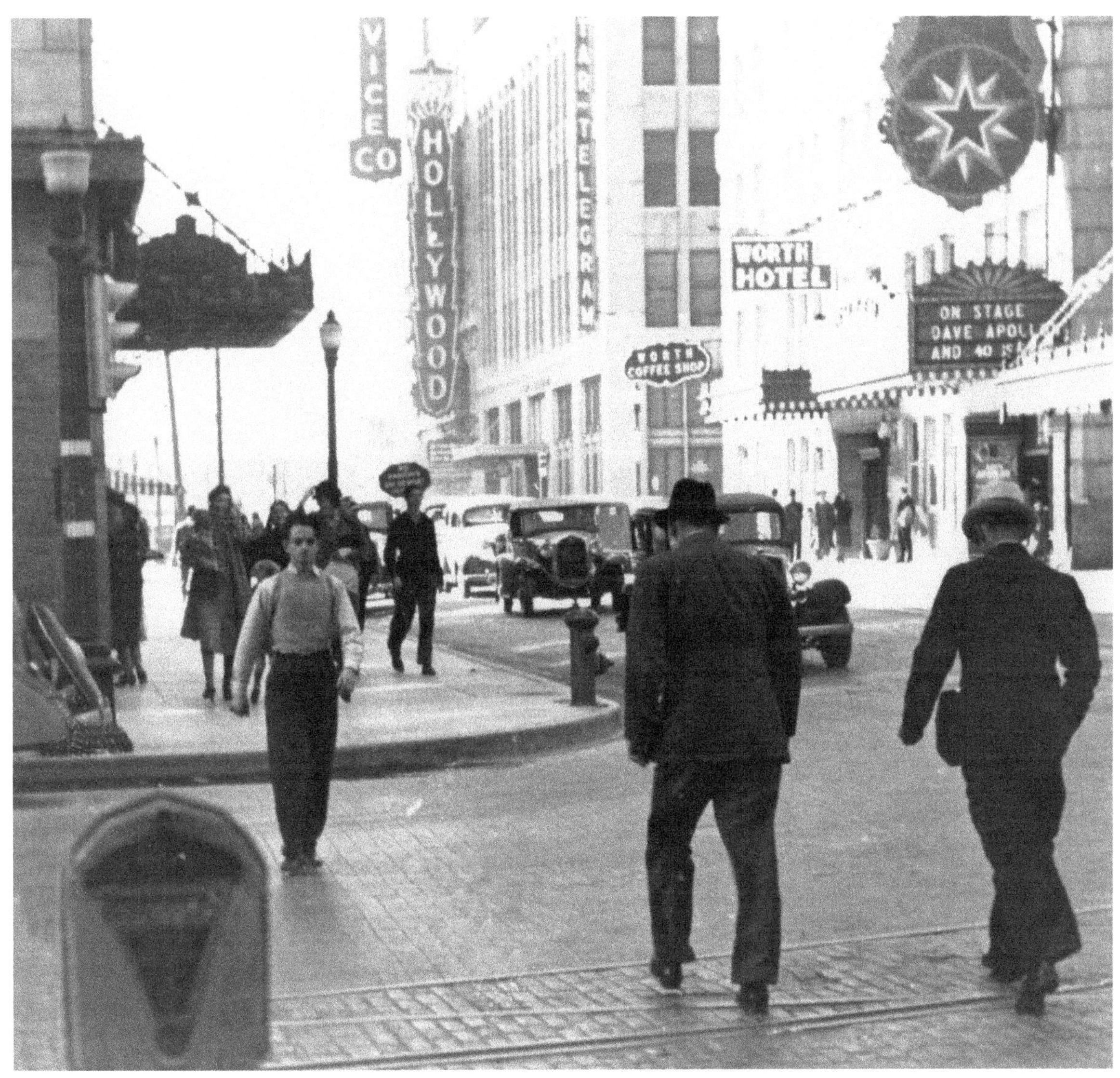


Pedestrians cross the intersection of 7th and Throckmorton streets in 1938. Headlining at the Worth Theatre is Dave Apollon, considered the greatest mandolin player of the twentieth century. He toured the country regularly, including several stops in Fort Worth before settling down to a recording and theatrical career in New York.

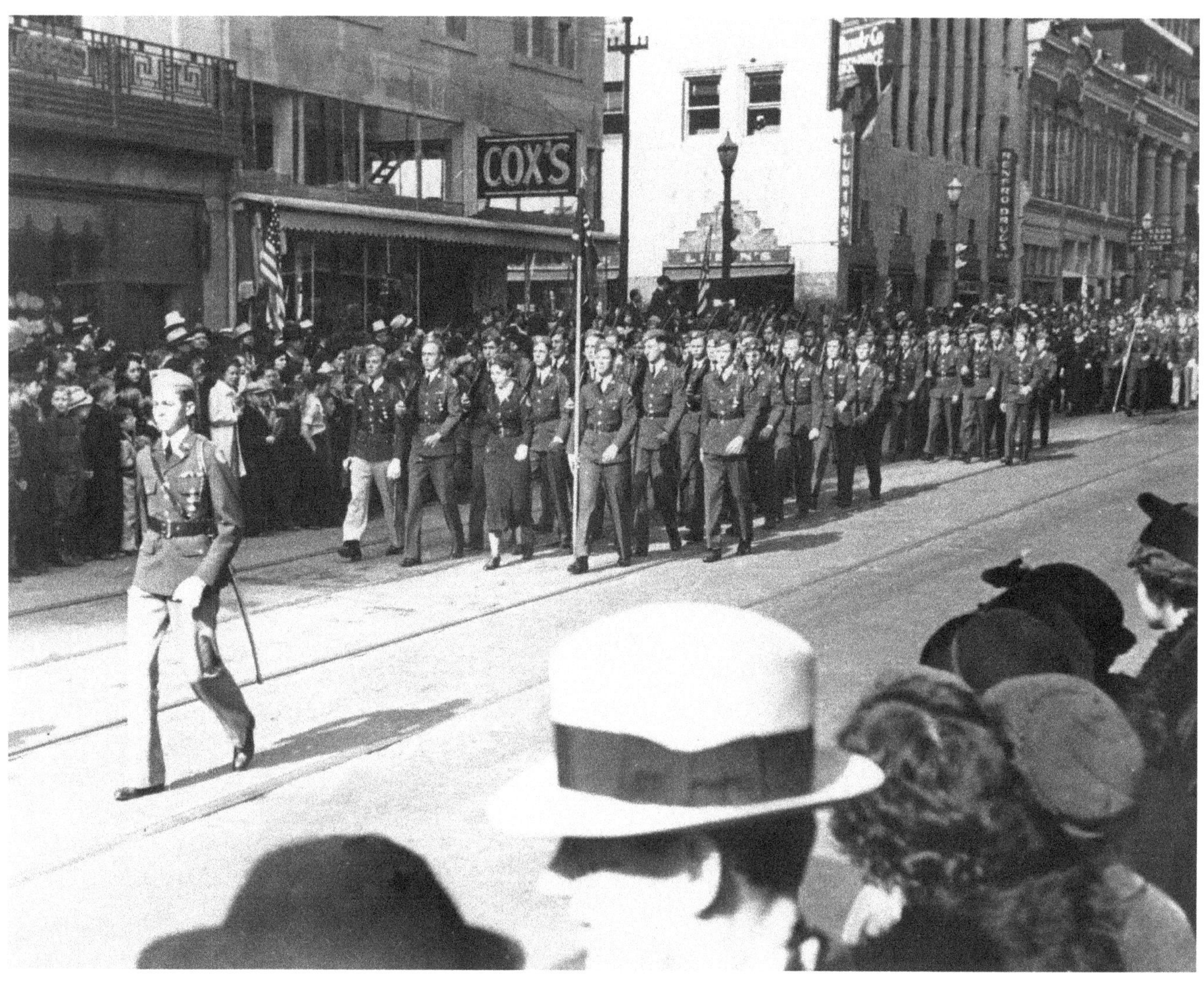


A column marches past the Sinclair Building during the annual Armistice Day Parade on November 11, 1936. Commemorating the cease-fire that marked the end of World War I, the holiday was an important one for Fort Worth, which had supported so many young men as they trained at Camp Bowie between 1917 and 1919.

A lone veteran of the First World War, identified as Charles L. Stowe, "Soldier, Politician, Publisher, etc." marches along Main Street during an Armistice Day parade honoring the service of his fellow soldiers from the 36th Division.

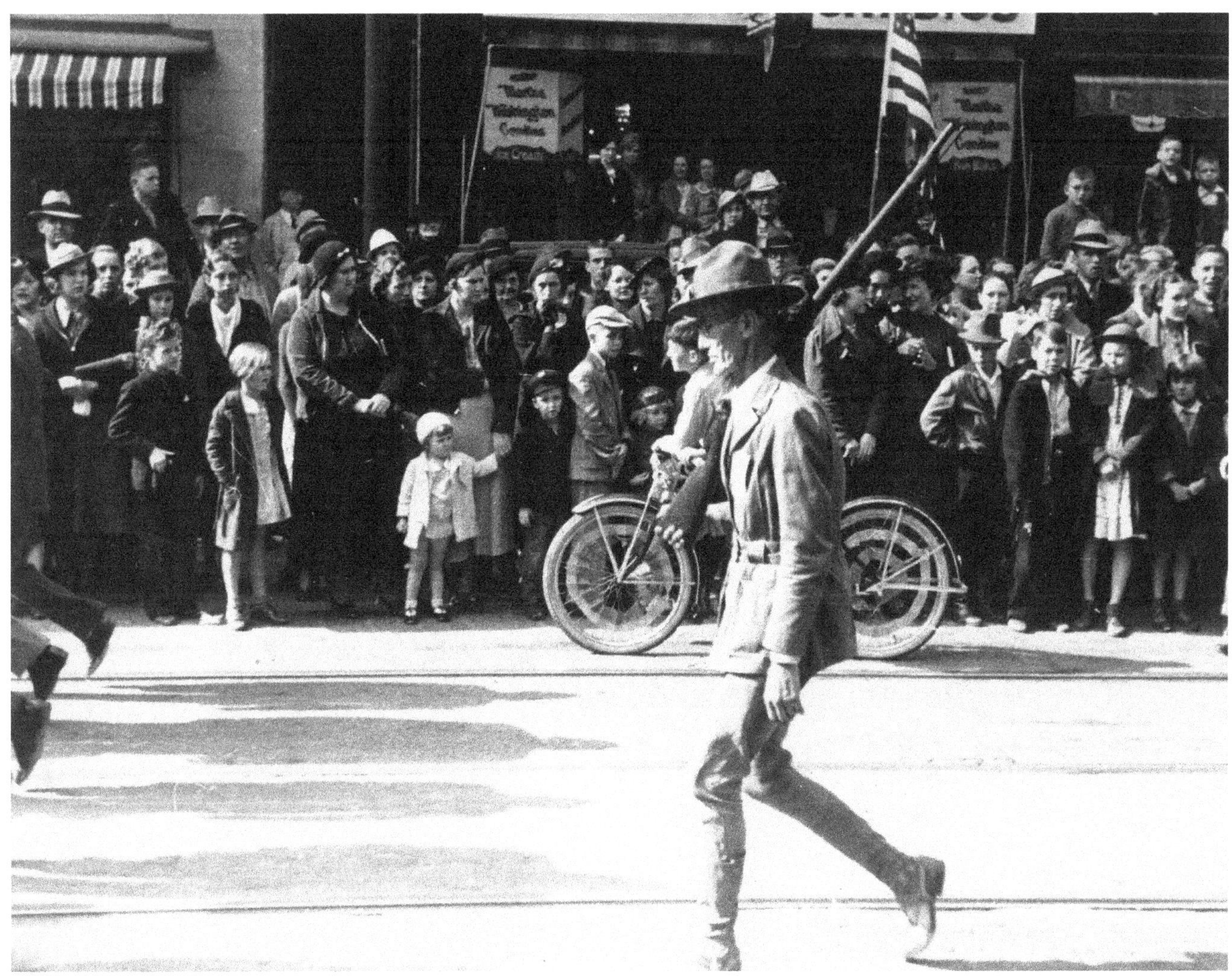

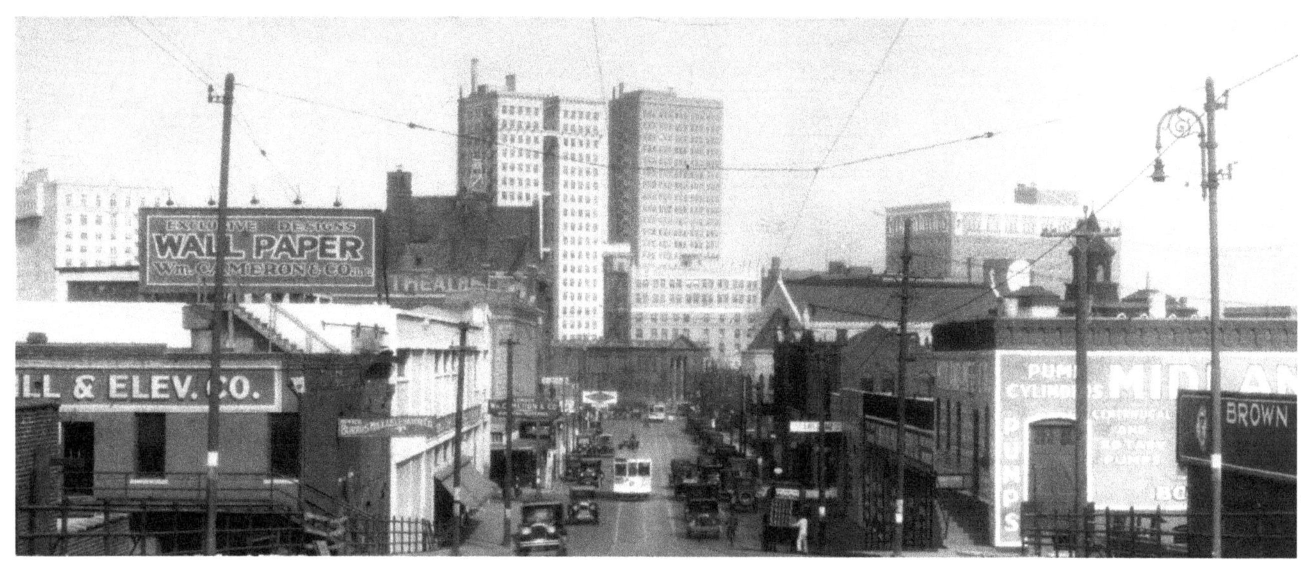


The Jennings Avenue viaduct provides a commanding view looking north toward the Carnegie Library in 1931. The next year, the viaduct was demolished and replaced with an underpass as part of the street and rail-crossing improvements jointly undertaken by the city and the T&P Railroad. The city was so grateful for the railroad's financial partnership that Front Street was renamed in honor of John L. Lancaster, the company president at the time.

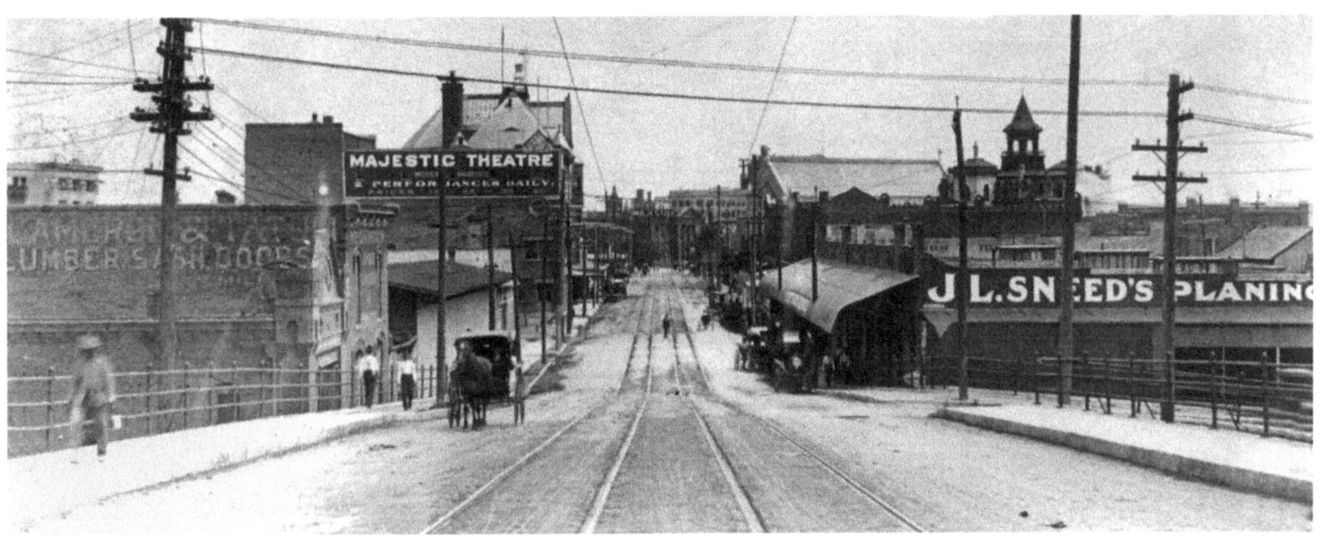


The same view from the Jennings viaduct as the preceding page, but taken over twenty-five years earlier, before the perfection of elevators allowed for the construction of high-rise buildings. The distinctive 1889 St. Ignatius Academy, and behind it St. Patrick Cathedral, remain today as benchmarks of the city's growth and progress over the years.

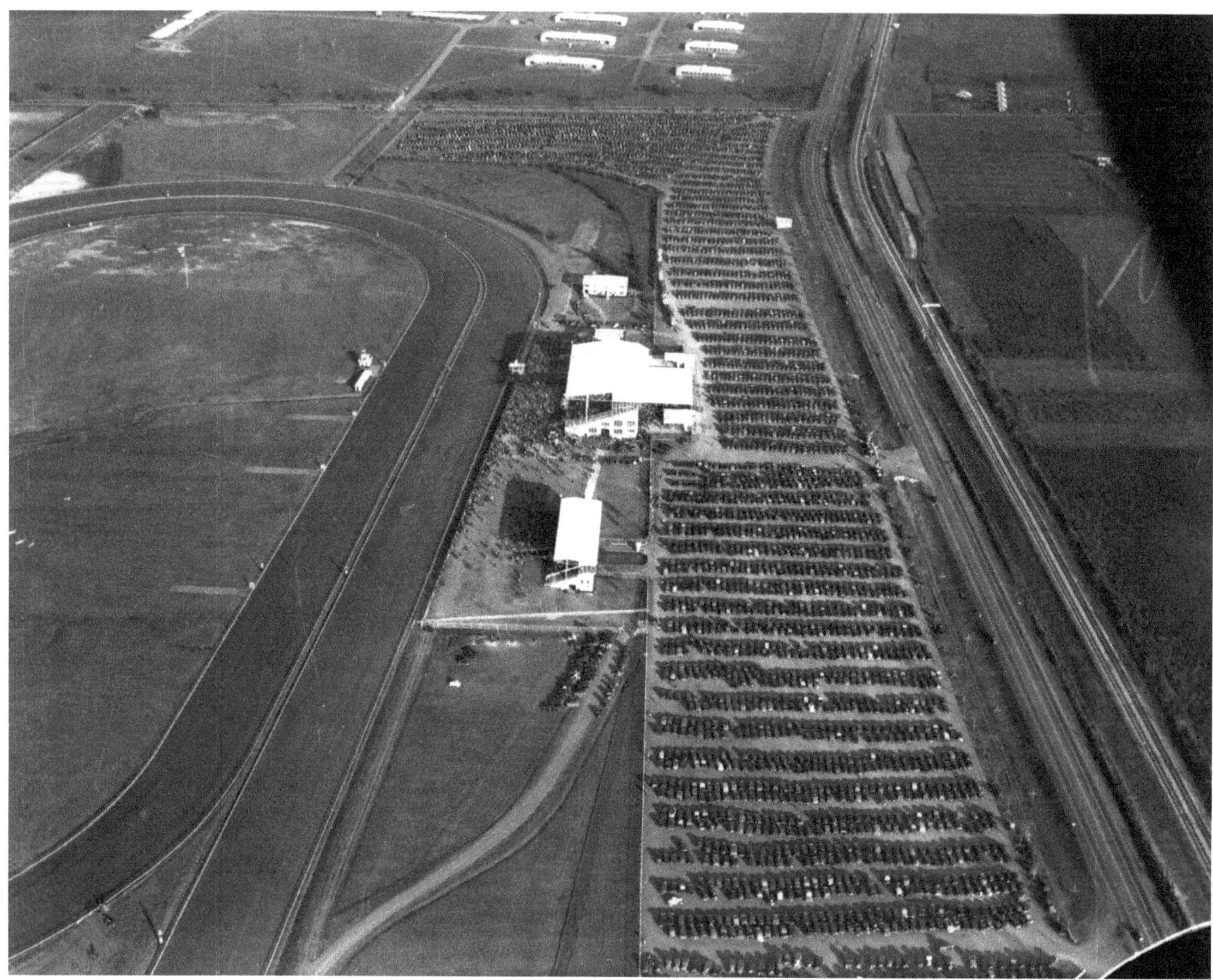

An aerial photographer captured Arlington Downs on a crowded race day in October 1933. Over 27,000 spectators gathered at the track, which was built by Fort Worth cattle and oil baron W. T. Waggoner sixteen miles east of the city to showcase his family's championship horse-breeding program. Considered the finest private racing facility in the nation when it opened in 1929, the track closed in 1937 after gambling opponents forced the repeal of pari-mutuel betting in Texas.

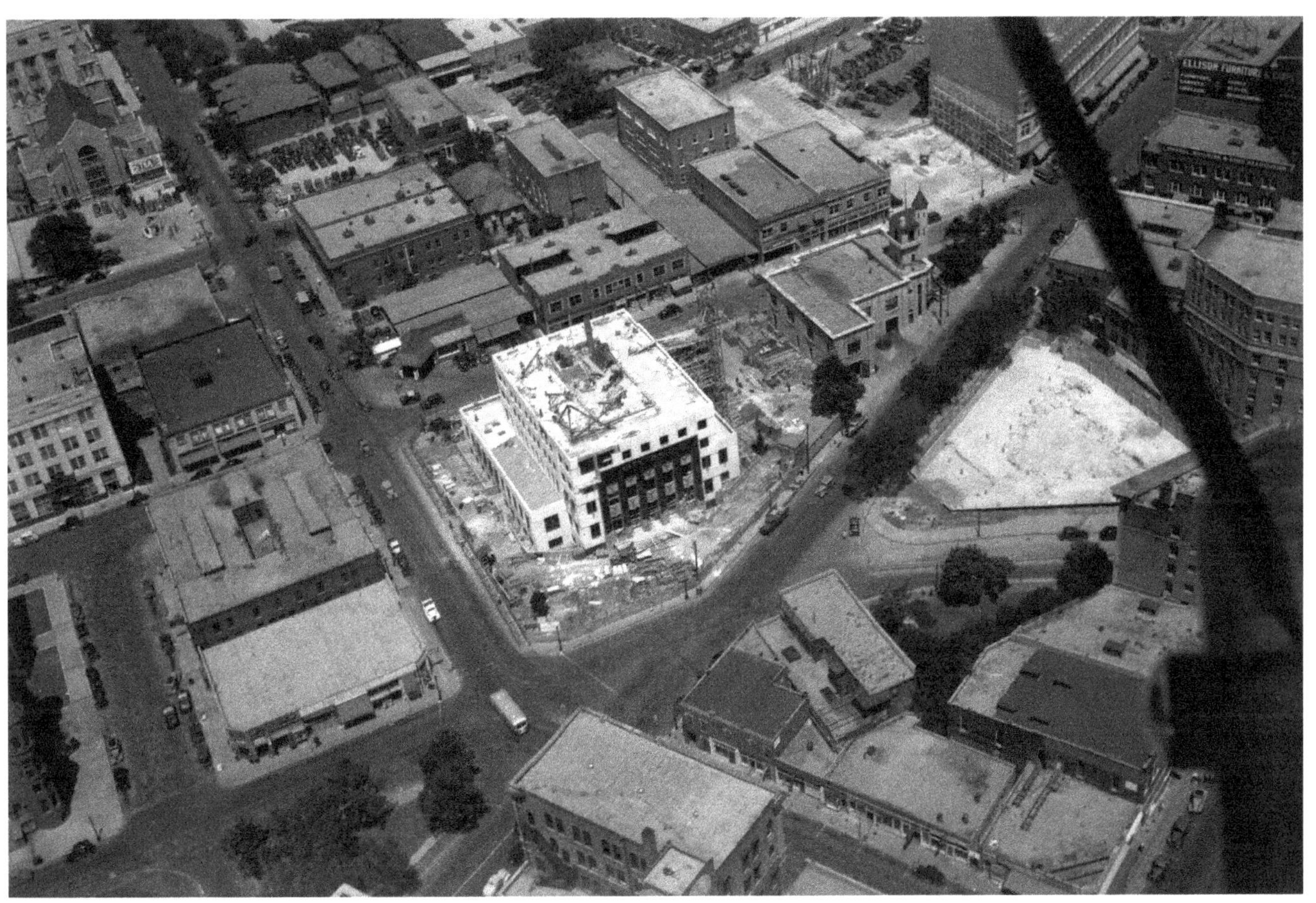

During the Depression, Fort Worth benefited from the power wielded in Washington by a strong Texas delegation that included local Congressman Fritz G. Lanham. With the aid of federal funds in 1938, the city built a new city hall on the site of the old 1893 municipal building. To the right of the new hall in this photograph, taken in February 1939, is the 1899 Central Fire Station and the foundation for the new public library on the site of the old Carnegie Library. At far left is the turreted corner of the nineteenth-century Federal Building.

Proprietor Charles Reichenstein moved his Worth Segar Store into the prestigious Worth Building at 7th and Main in 1932. Son of a German immigrant to Texas, the football standout from Texas A&M moved to Fort Worth about 1912. While building his businesses, he launched a nearly twenty-year career as a high school and college football referee, retiring in 1933 as the acknowledged dean of the profession. His store was the city's center for sports scores, tickets, and storytelling until the Depression economy forced it to close in 1938. "Charlie Rick" continued to operate his other store in the Livestock Exchange Building until his death in 1949.

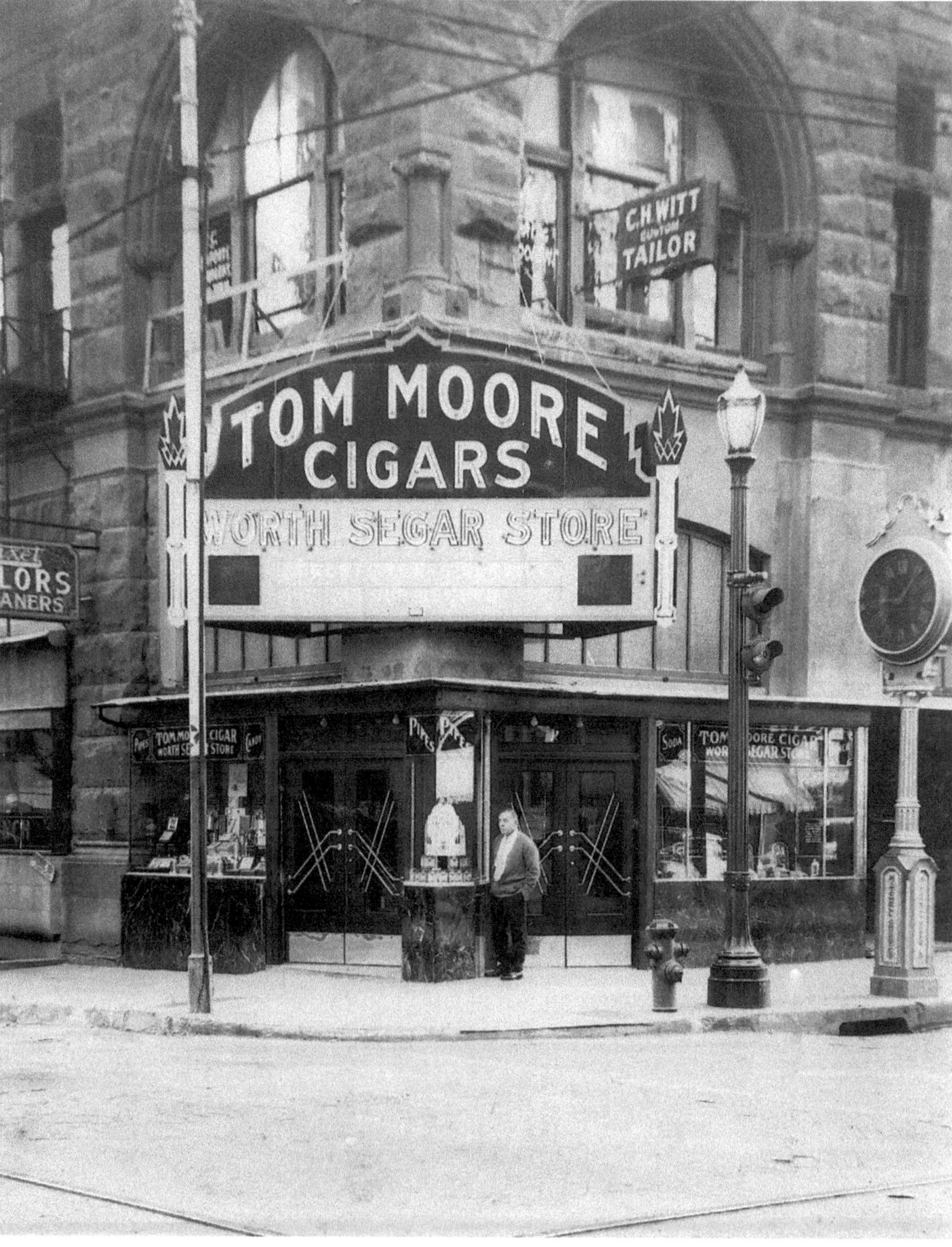

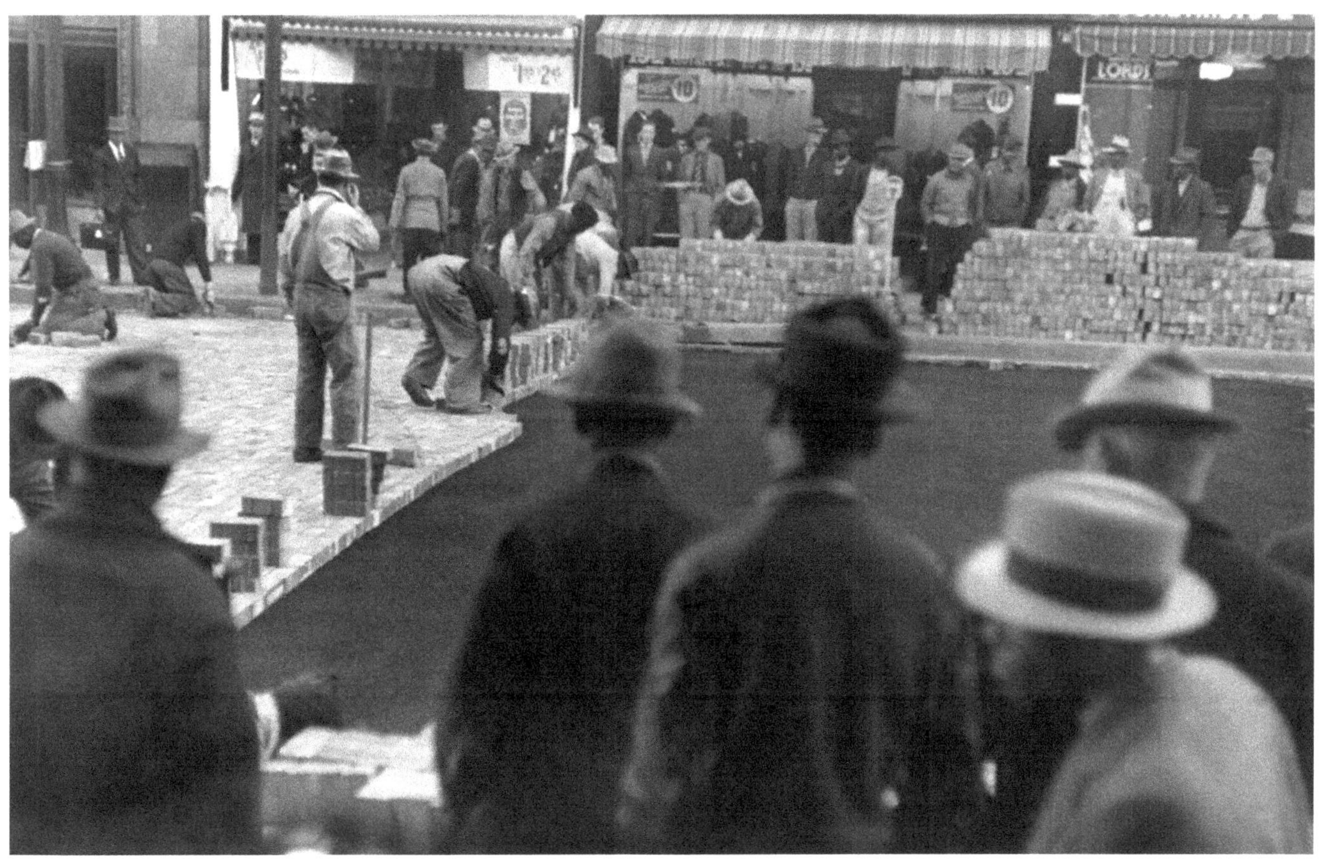


Among the many public improvements funded by city bonds and federal grants during the Depression was a massive street repaving program. During the spring and summer of 1938, downtown streets were recovered with hundreds of thousands of bricks, laid over sand and asphalt. In this image by the talented amateur photographer Lewis Fox, pedestrians have stopped to watch the professional bricklayers create a perfect street surface in the 700 block of Main Street.

The view west on 7th Street from Summit Avenue about 1936 shows Fort Worth's "Automobile Row," where most of the city's dealerships and shops operated. The recently completed First Methodist Church commands the skyline at left while the Neil P. Anderson Building, center at the head of the street, welcomes visitors to downtown.

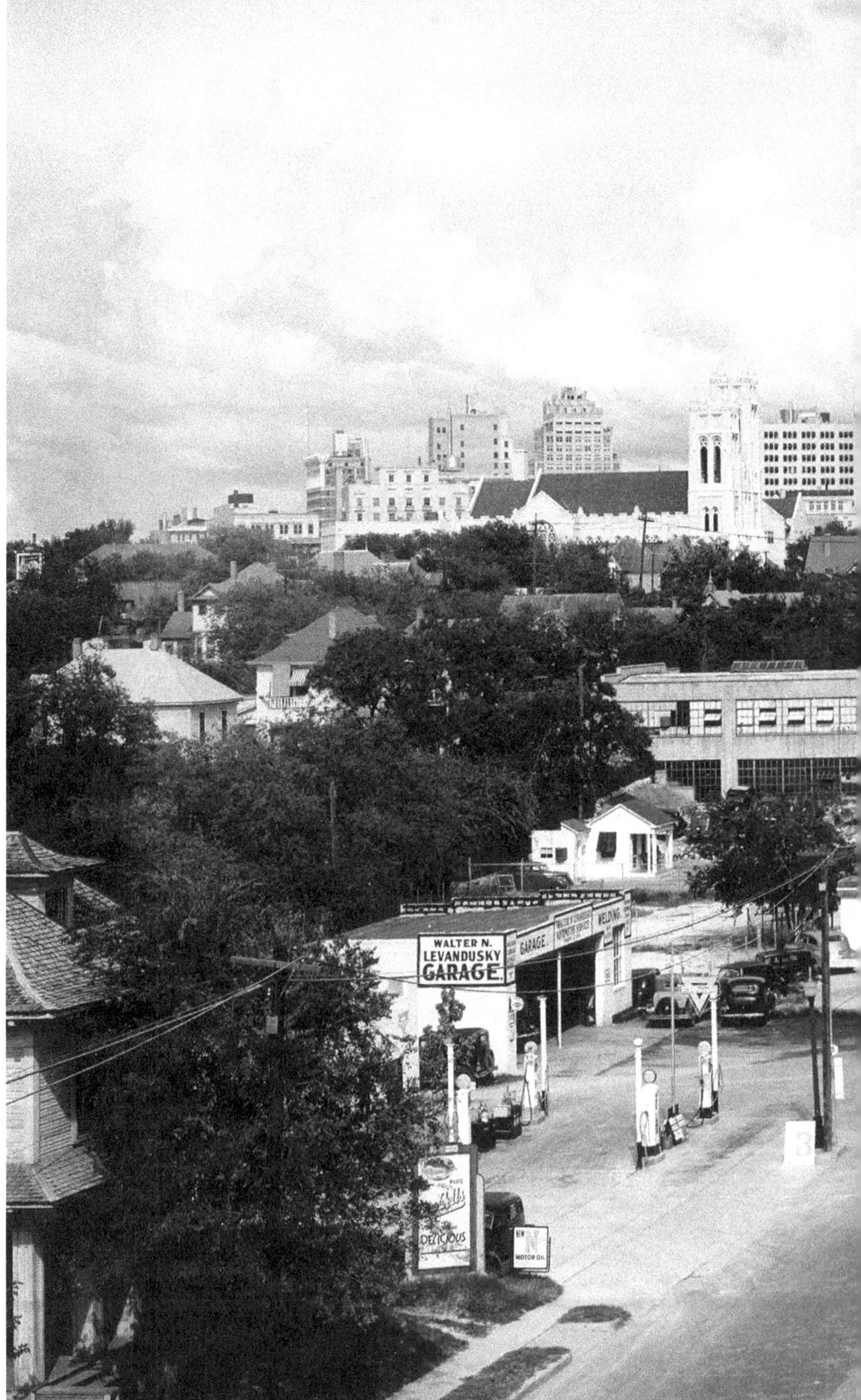

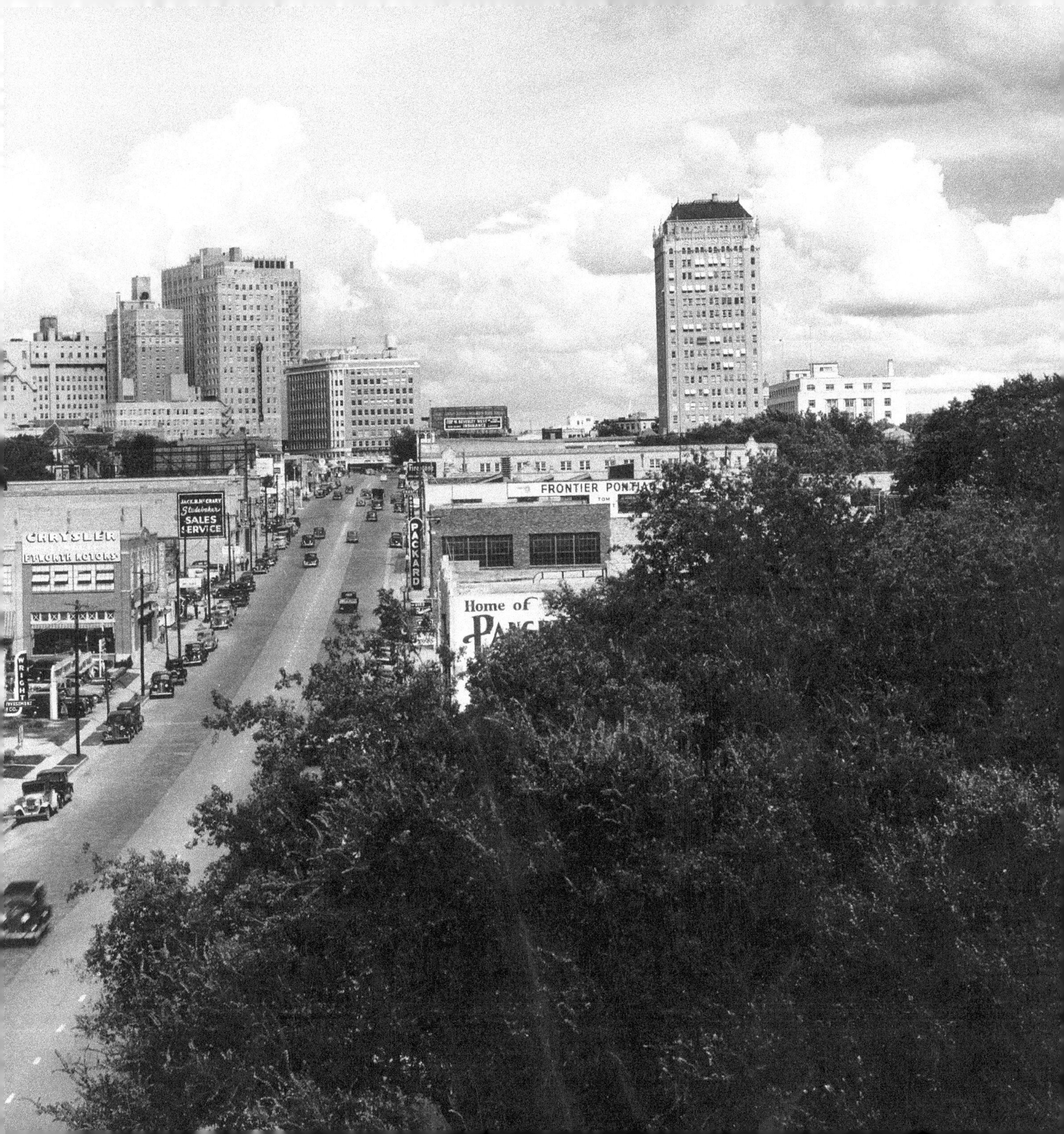

CHRYSLER
SALES
SERVICE
PACKARD
FRONTIER PONTIAC
Home of
WRIGHT

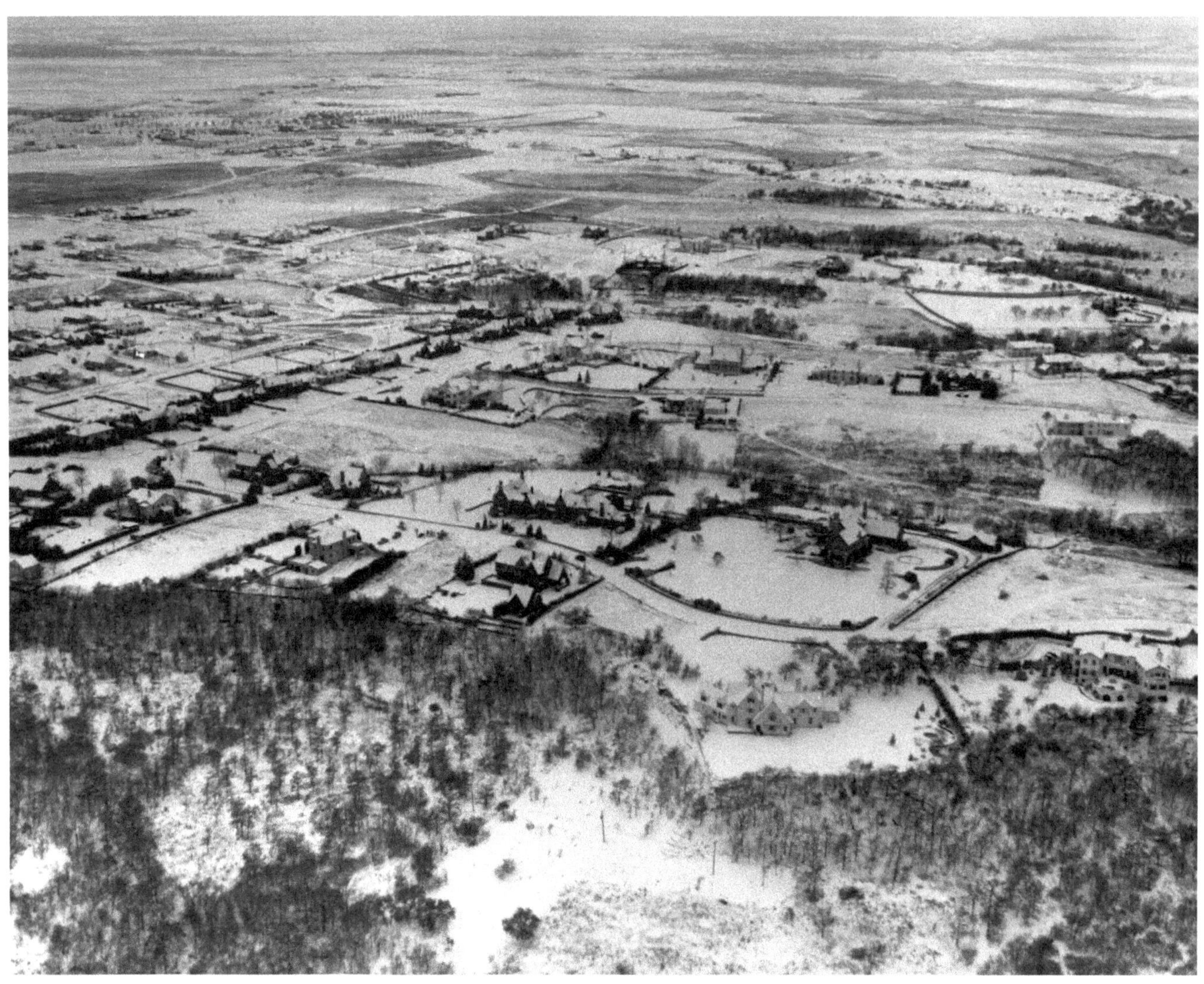

Incorporated in May 1937, Westover Hills remains home to some of the most influential families in Fort Worth. This photograph of the snow-covered residential enclave, taken the following November, shows a sparsely developed west side of town. The open fields at top center had been platted for the new Ridglea Development in 1928, but actual construction would not begin in earnest until a couple of years after this image was taken.

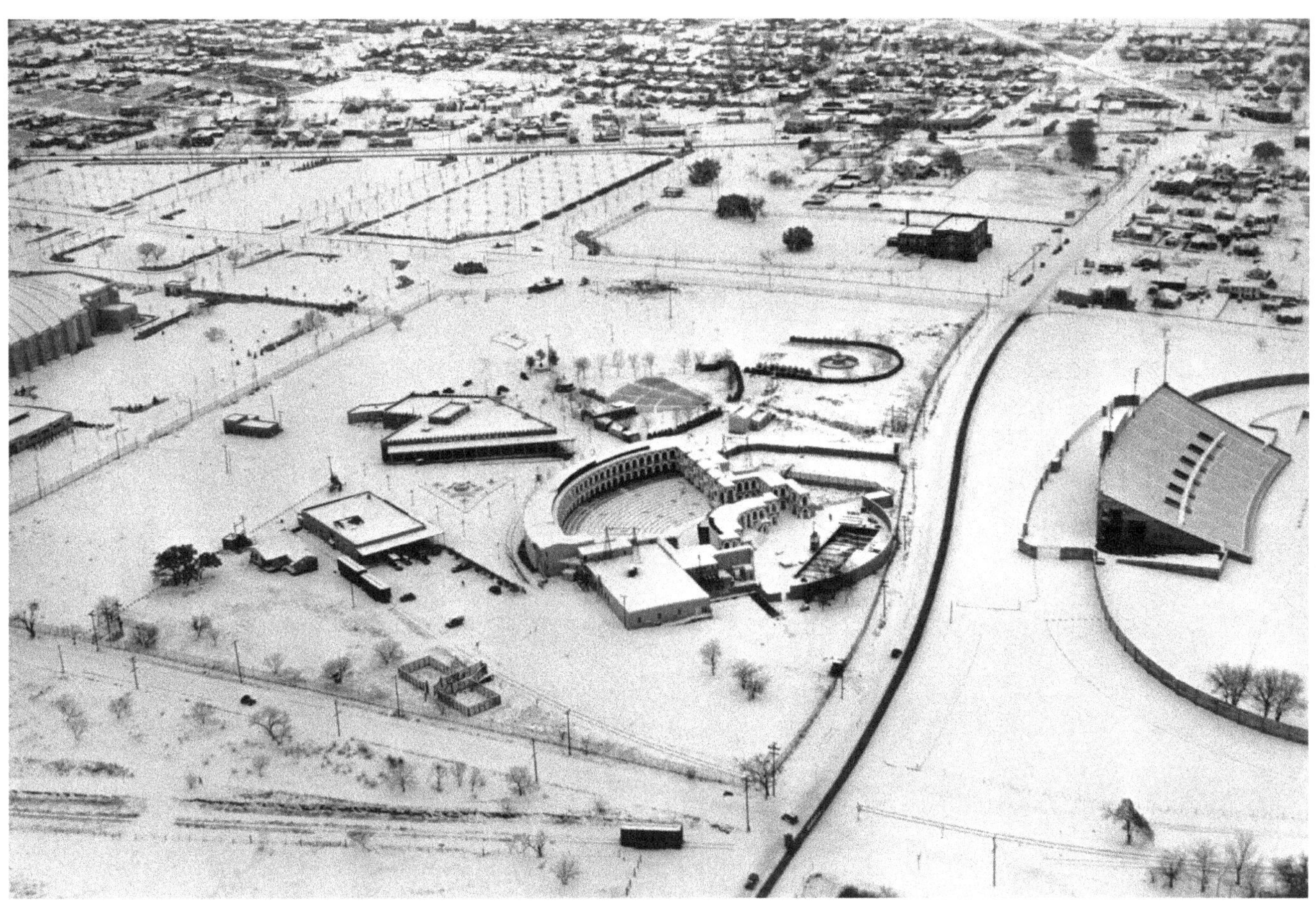

A January 1940 snowfall highlights the fairgrounds built for the Texas Centennial in 1936, and the area that would evolve into Fort Worth's Cultural District. Having seen its last season in 1939, the remarkable 4,000 seat Casa Manana amphitheater, at center, would be demolished in 1942.

From its very first year in 1896, the annual Stock Show has kicked off with a parade. At first, a few businesses decorated floats and wagons to accompany the working cowboys in a simple procession along North Main Street. Eventually, the parade moved Downtown and evolved into one of the longest non-mechanized annual processions in the world. Here, two riders move down Main Street for the opening of the 1938 show.

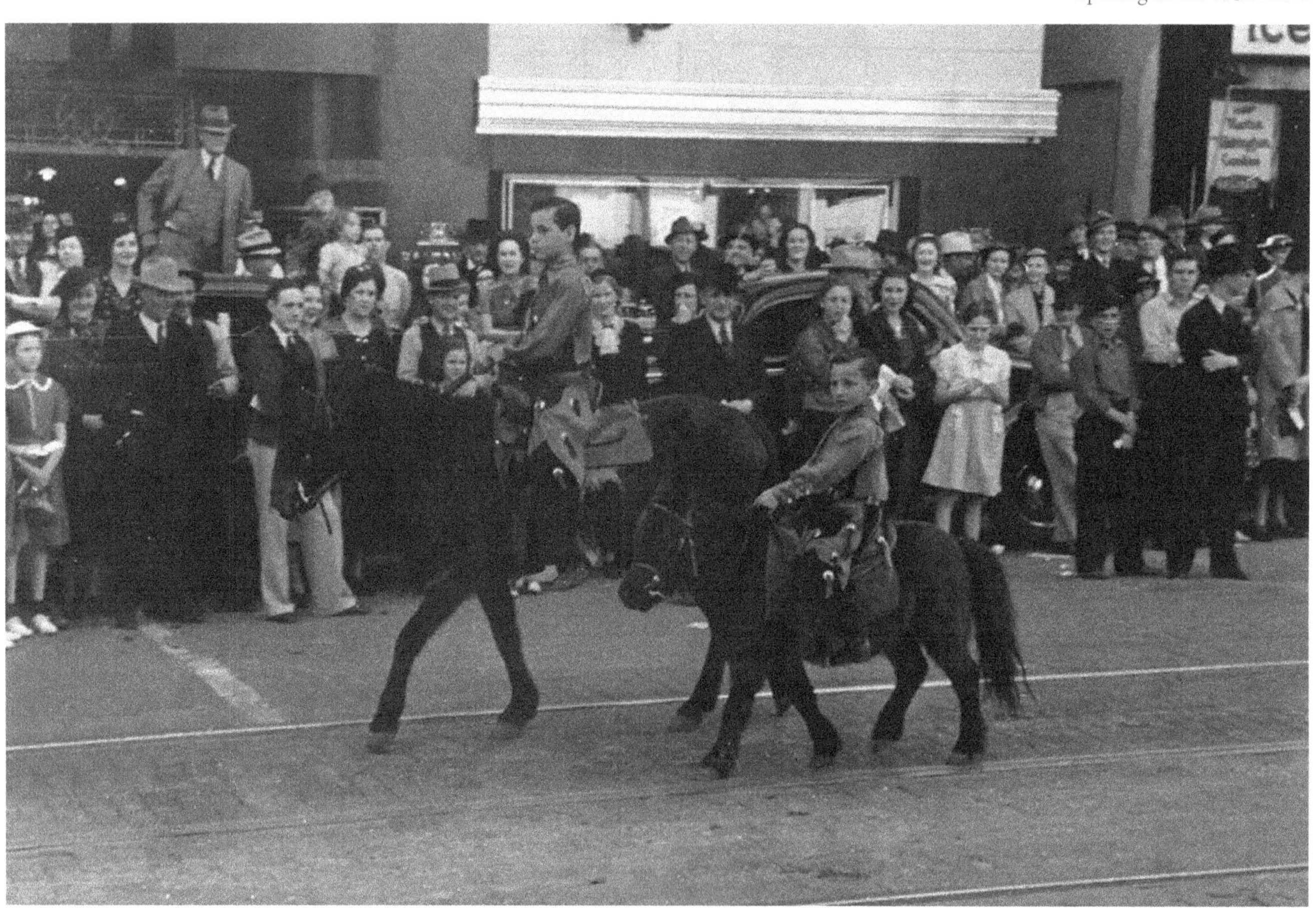

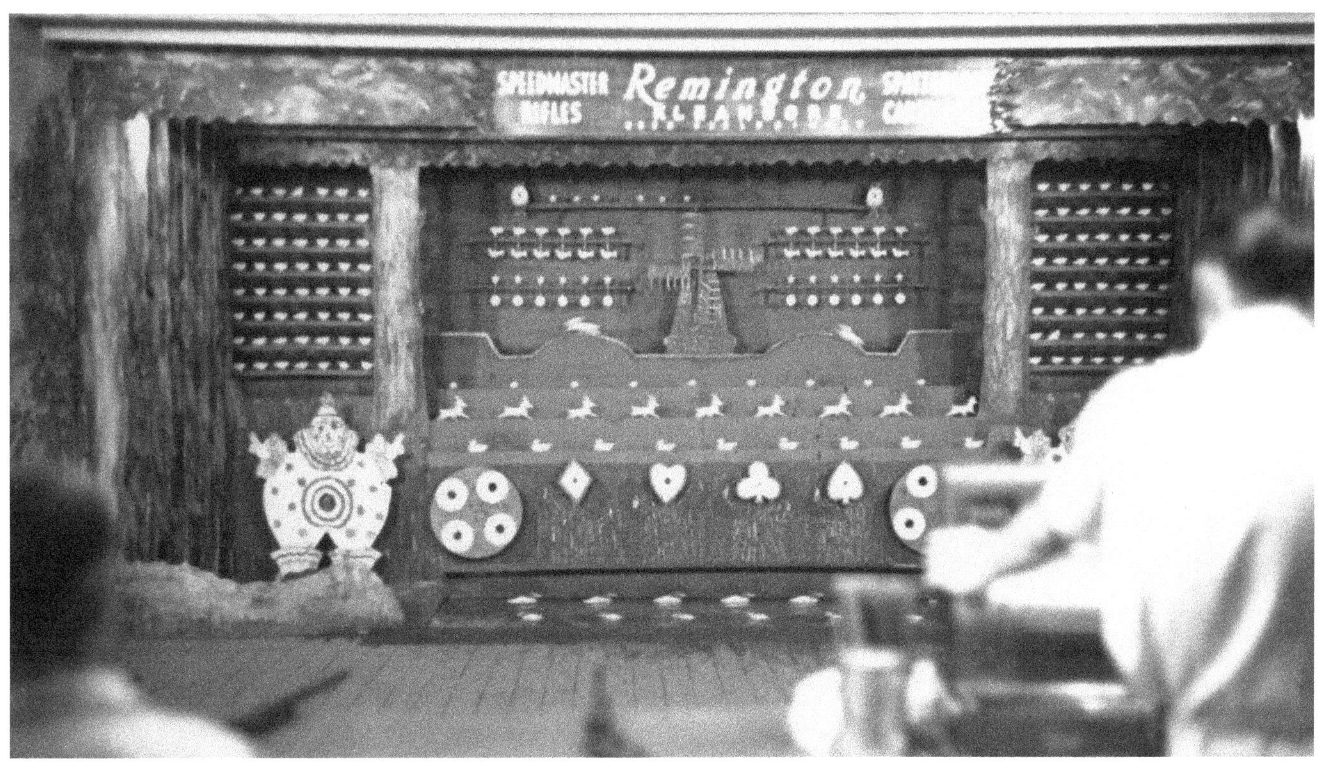


While Casa Manana was built to celebrate the Texas Centennial in 1936, the shows and fairground activities continued for a few more years as the "Frontier Fiesta." Always popular was the midway, with its peep shows, games and food. During the last year of the Fiesta, 1939, a marksman tries his luck at the Remington Shooting Gallery.

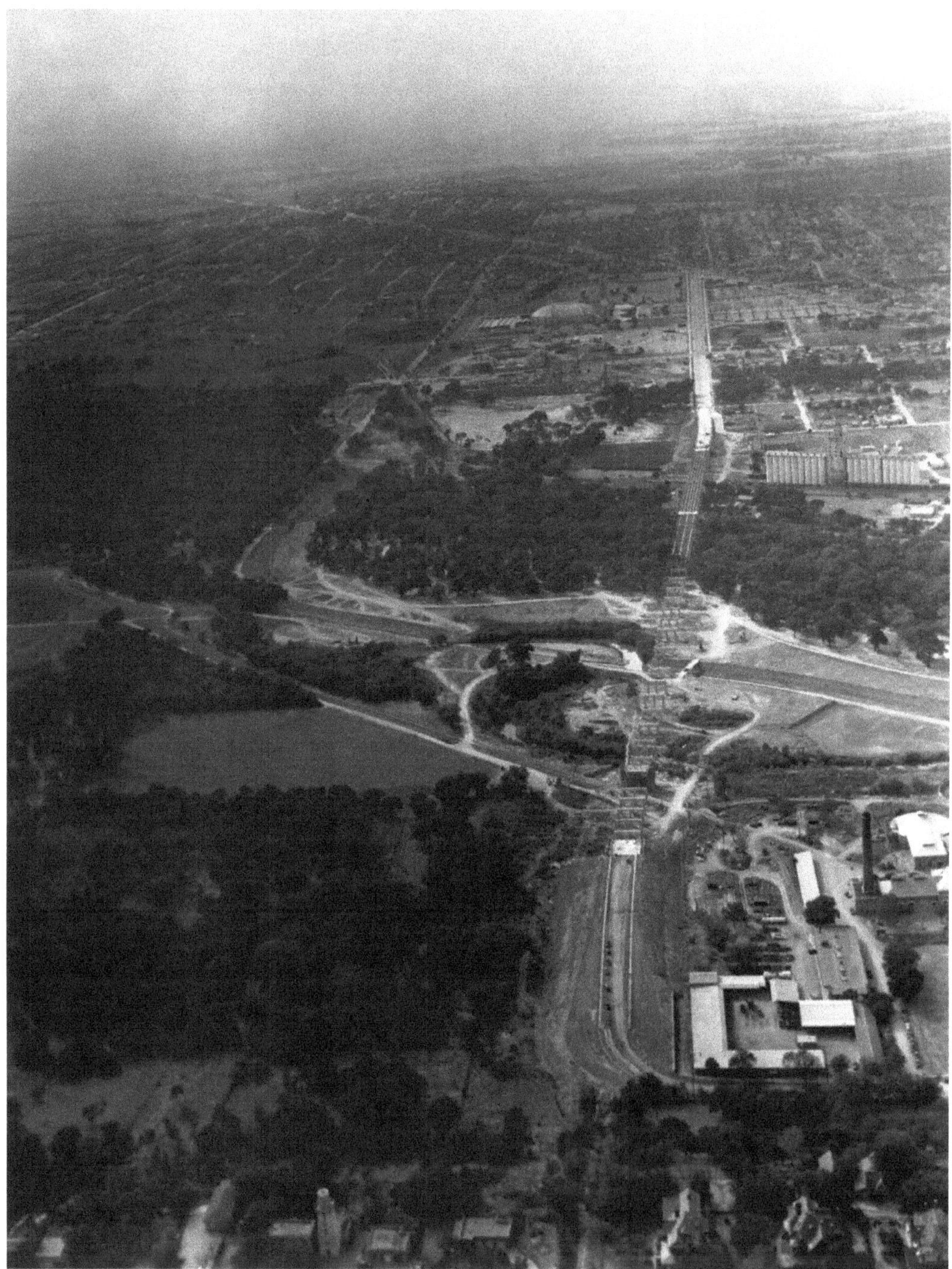

Both the old and new river channels are visible in this construction view of the Lancaster Avenue Bridge about 1938. Across the bottom of the image are the outbuildings of the mansions that faced Summit Avenue as well as three Penn Street mansions, two of which remain standing today. Across the river are the buildings of the Will Rogers Memorial Center, Casa Manana and the Centennial Fairgrounds, and a partially completed Farrington Field.

# Mid-Century Changes

## 1941–1965

Fort Worth's military connections once again brought prosperity to the city when the U.S. Army Air Corps and Consolidated Vultee Aircraft Corporation opened a bomber plant and airfield on the shores of Lake Worth on the city's west side. By 1943, the plant surpassed the stockyards as the area's largest employer, building over 3,000 planes by the end of World War II.

As Fort Worth prepared to celebrate its 100th birthday in 1949, it was struck by the worst flood in the city's history, leaving more than 13,000 people homeless and leading to the completion of flood-control levees and further channelization of the Trinity River. Once-elegant neighborhoods of Fort Worth's early elite made the transition to commercial use as the old mansions were demolished to make way for more modern enterprises. The transformation of downtown began with the removal of thirteen blocks around the area that had once housed the infamous Hell's Half Acre to make way for a new convention center and the Water Gardens. The elation of a presidential visit by John F. Kennedy on November 21, 1963, turned to grief a day later.

Throughout its history, Fort Worth has met challenges with frontier determination and a devout sense of humor born of its days as a true cowtown. The city combines many legendary elements of the growth of the American West—frontier outpost, cattle town, railroad center, oil boomtown and aviation pioneer. In the period following the 1960s, Fort Worth struggled with the challenges of a declining downtown, central city neighborhood problems and an identity crisis as it pondered how it wanted to be seen by the world. What emerged from the soul-searching is a great and vibrant city that celebrates its unique history and faces the future with the same optimism and spirit of those early settlers who moved into the abandoned fort buildings after the soldiers left more than one hundred and fifty years ago.

The photographs included here provide a glimpse into the life of Fort Worth over the years. Many of the places and most of the people are long gone, but so much of what they built and created still lives on in a city deeply grateful for their efforts and for their presence.

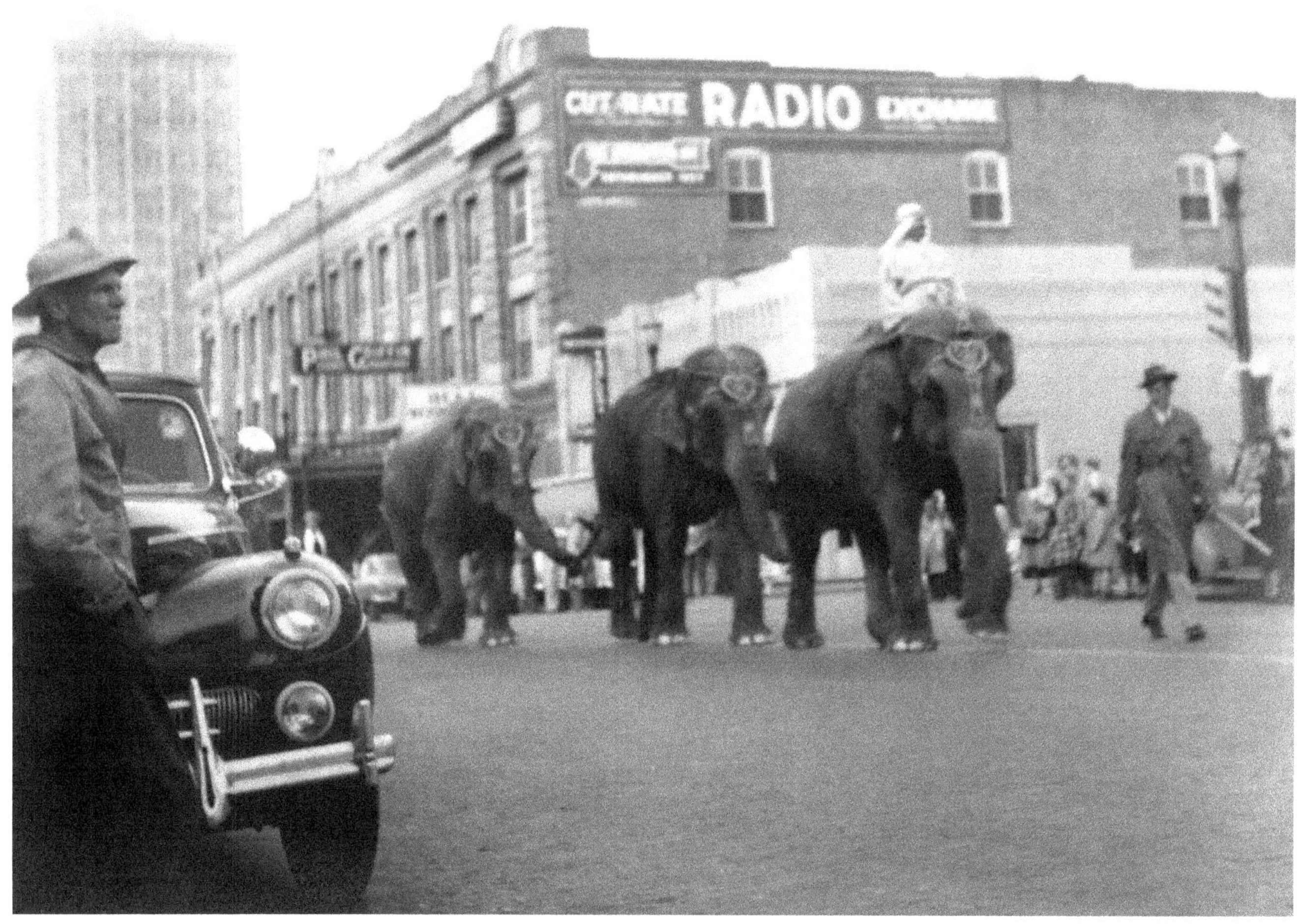


People lined lower Houston Street to watch the ever-popular parade of the elephants when the circus came to town. Before the availability of indoor facilities, the circus performances were often held south of the railroad track between Main and Jennings, near the site of the 1889-90 Texas Spring Palace.

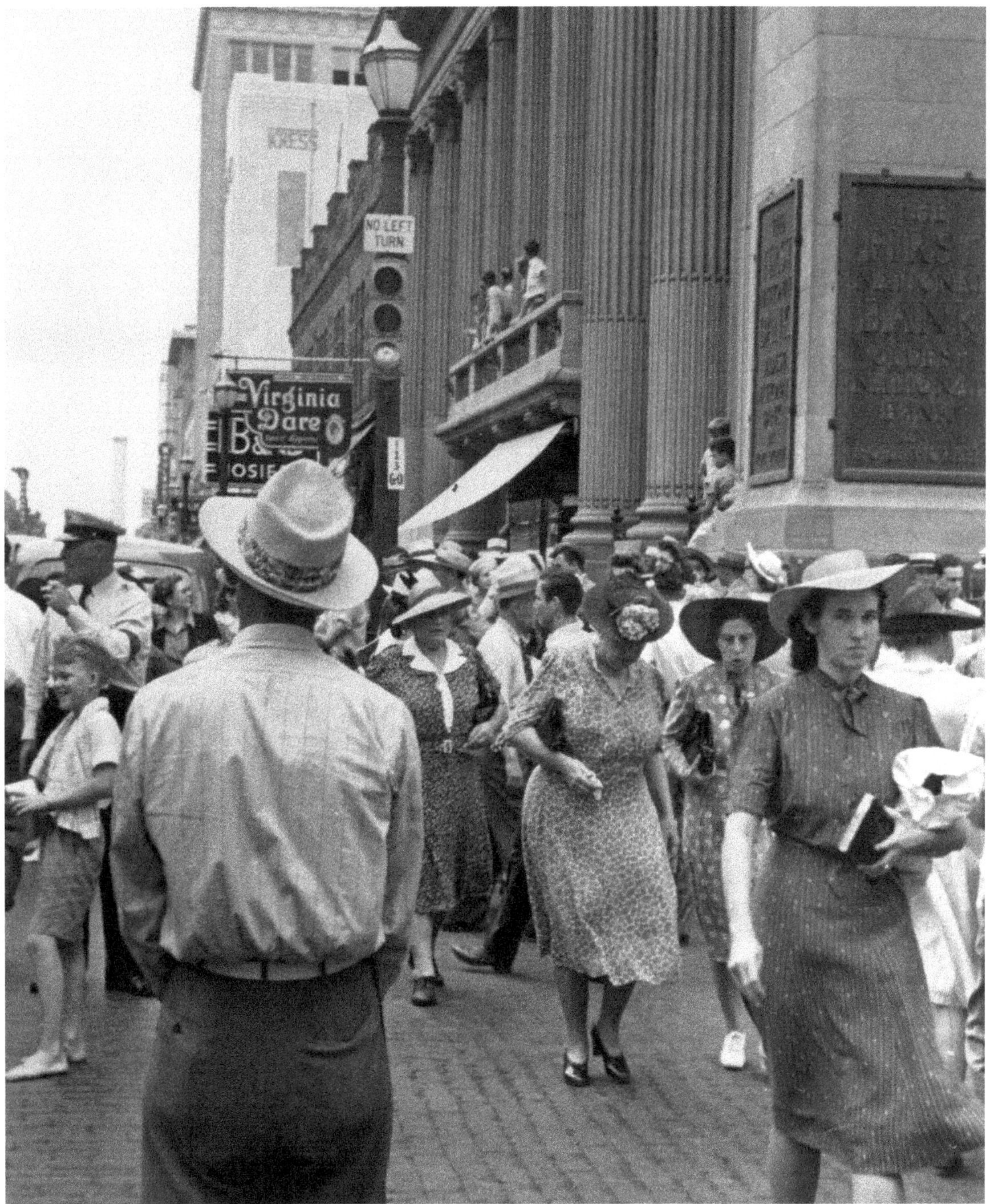


Other parades took on a more serious meaning after America entered World War II. This crowd gathered around the First National Bank for a parade promoting Defense Bonds in December 1941, less than a month after the bombing of Pearl Harbor shook the country out of its isolationist stance. Defense Bonds were soon renamed War Bonds.

During a national War Bond tour in 1943, the Japanese "midget sub" captured at Pearl Harbor in December 1941 made its way to Fort Worth. Displayed near the intersection of Houston and 9th Streets, the sub attracted enthusiastic crowds during its short stay. The vessel now resides within the Pacific War artifacts collection of the National Museum of the Pacific War, formerly the Admiral Nimitz Museum, in Fredericksburg, Texas.

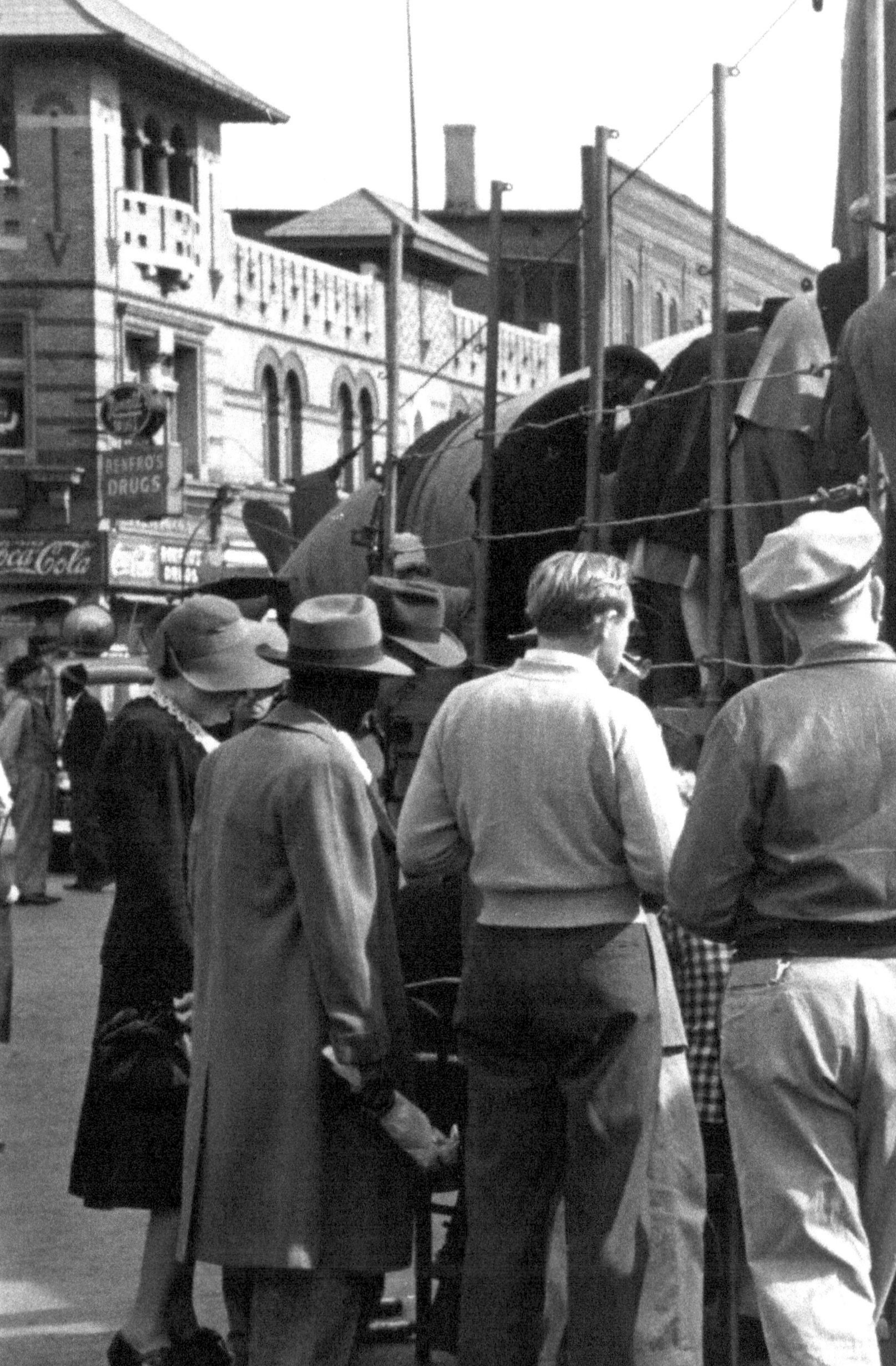

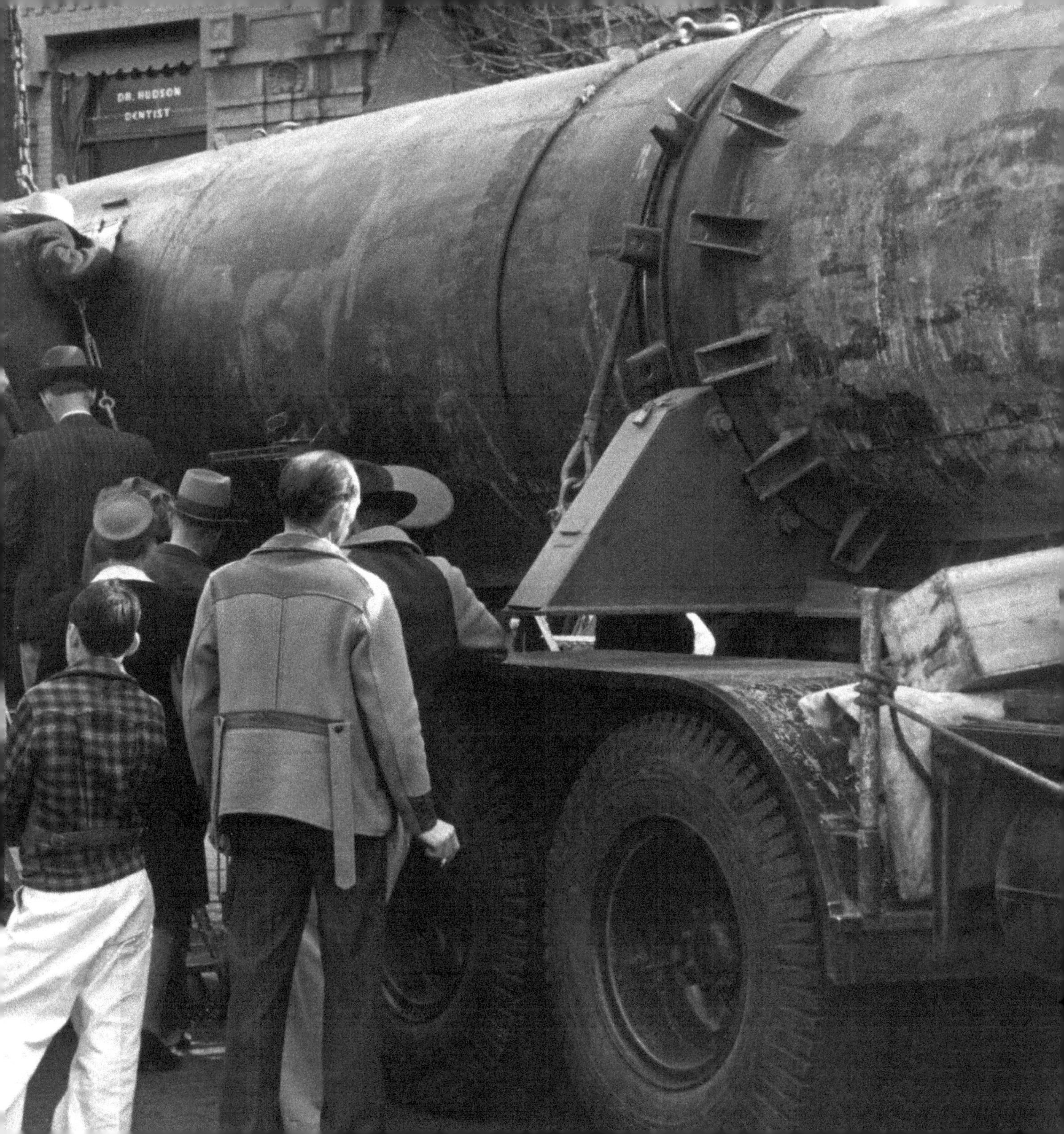
DR. HUDSON
DENTIST

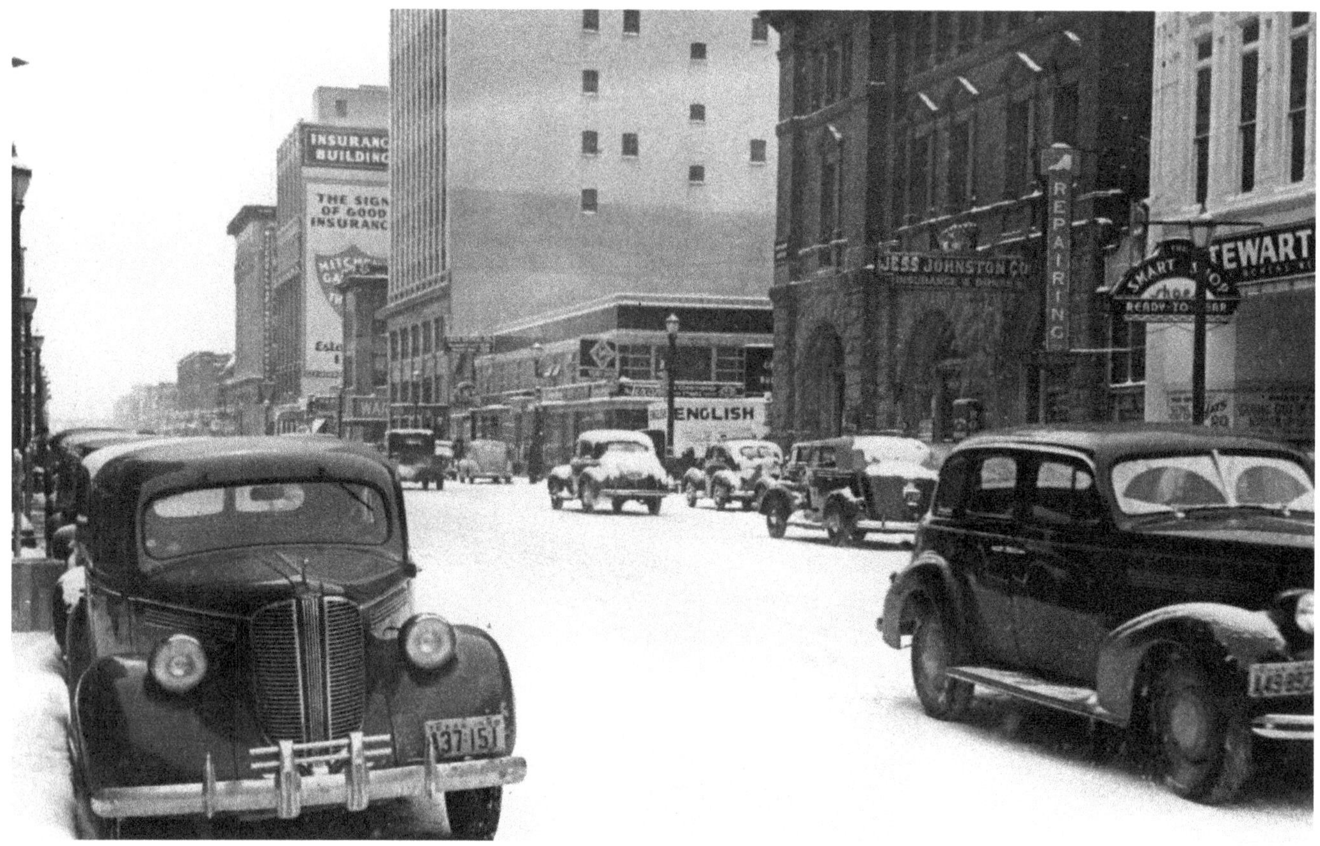


A light dusting of snow invited a photographer to venture out to capture Houston Street looking south from 6th. The ornate nineteenth-century Board of Trade Building would shortly disappear from its place on 7th Street, but the W. T. Waggoner Building in the next block and the Flatiron further down the street would remain.

Pedestrians dodging mounds of snow piled high in the center of Houston Street between 4th and 5th had plenty of opportunities to get in out of the cold in this heart of the Downtown shopping district where local retailers far outnumbered national and regional chains.

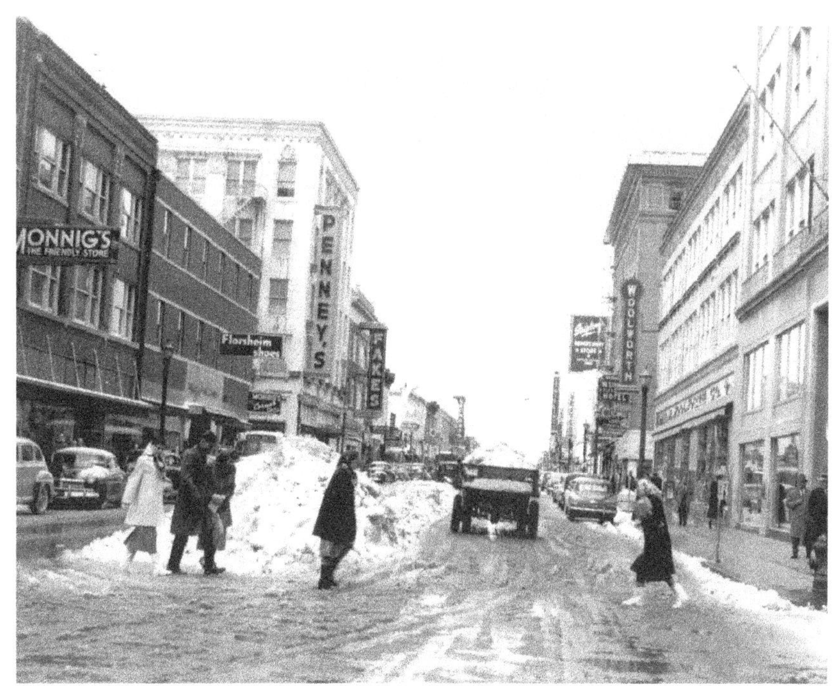

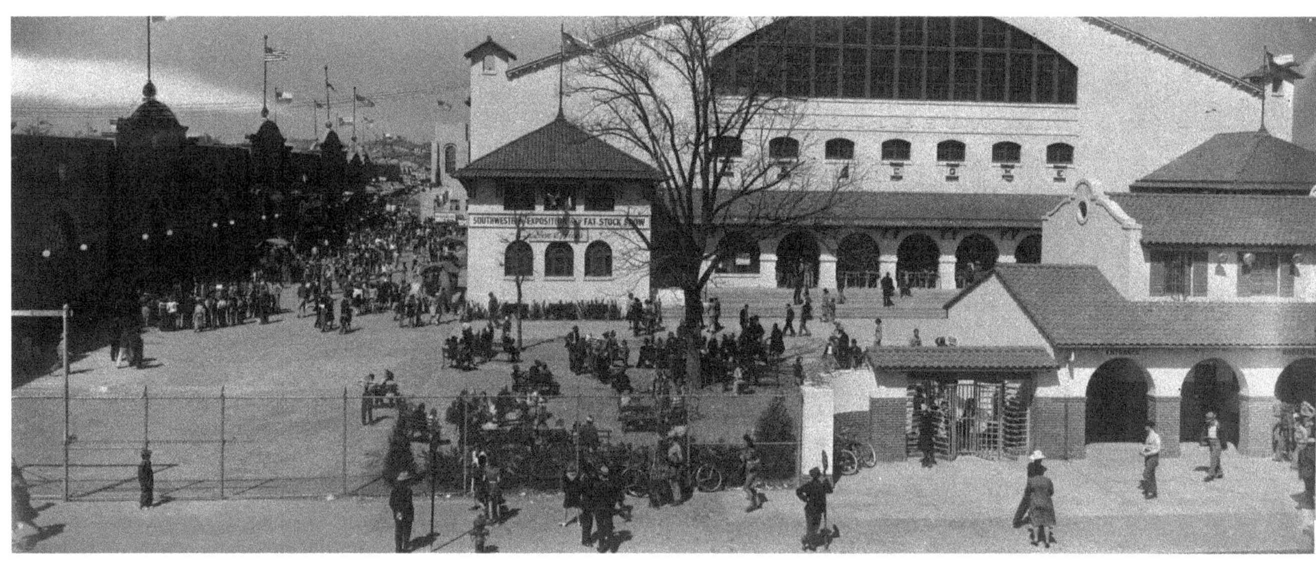

On April 9, 1942, just three weeks after the 1942 Stock Show closed, another of Fort Worth's devastating floods damaged so much of the property in the Stockyards that the show was cancelled for 1943. Wartime priorities hampered the show's regrouping, but when the exposition was fully up and running again in 1946, it had made a permanent move to the West Side and the Will Rogers Complex.

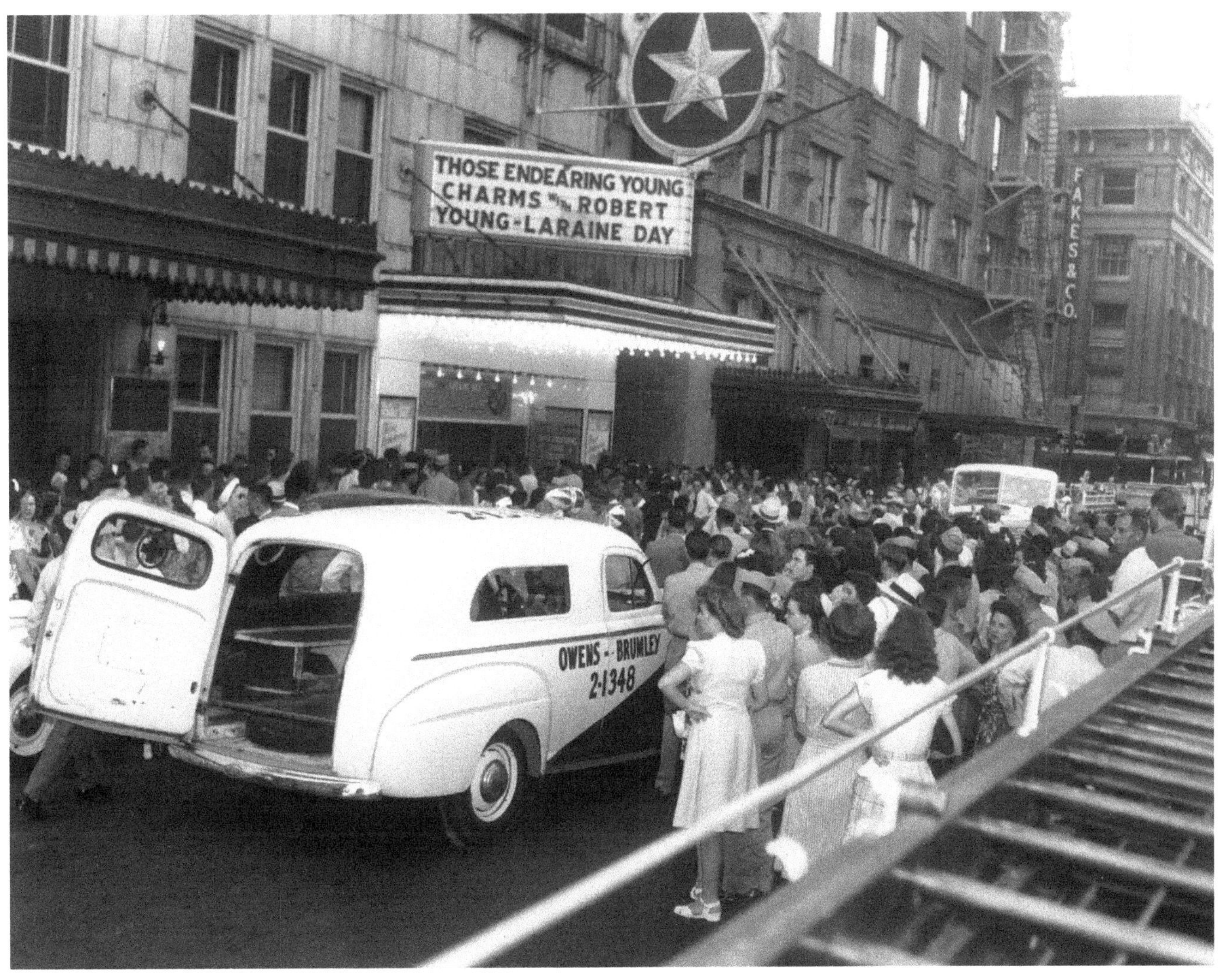


A crowd of evacuated moviegoers block 7th Street while emergency teams check the Worth Theatre for any damage. The Robert Young and Laraine Day film playing that afternoon was a light comedy that opened in June 1945, just a month after Victory in Europe (VE) Day. With the nation still fighting in the Pacific, it's a safe bet that most of the young men in uniform would have preferred a cozy, dark theatre to the excitement captured in this photograph.

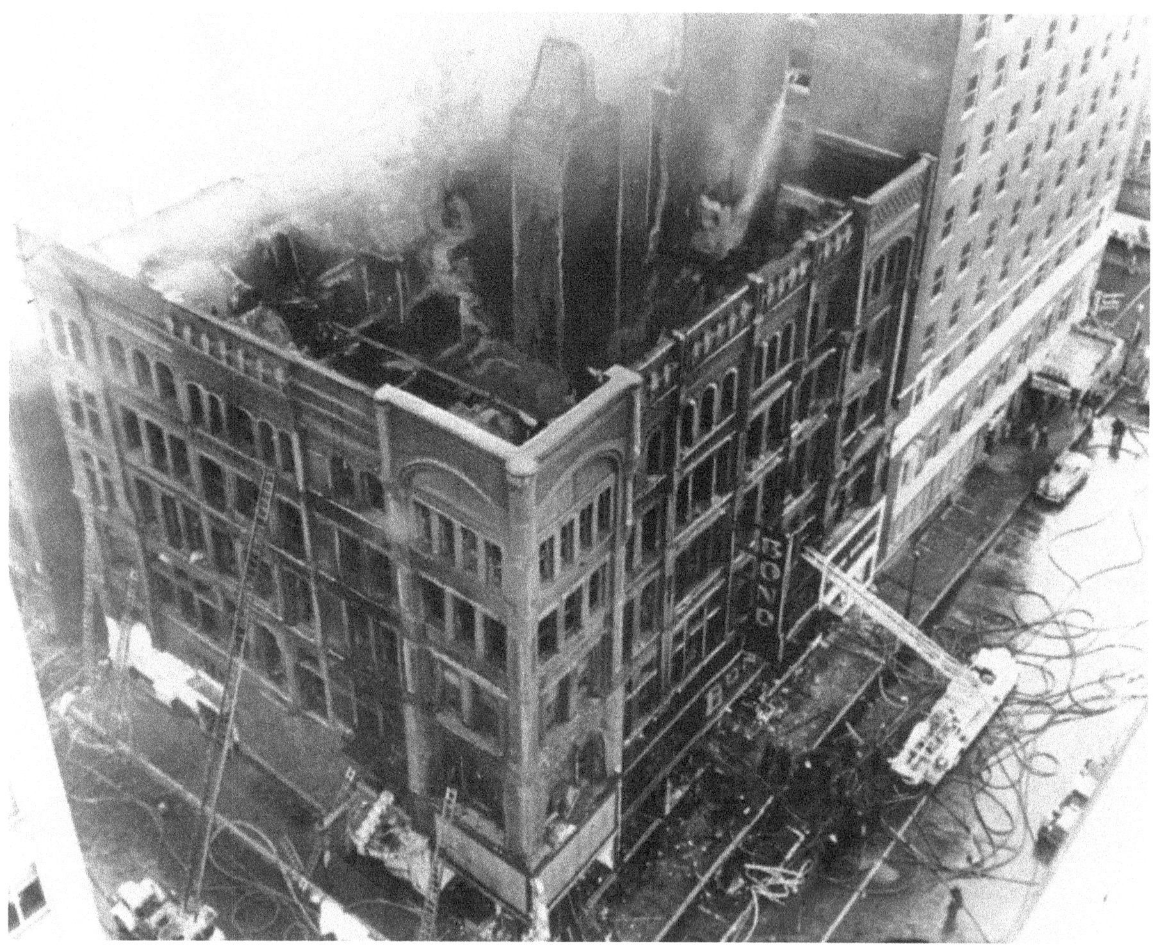


The once-elegant Worth Hotel, opened in the 1890s at 7th and Main streets, spent its last years as an office building. Gutted by an early morning fire in 1945, the remains were demolished, allowing for the expansion of the adjacent Texas Hotel, still operating today. In the aftermath of the fire, one witness recalled the contents of the destroyed basement liquor store being pumped out onto the streets and into the storm drains.

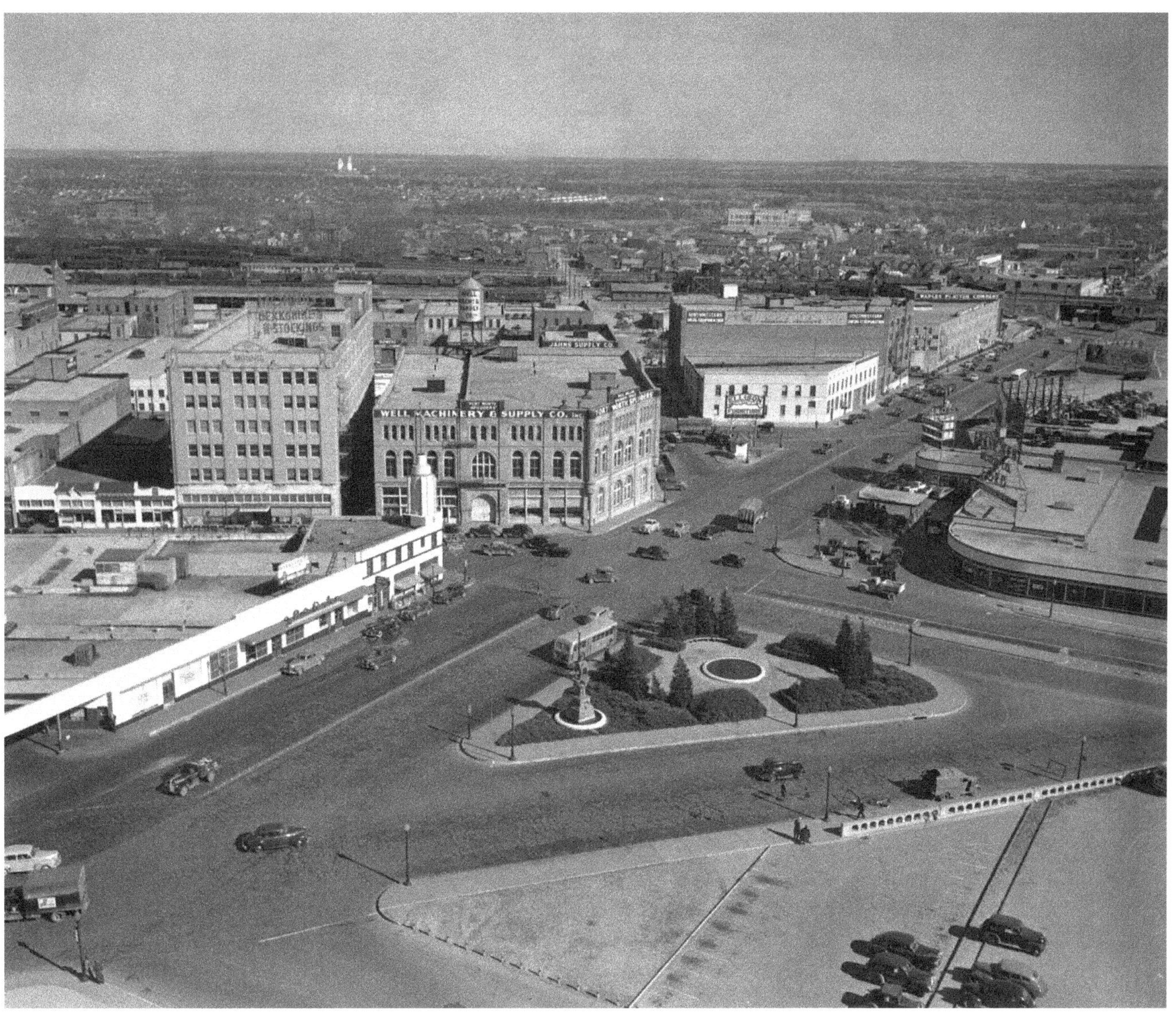


The 1893 Al Hayne Monument, center, presides over the much-changed intersection of Main and Lancaster in the 1940s. At far right, the Frank Kent Ford dealership occupies the site of the former T&P Passenger Station. Just below the horizon at right is the I. M. Terrell High School, completed in 1937 and named for the distinguished educator who came to Fort Worth in 1882 as head of the first school for African Americans here.

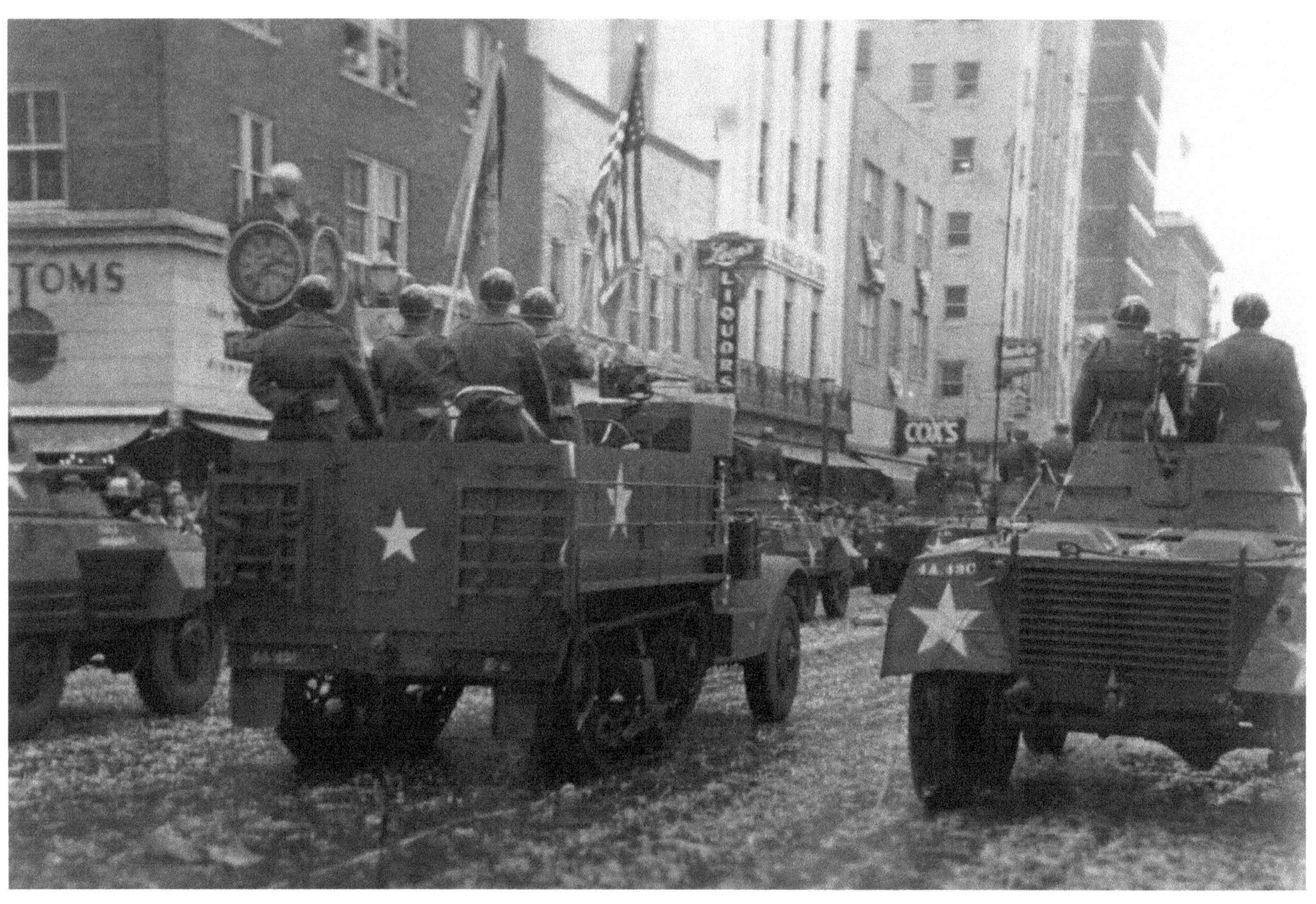


Army vehicles move north on Main Street during a parade to honor Jonathan Wainwright, the highest-ranking American taken prisoner in World War II. Temporarily promoted to lieutenant general on Corregidor, the Philippines, he was forced to surrender his force to the Japanese in 1942. After three years as a POW, he was present for the Japanese surrender aboard the U.S.S. *Missouri* in 1945 and returned to a hero's welcome in the United States.

Long before the construction of branch libraries during the sixties, the Fort Worth Public Library toured neighborhoods and schools, attracting young readers via the Bookmobile. The traveling library service began in 1948 under the auspices of Library Director Joseph Ibbotson, who also started the Friends of the Library organization.

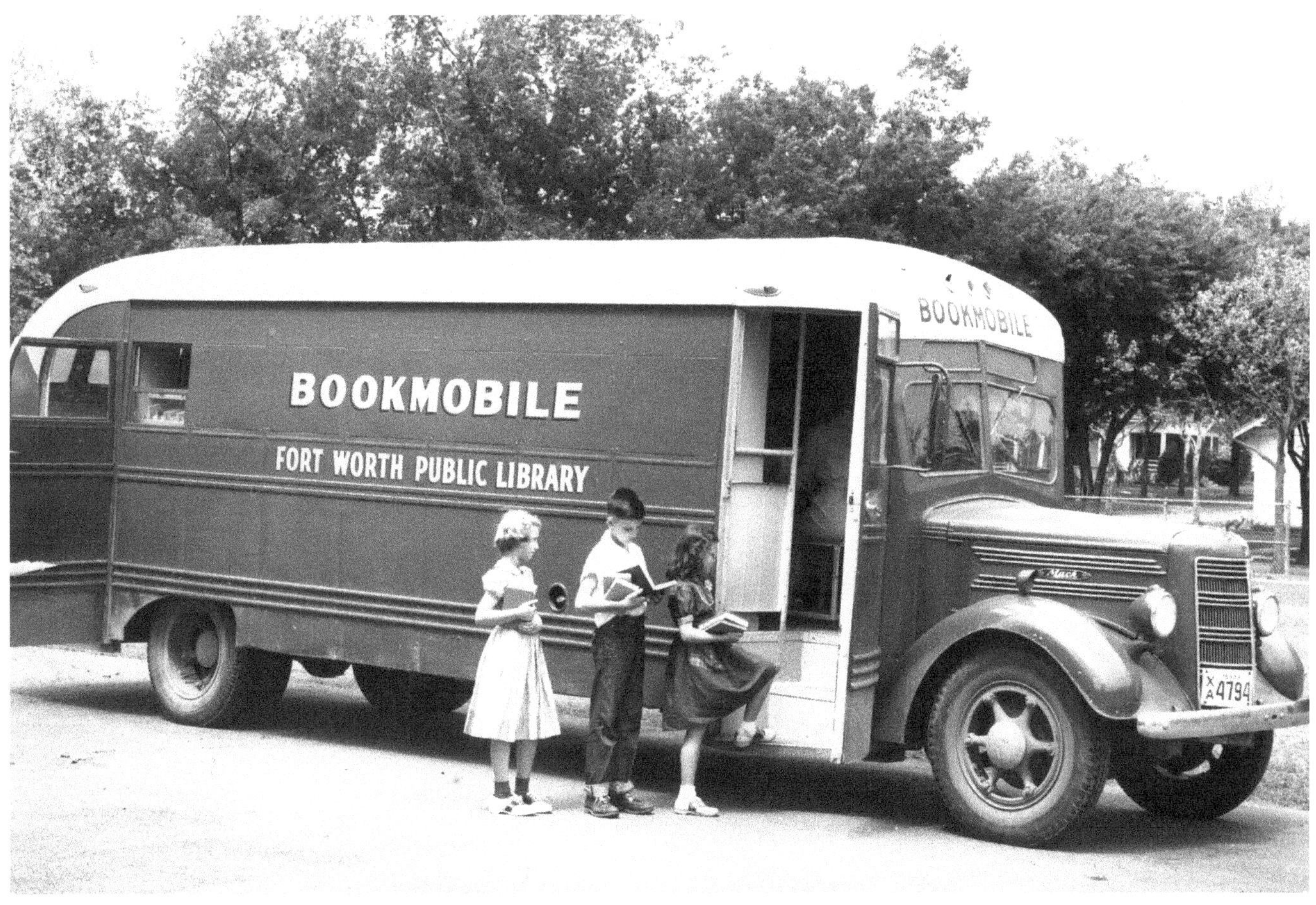

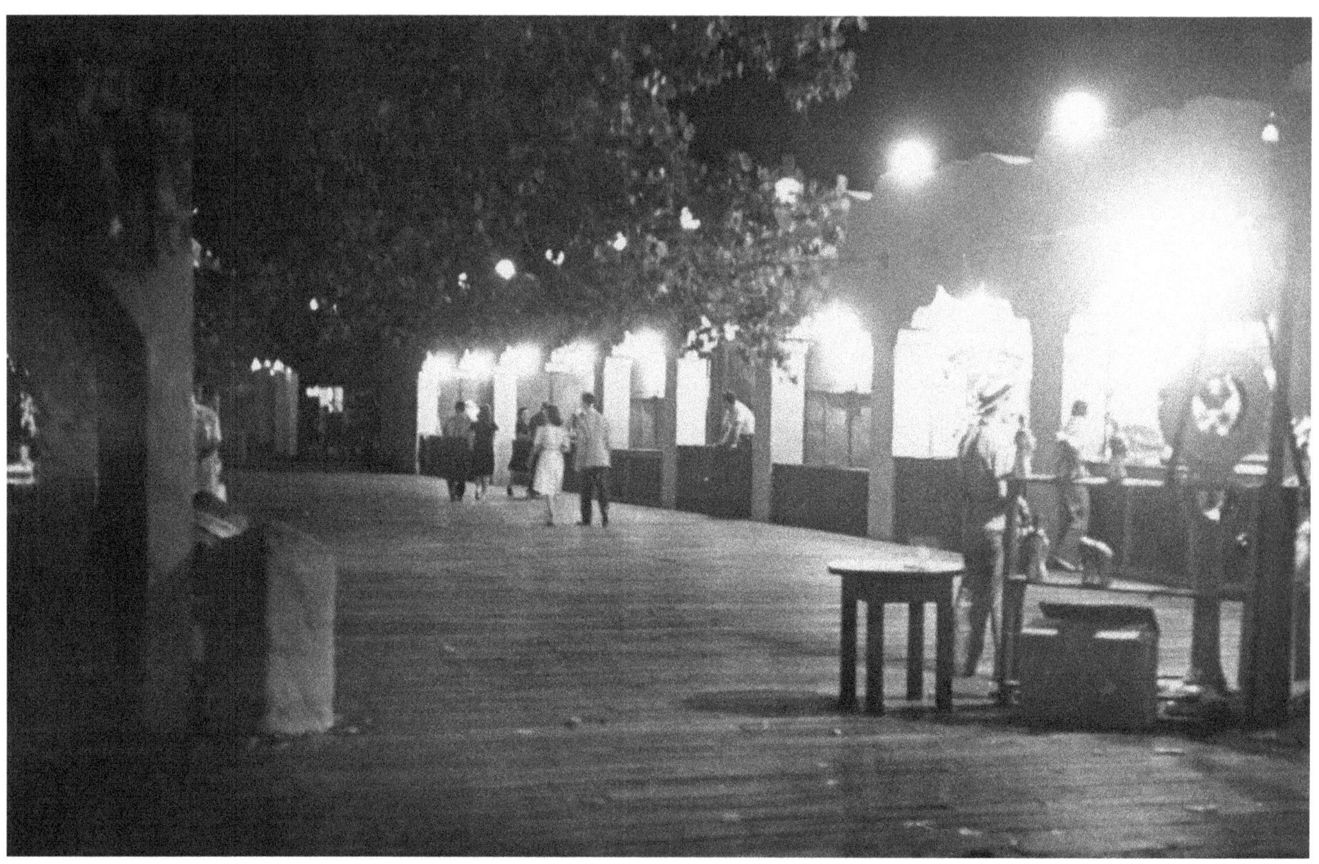

Lake Worth's Casino Beach Park was one of Fort Worth's most popular attractions from the late twenties through World War II. Boasting a 31,000-square-foot ballroom that could accommodate over a thousand couples, the park also featured, at nearly four hundred feet, the largest wooden boardwalk west of Atlantic City. The walkway, with its shops and midway was dismantled in 1941. The park continued to decline throughout the late forties and, after a brief renaissance in the sixties, finally closed for good.

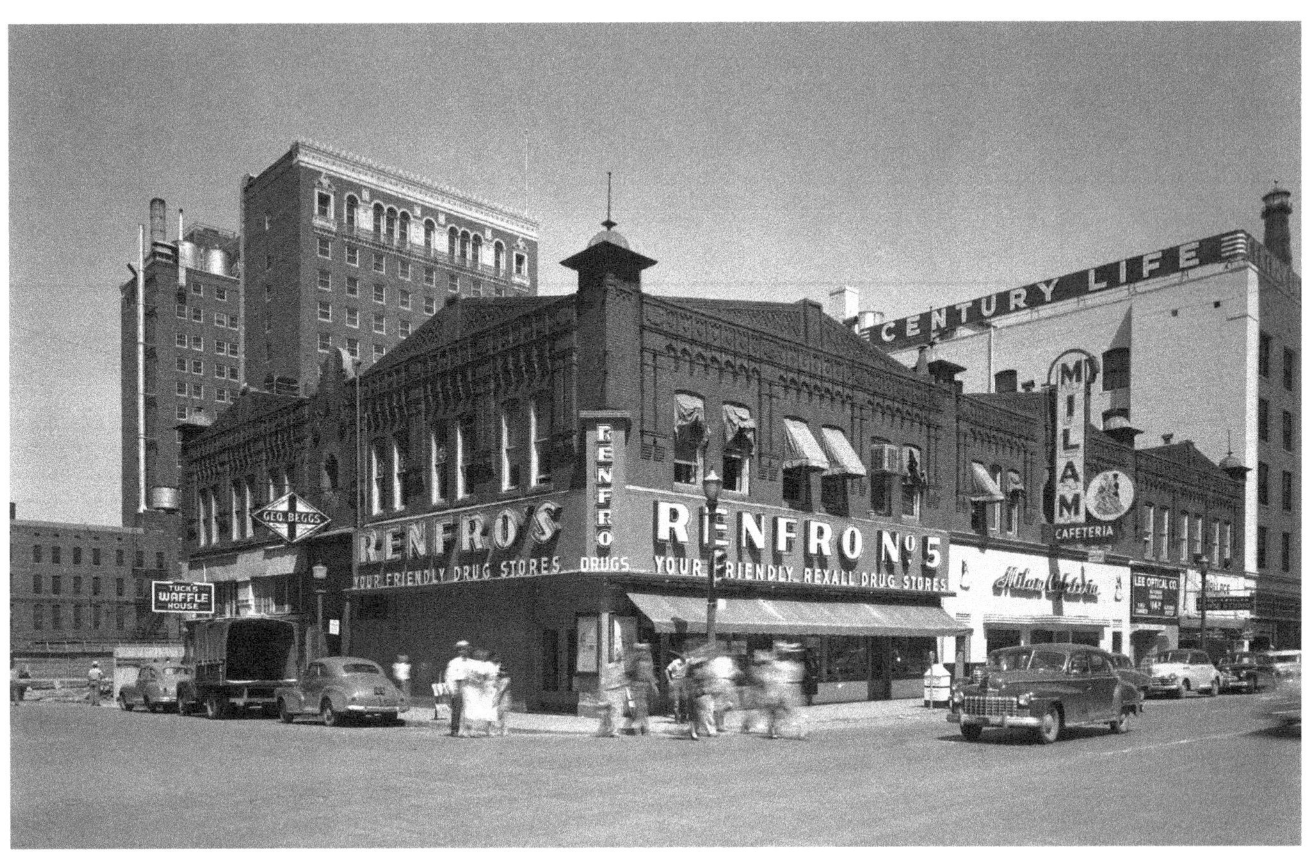


The two-story Dundee Building, built before 1898 on the southeast corner of 7th and Houston streets. Its tenants included the flagship store of Fort Worth's thirteen Renfro Drug Stores and the studios of pioneering photographers Charles Swartz and Roy Jernigan. The Fort Worth National Bank demolished the building in 1950 to erect a new skyscraper on the site.

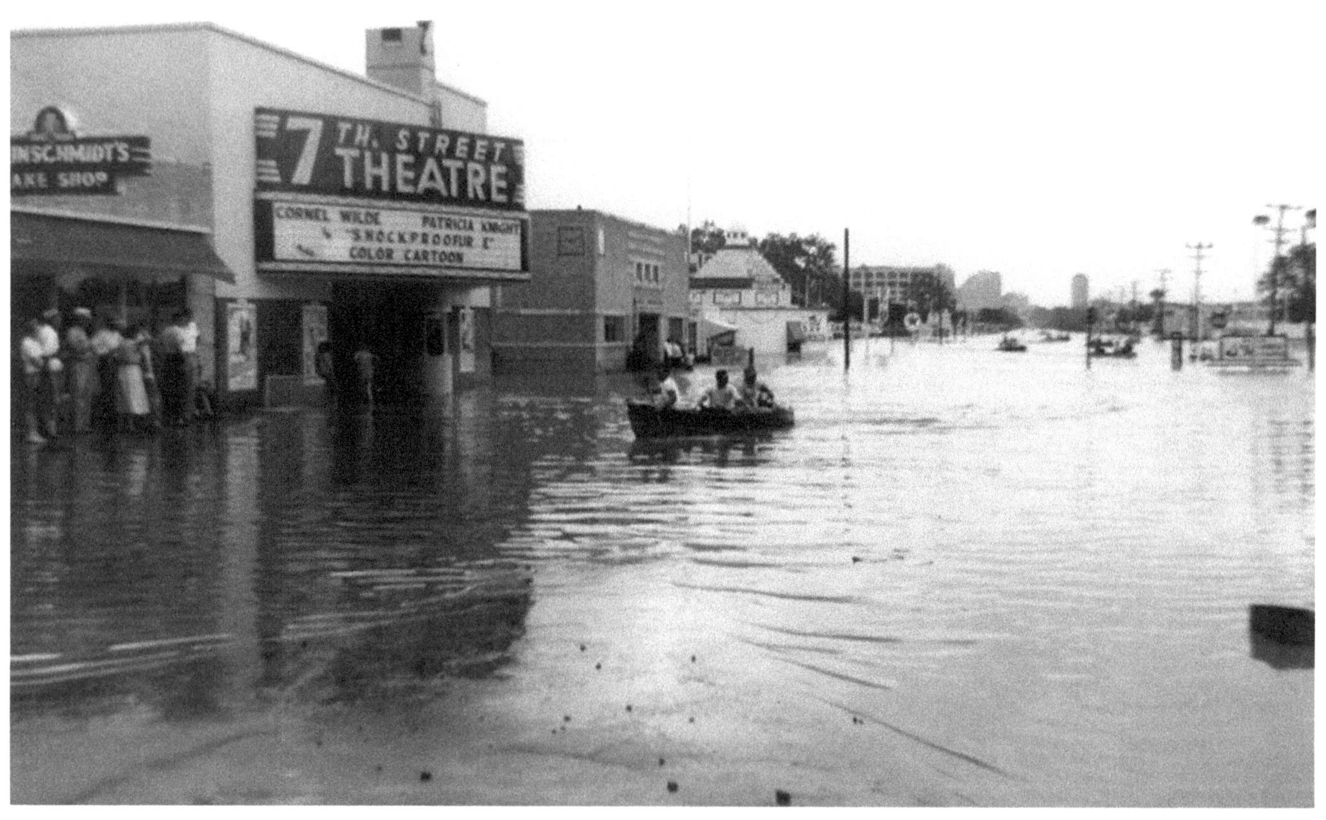


The Flood of May 1949 brought water close to the intersection of West 7th and Arch Adams Streets, allowing dockside service to both the Seventh Street Theatre and the renowned Kleinschmidt's Bake Shop. In the distance are Montgomery Ward's and the tower of the Medical Arts Building.

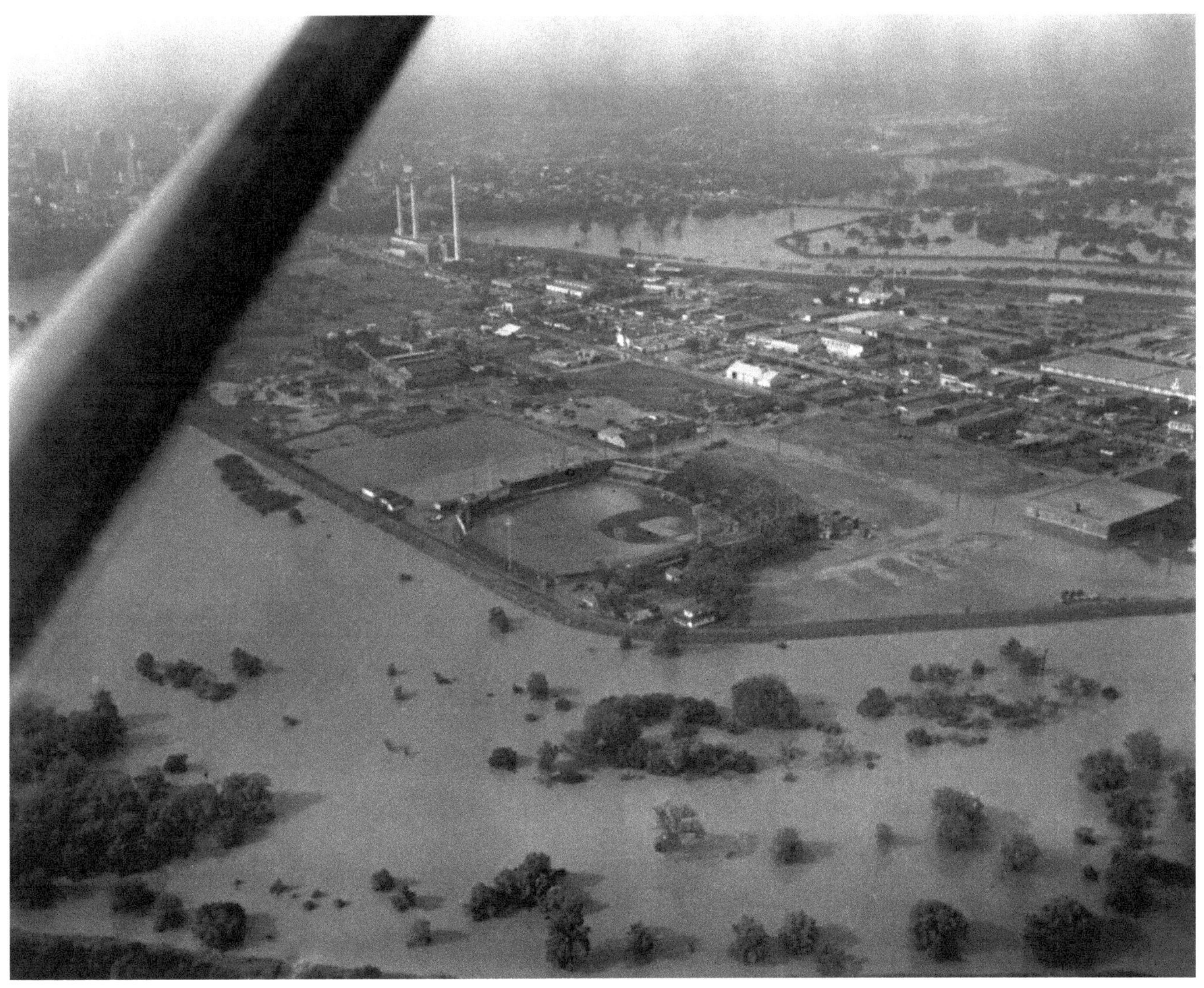

La Grave Field, center, home of the Fort Worth Cats, had just suffered the loss of its grandstand in a fire when the 1949 Flood inundated the area north of downtown. The signature smokestacks of the North Main Power Plant and the Paddock Viaduct are seen at top center. The receding floodwaters left behind over $11 million worth of damage and 13,000 homeless.

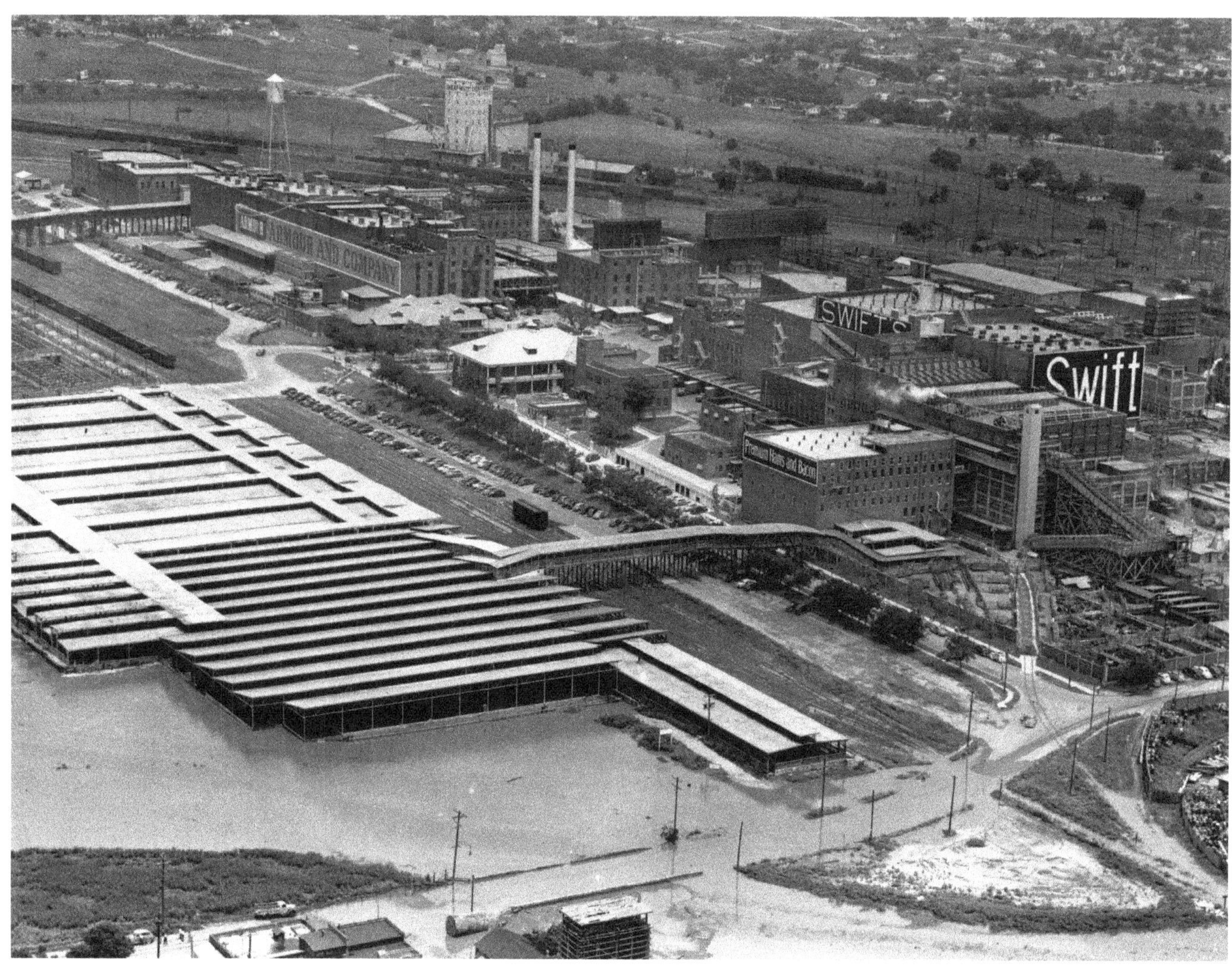


By the time of the May 1949 flood, the Fort Worth Stockyards had already started on the slow decline to closure after the peak year of 1944, when five and a quarter million animals were processed through the packing and rail facilities. Armour and Co. closed in 1962, followed by Swift's in 1971. The sprawling plants shown here have largely disappeared, with the exception of the columned Swift headquarters, center, restored in 2007. The hog and sheep pens, at left, were converted to the modern Stockyards Station, a major attraction in the National Historic District created in 1976 through the efforts of the North Fort Worth Historical Society, a volunteer organization whose museum in the District is dedicated to preserving the remarkable legacy of the livestock industry in Fort Worth.

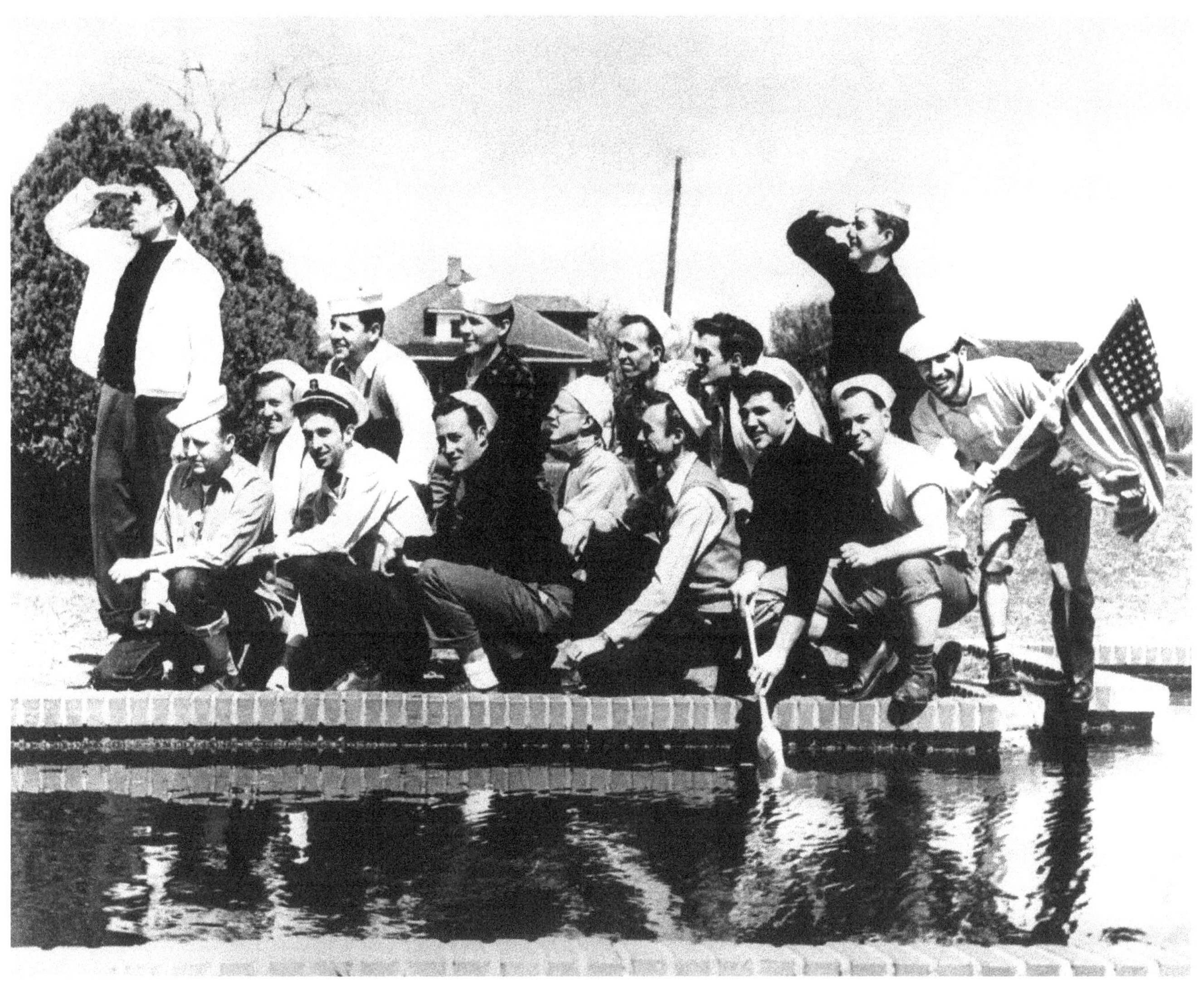

Across town, journalism students at Texas Christian University in 1949 established the whimsical TCU Yacht Club, commanding the waters of the fish pond in front of the Mary Couts Burnett Library. Among the "Admirals" of the club was Jack White, fourth from left, who went on to a long public relations career in Fort Worth and whose efforts to preserve the photographic history of the city helped protect for the future many of the images used in this book.

In commemoration of the one hundredth anniversary of the founding of Fort Worth, local riders reenacted the June 6, 1849, arrival of the 2nd United States Dragoons on the bluff overlooking the confluence of the Clear and West Forks of the Trinity River. Fort founder Major Ripley A. Arnold was portrayed by local celebrity Walker Moore as the soldiers paraded up Main Street and passed in front of the courthouse, built near the site of the original military camp.

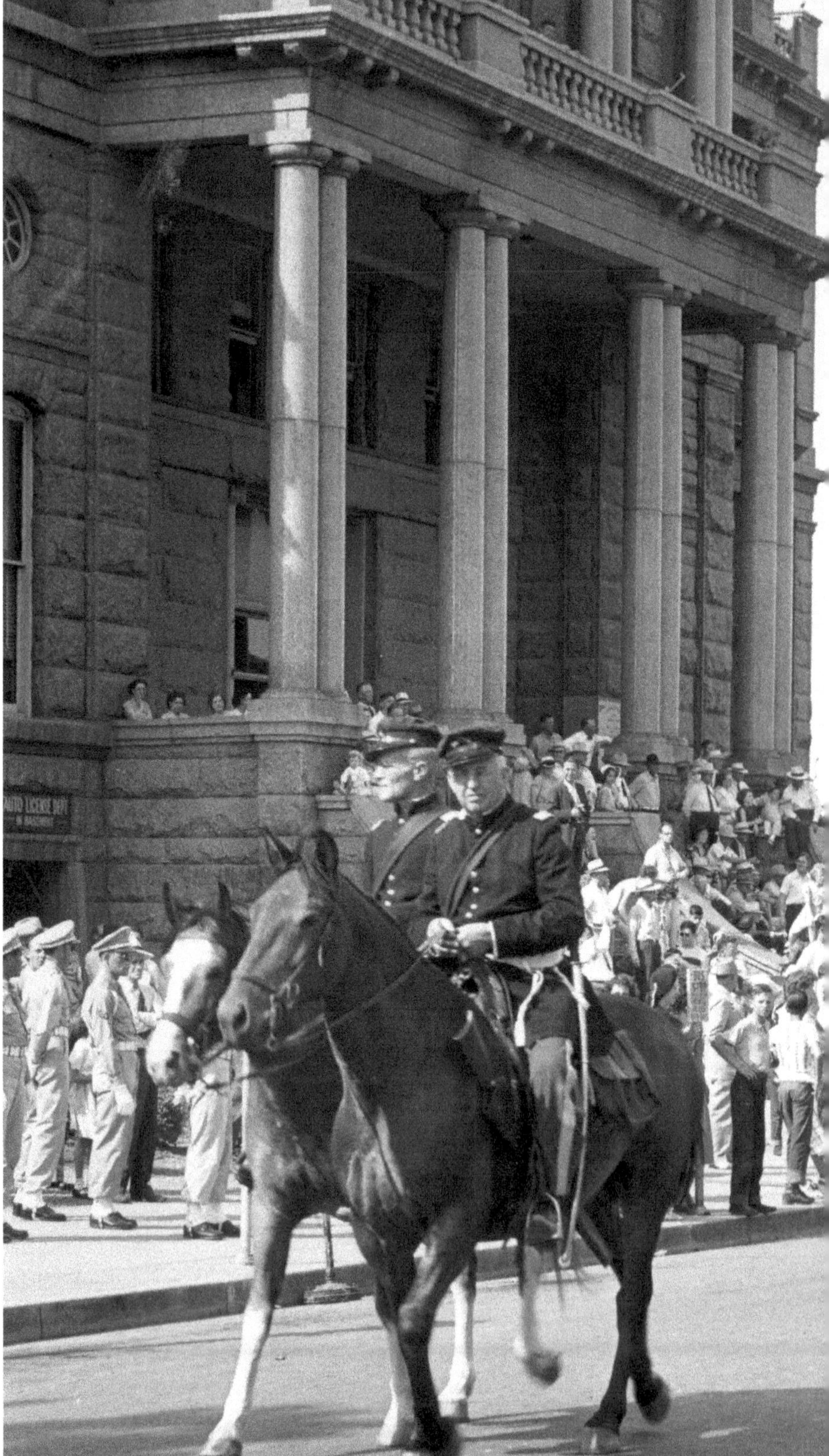

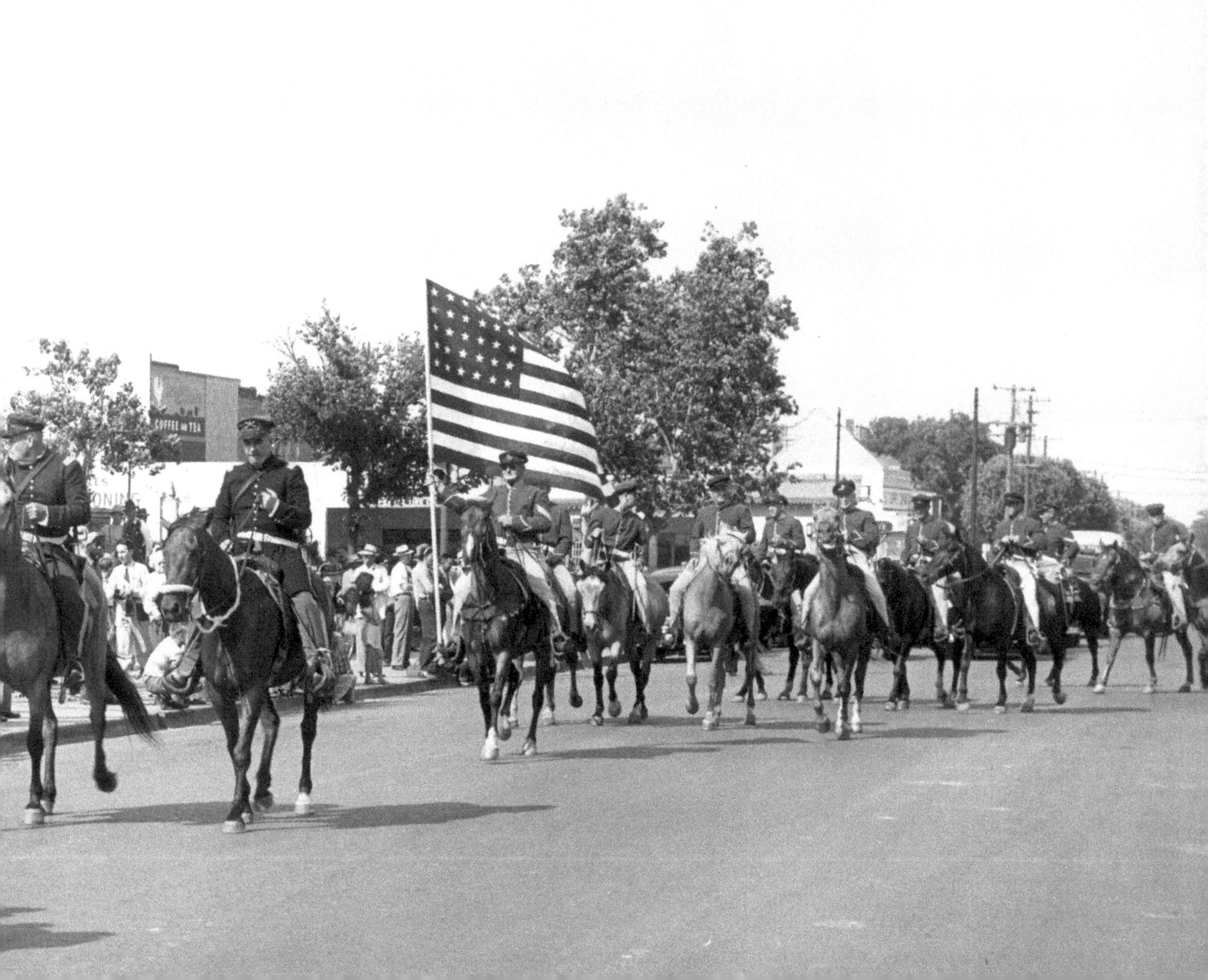

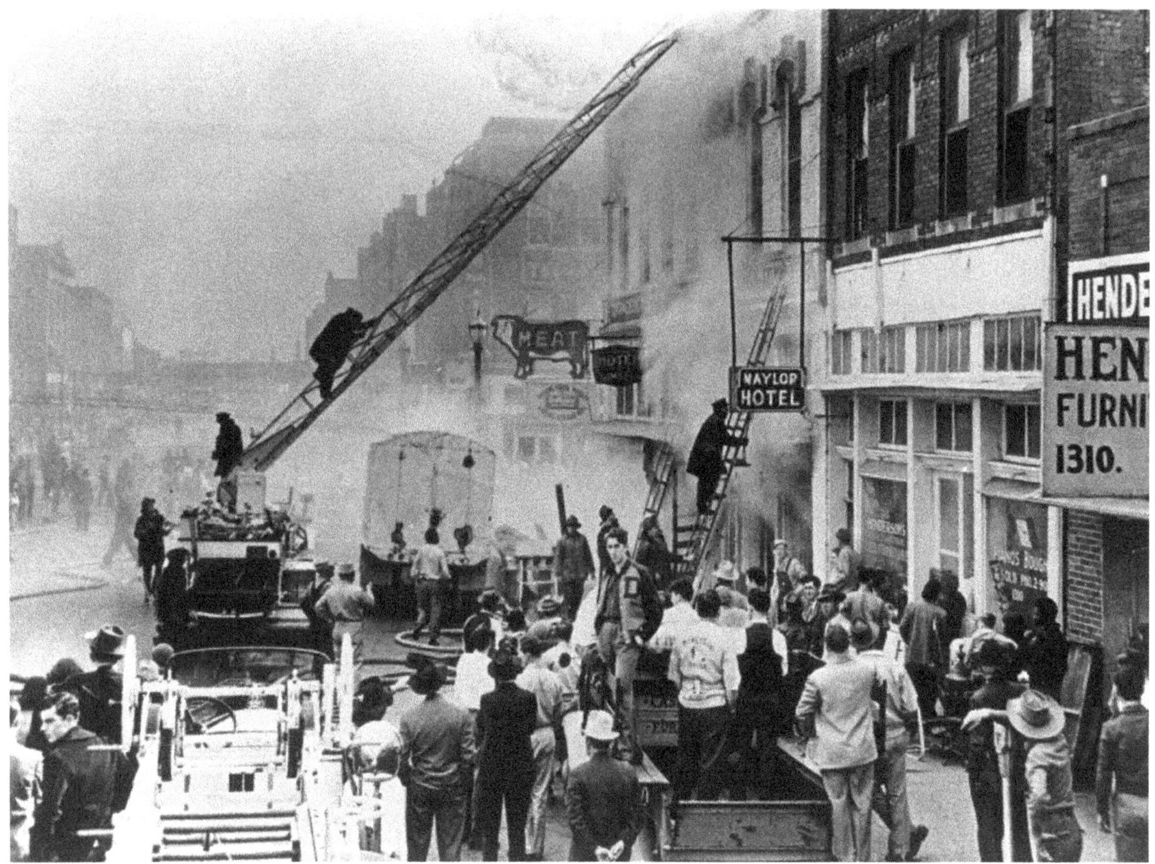


A crowd gathers to watch Fort Worth firefighters battle a blaze on the south end of Downtown about 1950. By that time, many of the old buildings in the once-vibrant business section had fallen into disrepair or were used for inexpensive housing—"flop houses," as one veteran firefighter recalled. Much of this area would be demolished a decade later to make way for the Convention Center.

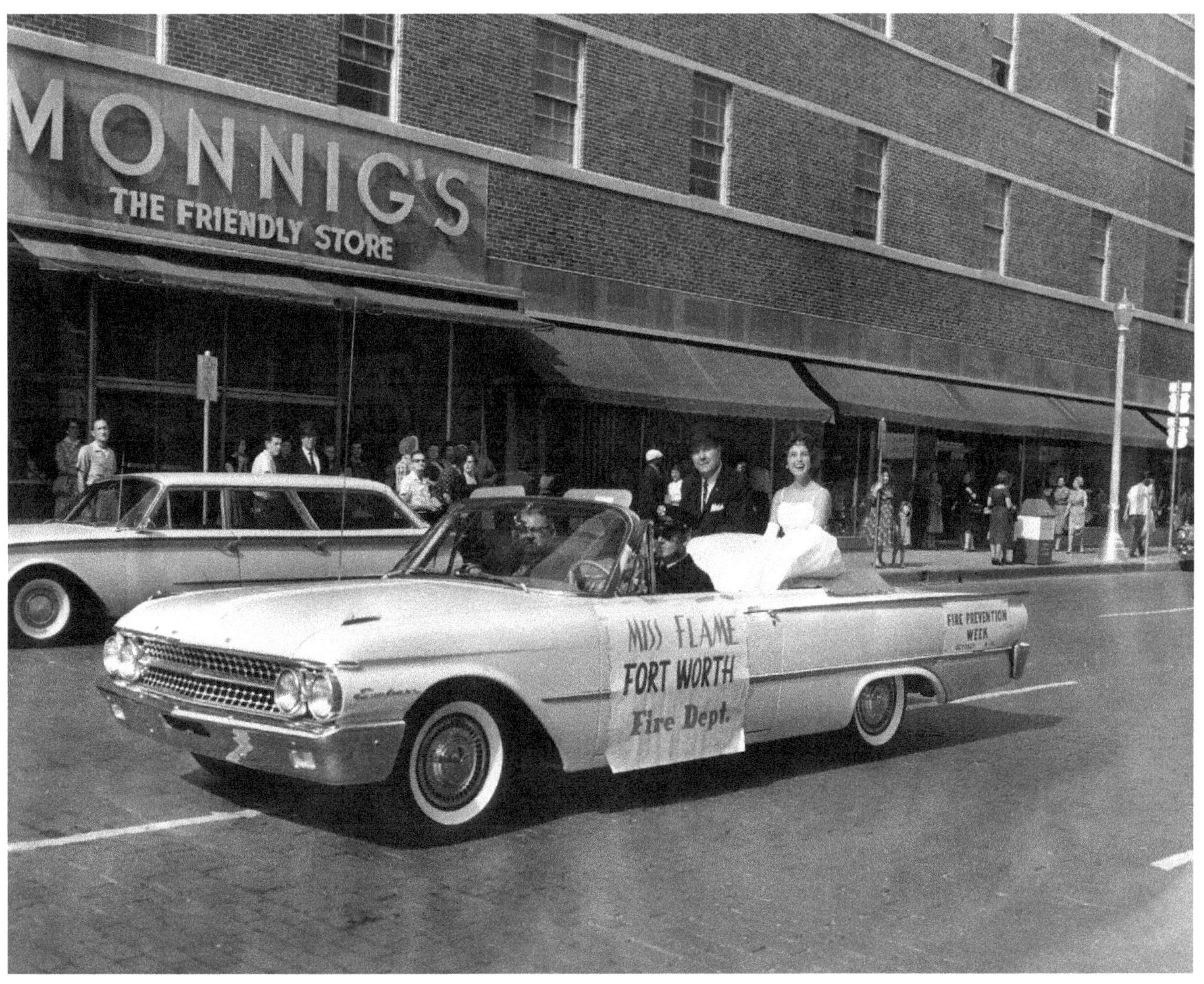


Fire Prevention Week was ably promoted throughout the sixties by the Fire Department's Miss Flame, whose duties included public appearances and parades. Behind her is one of Fort Worth's oldest stores, tracing its roots to 1889 when William Monnig arrived in Fort Worth to open a dry goods store. As owner of "the Friendly Store," Monnig served many leadership roles in the city, including heading up the Frontier Centennial Committee in 1936. In 1990, the company he founded was the last of the downtown retailers to move to the suburbs.

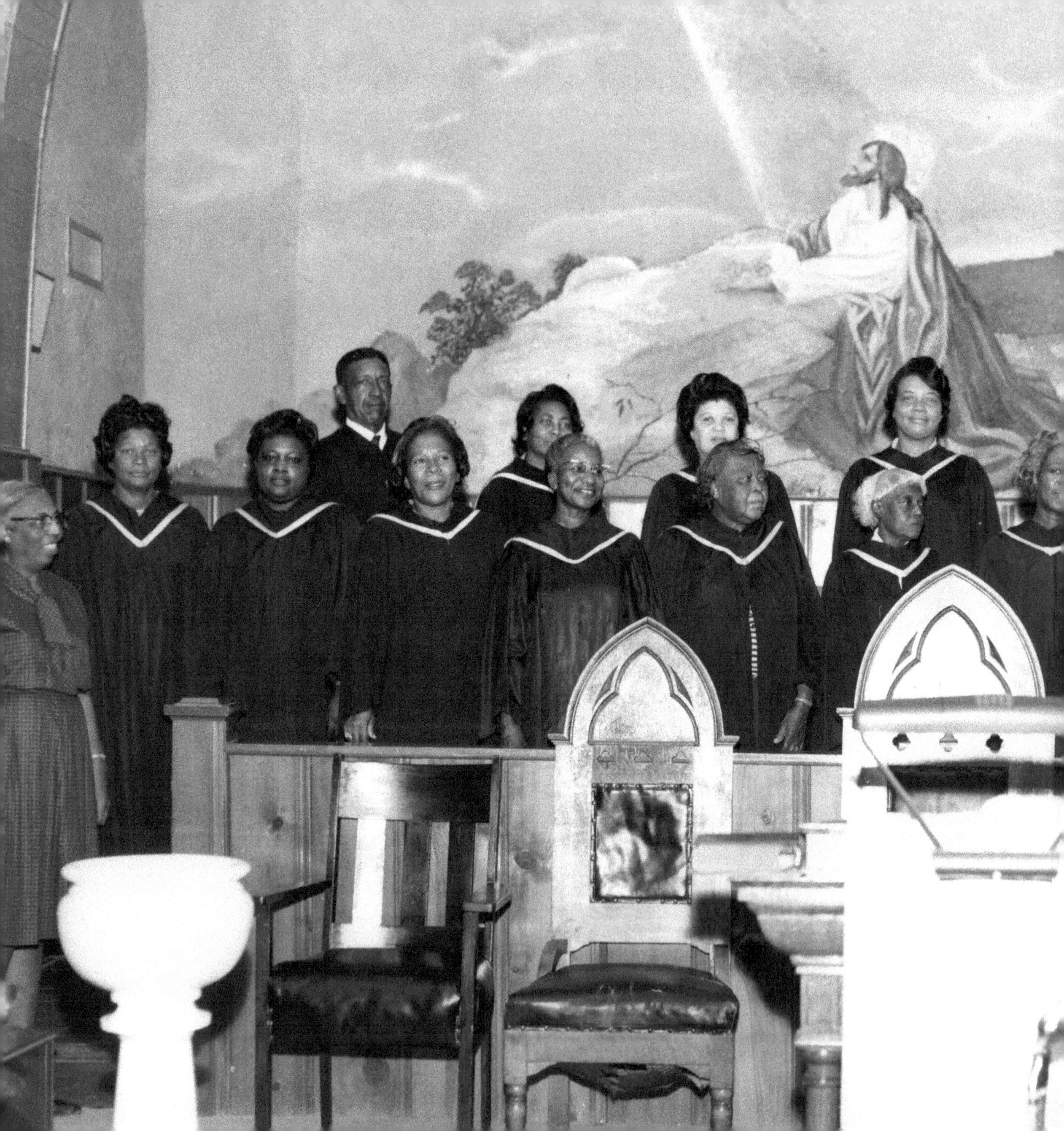

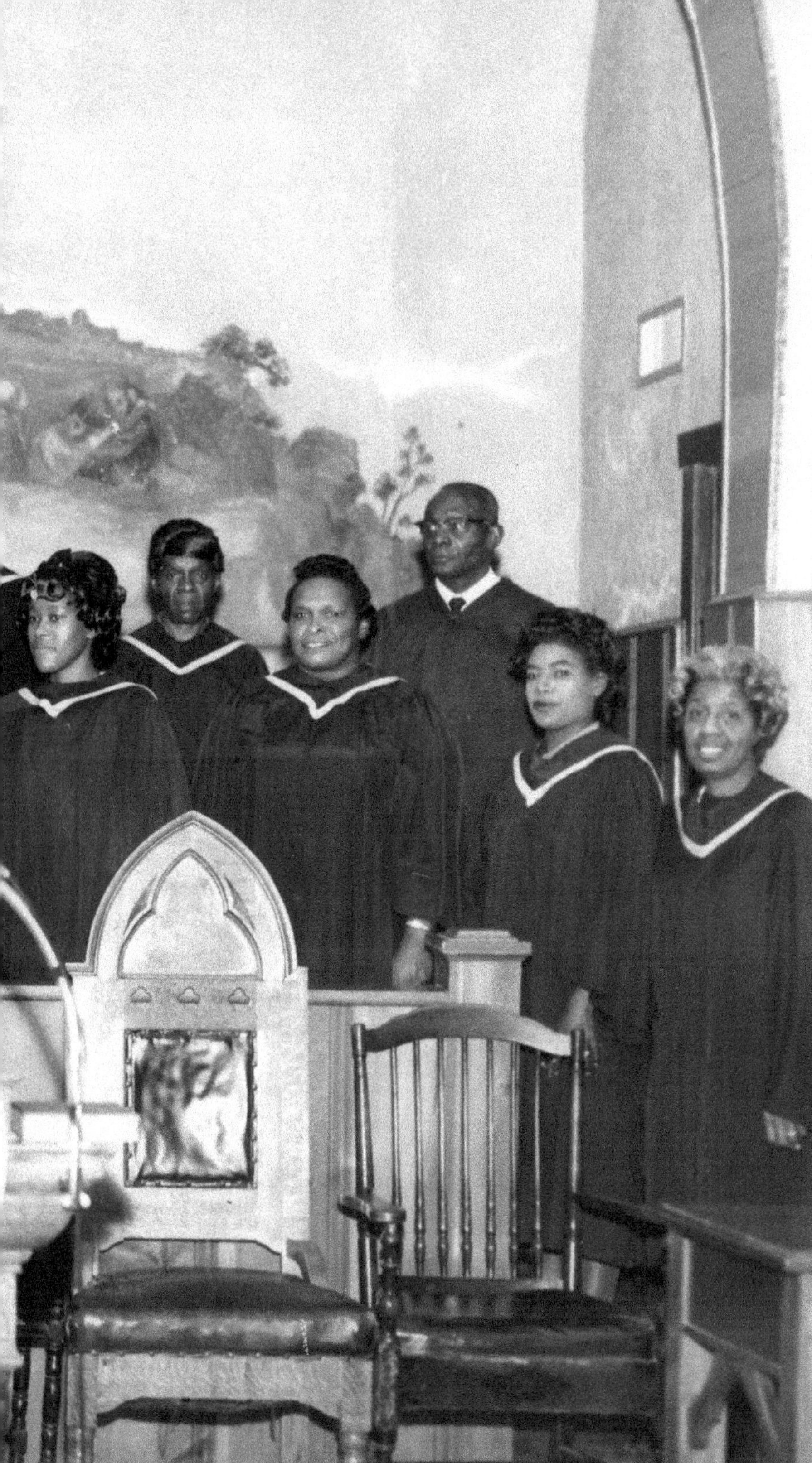

Fort Worth's oldest African American congregation was organized in 1866 and formally chartered in 1868 as Morning Chapel Colored Methodist Episcopal (C.M.E.) Church. In 1885, the church housed the first high school for African American students in the area, a program that evolved into the venerable I. M. Terrell High School that educated generations of community leaders. Nearly a century after the church's founding, members of the senior choir and their director, Mrs. Norvelle Stewart, far right, pose for a portrait by noted local photographer Calvin Littlejohn.

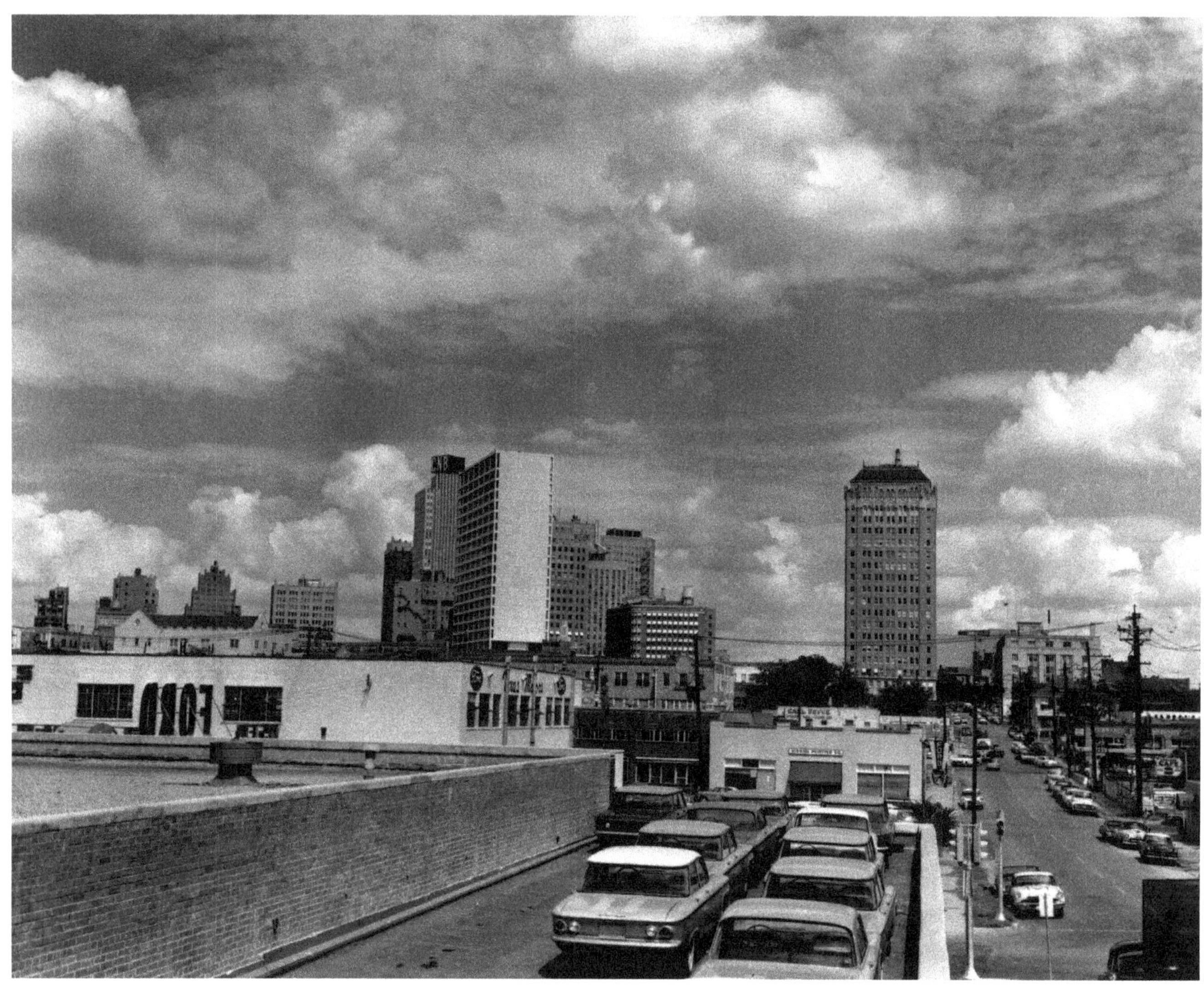

The new First National Bank Building, center, built in 1961 and designed by Skidmore, Owings and Merrill, introduced modern architecture to Fort Worth. This view, looking east on 10th Street from Henderson toward the Medical Arts Building and Federal Courthouse, shows the heart of the Automobile Row dealerships that extended along 7th Street. Texas Motors Ford started at this location in 1943.

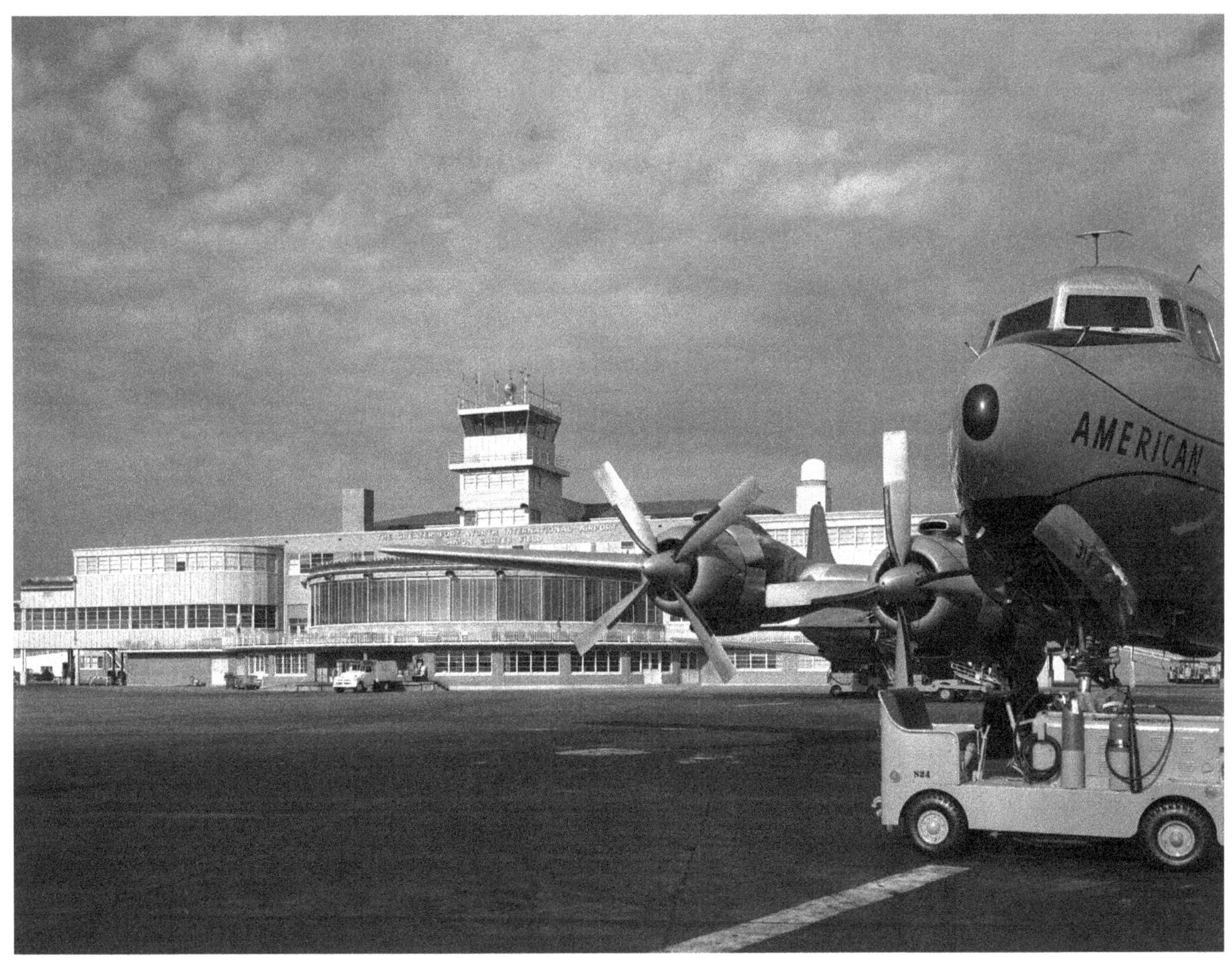


When construction began on Midway Airport in 1950, the new airfield was heralded as the long sought solution to settling the dispute between Fort Worth and Dallas over which city would dominate air services in the region. Dallas leaders balked because the airport lobby faced west to Fort Worth, and they refocused their energies to expand Love Field. The new airport built midway between the two cities was then renamed Greater Fort Worth International Airport. The two rivals eventually worked together to open Dallas Fort Worth International Airport in 1974, necessitating the closure of Amon Carter Field, as the midway facility had come to be called.

On November 21, 1963, President and Mrs. John F. Kennedy arrived in Fort Worth during a swing through Texas to rally Democratic leaders in advance of the 1964 elections. The Kennedys stayed the night at the Texas Hotel and attended a breakfast hosted by the chamber of commerce the next morning, before traveling to Dallas for a planned speech there. As he departed, the president greeted some of the sheriff's department mounted officers assigned to secure the area.

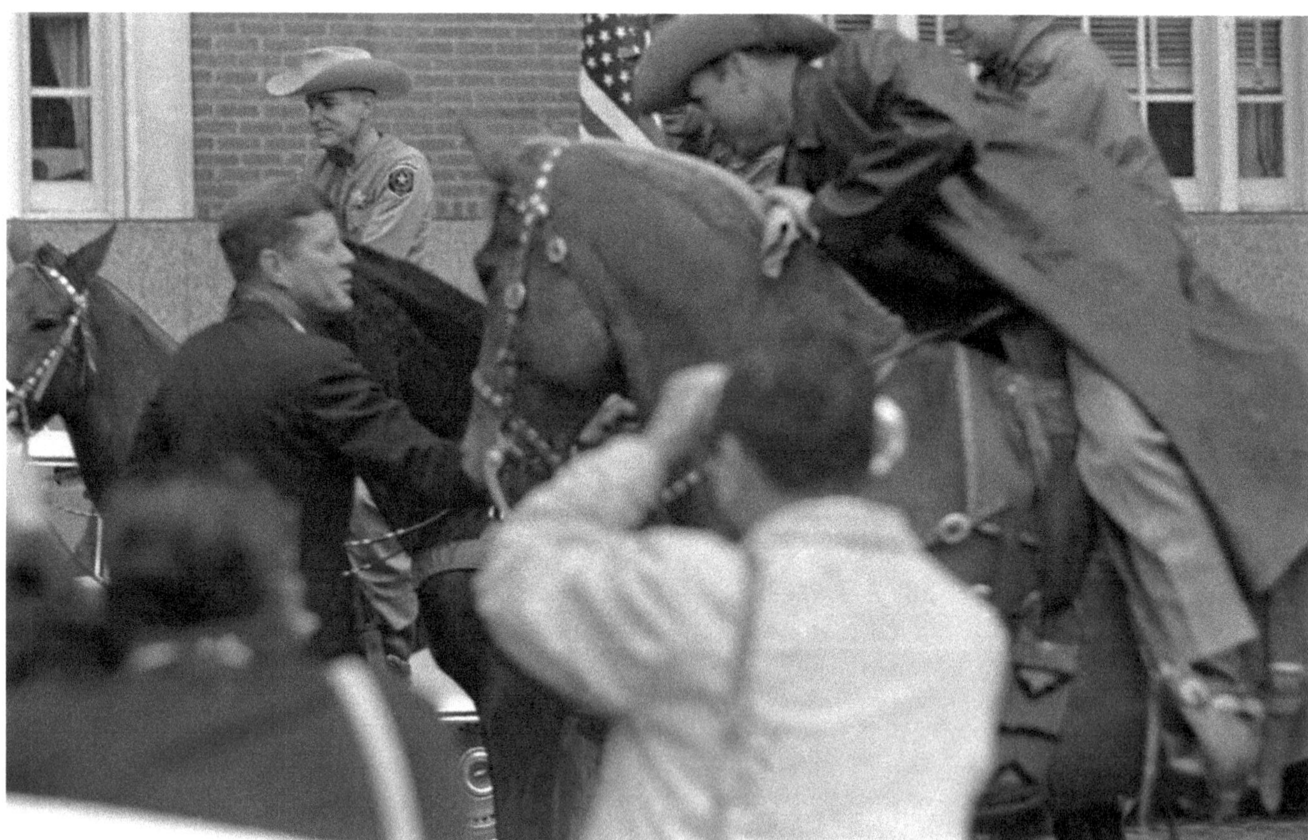

The president made a few remarks to a crowd of about eight thousand gathered outside the hotel on the drizzly morning of the 22nd and casually greeted some of the crowd before moving inside to the more formal chamber of commerce breakfast. Before heading to Carswell Air Force Base in a convertible borrowed from Ben Hogan, the Kennedys had an opportunity to enjoy a special art exhibit created for their hotel suite that included works borrowed from some of the museums and private collections in town.

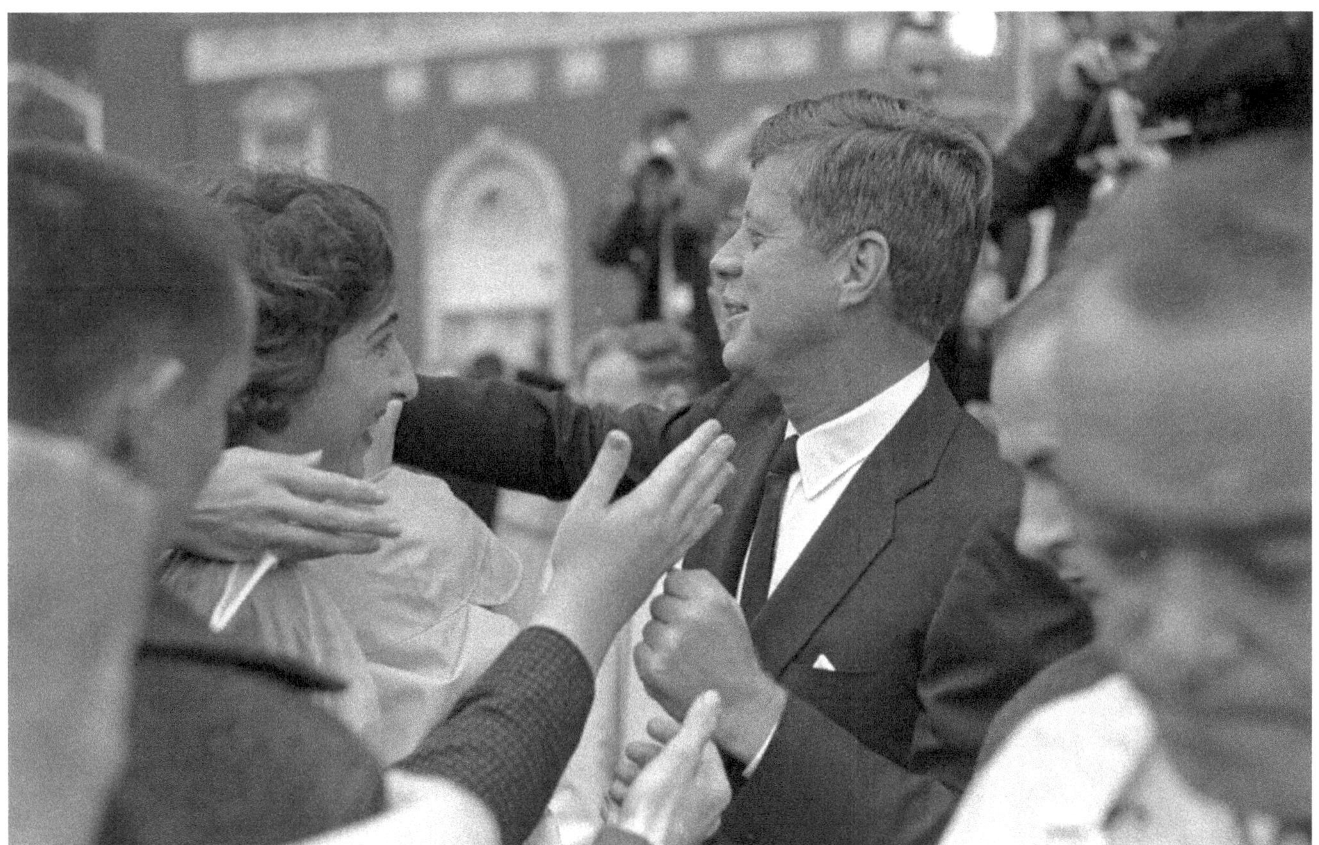

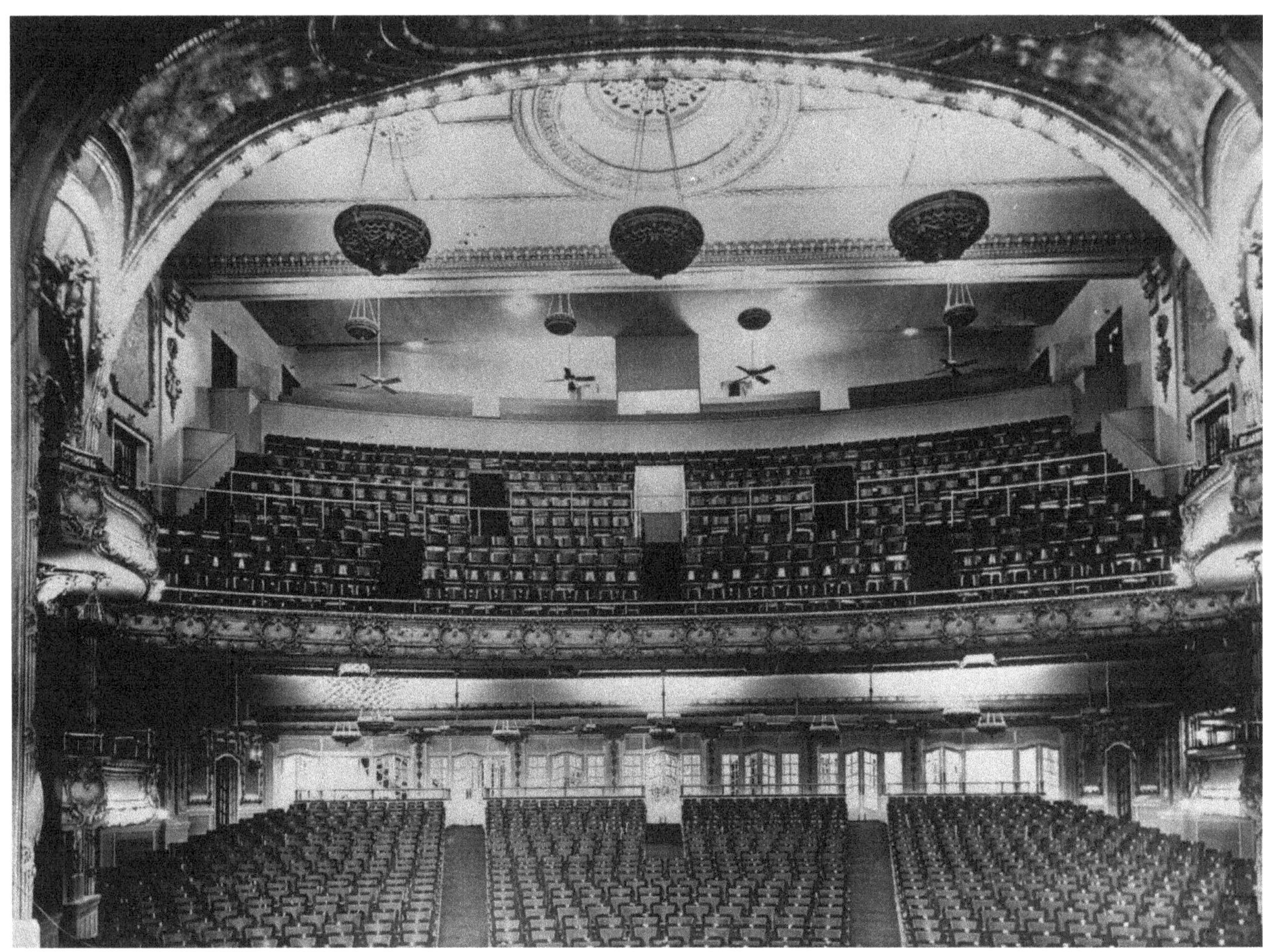

The face of Downtown began to change dramatically during the 1950s as once-bustling commercial areas and expensive residential neighborhoods began to show their age and fall to the wrecking ball. In 1966, the demolition of the magnificent 1910 Majestic Theatre at 10th and Commerce paved the way for the removal of thirteen blocks of buildings along Main Street below 9th for the construction of the Tarrant County Convention Center, completed in 1968.

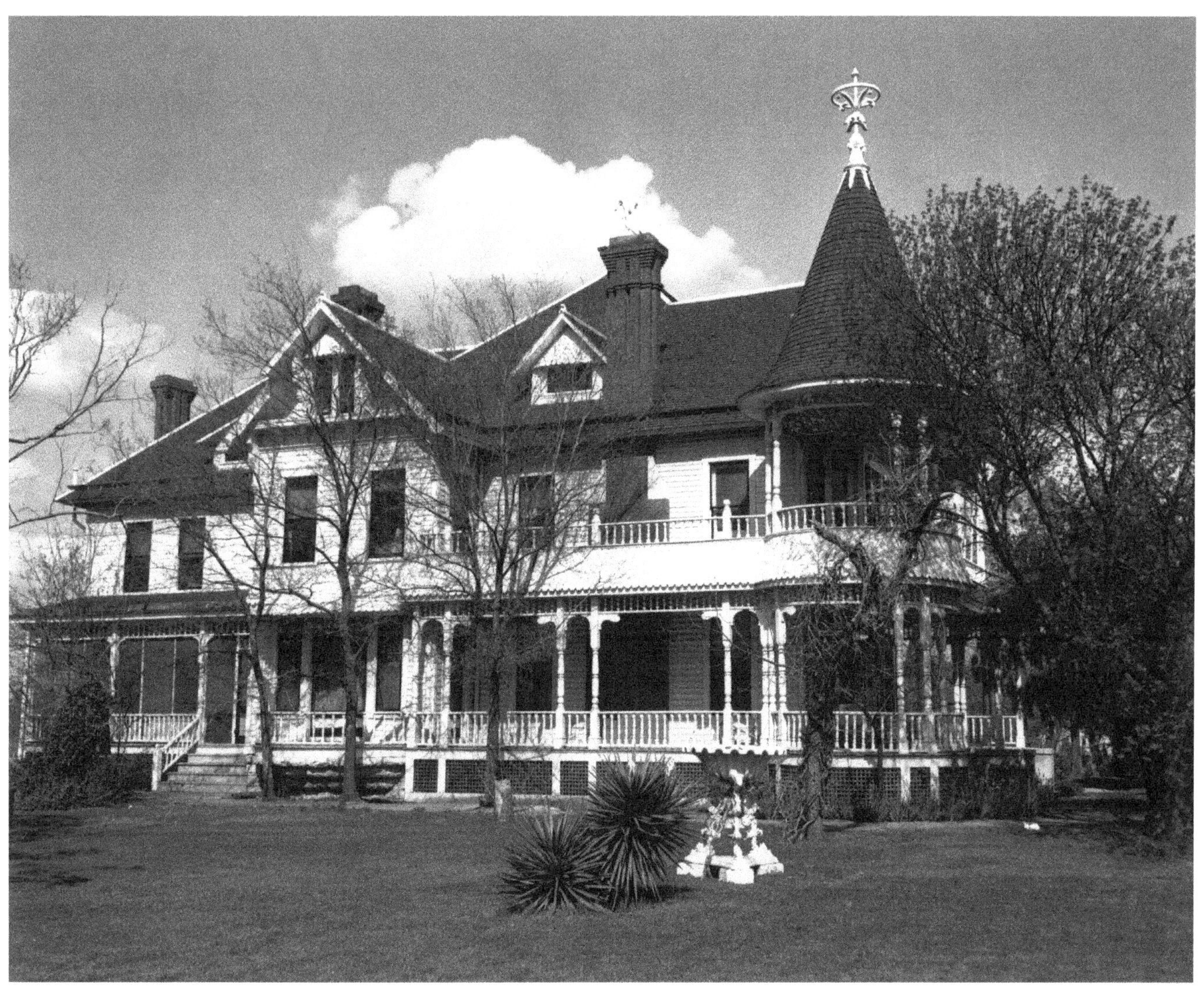

Built about 1889 as the first house in the new Arlington Heights subdivision, this classical Victorian home was probably constructed for the development's first president, George Tallant. Considered one of a dozen most important buildings worthy of preservation in Fort Worth in a 1969 study commissioned by Historic Fort Worth, the house was nevertheless demolished to make way for new development in 1970. Robert McCart, an early Fort Worth business leader who provided financial backing for the Texas Spring Palace and gave land for the development of Camp Bowie during World War I, owned the house for many years.

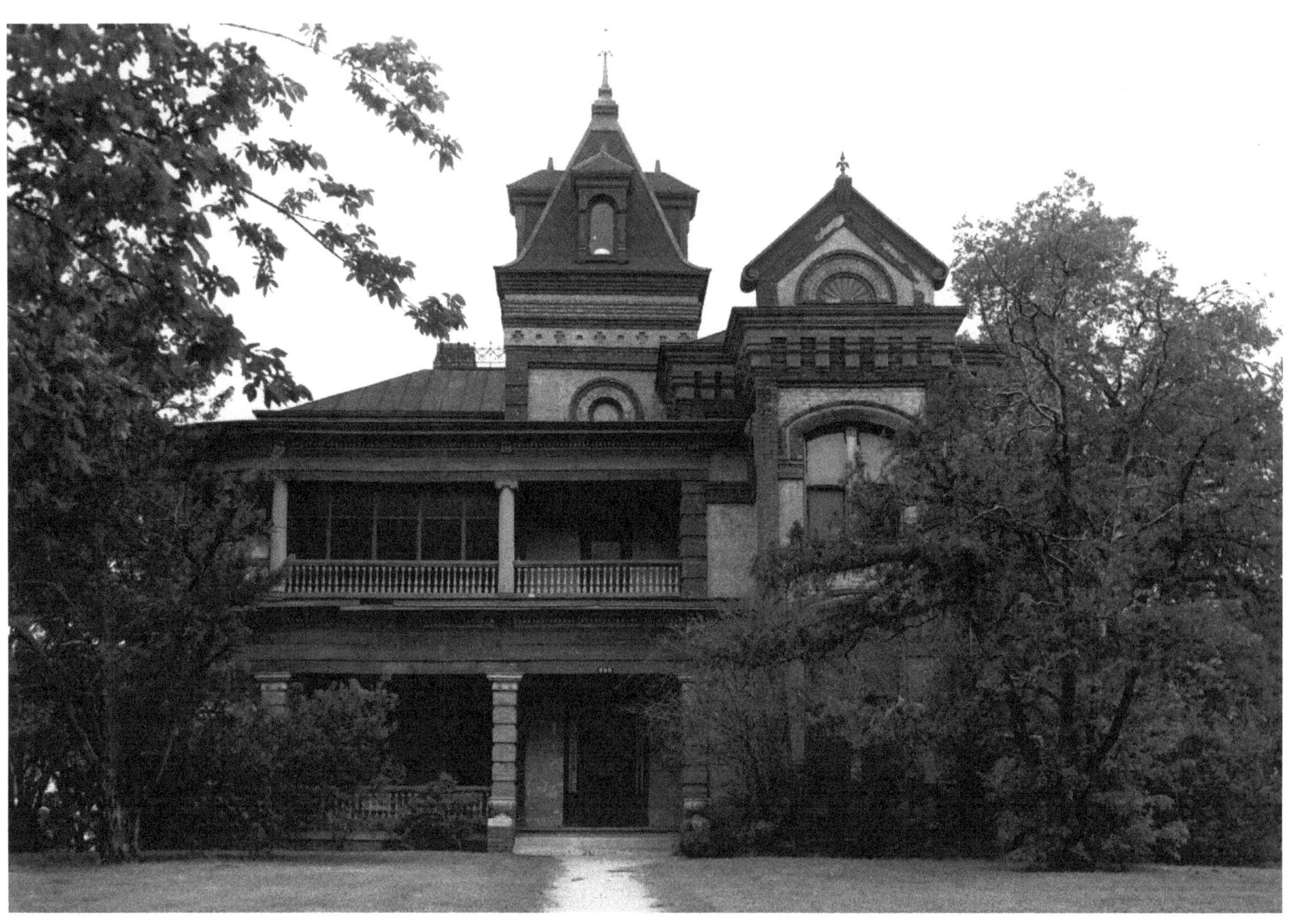

One of the classic homes on the nineteenth century "silk stocking row" along Summit Avenue and Penn Street, the K. M. Van Zandt house stood on downtown's western bluff at the southwest corner of 7th and Penn streets. The founder of the Fort Worth National Bank and early civic pioneer expanded his original 1874 home into the mansion seen here in a photograph taken shortly before its demolition in 1968. The site is now occupied by the Educational Employees Credit Union, which incorporated the limestone curbing that once surrounded the property into the landscape facing 7th Street.

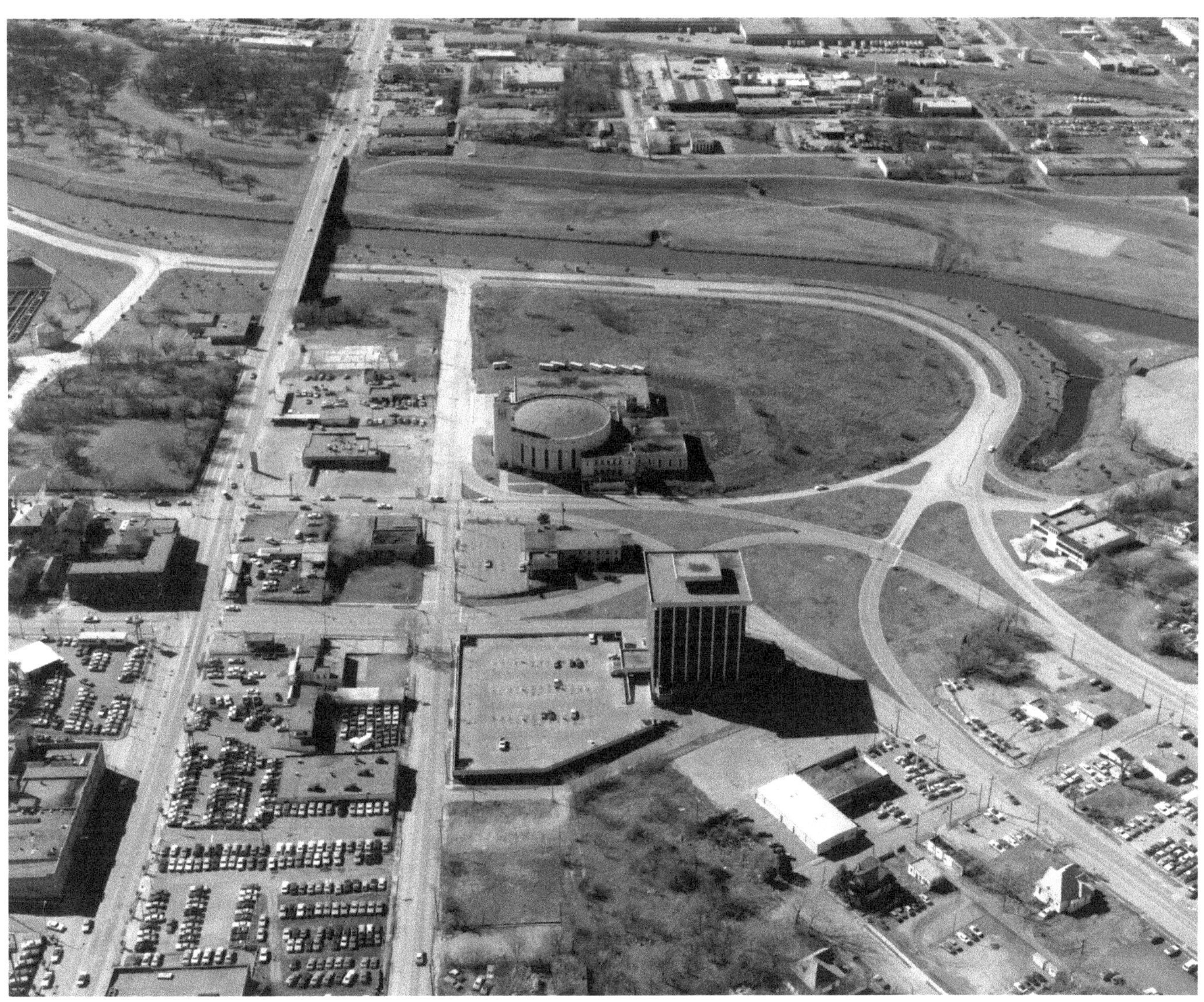

Taken about 1968, this image shows the newly completed Mallick Tower, bottom center, the first high-rise built west of Henderson Street. Just above it is the new home for the First Baptist Church at 5th and Penn streets, now the site of Pier One's headquarters. The small inlet at far right is the only remaining trace of Robinson's Branch, a creek that ran along what is present-day Henderson Street and named for Arch Robinson, the original owner of the land in the 1840s. The wooded lot, center left, along 7th Street, was the site of the recently demolished Van Zandt home.

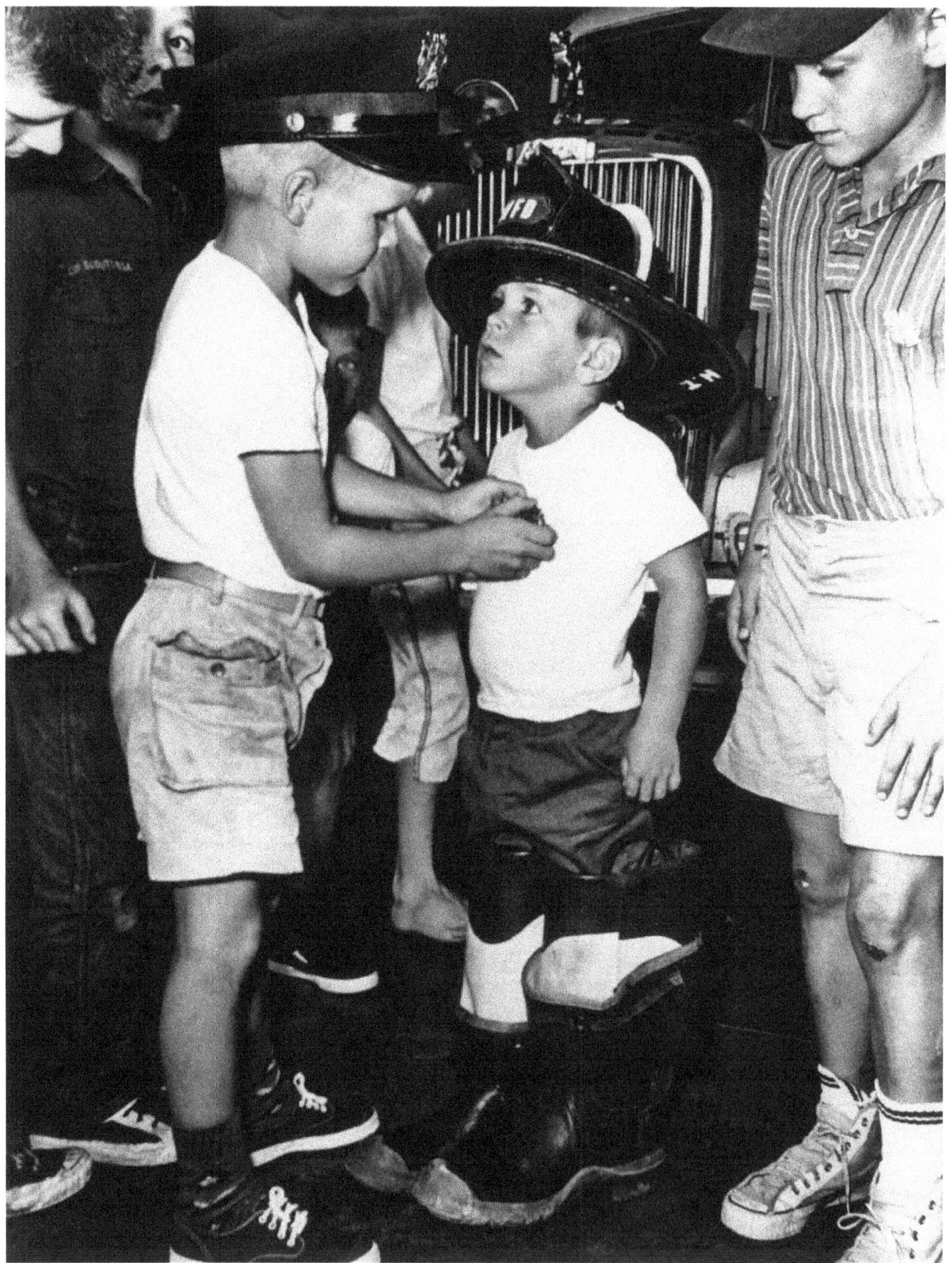

Fort Worth *Press* and later *Star-Telegram* photographer Gene Gordon captured this group of serious future firefighters during a "Sparky Party" at Station 26 at Hulen and Trail Lake in the early 1960s. Thousands of Fort Worth children learned fire safety from Captain William "Fireman Bill" Pierce, who, with Captain Luther Koch, created an innovative teaching tool, the "Sparky Fire Department," in 1954.

During a routine scuba training dive at Lake Benbrook in the late 1960s, members of the rescue team found a submerged 1947 Studebaker, verified by the police as having been stolen many years earlier. As the recovered car drained on shore, surprised firefighters heard something move in the trunk. This photograph of the 67- and 68-pound catfish that had evidently grown up in the back of the car hit the wire services and ran worldwide.

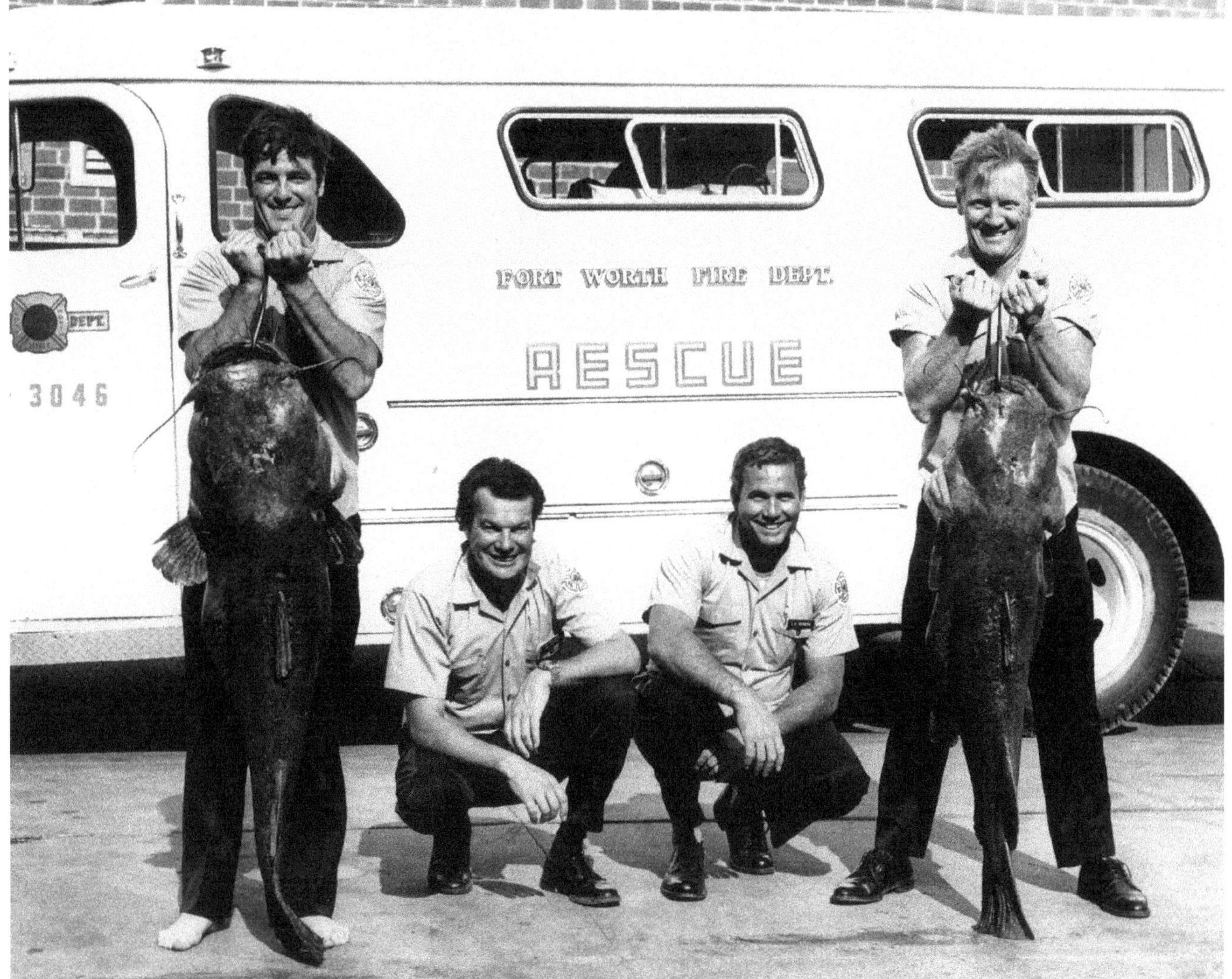

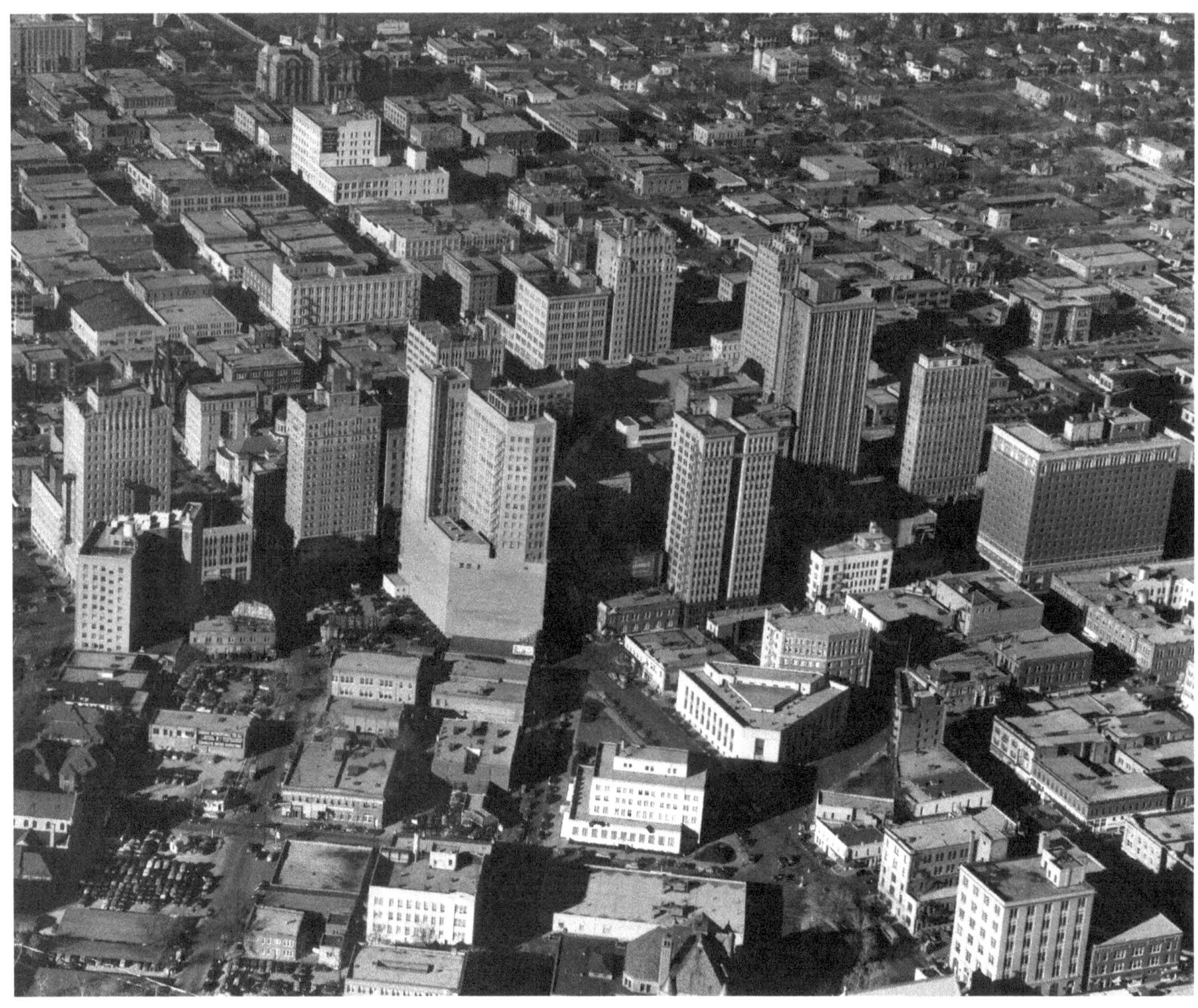

By 1950, few new buildings had been added to the city's skyline since the boom building years of the 1920s. The 1896 Federal Building can be seen at bottom center, and the tallest structure in town was still the 1921 Fort Worth National Bank Building at 7th and Main. Major changes were on the horizon as Fort Worth struggled with one of the pressing urban issues of the day—how to keep Downtown alive as suburban growth skyrocketed.

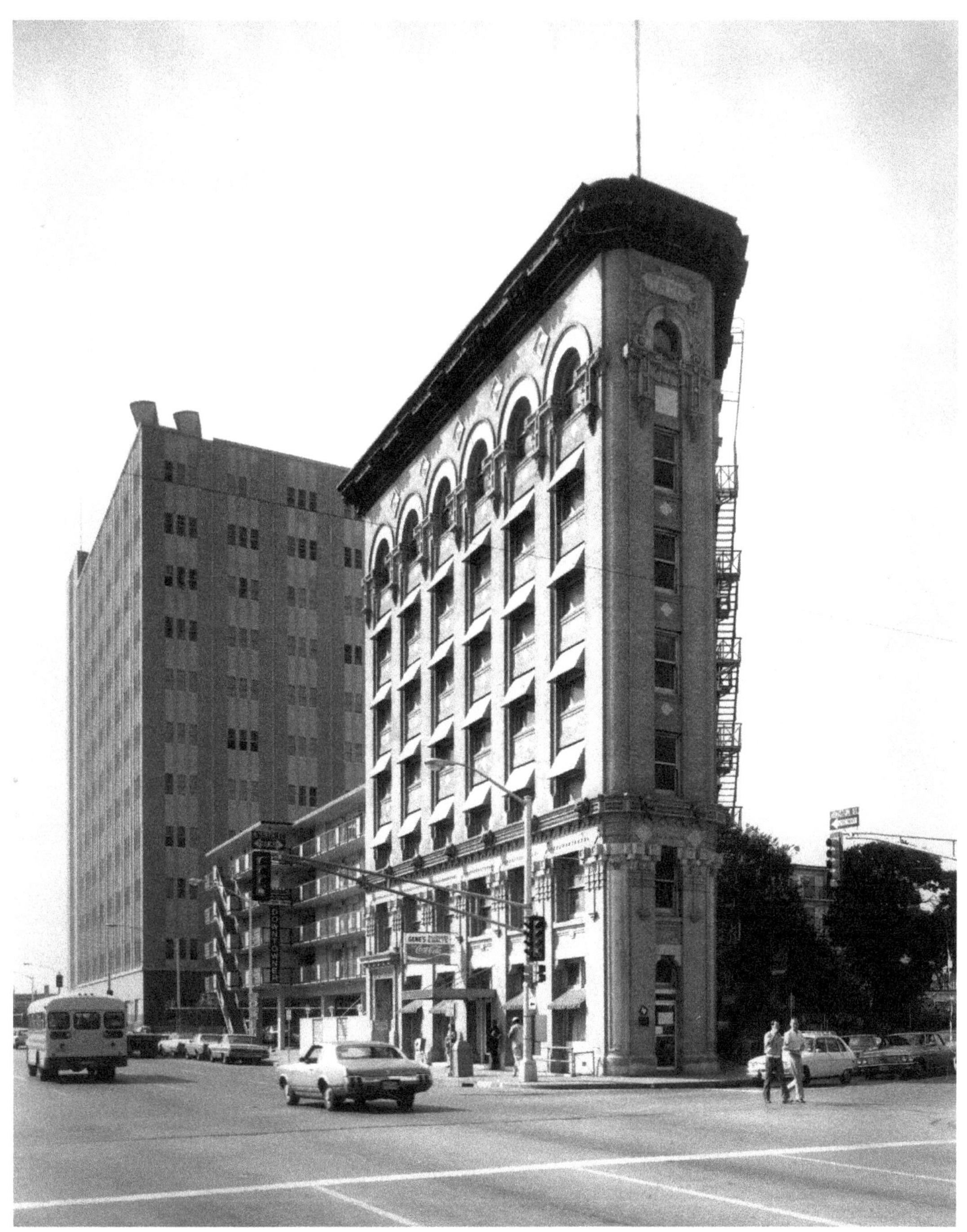

In this picture taken about 1968, the Flatiron Building's former neighbors, the Lyric Theatre and Robertson's Funeral Home, have been replaced by a hotel and the Southwestern Bell Building beyond it. Long considered one of Fort Worth's most important and beloved structures, the Flatiron enters its second century completely restored, a reminder of the early dreams of its builders.

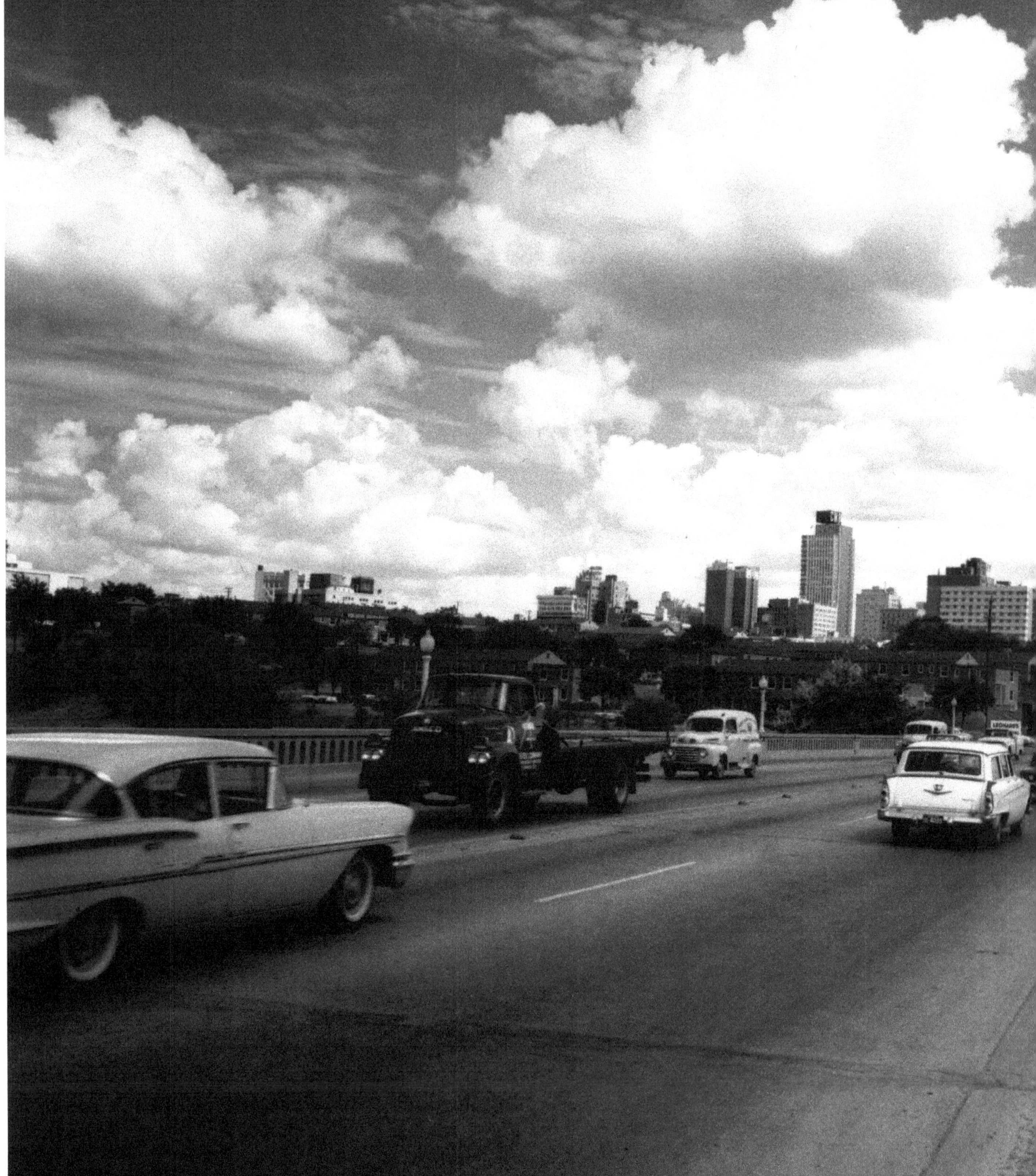

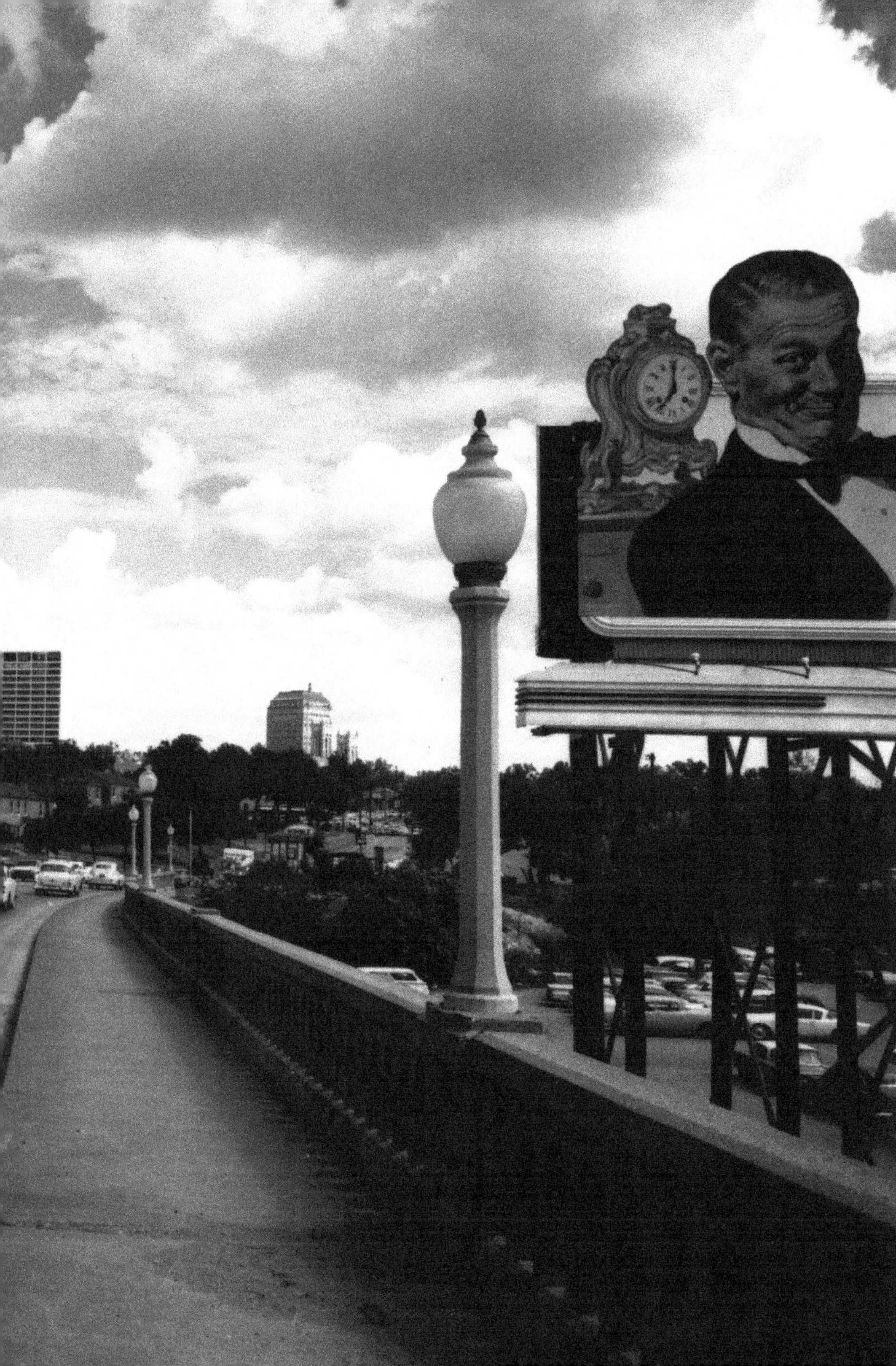

Drivers entering Downtown from the Jacksboro Highway across the Henderson Street Bridge were greeted for years by the elegant character on a liquor billboard, a not-altogether-unfitting reminder of the roadway's wild past. The 1957 Continental National Bank Building, with its enormous revolving clock dominates the skyline about 1962, after the completion of a new home for the First National Bank, seen just above the roadway.

Before its relocation to Sundance Square, the city's official Christmas tree, for many years sponsored by the Fort Worth Jaycees, turned Burnett Park into a holiday wonderland. The Downtown Building Owners and Managers Association made sure every major building in downtown was outlined in lights. With nature's lights adding to the display, the First National Bank, left, and the Electric and Neil P. Anderson Buildings glistened on a rainy night about 1965.

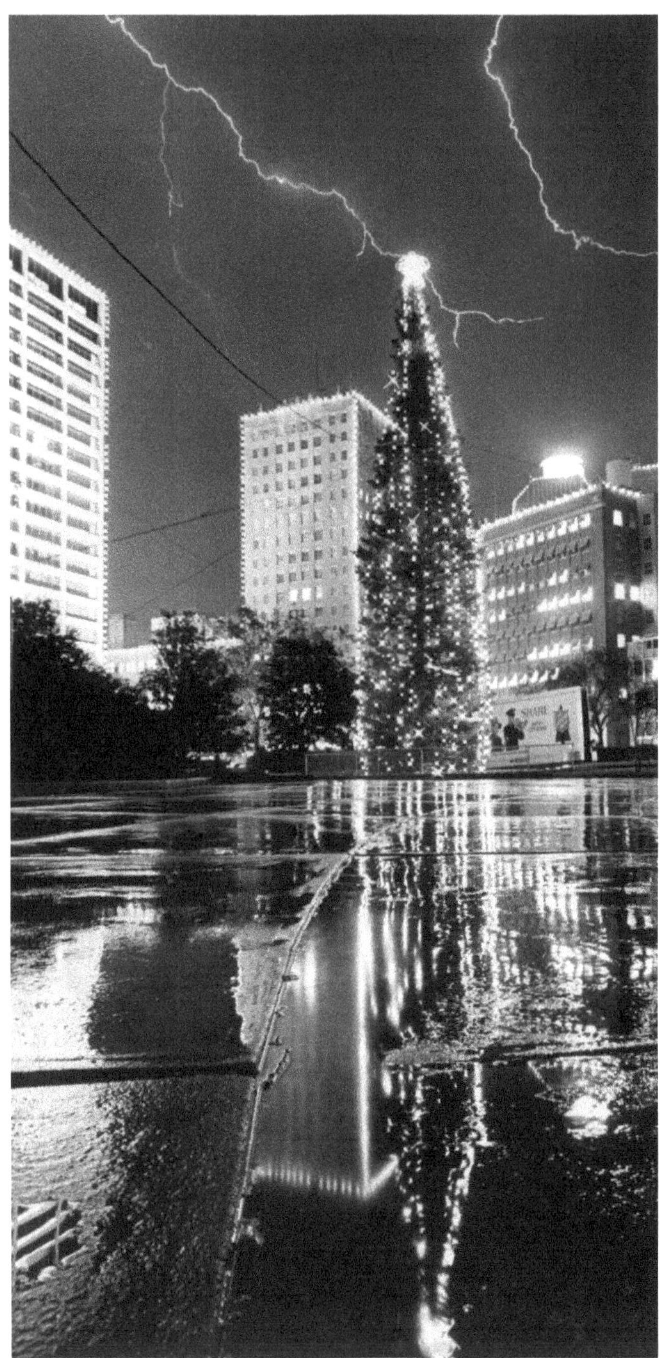

# Notes on the Photographs

These notes, listed by page number, attempt to include all aspects known of the photographs. Each of the photographs is identified by the page number, photograph's title or description, photographer and collection, archive, and call or box number when applicable. Although every attempt was made to collect all available data, in some cases complete data was unavailable due to the age and condition of some of the photographs and records.

**II Texas & Pacific Railroad Station**
Tarrant County Historical Society
Fort Worth Public Library
B-0023

**VI Will Rogers Statue**
Tarrant County Historical Society
Fort Worth Public Library
O-0024

**X Masonic Lodge No. 148**
Fort Worth Star-Telegram Collection, Special Collections
The University of Texas at Arlington Library, Arlington, Texas
AR406.1

**2 The Daggett and Hatcher Store**
Tarrant County Historical Society
Fort Worth Public Library
A-0033

**3 Market Day, Courthouse Square 1878**
Jack White Photograph Collection, Special Collections
The University of Texas at Arlington Library, Arlington, Texas
A-0019

**4 Tarrant County Courthouse**
Tarrant County Historical Society
Fort Worth Public Library
B-0007

**5 First City Hall, 1877**
Jim Noah Collection
The University of Texas at Arlington Library, Arlington, Texas
1stCityHall_1877

**6 Dugan's Wagon Yard**
Tarrant County Historical Society
Fort Worth Public Library
C-0092

**7 Boaz and Battle Cotton Yard**
Tarrant County Historical Society
Fort Worth Public Library
N-0009

**8 1876 Courthouse**
Jack White Photograph Collection, Special Collections
The University of Texas at Arlington Library, Arlington, Texas
1876 Courthouse

**9 1882 Courthouse**
Jack White Photograph Collection, Special Collections
The University of Texas at Arlington Library, Arlington, Texas
1882 Courthouse

**10 East Side Square 1884**
Fort Worth Star-Telegram Collection, Special Collections
The University of Texas at Arlington Library, Arlington, Texas
East side Square 1884

**11 Sam Levy House 1888**
Fort Worth Star-Telegram Collection, Special Collections
The University of Texas at Arlington Library, Arlington, Texas
Sam Levy House 1888

**12 Houston Street**
Tarrant County Historical Society
Fort Worth Public Library
A-0002

**13 Knights of Pythias Castle 1881**
Tarrant County Historical Society
Fort Worth Public Library
Knights of Pythias

**14 Lewis Blacksmith**
W. D. Smith Photograph Collection, Special Collections
The University of Texas at Arlington Library, Arlington, Texas
82-1-192

**15 St. Joseph's Infirmary**
Tarrant County Historical Society
Fort Worth Public Library
FW-101

**16 Main Street**
Tarrant County Historical Society
Fort Worth Public Library
A-0005

**17 Main Street 1900**
Fort Worth Star-Telegram Collection, Special Collections
The University of Texas at Arlington Library, Arlington, Texas
0003

**18 The Eberhard Anheuser Company Brewing Association**
Fort Worth Public Library
FW-106

**20 Railroads N. D.**
Fort Worth Star-Telegram Collection, Special Collections
The University of Texas at Arlington Library, Arlington, Texas
FWST# H178

**21 Polytechnic College**
Jack White Photograph Collection, Special Collections
The University of Texas at Arlington Library, Arlington, Texas
0056

**22 Texas Spring Palace, 1889**
Fort Worth Star-Telegram Collection, Special Collections
The University of Texas at Arlington Library, Arlington, Texas
48-1-59

**23 Texas Spring Palace**
Fort Worth Star-Telegram Collection, Special Collections
The University of Texas at Arlington Library, Arlington, Texas
0004

**24 Hotel Worth 1889**
W. D. Smith Photograph Collection, Special Collections
The University of Texas at Arlington Library, Arlington, Texas
76-1-176

**25 Cigar Store**
Tarrant County Historical Society
Fort Worth Public Library
Photo # 58

**26 Texas Brewing Wagon**
Fort Worth Star-Telegram Collection, Special Collections
The University of Texas at Arlington Library, Arlington, Texas
FWST# H102

**28 Tarrant County Courthouse Under Construction 1893**
Fort Worth Star-Telegram Collection, Special Collections
The University of Texas at Arlington Library, Arlington, Texas
AR406 #981

**29 Construction Foremen**
Jack White Photograph Collection, Special Collections
The University of Texas at Arlington Library, Arlington, Texas
AR407-1

**30 Post Office—Federal Courthouse**
Tarrant County Historical Society
Fort Worth Public Library
Photo # 105

**31 Jennings Ave., 1896**
The University of Texas at Arlington Library, Arlington, Texas
A-0006

**32 Bicocchi Grocery 1894**
Jack White Photograph Collection, Special Collections
The University of Texas at Arlington Library, Arlington, Texas
AR407-6-57

**34 Police Dept.**
Fort Worth Star-Telegram Collection, Special Collections
The University of Texas at Arlington Library, Arlington, Texas
FWST# 2502

**35 The Elks First Clubhouse**
Tarrant County Historical Society
Fort Worth Public Library
I-0005

**36 The Panthers**
Tarrant County Historical Society
Fort Worth Public Library
G-0041

**38 Fort Worth University 1889 College Ave.**
Jack White Photograph Collection, Special Collections
The University of Texas at Arlington Library, Arlington, Texas
AR407-6-57

**40 First "Skyscraper"**
Jack White Photograph Collection, Special Collections
The University of Texas at Arlington Library, Arlington, Texas

**41 Hurley Building Fire**
Fort Worth Star-Telegram Collection, Special Collections
The University of Texas at Arlington Library, Arlington, Texas
AR406

**42 Lee Whitsitt's Drug Store**
Jack White Photograph Collection, Special Collections
The University of Texas at Arlington Library, Arlington, Texas
AR430

**44 Easter Parade**
Tarrant County Historical Society
Fort Worth Public Library
H-0004

**45 South Side Grocery**
Tarrant County Historical Society
Fort Worth Public Library
C-0086

**46 Downtown Yard—Northern Texas Traction Company**
W. D. Smith Photograph Collection, Special Collections
The University of Texas at Arlington Library, Arlington, Texas
80-1-2

**47** **Jail, Traction Co.**
Fort Worth Star-Telegram Collection, Special Collections
The University of Texas at Arlington Library, Arlington, Texas
FWST# H050

**48** **Houston Street, 1900**
Tarrant County Historical Society
Fort Worth Public Library
A-0018

**49** **Main Street Looking North**
Tarrant County Historical Society
Fort Worth Public Library
A-0021

**50** **Streetcar**
Fort Worth Star-Telegram Collection, Special Collections
The University of Texas at Arlington Library, Arlington, Texas
FWST# H051

**51** **The Tarrant County Courthouse 1900**
Tarrant County Historical Society
Fort Worth Public Library
B-0003

**52** **Fort Worth Public Library Association**
Tarrant County Historical Society
Fort Worth Public Library
Photo # 57

**54** **Merchants Parade**
Tarrant County Historical Society
Fort Worth Public Library
Photo # 70

**55** **High School Football Team 1909**
Quentin McGown Collection

**56** **Bird's-Eye View**
Tarrant County Historical Society
Fort Worth Public Library
A-0017

**58** **Flatiron Building**
Tarrant County Historical Society
Fort Worth Public Library
B-0018

**59** **Bird's-Eye View**
Tarrant County Historical Society
Fort Worth Public Library
A-0017

**60** **German Verein**
Tarrant County Historical Society
Fort Worth Public Library
G-0038

**61** **8th and Houston Street**
Jack White Photograph Collection, Special Collections
The University of Texas at Arlington Library, Arlington, Texas
AR407-9-6

**62** **Main Street**
Tarrant County Historical Society
Fort Worth Public Library
A-0038

**63** **View from Texas & Pacific Station Tower**
Tarrant County Historical Society
Fort Worth Public Library
Photo # 45

**64** **First Banker and Employees**
Special Collections
The University of Texas at Arlington Library, Arlington, Texas
FWST# H153

**65** **T&P Fire 1904**
Special Collections
The University of Texas at Arlington Library, Arlington, Texas

**66** **Roosevelt Speech**
Fort Worth Star-Telegram Collection, Special Collections
The University of Texas at Arlington Library, Arlington, Texas
FWST # H153

**68** **Roosevelt Parade**
Fort Worth Star-Telegram Collection, Special Collections
The University of Texas at Arlington Library, Arlington, Texas
FWST # H165

**69** **First Cars**
Tarrant County Historical Society
Fort Worth Public Library
Photo # 135

**70** **Train of Interurban Cars**
Tarrant County Historical Society
Fort Worth Public Library
Photo # 11

**71** **Beautiful Lake Erie and the Pavilion**
Tarrant County Historical Society
Fort Worth Public Library
Photo # 39

**72** **Rosen Heights Streetcar 1905**
Fort Worth Star-Telegram Collection, Special Collections
The University of Texas at Arlington Library, Arlington, Texas
H051

**73** **Opera House at 7th and Rusk**
Tarrant County Historical Society
Fort Worth Public Library
C-0133

**74** **Park**
Tarrant County Historical Society
Fort Worth Public Library
E-0001

**75** **Fort Worth City Park**
Tarrant County Historical Society
Fort Worth Public Library
Photo # 38

**76** **Improved Order of Red Men**
Tarrant County Historical Society
Fort Worth Public Library
A-0023

**77** **The Hoxie Building**
Tarrant County Historical Society
Fort Worth Public Library
Photo # 59

**78** **First Methodist Church**
Tarrant County Historical Society
Fort Worth Public Library
P-0020

**79 Fire Station No. 1 1890s**
Fort Worth Star-Telegram Collection, Special Collections
The University of Texas at Arlington Library, Arlington, Texas
FWST # H219

**80 Horses, Talley-ho Wagon**
Tarrant County Historical Society
Fort Worth Public Library
Photo # 20

**82 Stock Yards Club Saloon**
Tarrant County Historical Society
Fort Worth Public Library
C-0146

**83 Fair Grounds**
Tarrant County Historical Society
Fort Worth Public Library
Photo # 56

**84 Houston Street Looking North**
Tarrant County Historical Society
Fort Worth Public Library
A-0032

**85 10th Street Looking East**
Tarrant County Historical Society
Fort Worth Public Library
Photo # 69

**86 Jennings Street Looking North**
Tarrant County Historical Society
Fort Worth Public Library
A-0015

**87 Board of Trade Bldg.**
Tarrant County Historical Society
Fort Worth Public Library
Photo # 48

**88 Electric Cars on Main Street, 1910**
Tarrant County Historical Society
Fort Worth Public Library
Photo # 29

**89 Mickle-Burgher Hardware Co.**
Tarrant County Historical Society
Fort Worth Public Library
C-0124

**90 1908 Flood from Viaduct**
Special Collections
The University of Texas at Arlington Library, Arlington, Texas

**91 1890 Main Bridge from River**
Special Collections
The University of Texas at Arlington Library, Arlington, Texas

**92 Horse-drawn Carriages Along Throckmorton Street, 1908**
Fort Worth Public Library
Photo # 68

**93 Central Fire Station**
Tarrant County Historical Society
Fort Worth Public Library
B-0010

**94 First Christian Church**
Tarrant County Historical Society
Fort Worth Public Library
P-0001

**95 First Christian Church 1914**
Tarrant County Historical Society
Fort Worth Public Library
P-0003

**96 Interior of Bound Electric Co.**
Tarrant County Historical Society
Fort Worth Public Library
C-0071

**98 Packing Houses and Stockyards**
Tarrant County Historical Society
Fort Worth Public Library
N-0019

**99 Elks Club**
Tarrant County Historical Society
Fort Worth Public Library
N-0004

**100 Fire Station # 8**
Tarrant County Historical Society
Fort Worth Public Library
B-0039

**101 Fort Worth Fire Dept. # 5**
Fort Worth Star-Telegram Collection, Special Collections
The University of Texas at Arlington Library, Arlington, Texas
FWST # H038

**102 Polytechnic College Militia**
Texas Wesleyan University Special Collections

**104 7th and Main**
Tarrant County Historical Society
Fort Worth Public Library
Photo # 74

**106 New First Baptist Church**
Tarrant County Historical Society
Fort Worth Public Library
P-0007

**107 Courthouse from North Main**
Fort Worth Star-Telegram Collection, Special Collections
The University of Texas at Arlington Library, Arlington, Texas
AR406

**108 Main Street and Ninth**
Special Collections
The University of Texas at Arlington Library, Arlington, Texas

**109 Jennings, Throckmorton, 1910**
Tarrant County Historical Society
Fort Worth Public Library
A-0003

**110 St. Ignatius Academy**
Tarrant County Historical Society
Fort Worth Public Library
Photo # 1

**111 First Flight 1911**
Fort Worth Star-Telegram Collection, Special Collections
The University of Texas at Arlington Library, Arlington, Texas
FWST # H236

**112 Paddock Viaduct**
W. D. Smith Photograph Collection, Special Collections
The University of Texas at Arlington Library, Arlington, Texas
AR430-85-1-300

**113 Cowtown**
Jack White Photograph Collection, Special Collections
The University of Texas at Arlington Library, Arlington, Texas
AR407

**114 Four Sixes Champion Livestock**
Fort Worth Star-Telegram Collection, Special Collections
The University of Texas at Arlington Library, Arlington, Texas
FWST # H115

**115 Stockyards Plant**
Tarrant County Historical Society
Fort Worth Public Library
Photo # 74

**116 Fort Worth Colored High School**
Tarrant County Historical Society
Fort Worth Public Library
Photo # 005

**117 W. T. Waggoner Building**
Fort Worth Star-Telegram Collection, Special Collections
The University of Texas at Arlington Library, Arlington, Texas
FWST # H230

**118 Main Street Looking South**
Tarrant County Historical Society
Fort Worth Public Library
A-0059

**119 Main Street Looking North**
Tarrant County Historical Society
Fort Worth Public Library
A-0063

**120 Houston Street Looking South**
Tarrant County Historical Society
Fort Worth Public Library
A-0061

**121 Fishburn's Steam Dye House**
Tarrant County Historical Society
Fort Worth Public Library
C-0022

**122 36th Division, 1918**
Tarrant County Historical Society
Fort Worth Public Library
H-0024

**123 Parade, 1919**
Quentin McGown Collection

**124 Frenchman's Well**
Tarrant County Historical Society
Fort Worth Public Library
O-0015

**125 Park Board Truck**
Tarrant County Historical Society
Fort Worth Public Library
J-0010

**126 Crystal-Pure Wagon**
Tarrant County Historical Society
Fort Worth Public Library
C-01376

**127 10th & Main, Hippodrome**
Jack White Photograph Collection, Special Collections
The University of Texas at Arlington Library, Arlington, Texas
AR407-9-29

**128 Star-Telegram Staff**
Fort Worth Star-Telegram Collection, Special Collections
The University of Texas at Arlington Library, Arlington, Texas
FWST # H081

**129 Thannisch Block Building**
Tarrant County Historical Society
Fort Worth Public Library
Photo # 19

**130 Lamar and 7th 1915**
Jack White Photograph Collection, Special Collections
The University of Texas at Arlington Library, Arlington, Texas

**131 Montgomery Ward Opening**
Howard McPeak Collection
Tarrant County Historical Society
Fort Worth Public Library

**132 Wards Stockboys**
Howard McPeak Collection
Tarrant County Historical Society
Fort Worth Public Library
Photo # 029

**133 Padilla Wedding**
Gilbert Anguiano Collection

**134 Fort Worth Business District, 1926**
Tarrant County Historical Society
Fort Worth Public Library
K-0021

**136 Quanah Parker's Relatives**
Tarrant County Historical Society
Fort Worth Public Library

**137 Sinclair Building**
Fort Worth Star-Telegram Collection, Special Collections
The University of Texas at Arlington Library, Arlington, Texas
88-1-103

**138 Belknap Overpass**
Fort Worth Star-Telegram Collection, Special Collections
The University of Texas at Arlington Library, Arlington, Texas
0006

**140 Casa Manana at Dusk**
Tarrant County Historical Society
Fort Worth Public Library
Fox 7

**141 White Front Store**
Fox Collection
Fort Worth Public Library

**142 Stock Show Parade**
Fox Collection
Fort Worth Public Library

**143 7th and Throckmorton, 1938**
Fox Collection
Fort Worth Public Library

**144 Armistice Day Parade**
Fox Collection
Fort Worth Public Library

**145 World War I Vet**
Fox Collection
Fort Worth Public Library

**146 Jennings Skyline**
Fort Worth Star-Telegram Collection, Special Collections
The University of Texas at Arlington Library, Arlington, Texas
AR406-1-32-5

**147 Jennings Avenue Viaduct**
Fort Worth Star-Telegram Collection, Special Collections
The University of Texas at Arlington Library, Arlington, Texas

**148 Arlington Downs**
Fort Worth Star-Telegram Collection, Special Collections
The University of Texas at Arlington Library, Arlington, Texas
0001

**149 Aerial of City Hall**
Fort Worth Star-Telegram Collection, Special Collections
The University of Texas at Arlington Library, Arlington, Texas
0002

**150 Worth Segar Store**
Charles Reichenstein Collection
Tarrant County Historical Commission

**151 Brick Layers**
Fox Collection
Fort Worth Public Library

**152 West 7th Street**
Tarrant County Historical Society
Fort Worth Public Library
K-0002

**154 Westover Hills in Snow**
Fort Worth Star-Telegram Collection, Special Collections
The University of Texas at Arlington Library, Arlington, Texas
0008

**155 Fairgrounds Aerial Snow Scene**
Fort Worth Star-Telegram Collection, Special Collections
The University of Texas at Arlington Library, Arlington, Texas
00071

**156 Stock Show Parade**
Fox Collection
Fort Worth Public Library

**157 Fairground Activities**
Fox Collection
Fort Worth Public Library

**158 Lancaster Bridge Under Construction**
Fort Worth Star-Telegram Collection, Special Collections
The University of Texas at Arlington Library, Arlington, Texas
0005

**160 Elephants on Houston Street**
Fox Collection
Fort Worth Public Library

**161 Defense Bond Parade**
Fox Collection
Fort Worth Public Library

**162 Japanese "Mini Sub"**
Fox Collection
Fort Worth Public Library

**164 Snow in Fort Worth**
Fox Collection
Fort Worth Public Library

**165 Snow**
Fox Collection
Fort Worth Public Library

**166 Stock Show Expo**
W. D. Smith Photograph Collection, Special Collections
The University of Texas at Arlington Library, Arlington, Texas
80-1-52

**167 Ambulance at Worth Theatre**
Jack White Photograph Collection, Special Collections
The University of Texas at Arlington Library, Arlington, Texas
AR407-9-7

**168 Worth Hotel Fire**
Tarrant County Historical Society
Fort Worth Public Library

**169 Main and Lancaster**
W. D. Smith Photograph Collection, Special Collections
The University of Texas at Arlington Library, Arlington, Texas
45-833-45

**170 Army Vehicles**
Fox Collection
Fort Worth Public Library

**171 Bookmobile**
Fox Collection
Fort Worth Public Library

**172 Boardwalk**
Fox Collection
Fort Worth Public Library

**173 Dundee Building**
W. D. Smith Photograph Collection, Special Collections
The University of Texas at Arlington Library, Arlington, Texas
50-48-40

**174 Flood, 1949**
Tarrant County Historical Society
Fort Worth Public Library
I-0023

**175 La Grave Field During the Flood**
Fort Worth Star-Telegram Collection, Special Collections
The University of Texas at Arlington Library, Arlington, Texas
0009

**176 Stockyards During Flood**
Jack White Photograph Collection, Special Collections
The University of Texas at Arlington Library, Arlington, Texas
00016

**177 Jack White and His "TCU Yacht Club"**
Jack White Photograph Collection, Special Collections
The University of Texas at Arlington Library, Arlington, Texas
AR407

**178 Fort Worth Centennial 1949**
Tarrant County Historical Society
Fort Worth Public Library
Photo # 102

**180 South End Fire**
Tarrant County Historical Society
Fort Worth Public Library
Photo # 160

**181 Miss Flame**
Tarrant County Historical Society
Fort Worth Public Library
Photo # 1364

**182 Morning Chapel Methodist Episcopal Church**
Beverly Washington
Morning Chaple CME Church

**184 Skyline**
Fort Worth Star-Telegram Collection, Special Collections
The University of Texas at Arlington Library, Arlington, Texas
00010

**185 Midway Airport**
W. D. Smith Photograph Collection, Special Collections
The University of Texas at Arlington Library, Arlington, Texas
58-48-22

**186 John F. Kennedy**
Fort Worth Star-Telegram Collection, Special Collections
The University of Texas at Arlington Library, Arlington, Texas
FWST # H157

**187 John F. Kennedy**
Fort Worth Star-Telegram Collection, Special Collections
The University of Texas at Arlington Library, Arlington, Texas
FWST # H4816

**188 Majestic Theatre Interior**
Jack White Photograph Collection, Special Collections
The University of Texas at Arlington Library, Arlington, Texas
00011

**189 First Arlington Heights House**
Jack White Photograph Collection, Special Collections
The University of Texas at Arlington Library, Arlington, Texas
00012

**190 Van Zandt Home, 1965**
Jack White Photograph Collection, Special Collections
The University of Texas at Arlington Library, Arlington, Texas
00013

**191 Aerial, Mallick Tower**
W. D. Smith Photograph Collection, Special Collections
The University of Texas at Arlington Library, Arlington, Texas

**192 Fire Boys**
Tarrant County Historical Society
Fort Worth Public Library
Photo # 1334

**193 Catfish**
Tarrant County Historical Society
Fort Worth Public Library
Photo # 1054

**194 Fort Worth View**
Tarrant County Historical Society
Fort Worth Public Library
K-0003

**195 Flatiron Building**
Tarrant County Historical Society
Fort Worth Public Library
C-0153

**196 Skyline from Jacksboro Highway**
Jack White Photograph Collection, Special Collections
The University of Texas at Arlington Library, Arlington, Texas
00015

**198 Lightning Christmas Tree**
Fort Worth Star-Telegram Collection, Special Collections
The University of Texas at Arlington Library, Arlington, Texas
1-32-5

**206 Tarrant County Courthouse**
Fort Worth Star-Telegram Collection, Special Collections
The University of Texas at Arlington Library, Arlington, Texas
ARD4DF-1

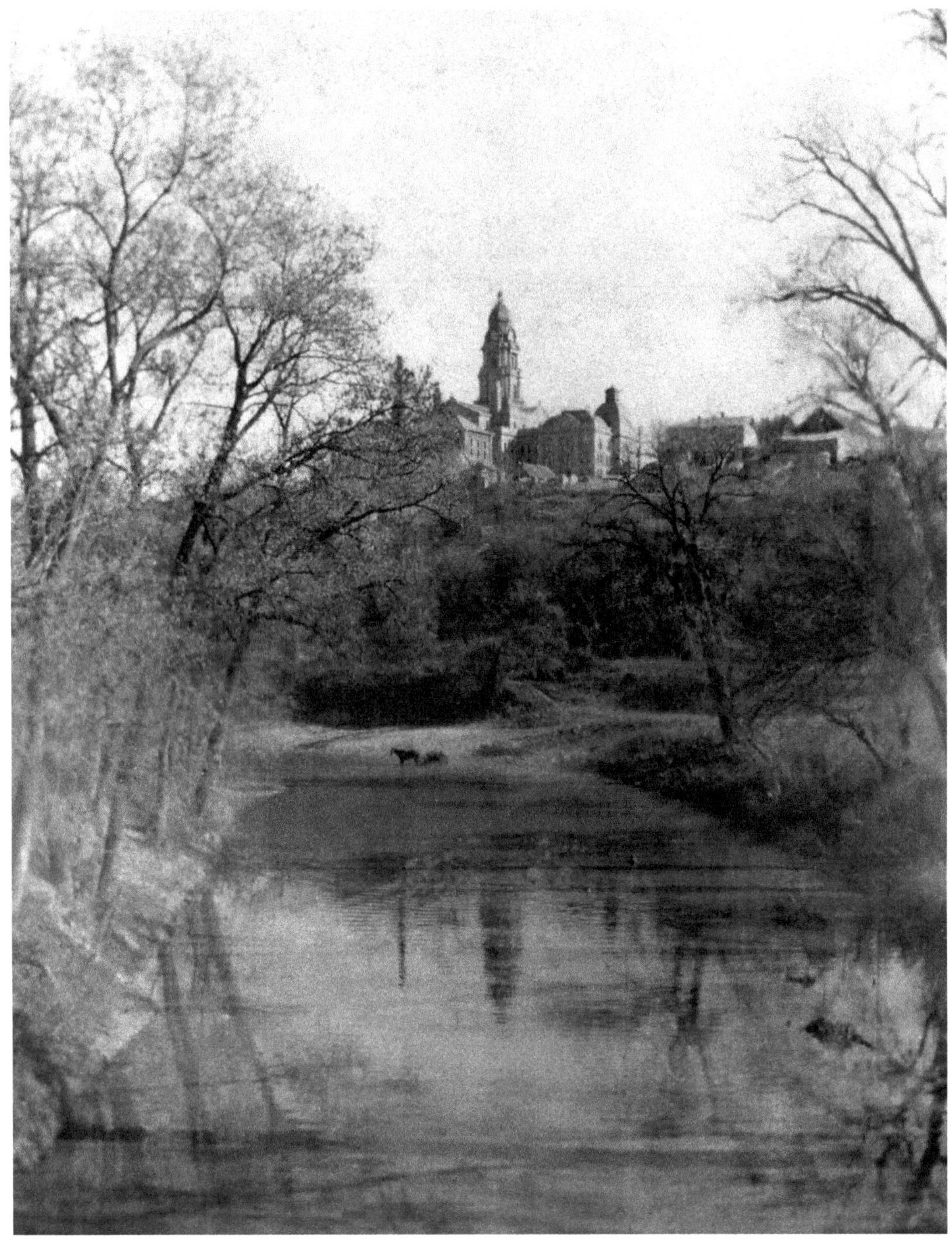

The new Tarrant County Courthouse rises majestically above a placid Trinity River in this view taken about 1896 from the 1880s-era iron bridge that crossed the river just below the confluence of the Clear and West forks. The lone horse and wagon make use of the old low-water crossing that had served the growing town, the soldiers of old Fort Worth and the Native Americans before them.

# HISTORIC PHOTOS OF FORT WORTH

Fort Worth is an American city quintessentially founded upon change. From its birth to the present, Fort Worth has consistently built and reshaped its appearance, ideals, and industry. Through changing fortunes, Fort Worth has continued to grow and prosper by overcoming adversity and maintaining the strong, independent culture of its citizens.

*Historic Photos of Fort Worth* captures this journey through still photography selected from the finest archives. From the Texas Spring Palace to Armour and Swift, the Carnegie Library to the Casa Manana and Frontier Centennial, *Historic Photos of Fort Worth* follows life, government, education, and events throughout the city's history.

This volume captures unique and rare scenes through the lens of hundreds of historic photographs. Published in striking black and white, these images communicate historic events and everyday life of two centuries of people building a unique and prosperous city.

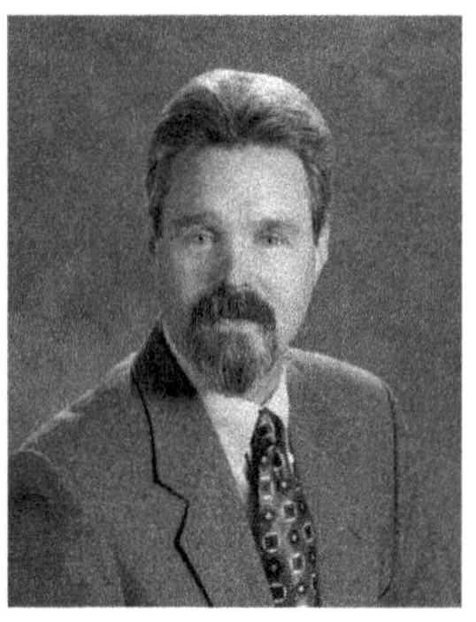

Quentin McGown is a sixth-generation Texan and fourth-generation Fort Worth attorney, with a lifelong interest in history. He served as General Counsel and Director of Gift Planning at Texas Wesleyan University, from which he graduated with degrees in theater and law. He served six years, three as chair, on the City of Fort Worth Historic and Cultural Landmarks Commission, and he is a past chair of the Tarrant County Historical Commission. He wrote and hosted the *Historic Fort Worth* series on community cable television, and served on the city's 1999 sesquicentennial history committee. He also co-chaired the Tarrant County Bar Association's 2004 centennial celebration. A member of the planning committee for the annual Red Steagall Cowboy Gathering, he serves on the board of the North Fort Worth and Tarrant County Historical Societies and the Outriders, the support organization for the Fort Worth Herd. He teaches courses on Fort Worth history for the Texas Christian University Extended Education program, and his book, *Fort Worth in Vintage Postcards,* was published by Arcadia Publishing in 2003. He and his wife, Laurie, are slowly restoring their 101-year-old downtown Fort Worth home.

WWW.TURNERPUBLISHING.COM